Self & Society

Self & Society

SOCIAL CHANGE AND
INDIVIDUAL DEVELOPMENT

Nevitt Sanford

ATHERTON PRESS
New York 1966

To Christine

Contents

Introduction

The major aim of this book is to help construct a basis in knowledge for planned action affecting individuals and groups. It offers a conception of the nature of practical problems and of the role of science in efforts to cope with them. It aims at being useful not only to students in psychology and the social sciences but also to professional workers who direct their efforts to people in trouble, people in psychologically dangerous situations, or people in need of further development.

There is nothing quite so practical as good theory and nothing so good for theory-making as direct involvement with practice. Just as professional workers may be guided by psychological and social theory, so psychologists and social scientists may contribute to systematic knowledge by directing their research to human problems—that is, problems defined in terms of their human significance rather than in terms of particular disciplines. This is a plea not so much for more applications of science as for the *practice of social science*. Human problems, such as neurosis, delinquency, or incompetence, usually confront the investigator or the practitioner, or the investigator-practitioner, with questions of how the behavior of individuals or of groups might be changed in some desired way. The scientist participates in the definition of the problem as well as in the determination of what sorts of solution might be satisfactory. Attemped solutions are at the same time experiments. In thinking about what to do and about the various possible consequences of actions, the investigator-practitioner formulates theory and hypotheses. Then, through observing the effects of these actions, he enlarges the empirical base of his formulations, and increases the predictive power of his hypotheses.

After presenting the value-orientation and the general strategy of research embodied in this approach to inquiry and action, this book reports studies on the problems of criminality, neurosis, anti-Semitism and authoritarianism, sex-role identity, the acting-out of impulses, and the inhibition of creativity. These studies show that theory can be generated through a coming to grips with human problems, and that empirical knowledge may be gained through the use of methods suited to the holistic and comprehensive approach such problems require.

The basic concern is with how to develop each individual's potentialities as fully as possible. Goals must be stated not only in terms of what is to be modified, corrected, or prevented, but also in terms of what is to be built up. Schools, colleges, correctional institutions, and mental hospitals as well as child guidance clinics and various programs for youth should be conceived, first of all, as institutions for human development. The book sets forth a developmental model to guide work in such institutions. This model is intended to supplement and to incorporate both the traditional medical model, which is concerned essentially with the causes and cures of disease, and with educational models which, although designed for personality-developing activity, tend to be restricted to cognitive functions. The model presented here holds not only for activities to modify existing disorders but also for activities designed to promote mental health. It should prove particularly valuable for programs in community mental health—that is, programs that marshal various community resources in efforts to improve the functioning of its people.

Efforts to develop the individual or to improve his functioning must be guided by both personality theory and social theory. Personality theory should aid our understanding of how different environmental stimuli may induce developmental changes in different parts of the person; social theory should guide inquiry into how arrangements can be made—either in an institutional setting or in the larger society—so that appropriate stimuli may be brought effectively to bear and inappropriate stimuli withheld. Ideally, we should have personality-social theory—that is, theory adequate to deal with the articulation of personality systems and social systems. Such theory would promote both more searching analysis of social systems in psychologically relevant terms and also an understanding of how relatively autonomous personality structures are constantly sustained by processes in the social system and tend to change as that system changes.

In the discussion of personality theory, full use is made of those aspects of Freudian psychology that have stood the test of time, chiefly the conceptions of the dynamic unconscious and the plasticity of drives. I join psychoanalytic "ego psychologists" and other personality theorists in an effort to develop a dynamic-organismic theory that is broader than classical psychoanalysis and more in keeping with contemporary social theory. More attention is given here than in classical psychoanalysis to the impact upon personality of events occurring in late adolescence and early adulthood, to the interaction of the adult personality and the social environment, and to the modification of personality structures that are not dominated by unconscious processes. This is done without giving up what is most fundamentally and most distinctively psychoanalytic.

Mine is a normative view of culture. Throughout, it is argued that a group's culture can be evaluated on the basis of its contribution to the development, toward full humanity, of the group's members. The analysis here of organizations and other social structures relies upon modern sociology, particularly upon conceptions pertaining to how these systems might be modified in the interest of the individual's development.

While preparing this book, I have often thought about the 1930s. This is partly because my studies of colleges and mental hospitals owe something to my work as a prison psychologist from 1932 until 1935. But there is something more which to me is very interesting: The 1960s are in some important respects like the 1930s. Each can be described as a period of revolutionary social and economic change. In the 1930s the gap between social science and social action was narrow, and—a natural accompaniment, it seems to me—the barriers separating the academic disciplines were relatively slight. Not only was the Keynesian economics being applied directly in the New Deal, but professors were carrying out as well as planning government programs. At the Norfolk Prison Colony in Norfolk, Massachusetts, for example, there was great optimism that social science would lead to big gains in the rehabilitation of criminal offenders. Howard Gill, the brilliant and resourceful warden, employed anthropologists, sociologists, and psychologists—and then mixed them together thoroughly. The anthropologists considered staff rituals and belief systems at least as interesting as those of the inmates. The sociologists, who were of Lloyd Warner's school, taught us that social status was not the same thing as economic status and that the new concept of status held for *all* members of our prison community. What the psychologists—some of them—were up to is illustrated by Chapter 8. They were applying the "new" and exciting psychoanalysis in their attempts to understand individual inmates. Gill was not content to employ young social scientists; he brought in as consultants the pioneers in scientific management, Elton Mayo and F. J. Roethlisberger, who made all hands aware of the "human factors" in the administration of large organizations.

Meanwhile, at the Harvard Psychological Clinic, Henry Murray, the great generalist and incorporator, was seeing to it that his students were exposed to as many people with ideas as possible, from whatever discipline, and his staff of psychologists, psychiatrists, lay psychoanalysts, anthropologists, sociologists, and humanistic scholars worked in intimate association, believing that this was normal operating procedure. During this period Murray was undertaking the research published in 1938 in his epoch-making *Explorations in Personality,* a book, characteristically, dedicated to Morton Prince, Sigmund Freud, Lawrence J. Henderson, Alfred N. White-head, and Carl G. Jung. There were twenty-eight contributors, but Murray himself did more than half the writing. This book remains a model for investigations that seek to follow up the implications of an organismic theory of personality. The basic approach in the original study, and in a few that have followed it, is to have a number of investigators apply a variety of procedures to the same subjects and then pool their findings in an effort to portray something of the wholeness of personality.

It was also during the early 1930s that Lawrence K. Frank of the Laura Spellman Rockefeller Foundation, and later of the General Education Board, was initiating interdisciplinary institutes, centers, and projects in the field of child development. One of the projects was the Harvard Growth Study of School Children in which I was engaged from 1935 to 1940.* Frank and Margaret Mead labored heroically, and effectively I believe, to convince students of child development of the crucial importance of seeing things in their "cultural" context. They insisted, for example, that what we found in a sample of children from a university and upper-middle class community might be more expressive of a particular subculture than of general principles of psychological growth. Margaret Mead also suggested that if we were interested in the effects on later childhood and adolescence of particular weaning practices, we should study a culture in which these practices prevailed.

It was assumed that all this work in child development would have practical effects. We all believed that the children we studied would develop beyond their parents, and that this outcome would be favored by our efforts. (Parents, I am afraid, were too often regarded as villains.)

In the 1960s we have something of a revival of the spirit of the 1930s. Social scientists, it is likely, will become increasingly involved in action programs, and new patterns of interdisciplinary collaboration will emerge. We may hope, however, that these activities will be on a higher level of sophistication than that generally attained in the 1930s. Then there was more sentiment in favor of social reform than there was knowledge of how it was to be brought about. Most of us at the Norfolk Prison Colony assumed that nothing short of radical social change was likely to reduce rates of crime and delinquency, and it seemed the most natural thing in the world for us to embrace socialist ideas. Our socialist fervor would have carried us farther, however, had we had a sociology that was focused on social structures and could tell us of the conditions and processes of their change. It would have helped, too, had our psychology of personality been more concerned with the articulation of personality processes and processes in contemporary social systems.

The influence of psychoanalysis was strong in the 1930s. Even social

* Nevitt Sanford, Margaret Adkins, Elizabeth Cobb, and Bretney Miller, *Physique, Personality, and Scholarship,* Monograph of the Society for Research in Child Development, 1943, 8, No. 1 (Ser. No. 34).

scientists who insisted that personality psychologists not neglect "the culture" were thinking primarily of the individual's past social environment. The "culture-personality" or "personality-culture" accent of the time was focused primarily upon the events of early childhood. The common belief, as expressed, for example, by Edward Sapir in his famous article in the *Encyclopedia of the Social Sciences* (1934), was that the personality was essentially formed by the age of two or three and remained essentially fixed after that. Culture shaped personality through the impact of the prevailing pattern of child training; and thus was the culture perpetuated in personality structure. A. L. Kroeber, one of the deans of American anthropology, could suggest at a seminar in Berkeley in 1940 that the Yurok were an "anal culture," as if the main theme of a whole culture derived from child-training practices—and from a single variable at that. Thus it was that the social change we advocated and promoted was to have its major impact in the next generation. And thus it was that when the opportunity to be psychoanalyzed presented itself, we were quick to seize it.

The scientific climate of the 1930s, then, provided some of the background for the earliest material in this volume. This material concerns *personality,* considered from a psychodynamic point of view. That we should see personality in its social context is strongly advocated in this material, but it was not until I observed the loyalty oath controversy at the University of California (1949–51), that I, as a participant-observer, seriously tried my hand at an analysis of strictly social processes in a particular social institution. The paper that resulted—and which has been used as the basis for Chapter 15—represents, I hope, the kind of approach that should be implied by the expression "person-in-a-social-system." It deals both with the authoritarian potential in the individual and with the social conditions that put pressure on the individual to behave in an authoritarian way. One could not understand why individuals behaved as they did without knowing something of the role structure of the university, the conditions of academic life, and the ways in which the general climate of the times impinged upon the university community. At the same time, one could not understand what happened without knowing something of how the primitive, emotional, often unconscious needs of men interact with similar needs in other members of a social group, and how these needs are "switched in" and begin to determine events as strain becomes increasingly severe.

This way of looking at things was clarified for me through a year's association with the Tavistock Institute in London, and it became fundamental to the frame of reference with which I approached the study of student development in college (at Vassar College, 1952–58) and the study of alcohol-related problems in our society (for the Cooperative Commission on the Study of Alcoholism, 1961–). These inquiries led to the formulation of the major themes of this book.

The integration of personality and social theory in the continuing search for useful knowledge is not going to be easy. Most university men would no doubt argue that the best course for a social scientist is to find a specialty and stick to it, leaving to someone else—undergraduates perhaps —the task of integrating knowledge and pointing out its relevance to practice. Even though personality and social structure are best conceived as one system, it is necessary to abstract parts from the whole for more intensive study. Why not then cut the pie along the lines of our existing departmental structure, with psychologists making specialized studies of personality, and sociologists, political scientists, and anthropologists making specialized studies of social structures and processes? My answer is that this is not the only way to cut the pie: we can just as well conceive of many personality-social subsystems and develop specialists in the study of them. At the same time, I am arguing against specialization itself—against too much or too narrow specialization. The tendencies toward disciplinary purity and toward the fragmentation of knowledge, which have been growing in the universities since World War II, have been widening the breach between the university and society and could lead to the university's becoming increasingly irrelevant. It is, of course, risky at this time to try to be a generalist; it is to invite one of the academic man's favorite epithets: "superficiality." There is no good defense against this, since any generalist is bound to touch upon many things that other people know more about than he, as well as upon some things that others refuse to inquire into. Probably it is up to those of us who have the least to lose, by virtue of age and academic tenure, to try to achieve a broad outlook. Perhaps we may hope to become specialists in breadth.

The basic question concerns training. A successful attack on human problems requires that we have people who are reasonably familiar both with the person and with the social system. The present account has shown something of the difficulties in the way of producing such people. Still, I believe it can be done if the task is undertaken with sufficient determination. It might be a good plan to have first-year graduate students in departments of psychology, sociology, political science, or anthropology—or in new departments—devote full time to field work. Let them take some responsibility for another person, in a setting such as an institution for training, rehabilitation, or correction. There they could learn that in order to understand the person and how he might change, it is necessary to understand the social structures in which he lives. The supervised reading of these students would be directed to helping them make sense of and act on what they encountered in the field, rather than to augmenting a conceptual burden perhaps already too heavy and certainly insufficiently related to experience. The formal curriculum and a specialized inquiry into some personality-social subsystem could come later.

The pressures toward early specialization are great, however, and its rewards are relatively large, tangible, and immediate. Departments are looking for young specialists, and the man who wants to get ahead rapidly will be best advised, in the short run at least, to acquire the most salable skills. A leading psychology department recently stretched a point and employed a young man who confessed that he was a "generalist interested in various cognitive processes"! Where such a young man will be after ten years is another question. It may be that in present circumstances, graduate school or even the upper division in college is already too late to capture students for the sort of approach being advocated here, that the appeal were better made to those natural generalists, freshmen and sophomores.

Most of the chapters that follow are based on or drawn from a collection of papers written over the past two decades. They have been woven together to form a book but each of them may be read independently of the others. The general reader might want to omit Chapters 6 and 7 which deal with some issues at the frontier of personality theory and were originally addressed to psychologists. On the other hand, it should be noted that most of the other chapters, though they include few technical terms (none that are not defined, I hope) and are ostensibly concerned with applied problems, are also oriented to basic theory.

Chapters 14, 18, and 19, and parts of Chapter 1, were prepared in connection with my work as Scientific Director of the Cooperative Commission on the Study of Alcoholism. (These papers, though they are intended to be general in their reference, were written with alcohol problems very much in mind.) The work of the Commission has been supported by a grant from the National Institute of Mental Health. A report of this Commission will be forthcoming; meanwhile none of its members, except me, can be held responsible for what is said in these chapters.

Obviously I owe thanks to a large number of people. First are those older scholars and scientists whose names have been mentioned; they all went to some pains to give me the benefit of their knowledge, insight, and wisdom. Chief among these is Henry Murray, my teacher and friend, to whom I owe more than I can say. I can offer one example of numerous areas of indebtedness: He taught me most of what I know about how to write. He did this by an extraordinary onslaught upon my Ph.D. thesis—the second draft as well as the first as I recall—and by then indicating how repairs might be made. I could not tell whether the draft was just too appalling to be left alone or whether it showed enough promise to deserve some special attention. It was years later before I learned (I did not really want to know) that he did the same thing for generations of Harvard Clinic Ph.D.'s.

Among those who have helped directly with the preparation of the book, William Henry stands first. He not only suggested that the book be prepared but he also stayed with the project to the end, offering encouragement, criticism, and wise counsel as needed. He was inestimably helpful in the determination of the over-all plan, in the selection of materials, and in the improvement of particular chapters. Members of a graduate seminar at Stanford—James Fadiman, Paul Kanzer, Peter Rogers, and Henry Selby—and also Roger Squire, addressed themselves to these same problems and made themselves indispensable. I owe a special debt of gratitude to Peter Madison. A visitor at our Institute during the time this book was in preparation, he took a keen interest in the project, familiarized himself with my writings, clarified through discussion a number of difficult theoretical issues, and made numerous valuable suggestions which influenced both the structure and the content of the book.

Members of the staff of the Institute for the Study of Human Problems—particularly Max Levin, Joseph Katz, Christian Bay, Howard Becker, and Thomas Plaut—not only provided intellectual stimulation but also were always available for help or advice. Different ones of these colleagues were especially helpful with particular chapters. Howard Becker saved me from overstating my case in Chapter 1. Joseph Katz helped me with the statement of an ethical position contained in Chapter 2 and edited the whole paper for inclusion in a book of his own (with Nochlin and Stover).* Thomas Plaut instructed me in the public health approach to mental disorders and gave a critical reading to Chapters 18 and 19. Christian Bay gave especially valuable editorial attention to Chapters 1, 14, and 20.

I am indebted, too, to numerous colleagues and friends with whom I was closely associated at times when particular papers were written. Erik Erikson was a colleague and intellectual companion at the Institute of Child Welfare in Berkeley when I wrote my paper on criminal types (Chapter 8), and his support and advice were crucially important to me. Alexander Meiklejohn (now deceased) not only provided inspiration and encouragement but also was a critical reader of the paper on the University of California loyalty oath controversy (Chapter 15). This paper, and particularly its theoretical ideas, owes much to Eric Trist, A. T. M. Wilson, and other members of the Tavistock Institute. A number of chapters were written at times when I was working on a project in collaboration with others, and I had the benefits of their stimulation, support, and tangible help: Donald MacKinnon and the staff of the Institute of Personality Assessment and Research, Berkeley, in connection with Chapters 12 and 13, my fellow authors of *The Authoritarian Personality*† in connection with Chapter 10, and the staff of the Mary Conover Mellon Foundation of Vassar College (Donald Brown, Mervin Freedman, Richard Jung, and John Bushnell) in connection with Chapters 2, 9, 16, and 17. To all these colleagues and friends, warm thanks. I have been highly responsive to their numerous suggestions, but I alone take responsibility for the shortcomings that may be charged to this book.

I also wish to acknowledge the kindness of the publishers who have permitted me to reprint my writings.

Mrs. Patricia Kollings of our Institute at Stanford edited the manuscript. Such readability as it has owes much to her sensitivity to style. She also performed with patience and care numerous of those other chores

* Joseph Katz, Philip Nochlin, and Robert Stover (eds.), *Writers on Ethics*, Princeton, N.J., Van Nostrand, 1964.

† T. W. Adorno, Else Frenkel-Brunswik, D. J. Levinson, and Nevitt Sanford, *The Authoritarian Personality*, New York, Harper, 1950.

that go into the making of a book. I am grateful for her serenity and loyalty as well as for her competence.

Signe Best, of Berkeley, over the years typed most of the papers—many of them more than once—included here and she did most of the typing necessary to the preparation of this book. I am deeply grateful to her not only for her superior competence but also for her enduring loyalty and willingness to be called upon on short notice.

Part One

CHAPTER ONE

The Study of Human Problems

The Economic Opportunity Act of 1964 called for the establishment of residential centers for poverty-stricken young women aged sixteen to twenty-one. Suppose a panel of psychologists and social scientists were asked to work out the guidelines for such centers, what would its members have to say? I suggest that discussion of this matter should revolve around three questions: What are these young women like now? What might one reasonably hope they would be like after one or two years in such a center? And what means should be adopted in order to realize these hopes?

Concerning the present status of these girls we may assume, as does the legislation itself, that although they are almost totally uneducated, they are not mentally retarded or delinquent; but we may also assume that, having been brought up in poverty, they bear some of the scars of it, and that, having been denied experiences that ordinarily develop individuals, their personalities are still in relatively undeveloped states. When offered a chance to learn a trade, they could hardly be expected to respond as would a lower-middle-class high school graduate who was temporarily out of a job. On the contrary, it seems highly likely that, in order to teach these girls the skills and social competencies that would make them employable, it would first be necessary to change attitudes, to develop different self-conceptions—indeed to undertake socialization on a broad scale.

3

This means that goals would have to be stated, not in terms of what was to be corrected or prevented, but in terms of what was to be built up. One might say that as a minimum it would be desirable to build up whatever was necessary in order for a girl to hold a job. A little further thought would suggest that such a girl would not be likely to hold a job unless she could see some point in it, and this would require that she develop in herself capacities for enjoying its benefits and taking satisfaction in it. More than this, in our changing world of work the sort of specific skills that could most readily be taught to an uneducated girl would probably not be salable for long. She would have to be given whatever it takes to acquire new skills rapidly, plus whatever is necessary to sustain morale when there was no job. In short, the general goal for such a center would be the fullest possible development of the personality in all of its aspects. In its general direction, this goal is not different from that which we would envision for any young person in our society.

The residential centers, then, would have to be conceived as institutions for personality development. Each of their constituent features, activities, or subprograms would have to be considered with attention to what it might contribute, and how, to the desired change in the person. The thinking about this should be guided by personality theory, particularly by conceptions of the structure of different parts of the personality and the processes by which they develop. Since development is progressive—that is, certain things have to happen before other events become possible—the whole enterprise would have to be planned with attention to what to do first and to the order of succeeding undertakings. It would have to be guided by a general theory of personality development and by knowledge of the stages that the young women had reached at various times during their residential experience.

This is the beginning of a "developmental model" for action affecting young people whose functioning we hope to improve. Its dominating objective is the maximum development of the individual's potential. As later chapters of this book attempt to show, the same general model holds for work with people of all ages; it should guide action to promote "positive mental health" as well as to prevent mental disorder or to modify existing disorder. It has been clear for some time that the "medical model," which is concerned with the causes and cures of disease, is not entirely adequate for programs of "community mental health"—that is to say, programs that involve all the resources of a community in efforts to improve the functioning of its people. An "educational model" might be more appropriate, for education in the broadest sense of the word means leading forth the potentialities of the person, but educational institutions in the United States, by and large, have insisted on restricting their activities to cognitive functions. Although schools and colleges would do well to give more attention than they do to other functions, they could not be asked to take over the whole task of developing the individuals in our society. What is needed is a theoretical model to guide the actions of various kinds of institutions and agencies that can promote individual development.

To have conceptions of what kinds of environmental stimuli will induce developmental change in different parts of the person is one thing; to know how to arrange an institutional setting so that appropriate stimuli will be brought effectively to bear, and inappropriate stimuli withheld, is something else. In planning a residential center of the sort under discussion, our natural inclination probably is to fall back on rules of thumb derived from experience in schools, camps, correctional institutions, and so forth, accenting what would appear to be practical. But the argument in this book is that a more practical guide to action would be sociological theory concerning the structure and functioning of organizations, and their interactions with the larger society.

What is needed is a conceptual model for an agency such as a residential center. In later chapters I undertake to develop a model for this or any other institution designed for the purpose of changing the people who pass through it. The scheme is sociological in that it seeks to formulate the structure and functioning of *organizations*; it is also psychological in that it formulates the processes of the *individual personalities* that occupy the organization's roles.

PERSONALITY THEORY AND SOCIAL ACTION

While the major focus of this book is on individual development within a change-oriented organization, what it has to say about personality theory should be equally pertinent to legal, administrative, and social actions which do not involve a specific organizational structure. These actions can still influence the individual in various direct and indirect ways and should be planned with some understanding of personality structure and development.

An example of action on this larger front, and of the kinds of questions which it can raise, is the whole problem of controlling teen-age drinking by law. Currently, nearly all states prohibit the purchase of alcoholic beverages, or possession of them in public places, by persons under twenty-one years of age.[1] Yet it is well known that a substantial proportion of high school students drink away from home, at least occasionally, and that the age at which they begin to drink is going down—thirteen or fourteen being common in some communities today. Let us suppose now that a change in the law is proposed, making the minimum age eighteen instead of twenty-one. The idea would be not so much to get rid of a law which is not enforced—and which, like most such laws,

[1] The State of New York allows persons eighteen years or older to buy any alcoholic beverage; in Hawaii the age limit is twenty. All other states place some restriction on the sale of alcoholic beverages to persons under twenty-one. Some states prohibit it completely; others allow purchase of beer or light wine at eighteen; still others allow purchase of distilled spirits at eighteen if the purchaser is married or has parental permission.

probably does more harm than good—as to remove some of the unhealthy emotional implications of illicit early drinking experiences. (Some studies suggest that when an individual's first experiences of drinking are in situations involving such emotions as rebelliousness and guilt, the chances of his later becoming a problem drinker are increased.) Changing the law might also make it possible for young people to become socialized in respect to drinking in ways that are more suitable than those prevailing at present.

But why set the age limit at eighteen? Could these things not be accomplished as well by doing away with all age limitations? At this point the legislator can no longer rely on common sense alone. If he hopes to find answers, he must seek them in scientific knowledge and theory about how adolescents develop. A personality theorist might offer him some such counsel as this: Drinking outside one's own family setting is properly defined as an adult activity. This definition rests on the assumption that people need to reach a certain stage of development before they can be said to be ready to take part in activities involving the release of basic impulses. Premature experience of this kind cannot be integrated into the developing personality. This means there is danger of uncontrolled impulse expression. Furthermore, the individual is unable to derive meaning and maximum satisfaction from the activity, and his future development is likely to be impaired. It seems safe to say that fourteen-year-olds have not reached the necessary stage of development, nor have many high school students. However, eighteen-year-olds have, on the average, developed enough capacity for control that external restraints may safely be reduced. This is not to say that delay of drinking until after eighteen, twenty-one, or even indefinitely might not be advantageous for many individuals, for personality development continues between eighteen and twenty-one, and beyond. But to try to force this delay by law has been futile and perhaps damaging.

Of course, there is good evidence that in their drinking escapades young people are not always after the sort of pleasure that comes with the release of impulse; often they are seeking identity through demonstrating that they can safely engage in adult activities. On this basis, teen-age drinking may be better understood as an effort by young people to cope with deeper problems, such as alienation, lack of identity, and a sense of worthlessness. A law aimed primarily at some surface manifestation of these underlying conditions could not be expected to contribute a great deal to a solution to the basic problem, but it would be a help. More than that, the public discussion that would be aroused by efforts to change the law, or to deal with the implications and consequences of a change, might set in motion processes of inquiry and action that would really come to grips with the problems of youth.

The change proposed here would have implications for a great many people besides teen-agers. Temperance organizations and the liquor industry, for example, could be expected to react to the merest suggestion that a change might be in the offing. Indeed, anyone interested in promoting a change would probably wish to consider first the power and intentions of these groups. Or, to take it the other way around, if one wanted to find out about these groups, a good way would be to begin promoting a change in the law. In any case, the change being discussed here would involve for the temperance organizations a change in ideology, and the liquor industry probably could anticipate further measures to regulate its operations.

The change would also have immediate consequences for various agencies and institutions that have responsibilities for young people, for it would create difficulties as well as new opportunities. For example, most colleges would have to change their rules governing drinking on their campuses. A consideration of this matter would bring us back to the conception of an agency designed to change personality. One would expect a college to plan its actions affecting drinking with strict attention to what would promote educational objectives. Some colleges, no doubt, would redouble their efforts to prohibit or restrict this activity; others, more enlightened, might see here an opportunity to create campus drinking places of a sort that could help develop meaningful folkways for those who drink and also serve as a means for cultivating educationally valuable student-faculty relations.

I have gone to some length with these examples in order to make the fundamental point that the theorist and the field worker have much of importance to say to each other. Human problems are in the last analysis the central concern of both.

THE KIND OF APPROACH THAT IS NEEDED

Psychology and social science have, of course, always been oriented to action, in the sense that they have proceeded on the assumption that their theories and empirical knowledge would eventually be applied. Psychology, when it has thought seriously about itself, has included among its aims "to promote human welfare." Sociology traditionally has been concerned with the solution of social problems and with "building a better society." The National Institute of Mental Health, which has supported so much research in biology, psychology, and newer social sciences, has been guided by the principle that such research should be "mental health relevant," but in practice any fundamental work in these fields has been considered to have this characteristic.

Yet there is no denying that at the present time there exists a wide gap between research and practice. Psychology and sociology, like biology, participate fully in the trend toward specialization and disciplinary professionalism that dominates in the universities today. These disciplines are much concerned to establish themselves as sciences, or to gain an increasingly respectable place in that hierarchy of sciences in which physics stands at the top. It must seem to many members of these disciplines that the way to achieve this sort of success is to display the visible attributes of the more prestigeful sciences: quantification, precision of measurement, elegance of experimental design, general laws. For the psychologists, clearly, the best way to achieve these things is to avoid the study of people, to stick to the study of simple part-processes, and to stay as close to biology as possible. For many sociologists, it seems, the best course is to be like the experimental psychologist.

There is, of course, a rationale for all this. It is not without some reason that the National Institute of Mental Health regards the so-called pure science of these disciplines as relevant to mental health. Science has always made progress through specialization. It can be argued that findings concerning simple and isolated processes will eventually add up to systematic knowledge that can then be applied to human problems.

There are two things to be said about this. One is that the "adding up" function is currently rather neglected, and the other is that many of these findings just do not add up. Concerning the first, the accent today is on the production of knowledge, in "knowledge factories" designed for that purpose, rather than on the organization of knowledge. There are few attempts at systematization of the sort that would put particular facts in perspective and show their significance. More than that, there seem to be few attempts to organize knowledge in such a way that its relevance to practice or to policy becomes apparent. A college president might examine a large number of issues of educational, psychological, or sociological journals without coming across anything that struck him as relevant to his purposes or helpful in the solution of his problems. It is not that all this material is irrelevant, but rather that the task of organizing and interpreting it is so largely neglected. Scientists write for each other. When they are looking for a problem to investigate, they turn to their professional journals instead of asking such questions as what might be troubling college presidents.

When I say that the study of simple, isolated processes does not add up to an understanding of more complex ones, I am assuming that human and social processes are organized on different levels, and that processes on higher (more complex) levels have a character of their own, are just as "real" as processes on lower levels, and must be studied directly. It is just as "scientific" to study, say, self-esteem in its relations to other factors of equal complexity, as it is to study the manifold conditioned responses into which self-esteem might be analyzed; it is just as scientific to study conditioned responses as it is to study by physiological methods the nerve processes that underlie them. The student of conditioning who is somewhat contemptuous of the vague globalism of the students of such personality needs as self-esteem could himself be regarded with contempt by students of the action of the nervous system.

I assume, further, that there is *interaction* between processes on different levels. Just as complex phenomena are to be explained in part in terms of the activities of constituent processes, so simple processes have to be understood as partly determined by the larger structures in which they have place. Truths may be discovered by abstracting parts from the whole and studying them intensively, but the whole truth can never be discovered in this way. It is the whole truth, and particularly the truth about wholes, that is needed for practice.

Thus one has to be concerned about a trend in science which puts all the accent on the study of abstracted part-functions. The main reason for this trend is the difficulty of studying complex processes by existing approved methods. In psychology theory-making itself is often guided more by consideration of what can be attacked by such methods than by an intellectual involvement with the problems of life. The kind of theory that is needed for the understanding of human problems is different from that which guides most laboratory research or is generated from it. Thus, instead of specialized personality theory and specialized social theory we need more general personality-social theory. We need theory that is not formal or mechanistic but dynamic, not elementaristic but holistic, not narrow and specialized but comprehensive, not concrete and tangible but on a level of abstraction that is appropriate to the problem at hand. Each of these ideas will be taken up in turn.

PERSONALITY-SOCIAL THEORY

It seems clear enough that for an effective approach to human problems we must have an integration of personality theory and social theory. This is not as easy as might first appear. Most sociologists seem to get along quite well without giving much attention to the individual personality, and probably the great majority of clinical practitioners rely on an "individual psychodynamic" approach that gives little attention to social and cultural factors. There is even a certain amount of interdisciplinary rivalry here; in discussions of such problems as prejudice or delinquency there is a tendency to oppose personality factors and social factors, and to argue about which is more important. But progress toward integration is being made. Certainly personality theory is far more "social" today than it was twenty-five years ago, and there is evidence, I think, that when sociologists note signs that their psychological colleagues are seeing the light, they are willing to go halfway toward *rapprochement*. What is needed is more knowledge of the articulation of personality systems and social systems. This requires more rather than less attention to the relatively autonomous personality structures and more searching analysis of social structures in terms that are psychologically relevant. The student of personality must, of course, focus on the internal structuring of personality, but he must grant that the hypothetical personality subsystems are not fully understood unless the conditions under which they change are specified.

I assume that there are social organizations that can bring out the authoritarianism in almost anybody, but I would also assume that when it came to changing a particular organization, the difficulty—and the strategy—would depend on how much authoritarianism in personality was found in people who occupied the key positions. To put this idea in more general terms: in order to induce change in personality it may sometimes be necessary first to change the role-structure in the organization in which the individual lives or works. By the same token, since we deal with a dynamic interaction between personality and social system, it may be necessary to change certain personalities in order to change the social system. Individuals use their social roles for the expression of their personality needs; hence a change in organizational role structure will be resisted by individuals in the same way that they resist change in internal adaptive devices that have been found to be more or less satisfying. The practicing social scientist needs to be familiar with personality dynamics.

DYNAMIC APPROACH

A personality, or an organized social group, seems best conceived as a system of interacting forces, a going concern in which energy is distributed among constituent parts and between the system (or its subsystems) and its environment. Dynamic organization refers to the way in which these forces or units of energy interact. Personalities and social systems also exhibit formal organization. They may be examined with attention to such over-all features as the number of different parts or the connectedness of parts, or to such formal relationships among parts as similarity, proximity, or inclusion. In general, the analysis of systems into states, conditions, or arrangements prepares the way for explanation in terms of dynamic theory.

Dynamic theory is essential when it comes to consideration of how a system might be changed. The question here, typically, is how to bring force to bear upon a particular subsystem that one wishes to modify. One might think first of bringing to bear upon the subsystem in question a potent set of environmental stimuli, and this might sometimes be effective. It usually turns out, however, that the particular subsystem is really being determined by other subsystems and by processes of the whole system. The problem, then, is to find out what within the larger system is determining of what, and then to get a purchase on the master processes. To take an example from the field of personality: an individual's prejudice toward minority groups may be due to a nagging but unrecognized sense of weakness in himself. In such a case it would do no good to give him correct information about minority groups; there would be no change in his prejudice until a way had been found to modify his sense of weakness. In an organization it might be generally recognized that a change in a certain process would increase production without loss in other essential values, but this would not mean that the change would take place as a matter of course. Whoever wished to promote it would still have to reckon with the implicit values of various segments of the power structure.

All this is not to deny the importance of information or of the mechanisms by which it is acquired. It is only to say that in dynamic theory information is instrumental to purpose. Just as, in an organization, the gathering, storing, and communication of information are put into the service of the organization's explicit and implicit functions, so, in the individual, perception and learning are organized in the interest of strivings.

Of course, perception and learning can be abstracted from their personal context and studied in and of themselves; this is indeed common practice. Consider, for example, the popular topic of programmed learning. It has been shown that when factual material is presented to subjects according to predetermined schedules of reinforcement, learning is more rapid and complete than in the usual hit-or-miss arrangement that obtains in the classroom or in solitary study. This could be a great boon to education, but we have to remember that from the point of view of dynamic theory we should not expect factual content to be retained for long, no matter how efficiently it was learned, unless it became integrated with the individual's purposes. But how such integration occurs is a complex question, which could hardly be answered unless individuals were carefully observed over relatively long periods of time.

Programmed learning of academic material also affords a nice example of some of the difficulties created when more or less general laws derived from the study of abstracted part-processes are applied in life situations, without anyone's remembering to put the part-process back into the living context where it belongs. If the psychologist fragments the person conceptually in the interests of research, many educators proceed to fragment their students by taking over the laboratory findings bodily and applying them directly.

The advent of the teaching machine seems so far to have played into the hands of those educators who believe that the learning of factual content *is* education, that this learning is neatly separated from everything else that might be going on in the student, and that these other things do not matter much anyway. The real educational problem is not how students may learn material well enough so that they can pass examinations at a high level, but how to make academic material sufficiently meaningful to them that it will play some part in building up in them the qualities of an educated person. How does the learning of factual material contribute to the development of such qualities as the ability to think well, self-understanding, sensitivity to ethical issues, intellectual integrity?

Promoters of teaching machines say that their main contribution will be to free the teacher from mechanical work so that he can get on with the really essential business of education, which is the development of the individual as a member of society. One can certainly agree with this. When we try to think of ways in which qualities such as courage or sensitivity are built up, we are led first to what the teacher does and is. We think of the complex interactions between the teacher and the student, and of what sort of model the teacher—like the parents before him—

provides. Many behavior theorists say that eventually the learning of personal qualities will go forward according to schedules of reinforcements of the same sort that are now applied to the learning of arithmetic. This may be doubted. Progress in this direction seems awfully slow. I should say that, although anything in behavior or personality can be translated into stimulus-response terms, once everything about it is known, at this stage we will do best to let a dynamic theory of the total personality guide our quest for knowledge that is relevant to education.

HOLISM

The essential idea of a holistic theory was introduced in our previous discussion of the neglect of complex processes. Particular phenomena, such as "a perception" or "a conditioned response," are almost always in part determined by—indeed their very nature depends upon—the larger organismic patterns and purposes within which they have a place.

The implications of this are great, and I would like to carry my argument further. The first point to be made is that few psychologists care to deny, on principle, the holistic premise. It seems to be almost universally understood and agreed that the way a stimulus is perceived depends on the context in which it exists at the moment; that whether or not an idea will be assimilated by a cognitive system depends on the degree of that idea's consistency with ideas already present there; that the meaning of a particular act depends on its place in a larger pattern of striving. It can be said with perfect safety that all personality theories are holistic in the sense that they are concerned with the relations of particular processes to larger personality functions.

What then is the argument about? It is not so much about high theory as about the strategy for research. The basic complaint against holistic theory is that it does not lend itself to testing by empirical methods. The very term "whole" has implications of unanalyzability, and American psychologists have been taught to be wary of anything "global." This argument would have force—complete force—if it were true that the study of part-whole relationships is impossible. But to confirm that this is not true one has only to point to the work of Klein (1951) on the relations of perception to the ego control system, that of Rogers and his associates (1954) on the relations of various attitudes and beliefs to the individual's self-conception, or the findings of Witkin et al. (1954) on sex differences in perception. The whole research undertaking that culminated in *The Authoritarian Personality* (Adorno, Frenkel-Brunswik, Levinson, and Sanford, 1950) was carried forward in accordance with a holistic orientation and indeed would have been impossible without holistic theory. The F scale for measuring authoritarianism in personality was developed by a process of going back and forth from observed behavior to hypothetical inner structure. The coherence of overt behavior patterns led to the conception of an inner structure of personality—that is, authoritarianism—and this conception was then used to predict other patterns of behavior.

It cannot, of course, be claimed that research carried out in accordance with the holistic orientation will ever achieve the high standards of precision and elegance that are often attained in laboratory experiments involving a few simple variables. Such research can be improved in these respects, but it cannot be expected to match the best laboratory experiments; it will have to aim at levels of rigor that are appropriate to the task at hand. Nor can one claim that this kind of research will be other than difficult and expensive. One might advise a graduate student to use the F scale, but one would never advise him to set to work to develop another instrument of this kind, for this would involve long and complicated interviews with many subjects as well as a complicated statistical operation. Not a suitable topic for a Ph.D. dissertation! For that matter, one would hesitate to advise any graduate student interested in "getting through quickly" to undertake an investigation to test some propositions of holistic personality theory. This would require the assessment of many variables, or the observation of subjects over relatively long periods of time; it might well be regarded as more than a one-man job. Unfortunately, today the conception of a suitable Ph.D. dissertation seems to be much the same as the prevailing conception of a supportable research project.

If the criticism of the holistic strategy is that it is difficult and expensive and relatively inelegant, the criticism of the strategy of abstracting part-functions for experimental study is more serious: this strategy, because of its very nature, is bound to fall short of the truth. Not only does it avoid the big problems; it fails to achieve its own chosen goal, which is to establish general laws of behavior. The main characteristic of such "laws" is their lack of generality. They break down as soon as a new variable is introduced into the picture. Since real life constantly presents new variables, or variables not taken into account in the laboratory experiment, such laws are most limited in their applicability. No teacher, for example, could possibly guide his work in accordance with the "psychology of learning," and the producers of this psychology make no such claim for it. The claim is for the *eventual* applicability of this kind of work.

There is an exception to this general statement about applicability. One can sometimes carry over into a life situation all the conditions that obtain in the laboratory and show that the general laws still hold. This is true of the teaching machine, which enables a student to learn material in just the way that laboratory subjects do. But unless the educators are very much aware of the limitations suggested above, they may in effect transform life into a laboratory experiment. Skinner himself, unlike many of his disciples, is fully aware of this danger. Yet he is deeply concerned with practice and cannot resist becoming involved with it. He says that his strategy of research is the slow but sure building up of a science from simple beginnings, and that so far he and his colleagues have attacked only the simple problems; but this does not prevent him from remaking school rooms and designing new cultures.

The preceding argument is the main one for holism as the best road to knowledge; there is an equally strong argument from the point of view of practice. If parts are really determined by the wholes to which they belong, and one wishes to modify a part, then clearly his best course is to bring influence to bear upon the whole. Thus in the psychotherapy of Carl Rogers (1959) the whole thrust is toward modifying the self-conception, because an inappropriate self-conception is believed to be determining of numerous specific unfortunate attitudes and patterns of overt behavior. The same principle applies to a social institution. A colleague tells me that he can infer the type of administration and the general climate to be found in a given mental hospital in California by noting the automobile speed limit posted on the grounds. If he were greatly troubled by the speed limit at one of these places and wanted to change it, he would probably waste his time by agitating for that change alone; he would have to direct his efforts to the inner core of the hospital administration. The same would be true of a school or college. Grading practices, course requirements, the organization of teaching, and so on are usually integral to the whole system and are not to be changed until after there has been some modification in the general character of the institution. This is far from being a hopeless prospect. Just as one may influence an individual's self-conception as readily as one could influence one of its constituent attitudes, so one might initiate a process of change in an institution's general climate with no more difficulty than would be involved in changing one of its most specific part-functions. Success would depend upon knowledge of the individual's or the institution's dynamics. Of course, a holistic approach to individual or social change involves for the change-agent a considerable responsibility: he should not seek change in whole-structures unless he is prepared for change in numerous particulars.

I have put the case for holism as strongly as I can; this entire book is very much in the holistic tradition. Yet I do not see how we can do without the intensive study of abstracted part-functions. The student of personality, after all, engages in this activity when he undertakes to explain the functioning of social groups. Here he might well be inclined to favor analysis in terms of the personality types of the group's members, but if he is a holist he would not be surprised or put off if a social theorist reminded him that there are things about personality that do not become apparent until the individual is seen in the context of the social group.

At a time when the holistic orientation seems rather neglected in psychology and social science, it seems proper to accent it as is done here. If we must abstract parts from wholes, let us be fully aware of the fact that we *are* abstracting; and let us devote as much energy to finding out how special bits of knowledge fit into the larger picture as we do to an-alyzing wholes in the conventional scientific way.

COMPREHENSIVENESS

The holistic orientation requires that we consider in what respects living systems function as units. It says nothing about the size or complexity of the unit. Such a unit might be the context of a perception, a pattern of striving that organizes particular acts, or the self that is expressed in numerous personality characteristics. The argument here is that we must examine large areas of the person and of society, and long sections of behavior; and we must have theoretical models that permit us to do this.

The whole that helps to determine a particular personality characteristic may be the whole personality, and not merely the whole self or the whole ego. Hence we need a theoretical model of the personality that permits us to deal with the relations of self to ego, of these relatively large structures to others of like kind. Similarly for social structures. One may study, holistically, a department of an industrial organization or a classroom in a school, but for full understanding one has to see the department or classroom in relation to the whole institution, and the institution in relation to the whole society.

Another argument for comprehensiveness is that the determination of human events is almost always complex. Multiple factors are involved, and it is the task of the scientist to find them. This always takes some imagination, but the right kind of theory can be a big help. Consider, for example, the phenomenon of compulsive drinking. A formula for this could be written out in terms of rewards and punishments; and in such a formulation the reproaches of the drinker's spouse might in some cases be put down on the side of punishment. But what about the case of a man who drinks in order to express hostility toward his wife and who welcomes her reproaches as signs that he is achieving his purpose? One could still describe what happens in stimulus-response terms, *after* one had discovered what the effective internal stimuli were; but in finding the stimuli the usual sort of learning theory and the knowledge that proceeds from laboratory tests of it would be of no help. The quest would have to be guided by theory and knowledge concerning the complex interplay of forces within the personality.

Other arguments for comprehensiveness flow from a consideration of the requirements of practice. In planning a residential center for poverty-stricken girls, we have to consider a range of personality needs—ideally, the total personality. Policy with respect to teen-age drinking has to be guided by a conception of long-range developmental goals and by knowledge of the relations of present events to future consequences. When it comes to intervening in the functioning of an individual or a social group with a view to changing some feature of it, a comprehensive approach is crucially important. Not only must we look far and wide throughout the system for determinants of the particular feature, but we must consider the implications for the whole system of a change in that feature. We must consider also that in dealing with human beings, singly or collectively, our actions respecting some particular feature or part-function—however nicely "on target" they might be—rarely affect this feature or function and nothing else. All this is well known to the experienced clinician and to the experienced administrator. It seems possible today to have theory that will enable us to describe what these practitioners do; our aim should be to develop theory and produce knowledge that will enable us to improve on common sense and intuition, and thus contribute uniquely to the planning of beneficial actions.

If we are to think comprehensively, it must be with the use of gross units of analysis. The psychotherapist, for example, faced with the task of making sense of vast quantities of verbal material, has no alternative to using coarse categories for bringing it all together. In the same way, when we wish to speak of elements which together make up the whole personality—elements defined with attention to the theoretical structure of the whole—we can do no better today than to use the Freudian conceptions of id, superego, and ego.

Suppose—to glance at a relatively broad aspect of the social scene—that one wished to compare the culture of San Francisco with that of Los Angeles, a matter which might be of great importance for some aspects of California governmental policy. It would hardly do to employ the highly elaborated schemes and finely calibrated instruments that are used in research on small groups. The investigator who had something less than a lifetime to spend on this undertaking would decide upon a few gross categories that seemed to him important, and then content himself with rough estimates of them.

Most scientists would probably dislike the loss of rigor involved in being comprehensive and would prefer to let George do it. And George, of course, has been very active. Decisions in big and important social matters are still based mainly on the observations and judgments of practical men. No doubt this will always be so to some extent, since in practical matters there is a place for wisdom and judgments of value as well as for scientific knowledge. Still, scientists often feel free to criticize the day-to-day decisions that affect us all and to complain that they are not consulted. This is an admission of their obligation to study complex problems and to show how their findings are relevant to practice. They may do this, as I have said before, without being any less scientific, in the best sense of the word, than the laboratory man. All they have to lose are the chains of respectability. Their procedure should be to suit their instruments to the task at hand and to make sure that the gross categories used are consistent with what is known at lower levels and lend themselves to reduction and systematic treatment.

LEVEL OF ABSTRACTION

When men are confronted with practical problems they naturally tend to think in terms of the concrete and the particular. The psychotherapist, faced with the task of taking action on short notice, has to deal with what is happening to a particular patient in the situation of the moment; he cannot stop to translate his thoughts into the terms of a general theoretical system. The test specialist who wishes to develop an instrument for predicting some practically important pattern of overt behavior does not need abstract concepts to stand for general dispositions of personality; he can go far with a set of concrete test items that correlate with the behavior in which he is interested. The businessman or the administrator of an organization is likely to see his problems as particular, local, and pressing, so he seeks solutions through manipulating plainly observable features of the immediate situation.

This kind of orientation to practical problems is a pretty far cry from the most characteristic work of the scientist. The scientist interested in psychopathology must use terms for describing a patient that are sufficiently abstract so that one patient may be compared with others and with nonpatients; the myriad specific acts of patients must be ordered to a conceptual scheme, so that future observations may be systematic, and general relationships among patients' processes may be established. As for organizations, one might say that we have hardly begun the scientific study of them until we have derived a set of abstract concepts, such as role, communication, and power, that apply to organizations generally; then we can carry over what we learn from one organization to the study of others.

If one uses abstract concepts, he must, of course, be able to go back to the concrete, showing that a given concept applies in a particular case; or, to take it the other way round, it must be possible to show that a given concrete phenomenon may reasonably be ordered to the abstract concept. Where everything under consideration is open to direct observation, this task is not difficult. "Response," for example, is a highly abstract psychological concept; yet, since it refers to something observable, it is usually not difficult to get agreement that a given phenomenon is indeed a response. "Unconscious wish," on the other hand, is an abstract concept that stands for processes behind behavior. By definition it is something inside the person that expresses itself in various ways; hence it is very difficult to show that a given observable phenomenon is a special case of an unconscious wish. We deal here with a hypothetical construct, something "dreamed up" by the psychologist, not to categorize his observations, but to make sense of them.

Strictly speaking, no elements or features of personality are observable with perfect directness; all are *inferred* from behavioral indexes. But there is wide variation in the degree of directness or explicitness with which the inferences may be made. The kind of theory that is offered in this volume, like most traditional personality theory, makes free use of concepts whose ties to what is observable are highly indirect.

This kind of theory does not go unchallenged by those scientists who consider that the essence of the scientific approach is accuracy of observation and precision of measurement. These "hard-headed" scientists have something in common with hard-headed men of affairs; both groups prefer to deal with the concrete and tangible, with "the facts," with what they can get their hands on. Hypothetical constructs smack of mysticism or "untried theory." This orientation gets the practical man into trouble because it leads to too narrow a definition of his problem and cuts off inquiry into the more complex, less observable patterns of events which may have largely determined his difficulty of the moment. The situation is similar for the scientist who places observability at the top of his hierarchy of values. The highest levels of observability and precision of measurement are attained in the laboratory experiment, but the psychologist who restricts himself to this mode of investigation denies himself the opportunity to study the whole personality. There are aspects of personality that cannot be experimented upon in the usual laboratory situation; for example, there are aspects of the person that become apparent only when he is observed in numerous varied situations, and there are aspects whose meaning cannot be detected unless they are seen in broad context. Also, at the present time, it is impossible or unfeasible to arouse in a laboratory situation motives and feelings that equal in quality and intensity some that are common in everyday life. In these circumstances it is natural for the convinced experimentalist not only to limit himself to problems for which his method is suited, but actually to conceive of personality as made up of elements—for example, measurable performances—that he can get hold of. In doing this, however, he often defeats his own purposes. As we have seen, those performances that he would like to know so well remain forever partially obscured, because they owe something of their nature to factors that have been excluded from consideration.

The issue of observable phenomena versus hypothetical constructs is an old one in psychology. The early psychology of personality, which stemmed mainly from the clinic, made free use of hypothetical constructs, but this practice was severely criticized by academic psychologists, who were eager to establish their discipline as a science. For the latter, objectivity was the watchword. When the "operationism" of Bridgman (1927) appeared on the scene, they embraced it wholeheartedly. It became something of a fashion in psychology to reject, as outside of science, concepts that could not be "defined operationally"—that is, in terms of the steps taken to obtain an objective index of a given concept. During the years since the late 1920s the struggle between the operationists and the traditional personality theorists has continued. The personality theorists have been largely vindicated, but they have been forced to give some ground. Today it is pretty generally recognized that there are practically no theoretical statements that can be completely and directly verified by observation, and that hypothetical constructs are not only necessary to intellectual activity but have led to the best success in predicting and explaining behavior. Modern operationism does not require that every concept be defined in terms of operations; it does require, however, that every concept be connectable, at least indirectly, with some kind of observable phenomenon. Personality theorists, while now perfectly free to use hypothetical concepts, still have to proceed with attention to conceptual clarity, to objective indicators of their concepts, and to the question of just how their theoretical formulations might be proved or disproved by observation.

I am arguing that abstract theory is not only necessary to the development of a science of personality and social systems but also most useful in practice. It is mainly through the use of hypothetical constructs that science gets beyond common sense, and it is in getting beyond common sense that its greatest usefulness lies. Let us revert to the example of prejudice. Most of what psychologists and social scientists have said about the situational, social, and economic determinants of prejudice conforms well with what everybody knew already, but to show that prejudice in some of its aspects springs from a hypothetical deep-lying structure of personality is to go beyond the depth of the man in the street, and at the same time to state a proposition whose implications for practice are very different from those that flow from the "conventional wisdom."

THE PRACTICE OF SCIENCE

My argument rests most heavily upon a conception of the nature of practical problems and of the role of science in efforts to solve them. We must inquire further into these matters. A look at the history of psychology shows that there was a time when this science was far more concerned with practical problems than it is today, and that the results were not always good. For example, the early, very practical concern with psychological tests led to many misapplications and contributed little to the advancement of psychology as a science. Again, the experiments of Thorndike and Woodworth (1901) on "transfer of training" were carried on in an educational setting, with practice very much in mind. Their major conclusion—that learning was specific, that what was learned in one area of content or skill was not transferred to others—was immediately and very generally applied in the schools. This led to the introduction of all kinds of technical subjects, the proliferation of courses, the fragmentation of the curriculum. If children had not gone on transferring their training anyway, and if teachers had not continued to use their common sense, the results might have been even more serious. Experiences of this kind led the universities, in time, to become exceedingly wary of practice and "service," which were seen as restrictions upon the scientist's freedom to be guided solely by his curiosity and to look for answers anywhere that he pleased. Hence came the present accent on pure science, and the relegation of members of the professional schools to second-class citizenship.

I am arguing that the pendulum has now swung too far in the other direction; psychology and social science have become too far removed from practice. While science has gained from its period of withdrawal into "purity," it can now afford to become involved with practice again. In doing so it will fulfill its obligations and derive benefit for itself.

This time, however, we must proceed in a different way. For one thing, we have to consider that a practical concern involves setting goals, which raises the question of who is to do this setting. When individuals or organizations look to science for help, their interest is usually focused narrowly upon a specific problem that seems very pressing, and they often have an overrealistic conception of what they desire. Often in such cases the most useful thing a scientist can do is to bring about a reconsideration of the goal. A teacher, for example, might want science to tell her how to keep her pupils quiet—that and nothing more. This problem would rapidly become secondary if the teacher could be led to give serious attention to educational objectives. Again, psychologists have been asked to devise tests that will predict success in college. This being something they are good at, they have gone about it with extraordinary singleness of purpose—even before the question "What is success?" was satisfactorily answered. Where grades have been regarded as the only practicable criteria of success, the testing has gone forward, usually without anyone's asking what grades have to do with becoming educated, or what success in college, measured in this way, has to do with success in life.

Practice is not a matter of putting science at the disposal of anyone who can formulate a problem and afford to have some work done on it. The scientist must participate in determining what the problem is and in deciding what sort of solution will be satisfactory. This, as already indicated, will be good for the individual or group most immediately concerned; at the same time the scientist has an obligation to seek a solution that is good for *all* concerned. No scientist would lend himself to an enterprise designed to help the management of a firm more effectively exploit its employees, or to help teachers exploit students. When he works in an organization, he must consider the interests of all departments, factions, and subgroups. When he devotes himself to public questions, he must seek solutions that are in the public interest. This follows from the fact that science belongs to everybody; its commitment to truth necessarily involves for it commitment to an array of humanistic values. From this general point of view it would appear to be poor practice for a psychologist to devote himself to predicting grades in college without raising any further questions about the implications of his work or about what is being left out of consideration. No one is in a better position than he to see things impartially and whole, and to be aware of the interests of students, parents, and society generally, as well as those of colleges that want to improve their work.

For the scientist to adopt this conception of his role and to proceed accordingly is to interfere in no way with his pursuit of knowledge. On the contrary, this is to open the way for scientific inquiry into complex matters. By insisting that practical problems are complex, interwoven with other problems, and tied to long-range human and social goals, the scientist puts himself in a position to ask questions of general scientific interest. He may now adopt the simple rule that no problem is worthy of his attention unless it can be regarded as a special case of something more general, unless it can be phrased in such terms and attacked in such a way as to promise some addition to systematic knowledge. Thus he will be able to resist pressure to produce results at once and to avoid involvement in local, *ad hoc*, or fragmentary studies (often called "practical") that contribute nothing to science and do little for the individual or group seeking help.

The scientist may, of course, offer consultation on the basis of what he already knows, and technologies may sometimes be designed in accordance with general scientific knowledge, but most practical problems call for study, for an engagement of the scientist with the problem and its ramifications. It is here that the general approach which I have outlined recommends itself.

In adopting this approach to an individual or a group asking for help, the scientist must accept the task of explaining what he is up to. Individuals who enter into counseling or psychotherapeutic relationships can usually be led without difficulty to understand that they are to participate jointly with the scientist in an inquiry that promises to be mutually helpful. One may safely say that they will usually respond better to a situation defined in this way, a way that protects their dignity, than to one in which it is understood that they are to get answers from an authority. The case is not essentially different from that of research subjects who volunteer to be studied intensively in the interests of science and who, when the inquiry is conducted in the right way, regularly report that they derived benefit from the experience.

When an organization or social group calls on scientists for help with its problems, the task of explaining the scientific approach is more complicated. Now several individuals, in various relations to one another and each with his own view of the matter, are involved. However, it often happens that by the time the scientist has finished explaining his role and procedure to all concerned, the original problems are already being defined differently—and the scientist has already learned a great deal about the social structure he is planning to study. This whole problem of the scientist's approach to an organization or group that asks for help, or that he seeks to study, is discussed at length in the last chapter of this book. It suffices to say here that the main points for the scientist to make clear are these: that he must proceed in his own way; that he cannot restrict himself to some particular problem, however glaring, but must see it in its context; that he cannot limit his inquiries to one department or subsection of the organization but must be free to look anywhere for relevant facts; that since he is going to state problems in general terms and communicate his findings to a general audience, his activities may be useful not only to the organization in which he works but to other organizations and to science itself. Organizations that cannot accept these conditions are of course free to apply science as they see fit, but they may have difficulty in getting scientists themselves to become actively involved with their problems.

In the domain of public affairs, where the concern is with such problems as helping culturally deprived people or regulating youthful drinking, there is little reason, save insufficient public enlightenment, for conflict between an interest in solving problems and an interest in advancing social science. Support for both of these kinds of activity comes ultimately from the same source—namely, the people, expressing themselves through public agencies. Here the ideal is to build the research function into planned social actions, and to state research problems in terms of how to induce desired effects. Inquiry and action thus become two aspects of the same humanistic enterprise.

Part Two

This section presents an overview of the whole book. It introduces the major concepts that are used throughout the book and states its major theme: intervention in individual and group processes with a view to promoting desirable changes. Although personality-in-the-social-system is conceived as a single system, analysis must proceed by abstracting from this larger whole (*a*) the personality, (*b*) the social system, and (*c*) their interactions. Chapter 2 discusses positive goals for the individual and outlines a general theory of how personality develops in interaction with the social environment. Chapter 3 is concerned with the workings of the social system itself, and its interaction with the larger society in which it exists. The central question here is how it may be possible to intervene in the functioning of the system in such a way that changes in its parts or in the whole might further the health and development of its members.

Chapter 4 offers a preliminary view of the complex interactions between the individual and the social system—in this case a college. A case study is used to throw light upon some of the conditions and processes of change in a student during four years of college, to show something of how a change in one part of the personality affects other parts, and of how different features of the college environment interact and combine to induce personality change.

CHAPTER TWO

Action to Promote Personality Development: Some Basic Concepts

If one wishes to improve himself, as we in America so often do, but cannot point to any illness that needs to be cured, he is very likely to conceive of his goal in developmental terms: to be more "mature," to grow in this or that respect, to develop this or that quality of character or of performance. And if we ask ourselves what can or should be done in the interests of individuals for whom we have some responsibility, professional or other—say we are educators or counselors or consultants—we inevitably find ourselves thinking in developmental terms of the same kind.

Again, psychologists of today, when they try to formulate what they hope to accomplish by psychotherapy, are likely to state their objectives in the terms of a developmental psychology. For example, the Commission in Psychology for a Conference on Psychotherapy and Counseling, a commission made up of psychologists of quite varied theoretical outlook (including the present writer) agreed on the following statement (Sanford et al., 1955):

"We also applaud what appears to be a growing accent upon a psychological approach to personal problems. This approach rests upon a psychology of personality development and seeks to conceptualize the goals of such development—differentiation, wholeness, autonomy, utilization of

This paper is based upon a manuscript prepared for the Joint Commission on Mental Illness and Health. It was adapted by the author and published in J. Katz, P. Nochlin, and R. Stover (eds.), *Writers on Ethics* (Princeton, N.J.: Van Nostrand, 1962).

potentialities, and the like. Psychological well-being, from this point of view, does not mean absence of disease but rather a state of relatively advanced development. Psychological maladjustment is conceived of as relative failure with respect to the diverse goals of development. Psychological diagnosis—or, as we should prefer to say, psychological analysis of the problem—is an attempt to assess the developmental status of the individual with particular attention to the potentialities for and the obstacles to further growth, and to formulate in psychodynamic terms the reasons for this state of affairs. In his practice of psychotherapy, the psychologist seeks, most essentially, to further the growth of the individual, to help him to become what he can."

I should not like to argue that studying health is more important, or in any way more virtuous, than studying illness. It must be admitted, however, that in the present state of our knowledge intensive studies of normal people may contribute to the formulation of a general theory that will further our understanding of both illness and health. Nor would I like to argue that it has been a mistake to derive so much of our personality theory from studies of the abnormal, or that our attention to psychopathology has given us a false conception of the nature of man. Personality, like other functioning systems, can be best observed and understood when something goes wrong; if there has been a delay in studies of the normal, this has not been due to the morbid preoccupations of certain theorists, but to our natural inclination to give first attention to the more vivid and pressing human problems, and, in the development of a new science, to postpone the conceptually and methodologically more difficult. Still, if one works with people who are in no sense ill but who nevertheless wish to improve, and whose improvement is earnestly sought by others and by society at large, he has no alternative but to conceive of desiderata and to seek for means by which they might be attained. (This is the position of those who, like the present writer, work in educational institutions.) In this circumstance psychopathology is not enough, not because it has led to a wrong conception of personality, but because it has not considered all the desiderata and the conditions that favor them.

Actually the psychological and social sciences have not neglected positive goals altogether. Erikson (1955) has remarked: "A system must have its utopia. For psychoanalysis the utopia is 'genitality,' "—an ill-defined but no doubt blessed state. In a similar context Erikson later quotes Freud's famous but possibly apocryphal remark when asked what he thought a normal person should be able to do well: "To love and to work." Erikson then goes on to spell out some desiderata of his own, which reflect his well-known stages of ego development and reach their culmination in "ego integrity"—a state which he describes as "the ego's accrued assurance of its proclivity for order and meaning . . . a postnarcissistic love of the human ego—not of the self—as an experience which conveys some world order and spiritual sense, no matter how dearly paid for." The absence of ego integration is signified by fear of death. R. W. White (1952b), in summarizing much recent thought in the area of developmental goals, distinguishes four major "trends of natural growth": the stabilizing of ego identity (with credits to Erikson), the deepening of interests, the freeing of personal relationships, and the humanizing of values. This is reminiscent of the earlier effort by Allport (1937) to set down the marks of the mature personality: "extension of the self," "self-objectification," "autonomous interests," "unified philosophy of life." Also to be mentioned in this connection is the "self-actualized person" of Goldstein (1939) and of Maslow (1954).

In all these schemes there is the assumption of a connection between growth and the possession of these desirable characteristics. There is the assumption of natural tendencies for people to grow in these directions, but it is not held that every adult, or even the average adult, ever attains these high levels of development. Actually these are ideals; they can be attained—have been attained—by many people, and apparently any person can conceivably attain more of them; and the mechanisms or processes by which they are attained come under the heading of development. In a great deal of more or less popular literature the term "maturity" is used to stand for these patterns of ideal or eminently desirable traits or features, although the connection with facts or theories of natural growth may be remote.

Perhaps it is not surprising that when writers have turned their attention to health many of these same desirable human features enter prominently into the picture. Thus, for example, Barron (1957), in summarizing a study of personal soundness conducted at the University of California Institute of Personality Assessment and Research (Barron, 1954), writes as follows:

"The most general conclusion arrived at by the psychologists who conducted the study was that personal soundness is essentially a way of responding to the problems set by life, and that its marks are realism, adaptability, and the development of a sense of responsibility based on internally determined principles."

Barron (1957) later goes on to propose an interesting conception of mental health:

"I think that some such concept as that of elegance is needed if we are to talk meaningfully of psychological health. A person may be said to be most elegant, and most healthy, when his awareness includes the broadest possible aspects of human experience, and the deepest possible comprehension of them, while at the same time he is most simple and direct in his feelings, thoughts, and action."

Obviously, it is not easy to distinguish between maturity and health or, one might better say, among maturity, health, and ideal goals of development. Value judgments shape our conceptions of all these things. In discussing them we must be careful to separate fact from value and to remember that our own values are not likely to be universally shared.

Representatives of the psychological and the social sciences have joined with other citizens in producing a multiplicity of conceptions of the desirable in human behavior and personality. Not only do we have health and maturity, but also social adjustment, efficiency, creativity, various conceptions of education, and so on. Specialists differ in their preferences among these things almost as much as other people do. The whole matter is to a large extent relative to time and to place—that is, to historical phase and to social and cultural setting.

For example, for a long time after the rise of applied psychology in America most workers in the field shared with the mass of our citizens the tendency to place very high value upon social adjustment. Today, when most of our intellectuals worry about conformity, or the loss of individuality to the social group or to the organization, social adjustment as a desideratum comes in for much severe criticism, both from within (White, 1952a) and from without the ranks of the interested professions. Again, the value for social adjustment may be declining in America, but this does not yet prevent British psychoanalysts from scolding American psychoanalysts for having or seeming to have the wrong objectives. Thus Marjorie Brierley (1951) accuses Alexander and French (1946) of participating in the American therapeutic concern for fixing people up so that they can take their place in the productive machinery of the nation, instead of adhering to the true goal of psychoanalysis—that is, the wholeness of the individual. The argument undoubtedly reflects a deep-seated difference between the British and American cultures.

The notion that people should develop their potentialities to the fullest possible extent, or in the words of the Commission in Psychology, that the individual should be helped to "become what he can," has the advantage of being in keeping with the spirit of Western civilization, and it serves as an antidote to the extreme cultural relativism that marked the period just prior to World War II. And a great many other values flow from this major one. But people can become a great many things, including things as yet unknown, so we shall not be spared the necessity of making choices.

Happily, the existence of pluralism and relativity with respect to goals does not prevent the social scientist from getting on with the work of discovering the determinants of various desired states and processes of the person and, in appropriate circumstances, doing what he can to promote these desiderata. He can work in the interests of some objective without considering that it is the only "good," or even that it occupies a particularly high place in a defensible scheme of values. If he wishes to function as a valuing individual, however, he should take care to insure that what he does in the interests of a particular objective does not interfere with the attainment of other objectives that he considers more important, or that what he does with one purpose in mind does not have incidental consequences which he believes to be bad.

A major argument of this chapter is that health, maturity, and maximum development can and should be distinguished—difficult though this is to do at the present time; that they are independently variable and, when large samples of the earth's population are considered, not necessarily positively correlated; and that they appear in different combinations, some of which seem far more ideal than others. Social adjustment, social effectiveness, creativity, educatedness are, in their turn, different from health, maturity, and maximum development, and from one another. If we can define such desiderata clearly enough, and work out sufficiently valid indices of them, it will become possible to demonstrate their relations to present and to antecedent conditions. Out of this kind of inquiry there may eventually emerge clearer conceptions of the desirable.

HEALTH

A discussion of mental health may well take as its point of departure Kubie's important paper on "The Fundamental Nature of the Distinction Between Normality and Neurosis" (1954). Kubie writes:

"One quality *however is constant and sets a normal act apart from one that is a manifestation of the neurotic process.* This is not a judgment of value, but rather a clinical description of that one attribute of behavior common to every neurotic action and absent from every normal act. If we are to understand the difference between the two, it is essential to keep this characteristic clearly in mind. *This clinically derived distinguishing trait centers around the freedom and flexibility to learn through experience, to change, and to adapt to changing external circumstances.* Thus, *the essence of normality is flexibility,* in contrast to the freezing of behavior into patterns of unalterability that characterizes every manifestation of the neurotic process, whether in impulses, purposes, acts, thoughts, or feelings. Whether or not a behavioral event is free to change depends not upon the quality of the act itself, but upon the nature of the constellation of forces that has produced it. *No moment of behavior can be looked upon as neurotic unless the processes that have set it in motion predetermine its automatic repetition irrespective of the situation, the utility, or the consequences of the act."*

Kubie goes on to make it clear that the processes underlying the neurotic act are *unconscious.* Neurotic acts are unconsciously determined; normal acts are not. One of the great virtues of this conception, as Kubie shows, is that it points up the relative superficiality of various phenomena that have long been associated with mental illness or with mental health, but which could never be made to stand as reliable indices of it. By separating underlying determinants from overt manifestations, Kubie's conception aids our understanding of the latter without imposing on them the burden of maintaining the essential distinction between neurosis and normality. Thus, exhibiting symptoms, suffering psychologically, causing pain to others are not necessarily neurotic; these phenomena may be conscious responses to unusual strains, rather than expressions of unconscious processes. The pathology, in other words, may be in the environment rather than in the individual. Similarly, the usualness or frequency in a population, the conformity with social norms, the social utility, the pleasantness or comfort to the individual, the interpersonal smoothness, of a behavior pattern are not highly reliable signs of mental health, since any of these features may be largely determined by unconscious processes.

But it seems that a somewhat more general frame of reference is needed. Why is it important to the individual that he be flexible and adaptable, and that his psychological processes be predominantly conscious —or capable of becoming so (preconscious)—rather than unconscious? Because, it would appear, this enables him to function well, to manage strains of whatever severity in a way that permits him to maintain himself and that minimally impairs his capacity for dealing with future strains. When processes are predominantly conscious and preconscious, the possibilities of intercommunication among them are maximized, so that optimal functioning in one area is favorable to optimal functioning in others, and so that when a strain occurs, as many resources as are needed may be brought to bear upon it. And, similarly, when such possibilities of intercommunication among differentiated parts exist, the individual is able to handle a given strain with no more of his resources than are necessary; he does not, so to speak, become overcommitted on a given front, thus weakening himself on other fronts or unnecessarily exposing his general position.

We are saying, with Kubie and with Barron, that mental health is a way of meeting and dealing with life's problems. It is not a matter of stability, in the usual sense of the word.

Barron finds that people who come to a clinic seeking help for psychological problems are readily differentiated into the relatively healthy and the relatively unhealthy. And the characteristics that distinguish the healthier are, in general, the same as those found to be outstanding in a group of graduate students rated high on personal soundness—that is, "realism, adaptability, and the development of a sense of responsibility based on internally determined principles." Health is thus a potential for dealing with strain.

Stability, on the other hand, may be due to an absence of strain of a kind that would disturb equilibrium, or to the existence of equilibrating devices in the environment. A person might be so well adjusted to his environment, or his environment might be so simple or so protective of the individual, that he was not called upon to manage any severe strains. He might have all the health he needed in the circumstances, or even all he would need for any foreseeable future, but still be relatively lacking in what it takes to deal with a variety of severe strains. But in our complex society virtually no one is free of strains, diverse and taxing; the healthy person certainly has his share, and as we observe him over time we note that periods of stress are followed by periods of relative stability and that a kind of fundamental stability is maintained. The person changes, as he must in order to adapt, but he does not change altogether, or even, as a rule, in large areas of himself; and the changes made are consistent with what he was before. The healthy person is upset by strains, but not too much; and the equilibrium that he gains is not the same as that which he enjoyed before; it is on a higher level, but this higher level of functioning is no more different from the earlier one than it needs to be in order to incorporate adaptations to the new strain.

As with stability, so with "integration." Health is not a matter of integration pure and simple, nor does integration seem to be the major requirement. Integration is maximum in the mass action of the child, and perhaps in the rigidly maintained unified scheme of things sometimes found in much older people. Being unified or all of a piece, so that the whole system goes into action in response to a stimulus, is hardly the way to cope effectively with a variety of strains. We say, then, that we want integration after differentiation has taken place. Yet, even in the highly differentiated person—one in whom more different functions are being performed and being allocated to more different parts—integration as a feature of health may easily be overaccented. There is still the possibility that it will be attained or maintained at the expense of breadth or richness, and leave the individual in a poor way to adapt to changed circumstances. Health, according to the present conception, may very well involve the giving up of integrated structures if this is required in order to manage strains in the most appropriate way. As Barron (1954) has put it, "It is . . . a sign of greater inner resources to be able to upset one's own balance and to seek a new order of self-hood."

Integration may also be externally determined, as a result of the organization of the individual's environment. For instance, an individual who becomes well adapted to a total institution such as an asylum or army bootcamp will display integration of a sort, but this would hardly increase his potential for handling future strains if his environment changed radically.

Yet, in spite of all this, there seems to be no doubt that integration should have a place in the formula for health. We might say that the healthy person has a marked capacity for integration and is always moving toward it. At the same time, we must remember that he is becoming more expanded—that is, more parts are being added and the parts are growing larger—and more differentiated. As long as his complexity is increasing, integration will be incomplete. He will remain, as it were, somewhat open-ended, always ready to include more. Thus it is that such a person may at any time embody contradictions and conflicts and exhibit surprising, seemingly unrelated "sides to his nature." But we do not detect any particular effort to bring all these things together; he acts as if he could wait. What we do observe is that most of the time he seems integrated enough, that in a critical situation he brings up the resources which are needed, and that these might very well include some of his less characteristic—we might say less integrated—processes. We might, of course, call this condition of flexibility, of heightened possibility for communication among diverse parts, "integration," or fundamental integration, were it not that this term has too many connotations of unity or harmony or all-of-a-piece-ness. "Integrative potential" might do for the time being.

MATURITY

There is no doubt that the present conception of health includes much that other writers have brought under the general heading of "maturity." And we have not been able to steer altogether clear of maximum or ideal development. The proposal here is that we may avoid confusion if we go back to an earlier—and, as it seems, "common-sense"—meaning of maturity, and if we distinguish it from health as here conceived and avoid strictly the temptation to use the word to stand for ideal developmental goals or general patterns of values.

In the classical literature in developmental psychology, maturity is a stage of development, like childhood, adolescence, and old age; each of these stages has features which, in general, distinguish it from the others. A highly mature person would be one that possessed a great deal of that which generally distinguishes adults from younger or older people. Tied as it is to the ground plan of organic life, this conception does not permit an adult to become more and more mature as he grows older; instead—and quite impersonally—it requires him to become more like an old person, who in some ways is more like a child than like the mature adult. Nor does this conception have anything to do with our desires in the matter. Obviously some traits generally considered desirable in anybody are more characteristic of children than of adults. Spontaneity, the naive eye, whole-heartedness, genuineness, and of course honesty might be examples. In the common-sense view, adopted by many psychologists, maturity is simply the predominance of the efficient, the discriminating, the differentiated and realistic over the primitive, the impulsive, the passionate. When maturity is conceived in this way, we are left free to do what we have done about health; instead of thinking of it in terms of the predominance of certain dimensions, we think of it as a way of functioning involving all dimensions.

The mature person may be healthy or unhealthy. One has only to imagine what extreme predominance of the rational processes would mean —constriction, overorganization, emotional coldness, preoccupation with detail, overintellectualization, and the like—in order to see that it may be an accompaniment of some forms of pathology. Or consider the more usual picture: a steady man with a steady job which he performs conscientiously and well, a good husband and father and citizen—in short, a man who performs adequately and comfortably and with gratification in a variety of functionally significant social positions. Or take the folk conception of maturity which we see displayed in the liquor advertisement: "A man for whom all things are important chooses his friends, his club and his whisky with taste and discrimination." No one but a youthful spirit, or perhaps a new Ph.D. in psychology, would care to say that such men are not mature. But health is another matter. It may very well be that these patterns of maturity are sustained by too heavy an admixture of unconscious processes and, hence, that there is inadequate capacity for managing varied strains. On the other hand, there is nothing about the patterns in and of themselves to suggest ill health. Only rather searching analysis, or else observation over a fairly long period of time, would tell.

DEVELOPMENT

At the same time, we are not saying that these mature men cannot go on growing and developing. Adults are not only more mature but more *developed*. A person might strike us as complex, rich, interesting, and still not strike us as mature. Although he displayed discrimination, efficiency, and responsibility, he would lapse often enough into overgeneralization, regressive integration (such as throwing oneself into the teen-age "gang" style of relating to people when in social difficulty), or primitive adaptation to be found to have an aspect of immaturity.

This way of looking at the matter requires that we stick to certain definitions of development—and of growth. In general systems theory, for example, according to Boulding (1956), the growth of something—an organism, an institution, or a city—is simply expansion, the enlargement of parts and the addition of parts, while development refers to increasing complexity. This accords well enough with what seems to be the prevailing view in developmental psychology. According to C. Buhler (1951), growth involves "(a) the interaction of exogenous materials in the formation of new units and (b) relatively irreversible time changes in magnitude of measured dimensions or functions," while development is "the directive coordination of the diverse processes into an adult . . . into an organized heterogeneity." "Organized" here would not mean harmoniously or otherwise ideally organized but simply that the diverse processes are functionally related one to another and to the whole.

How are growth and development to be distinguished from health? In general, as we have seen, we may accomplish this simply by restricting the definitions of the two former to expansion and complexity and being faithful to our conception of health. Can we conceive of a person who is expanded and complex but not healthy? It seems that we may. Indeed, one might as well ask whether one can conceive of an unhealthy person who is not, in some fair degree, expanded and differentiated, for it would appear that only in such a state would we find the conflicts so characteristic of neurosis. The fact is that as people grow from infancy to adulthood, as their life space increases, their susceptibility to strain becomes greater. But with expansion and differentiation the possibilities for health also increase; so it is of interest to note the relatively highly developed but unhealthy person. He is not hard to find: the interesting, colorful, contradictory, and tortured person to be encountered occasionally at any clinic —or cocktail party.

We have to say also that a person who is unhealthy is not thereby prevented from growing and developing. The neurotic adult is readily distinguished from a neurotic child, and a man who has been neurotic since childhood is far from being the same now as then. The differences are matters of growth and development—and maturity. Neurotic defenses have to evolve in order to continue at the same level of effectiveness, for forces that would undo them increase in variety and strength. Even a paranoid system has to go on expanding and increasing in complexity in order to maintain itself. But obviously such growth and development are not normal, in kind or in rate. The important and sobering fact is that growth, normal or abnormal, is progressive; early distortions and dislocations tend to follow their own course and to ramify throughout the whole system.

But what about health in the relatively undeveloped person? Margaret Brenman, in raising a question about Kubie's conception of health, drew attention to a group of uneducated and underprivileged girls with whom she had worked; they seemed healthy, untroubled, stable; yet one could not see that their behavior was being determined predominantly by conscious and preconscious processes. And similarly, consider the member of some simple, underdeveloped society, an individual whose differentiation is minimal but who performs all the functions required of him and seems happy and stable. One is reluctant to say that such people are lacking in health. Here, of course, we have to remember that stability may be very largely due to an absence of strain; and that Margaret Brenman's girls and our citizen of the simple society might indeed be far less healthy than a person who, with plenty of signs of tension, is adapting himself to the complexities of the modern world. Indeed, these girls and this primitive might easily break down if the expansion and differentiation which would follow upon education and privilege and experience in a complex society were not accompanied by a commensurate increase in health.

Now what about the healthy child? These same considerations would seem generally to hold. Certainly the adolescent of our society is in a pathogenic situation. We do not gauge his health by the amount of tension and instability that he exhibits right now; rather we try to get a conception of where he is going, and we are reassured about his health if it seems that the strains he is under are going to be managed. This, according to our general formulation, will depend upon the degree of intercommunication among the various processes of his personality. A bad outcome would be indicated by a predominance of unconscious forces or by a tendency to make processes unconscious right now. The question is, how far back into childhood may we carry this formulation? Perhaps the younger the child, the less health depends upon what is inside his personality and the more we take into account his probable future in estimating his health. We should be seriously concerned if strains upon the child were of such severity that he had no recourse but repression and so tended to expand the areas of behavior dominated by unconscious forces.

What would seem to be very desirable is a high degree of health in highly developed persons. It is this consummation that is wished in the various proposals concerning the goals of development—for example, those of Erikson (1955) or White (1952) or the Commission in Psychology. But this does not mean that we have now arrived at the psychologist's conception of the greatest good. Health and development are different, and people are free to prefer one or the other. Or they may place higher value upon maturity. Or they may prefer one or another of the different combinations in which these three desiderata may occur in different people.

Thus it should be clear that we are far from having set up any absolute values which would restrict the function of preference in human affairs. The main effect of psychological inquiry into behavior is to reduce the element of subjectivity in value judgments. As we learn more and more about health, maturity, and development—their conditions, interrelationships, and implications—we increase the likelihood that choices will be made on the basis of knowledge of fact rather than on the basis of wishes or fears.

THE DEVELOPMENTAL FUNCTION OF PSYCHOLOGICAL STRAIN

We have seen that desiderata of the kind proposed by Erikson, White, or Maslow are sometimes regarded as the natural outcomes of normal growth. The implication is that we come by these things just by virtue of our being human, unless of course, we are so unfortunate as to encounter pathogenic circumstances. Such a view is an expression of what Allport calls the "Leibnitzian point of view," the view that it is in our nature to become unified, to extend ourselves, and so on, and that the process by which we become so is a kind of unfolding of what was there in the beginning.

There is no doubt that some aspects of growth and development have this characteristic. It is usual in the literature of developmental psychology to think in this way of changes due to maturation, as distinguished from changes due primarily to experience. Where there is apparent unfolding in accordance with a ground plan of life we expect physiological correlates to loom large. Thus the sequence of Freud's stages of libidinal development is closely associated with a sequence of known bodily changes. But when we come to Erikson's stages of ego development, things become somewhat obscure. Does the sequence of these stages, assuming that it holds generally in our society, actually conform with a ground plan of life or is it in large part a result of the pattern of our culture and social organization? The point would appear to be moot. It would appear no more *natural* for a person in our society to be concerned about his ego identity than for a man in a primitive society to remain so undifferentiated that he has no conception of himself apart from his family and tribe. We do not question that development is naturally sequential, that if, for example, our primitive man should become more differentiated, an inevitable tendency toward integration would arise. What we are doing is—granted some human potential for differentiation—putting considerable emphasis upon the environmental circumstances in which it occurs or does not occur. And of course we assume that whatever happens is in accordance with natural law.

Growth and development as they have been defined here—expansion and increasing complexity—are certainly the best candidates for the status of natural tendencies. They may safely be accorded this status, provided we do not use this as an excuse for not trying to explain just how they occur and provided we do not underestimate the possible influence of varying environmental conditions. But expansion and differentiation are very general and very abstract conceptions; we cannot deduce from them such things as "humanized values," "ego integrity," or autonomy. These desirable states or processes, like health, maturity, education, and other developmental goals, depend heavily for their attainment upon external circumstances, upon what is thus conceivably within our power. What this adds up to is the general view that with respect to these desiderata we cannot adopt an attitude of "leave them alone and they'll come home"; these are things that have to be worked for. But this view is not an all-out environmentalism either. There is a notion from Gestalt psychology, and general systems theory, that is intended to transcend the old nature-nurture controversy; this is the notion that the new Gestalts, the higher-level organizations that the individual comes to in the course of his development, are not the direct results of an unfolding or the results of the internalization of a culture pattern; they are new stages of equilibrium embodying both the person's tendency to remain what he is and the changes that have been required in order to reduce strains.

Writers of the Leibnitzian tradition, who consider that man does more than "just adjust" and that his potential for "higher things" is there from the beginning, tend to be particularly critical of the "tension-reduction" theory of motivation and personality change. This theory, fundamental in stimulus-response psychology and psychoanalysis, holds that all behavior is initiated by some kind of disequilibrium or tension and proceeds in the direction of restoring equilibrium. In its most general formulation, it is the principle of homeostasis.

Criticisms are of two sorts. One is that the disequilibrium-equilibrium formula is too simple, and the other is that organisms and particularly humans do other things besides seek ways and means to reduce tension or restore equilibrium. The first type of criticism has been directed particularly against the notion, found in some of the older theories, that the final state of equilibrium is the same as that which existed before the disequilibrating circumstances. It is easily answered by the generally accepted modern view that the final states of equilibrium tend to be on progressively higher levels than the initial states.

More controversial is the view that equilibrium, however new or however high its level, is not enough. Thus for Goldstein (1939) "self-actualization" is the drive that carries the organism on to activity after equilibrium has been reached. Similarly, Maslow (1954) distinguishes "expressive behavior" from "coping behavior"; Mowrer (1950) distinguishes "sign learning," which is "problem making," from "solution learning"; while Murray and Kluckhohn (1955) list "process activity" and the "generation of tension" alongside tension reduction as major functions of personality. None of these writers proposes to do away with tension reduction; they merely wish to supplement this conception with something else. The generous attention devoted to this "something else" nowadays may tend to obscure what seems to be the central fact: that the homeostatic principle is still of fundamental importance. It may have to be supplemented, or it may in the future be incorporated in some more general theory, but it seems at the moment to be the best principle we have for formulating the phenomena of growth and development and health. It still seems our best approach to an understanding of the systematic causation of growth or developmental changes. To say with C. Bühler (1951) that "life's basic tendency is toward expansion" and that the individual may change direction without benefit of any disturbing external stimulus is to skirt the vexing question of what makes expansion or development occur. It seems better to say that organisms are irritable and open to disequilibrating inputs, to manage some of which they have no alternative but to expand. We are thus offered an explanation of the well-nigh universal phenomenon of expansion at the same time that we are offered a basis for hypotheses concerning any kind of change in behavior or personality.

Sticking, then, to the homeostatic principle, we have to say that in order to induce a desirable change—toward further growth or development or toward greater health—we have to think in terms of what would upset the existing equilibrium, produce instability, set in motion activity leading to stabilization on a higher level.

This formula, as we shall see in a moment, seems to work very well when we address ourselves to the problem of how to increase health and development in normal youths or adults. When we concentrate on children, and particularly when we have ill health primarily in mind, we are struck of course by the bad effects of strain. We are likely to think mainly of protecting the child from strain, so that he may "grow naturally." Here it is necessary to think in terms of the intensity of the strains relative to the child's capacity for managing. When strains exceed the limits of the child's normal adaptive capacities, he seems to fall back upon primitive adaptive mechanisms which, though they may suffice at the time, tend to persist and make later adaptations more difficult. The classical case, of course, is that of the child who in dealing with some traumatic experience has to repress or deny—to wall off—some part of himself. This adaptation impairs health and development because the child, fearing a repetition of the original trauma, has to go on repressing or denying, and thus his capacity to learn from experience is reduced. To bring these disconnected or walled-off parts of the personality back into the picture, into the adaptively functioning part of the personality, is the primary task of psychotherapy, and to guide development in such a way that the strains to which the child is subjected do not exceed the limits of his normal adaptive capacities is the essence of mental hygiene.

But these considerations should not lead us to overlook the fact that the progressive changes we desire are also induced by strains and preceded by instability, though in this case of course the adaptive changes are within normal limits—either because the strains were not too great or because the environment helped to supply equilibrating devices. When the individual is able successfully to manage severe strains, health and also growth and development appear to be increased. On this basis we could explain why it was that the unusually healthy young men described by Barron and the outstanding people described in the Office of Strategic Services study (1948) uniformly reported a variety of painful and disturbing childhood experiences.

It does not follow from this that in order to attain high levels of health and development we must deliberately traumatize children. But it does follow that as adaptive capacities increase we would be wise to put less emphasis upon the hope for "natural growth" and more emphasis upon experiences that would lead the individual to stretch himself. After the special strains connected with puberty and its aftermath have been more or less mastered, the major obstacle to further development and to increased health would appear to be premature integration or structuration, particularly if the internal structures are continually reinforced by adjustment to a social group. In such circumstances, and also in the case of the average, mature adult who has reached a stable adjustment, the procedure for increasing health and furthering development—and perhaps also education—would seem to be to stir people up enough so that the existing organization was disturbed. But, of course, no one would wish to do this unless he was prepared to deal with some fresh instability, unless he had reason to believe it would not exceed the individual's adaptive capacities, and unless he could see a way to stabilization on a higher level.

This general way of looking at things is supported by studies of college students. Reports by Webster (1956), by Freedman (1956), and by the present writer (1957) show that young women in college changed quite measurably in four years in the direction of greater health and higher levels of development. But these reports also show that seniors are considerably more unstable than freshmen. The interpretation offered by these writers—one that is consistent with the major themes of this chapter—is that the college is to some extent successful in upsetting the more or less stable organizations that freshmen present upon arrival, and in inducing very considerable expansion and differentiation—even in shrinking to some extent the area of behavior that is dominated by unconscious forces. But it does not go so far as to establish a new equilibrium; indeed one should not expect to find a stable organization in people who are about to leave an environment to which they have become more or less adapted and enter another which, though it is largely unknown, they can expect to be in some respects radically different.

It is important to note, finally, that these considerations hold only for people who are already more or less healthy. The approach one takes to the problem of increasing health and development in students or in adults will depend upon how healthy he perceives them to be, on the average, or perhaps upon whether he believes that expansion of the healthy parts of a personality, leading to a healthier total personality, can take place without the unhealthy parts having first been attended to. It is interesting that Kubie, when he addresses himself to problems of college education ("The Forgotten Man of Education," 1954a), stresses almost exclusively the task of shrinking the areas dominated by unconscious forces; and the procedures by which this is to be done must perforce be those that increase self-insight. But psychologists—for example, White (1952b) and the present writer (1956)—have proposed numerous other conditions and processes of increased health and development, such as having one's values challenged, being forced to perform in new social roles, encountering people who do not accept the transference upon them of infantile imagery, and so on. From this point of view one would say that perhaps the Russians or well-adapted Californians (that is, those who have been in California for ten years) need not so much to be psychoanalyzed as to travel. Kubie's answer would be that there is no use in offering people a chance to broaden their experience if their unconscious processes prevent them from *having* experience; that there is no use in requiring new role-performances if the unconscious dictates that they endlessly repeat the role-performance they have already learned. He is largely right, of course. I should not wish to encourage any bland underestimation of the extent to which the behavior of people in our society is dominated by unconscious forces.

We may all join Kubie in the effort to find ways for increasing self-insight that can be practiced elsewhere than in the consulting room. But it would also be a mistake to approach young people as if they were on the average more neurotic than healthy. All of course have areas dominated by unconscious processes; many efforts to broaden their experience or to induce new responses will on that account fail. It is a safe assumption, however, that all have areas of functioning in which conscious and preconscious processes predominate and which can be expanded and developed by methods available to the educator, the counselor, or the social reformer. Whether one could ever in this way modify or shrink unconsciously determined areas of behavior is an unanswered question, but one could certainly increase the ratio of the healthy to the unhealthy and perhaps thereby set in motion processes by which the latter would finally dwindle to relative unimportance.

CHAPTER THREE

Personality Development in a Change-Promoting Institution

In every human society there evolve institutions for the socialization of its members, or, as we would say, agencies of personality development. It is as if the society understands implicitly that it cannot leave the development of the individual personality to natural maturation and chance encounters with psychological strain. The family is the first institution of personality development. As societies become more complex, other such institutions proliferate. In our society, for example, we have schools and colleges, summer camps, military training programs, the Peace Corps, penal institutions, the psychotherapeutic relationship, and a wide range of other similar agencies and programs. While their goals may differ, these are all agencies through which an individual passes for a limited time for the purpose of being changed in some desired way.

Let us consider, as an example, the freshman student who enters a college. After being subjected for a specified period to a variety of modifying and improving processes within the institution, he will, ideally, emerge a larger and more differentiated individual. It should be noted here that there is an optimum time during which this development is expected to take place. Too prolonged a stay becomes unhealthy for the individual. The "perennial sophomore," or the child who stays in the family too long, becomes a source of concern. On the other hand, being

This chapter has been adapted from a paper presented at the Conference on Higher Education and Mental Health, in Gainesville, Florida, September 25–26, 1963.

prematurely ejected from one of these institutions also has bad consequences. Schools worry about drop-outs, and psychiatrists worry about the patient who leaves treatment after just one interview, telling himself that he is now all right.

How effectively the institution will use its allotment of time to change or develop any given individual will depend on a number of factors within the individual and within the institution. A closer look at our freshman and the college of his choice may bring these factors into focus.

DEFINITION OF GOALS

First, let us consider what kind of changes the college would encourage a student to undergo, some clear conception of its goals being fundamental to any institution of change. For a college these goals are likely to include, in addition to the inculcation of knowledge and skills, some balance of mental health and enriched development. All three are implicit in the professed goal of *education*—the educing or leading forth of whatever potential lies within the individual. Of course, merely proclaiming "education" as a goal is not enough; it must be carefully defined. True education is liberating and differentiating. If it is successful, it makes every individual different from every other. Colleges also pursue *training,* but that is quite a different thing from education. Training tends to process individuals so that they become more alike, speaking the same language, sharing the same professional baggage, engaging in the same kinds of activities in the same more or less prescribed way. While training is necessary, it is to some extent the enemy of education and should be postponed as long as one can afford it.

In defining their goal of education, colleges must also distinguish it from indoctrination. There is a common conception that education somehow transfers certain beliefs, attitudes, values, and knowledge from the minds of the teachers into the mind of the student. This can be done, and is done, but it cannot properly be called education. It does nothing to liberate or develop the individual. Insofar as colleges undertake to introduce into the minds of young people prescribed facts or notions which they insist that everybody know or believe, they are not educating but rather are offering a kind of training which makes people more alike. The individual who passes through such a college will emerge well schooled in the symbols of our culture knowing language, mathematics, and other skills. But, unless at the same time he has been modified in such a way that he can act in accordance with larger purposes, he may use these symbols in the service of ends that are quite destructive to himself and to society.

Thus the educational goal of our hypothetical college might well be the maximum development of the individual, bringing forth as much of his potential as possible, and setting in motion a process, that will continue throughout his lifetime. This goal implies the development of certain qualities in a person which exist independently of any specialized skill or knowledge, qualities which are favorable to his leading a rich, productive life himself and to his performing effectively as a citizen in a democratic society. These qualities would include such characteristics as independence of thinking, readiness to take social responsibility, openness to democratic values, and others which our culture has recognized as good and would like to see developed in students.

Sometimes the goals of an institution, or the means of achieving those goals, come into conflict with one another. For example, the college which declares that its primary aim is education may also wish to promote positive mental health among its students. However, when one remembers that development often takes place as a response to strain, it becomes clear that the same strains which further education may present a threat to mental health. In practice, the institution must weigh its various goals and arrange them into a sort of hierarchy.

THE PERSON TO BE CHANGED

To understand and appraise the personality development which takes place within an institution demands also a clear conception of the entering individual. By the time our freshman comes to college, his personality has already undergone a considerable amount of development. He is already a whole, embracing various parts which interact with one another. However, these parts are still relatively few and not yet highly integrated. By comparison, the parts of the graduating senior are more numerous and more complicated. They can now act in concert so that what happens in one area is easily brought into communication with happenings in other areas.

One of the major parts or subsystems which becomes modified under the impact of the college system is the impulse life of the individual— those basic emotional needs that underlie his creativity and make his life passionate and real. Another is conscience, which includes the internalized standards and aspirations of society, his own feelings of what he ought to do, and the internalized pressures that make him do it. Still another is the ego system, that aspect of the person which exercises control over emotional impulses and deals with the demands of life in a more or less realistic way.[1] In the ideal college system all these components of the personality are helped to develop. The impulse life becomes expanded and differentiated. It is fuller and richer because what is learned can be used in the service of emotional expression. Conscience becomes more individualized and enlightened, the individual's moral standards and values being more and more fully supported by his own knowledge, thought, and judgment. The ego's capacity to discriminate and be reasonable increases

[1] For a further discussion see Chapter 5, "Elements of Personality: Id, Ego, Superego."

directly as it meets with success in performing the increasingly difficult tasks imposed by the educational process.

Just how much have these systems developed by the time a student enters college? What are his particular susceptibilities and his particular strengths? First, he is a late adolescent; some of the major adolescent conflicts are over. He has attained some mastery of his impulses, so that he is able to act as if he were a more or less grown-up person. But typically he has accomplished this mastery by accepting very fully the value orientation of his family and immediate community. Indeed, he usually adheres too rigidly to these values, acting as if he were already grown-up and as if no foolish indulgence would ever cross his mind. Of course, impulses for foolish indulgences are still there and express themselves from time to time when he cannot help it. Consequently the freshman is susceptible to feelings of guilt over betraying the values of his family while at the same time being plunged into a situation in which many people are trying to persuade him to betray them. Fellow students suggest behavior that would never receive family approval. At the level of beliefs and ideology, the faculty does the same thing, challenging the belief system that his family has taught him is the only one worth holding.

If the freshman is to be educated, the value orientation with which he arrives must be challenged. Should this freshman have a neurotic necessity to adhere strongly to his parents, he is highly susceptible to trouble. He faces a difficult choice: to remain loyal to his traditional values, making true education impossible, or to make a painful break with them. If he dares to make this break, he will probably need a good deal of support from the faculty, fellow students, and the whole educational community.

Another characteristic of the entering freshman is the instability of his self-esteem. He simultaneously hopes for the best and fears the worst. Since he has not yet encountered the major challenges of life, he is not sure how successfully he will be able to meet them. His family, friends, and high school teachers have typically told him that he is "pretty good," but before he is on the campus long, he has experiences that suggest he may not be so good after all. When a student suddenly discovers his own limitations, he may feel that he has disappointed his parents and himself. His self-doubts usually extend not only to academic achievement but also to interpersonal relationships. He is concerned about his skill in the realm of heterosexual relations. In fact, he is not even sure how well he can handle friendships with students of his own sex. So he vacillates between underestimations and overestimations of himself. Sometimes he will display depression and withdrawal, feeling that he is worthless. Again he will exhibit bravado and arrogance, trying to convince himself that he is all that he has been told he was. If these normal strains are complicated by strong neurotic susceptibilities, he may be in for serious trouble.

Every freshman arrives at college with some neurotic elements in his makeup. Remnants of maladaptive devices that have been used in the past are still with him. In fact, in this population as in any other, there will be a certain percentage that need psychiatric help immediately. However, the educator's hope is that enough of the student's personality is free of neurotic entanglements so that he can respond to the educational environment. If so, he will not have to concentrate on changing his underlying personality before he can go on to develop in the general framework of the college. Where psychiatric help is needed, its goal should be to get the student back into harness as rapidly as possible. Resolution of his neurotic problems is not the primary purpose for which he came to college; he is there to be developed as an individual. As long as there are parts of him which are capable of responding to the educational challenge, these are the parts to which the college should direct its efforts.

CHALLENGE AND RESPONSE

Once the institution possesses clear pictures both of the individuals who are entering it and of the kind of individual that it hopes will emerge, it is in a position to plan effective procedures for bringing the desired change about. The techniques will vary, of course, for each type of institution. Here we will discuss only those which would seem appropriate for our hypothetical college, although they are based on the same fundamental principle which underlies all institutional efforts aimed at individual development—the principle of *challenge and response.*

This approach to developing the individual grows out of the belief that people do not change unless they encounter a situation to which they cannot adapt with the use of devices already present. They have to innovate, to generate some new response to meet the new situation offered them. Children develop in this way from infancy. The reason they develop so quickly is that they are constantly confronted with new situations. They must constantly find suitable new means of response to reduce tension and free their attention for other things. Thus the person expands and becomes more differentiated. It is the job of the change-inducing institution to present the person to be changed with a succession of new challenges which will stimulate the desired new responses.

While children are challenged amply—perhaps too much—college students are often not challenged enough. By and large, those who have no basic neurotic difficulties find quite comfortable ruts on our college campuses. They are usually upset for about two weeks after they arrive; then they settle in. They "learn the ropes" and soon fall into a fairly complacent pattern of life. They master the content without too much trouble, but often their teachers believe that nothing very exciting is happening within them. It is the teacher's task to find a way to reach these students, challenge them, jolt them out of their ruts, so that they will revise their ways of looking at things and thus be required to generate new perspectives and systems of response. One way to do this would be deliberately to change the situation to which the student has grown accustomed—for example, to bring a group of students who do not know one another together at a weekend seminar. By placing the student in a strange situation, we free him from his usual role with its expectations and accustomed modes of behavior and force him to adapt in new ways. By creating a little anxiety in him we open him to learning. He is likely to learn more in that weekend than in an entire semester of routinely going to classes, then routinely meeting his friends afterward and probably forgetting what was learned in class.

It is frequently remarked by those in student personnel offices that getting into trouble and falling into the hands of the deans can be one of the best things that can happen to a student. This may be the first time in his college experience that any adult has taken the trouble to treat him as a human being, look at his problems, and try to see things as he sees them. This crisis can be the occasion for a student's really changing his perspective and taking a new lease on college life.

Important as the challenge-response process is to positive development, it also carries a potential for trouble. While the teacher believes that students need above all to be shaken out of their ruts and set into conflict with some of their traditional value orientations, the college psychiatrist may be equally sure that the stress which students feel is already too great. In order to keep the individual mentally healthy and at the same time develop him, an institution should present only challenges which are at once disturbing enough to force him to find new responses and not so disturbing as to cause him to fall back on primitive responses that have served him in the past. This, of course, is an ideal. In practice, there will always be some risk. A college which tried to insulate its students from all stimuli which might threaten mental health would also be depriving them of many of the challenges which help them to develop. The college must take a calculated risk similar to that taken by a democracy, which offers all its citizens freedom even though this may result in mental ill health for some who are not prepared for such independence.

Presumably, the colleges which do the most to upset students in order that they may learn should also be the ones which give students the most access to the student health service. The most effective college might well be one in which half of the people were working at challenging the students and the other half at seeing that these challenges did not become overwhelming.

St. John's College in Annapolis, Maryland, was, when the author knew it in the middle 1950s, a great place for upsetting students. Everything that they suggested in a seminar was immediately challenged and knocked down, either by the professor or by fellow students. By the end of the freshman year, the student felt that he had lost everything, that all he had ever believed was probably wrong. This was a marvelous technique for making him wonder who he was and what living was all about. However, it was an enormously upsetting situation. The college had no psychiatrist on its staff, so a considerable number of students either dropped out or sought help from psychiatrists in Washington. Those who survived this ordeal together developed strong bonds of friendship, and like old soldiers they continue to meet whenever possible to talk about the "old days." They have the benefits of having coped, which is one way to mental health but very strong medicine. Probably more would have survived, and survived more comfortably, had St. John's provided some maternal influence on the campus to pick up the pieces after students had been thrown into this richly developmental but chaotic experience.

On the other hand, overconcern about mental health may lead us to mistake a temporary crisis to which a student is responding for a serious neurotic situation. We may treat as a neurosis what in fact is growing pains. The author recalls such an incident during the early days of the Mellon research program at Vassar College.[2] The study group presented to its advisers—psychiatrists, psychologists, and sociologists, all oriented to the mental health value system—the case of a freshman girl with whom there had been four interviews. This student was being exposed to the unsettling influences which all freshmen face and in addition demonstrated some neurotic tendencies involving achievement and an alliance with her father against her mother. As soon as the material was presented, the committee immediately turned its full attention to the problem of the girl's neurosis and the sort of treatment that should be undertaken. What escaped these experts was the fact that, in spite of her neurotic symptoms, this student was bright and, in large parts of herself, open to development. While there were some unconscious complexes present, there were also aspects of her personality that were not involved but were still open to learning in the usual way. In fact, this case had been chosen for presentation precisely because the interviewers considered that she was the most promising of all the freshmen interviewed. (This appraisal was later substantiated. She made an excellent record in college and is now the wife of a scientist, the mother of three children, and a leader in her community.)

To summarize, the institution which would lead an individual toward greater development must, then, present him with strong challenges, appraise accurately his ability to cope with these challenges, and offer him support when they become overwhelming.

THE CHANGE AGENCY AS A SYSTEM

A college, or any other change-inducing institution, may be conceived of in much the same way as an individual—that is, as a system embracing a number of subsystems. In a college, the most important subsystems are those originally designed to serve some function in changing the enter-

[2] The research program conducted at Vassar is described more fully in H. Webster, M. Freedman, and P. Heist, "Personality Changes in College Students," in N. Sanford (ed.), *The American College* (New York: Wiley, 1962).

ing freshman in some desired way. They include the curriculum, the departments, the organization of teaching, the residences, the extracurricular activities—all those sources of stress and relief which represent instituted parts of the larger college system.

Together, these part-systems form a unit; what occurs in any one of them affects, and is affected by, the whole. For example, simply changing the undergraduate curriculum in English can evoke a surprising amount of dissension from persons in many quarters of the college. They perceive, and rightly, that in one way or another a change in the English department will have repercussions within their own departments. Even beyond its direct effects on English students and faculty, and its indirect effects on curriculum policy in general, the English curriculum makes some small contribution to that larger, vital but intangible factor which, for want of better words, we call "college climate," "campus atmosphere," "student morale," or "student-faculty rapport." Whatever it is called, this factor is a palpable force that stimulates good minds to achieve excellence, and excellent minds sometimes to achieve greatness.

A few institutions possess this special quality; some do not have it at all; many seek it uncertainly. It has something to do with the caliber of students, the quality of faculty, the physical resources and traditions of the institution, but is more than these. Without it, all of these other conditions, however satisfactory, are not enough. Conversely, this element more than compensates in many cases for other imperfections. Colleges which lack top-notch students, nationally distinguished faculty members, first-rate libraries and laboratories, idyllic settings, or 300-year-old traditions have nevertheless achieved it in significant measure, sometimes in a relatively short time.

Certainly one important component of this "climate"—and one which has been seriously neglected in research on higher education—is the administration. When things are running smoothly at a college, the role of the administration in the lives of the students appears small. A new president may appear on the scene, accompanied by wholesale changes of personnel in the upper ranks, without the students showing much interest. Yet in times of crisis the administration looms as an influence of crucial importance. For example, when there is a disruptive student riot, investigation will often show that the outbreak was merely the culmination of unfavorable conditions that had been in the making for some time.

Particularly striking are cases in which the students suddenly become aware of some moral failure of the administration, as when a president compromises with the natural enemies of the college or when he becomes personally involved in some kind of scandal. The students' sense of betrayal is marked. If not expressed in outbreaks of destructiveness, it will at least show itself as cynicism and demoralization. Episodes of this kind strongly suggest that, during the preceding quiet time, when the students were apparently taking the administration for granted, they were actually counting on it to represent the durable values of the college and society.

One might even say that the administration had been to some extent internalized by the students, so that when it failed, they had to deal with a disturbance in their inner psychological households.

Related to these are cases of prolonged misadministration. Occasionally, the highest officials of a college or university fail to meet minimum standards of culture, intelligence, decency, or courage. They sometimes consistently dodge responsibility, or act as if the major business of the college were public relations, saying one thing to the public and something else to the students. In places like this we find prolonged disaffection and alienation from the basic value orientation that the college supposedly represents. Students will say, "You can get an education here, but you have to do it outside the system."

If administrative failure has harmful effects upon students, might we not suppose that conspicuous greatness in the administration, or even moderately good leadership, would have beneficial effects in similar degree? Although we agree that students need models, we usually assume that members of the faculty will serve this need. It is doubtful, however, that individual faculty members can represent the ideals of the whole college or express for the student the aspirations most deeply imbedded in our national culture. This is the job of the president. As citizens we do not look to members of the Congress for someone who embodies our highest ideals, but rather to the President of the United States. Granted that what we see in him is largely of our own making, who he is and what he does makes a great deal of difference in our lives. The president of a college can have, should have, and sometimes does have the same significance in the lives of the students.

STRAINS WITHIN THE CHANGE-AGENCY

The college as a unified whole exists, as does the individual, within the larger society. Much that happens inside depends on what happens outside. In thinking of a college as a social system we must consider the kinds of outside publics which it is trying to serve, and the kinds of pressures by which they would determine, if they could, what goes on inside. One measure of the health of a college is how well it deals with these pressures. Too often it behaves in a very unhealthy fashion. Let us suppose that a college is confronted by an angry citizens' group that demands that it dismiss a certain professor. The first internal response is likely to be a sharp split throughout the whole system, with some faculty members saying, in effect, "Good riddance!" and others arguing, "We must defend our right to decide these things for ourselves." At times of such controversy, an institution may display characteristics which can best be described as neurotic. Present issues reopen past wounds. A faculty meeting which begins with rational discussion may, without apparent reason, become passionate. People take increasingly rigid positions, and soon the meeting breaks up with no decision except to send the whole problem back to committee. At the next meeting, the same performance is likely to be repeated. Gradually it will become apparent that the alignments on the current issue are in reality alignments that were worked out twenty years earlier when some other issue split the community. Friendships and enmities made then still persist. In an institution, as in the neurotic individual, a situation which cannot be settled immediately on realistic terms threatens to bring about a split along lines of previous stress. In a situation of this kind, it is up to the president or some other administrative officer to offer the necessary therapy.

By contrast, a healthy college would be able to mobilize all of its resources to deal with the externally caused strain. Its success in doing so would be a function of the amount of communication among various parts of the system—just as, in the individual personality, the command of the resources needed to deal with an external threat would depend on the degree of integration of the individual's different parts.

It is interesting to contemplate the effects of an unhealthy lack of communication in a college. If, for example, the psychology department is not speaking to the education department but instead is making up fantasies about it, a paranoid situation may develop. As the two departments compete for budget or students, the situation is right for each to imagine that the other is doing all kinds of wrongs—usually the very things which it would do itself if it dared. A similar split may occur between faculty and student personnel officers or between members of the faculty within a single department.

When such unhealthy conditions prevail within a college, their effects on the developing student are bound to be unhealthy, too. In the preceding example, any student who feels some identification with both of two feuding departments or professors will be split internally. He will be caught in a situation in which he must be beholden to both parties, as is the child whose parents are quarreling. Since he cannot accept the disloyalty which would be involved in supporting either side, he will be torn with conflict.

Thus we see that each individual's development depends on factors within himself and also on factors within the institution through which he is passing. For the identification and removal of individual obstacles to development, the counselor remains indispensable. For detecting and correcting institutional obstacles, however, we must use a different approach, one based on a scheme for the analysis of social structures. If an institution is a system of subsystems, and if a change in any one of them can change the whole, then it should be possible to make certain modifications in a college program which would reduce over-all rates of mental illness among students, or increase the over-all level of their development.

In practice, it is not always easy to determine just what kinds of modifications are needed in a given institution at a given time. Those who are entrusted with planning such changes will need all the knowledge and vicarious experience which research can make available. In education, for example, it would be useful to make epidemiological studies of the rates of student development, scholastic achievement, or mental health in colleges known to have favorable "climates" and in those of lesser reputation. Similar studies might compare the effects of contrasting subsystems (such as living groups or academic departments) within a single college.[3]

Sometimes the weaknesses in a particular college system will come to light in a time of crisis, such as the dismissal of a controversial faculty member. Again they may be inferred from crises in the lives of students who find the pressures too great and end with emotional or disciplinary trouble. But other weaknesses may never erupt into crises which have visible symptoms. They may remain hidden for years, all the while interfering with the effective pursuit of the institution's goals.

Consider, for example, the phenomenon of declining friendship among men students at a large private university. This first came to light during the author's conversations with small groups of students and was later confirmed by other observers. Apparently these young men could not reveal themselves to one another enough to establish intimate relationships. They saw one another as competitors, as people to be manipulated, as onlookers who could make one feel big or little—as everything except genuine objects of human relationship. This problem seems to be particularly acute in the most prominent institutions, the places that young people want to get into and get a sense of status from being in.

The high incidence of the friendship problem suggests that it must be a function of the whole social system of the institution, which is in turn a function of the place of the institution in society. Traditionally, college has been seen as a moratorium, during which people have a few years to discover themselves and to learn how to relate to other people, but today it is being subjected to great outside pressures to become a processor for vocations or a status-giving set-up. Until these pressures, or the institution's response to them, are changed, the symptoms at the individual level are likely to persist and development will be impeded.

This is not to advocate a blanket reduction in the demands on students. One dean recently commented that the students on his campus were working too hard, were too busy, to become ill, and he may have been right. It is not so much the quantity of work that matters as the kind of work and the circumstances under which it is done. In London during the blitz, or in certain Negro communities in the South today, where the whole group is threatened and everyone plunges into concerted action, it is literally true that people are too busy to become ill. They have a purpose, something to work and fight for. But how rare it is that students, except perhaps athletes, have the chance to engage in teamwork, or group work in which their efforts make a difference to the whole group. Analysts of our society have pointed to the increasing impersonality of our relationships. It has been said, for example, that the only human community to which the average American businessman belongs is the car pool which takes him to work. He has few genuine relationships with his neighbors in the suburbs. At the office, it is a matter of whom he can

[3] See Suggested Readings at the end of this chapter.

manipulate and who can manipulate him. The plight of the friendless college male may really be a reflection of the wider problem in contemporary society. There is one encouraging difference: complex though it is, the college society is vastly simpler than the society at large and therefore, we may hope, more amenable to change.

There should be no conflict between individual and social approaches to mental health and development. On the contrary, they should be mutually supporting. The individual is, after all, at the center of both. The campus psychiatrist who takes cognizance of the broader social system will be a better psychotherapist as well as a valuable aid to the larger system in detecting its adverse effects. On the other hand, the larger system must never lose sight of the individual or cease adapting itself to increase his chances for full and healthy development. We want sound minds in a sound body politic, and we want continuously developing individuals in a healthy institution.

SUGGESTED READINGS

The reader interested in knowing more about the research which has been done in this area may find the following helpful:

C. R. Pace and G. G. Stern, *A Criteria Study of College Environments* (Syracuse, N.Y.: Syracuse University Psychological Research Center, 1958).
Development of College Characteristics Index which offers a means of describing college climates.

D. L. Thistlethwaite, "College Press and Student Achievement," *Journal of Educational Psychology,* 50:183–91, 1959.
Association of variations in College Characteristics Index with general levels of academic achievement.

R. Goldsen, *et al., What College Students Think* (Princeton, N.J.: Van Nostrand, 1960). Also P. E. Jacob, *Changing Values in College* (New York: Harper, 1957).
General descriptions of patterns of student attitudes at different kinds of institutions.

Lois B. Murphy and Esther Raushenbush (eds.), *Achievement in the College Years* (New York: Harper, 1960).
Studies at Sarah Lawrence College in which students were systematically questioned about all aspects of their college life; general observations about freedom and authority on the campus.

G. Stewart, *The Year of the Oath* (New York: Doubleday, 1950). Also N. Sanford, "Individual and Social Change in a Community under Pressure: The Oath Controversy," *Journal of Social Issues,* 9:25–42, 1953.
Institutions in crisis.

D. Riesman and J. Jencks, "The Viability of the American College"; J. Bushnell, "Student Culture at Vassar"; F. Pinner, "The Crisis of the State Universities: Analysis and Remedies"; all in N. Sanford (ed.), *The American College* (New York: Wiley, 1962).
Theoretically oriented observational studies of colleges.

C. Bay, "A Social Theory of Intellectual Development"; T. M. Newcomb, "Student Peer Groups"; both in N. Sanford (ed.), *The American College* (New York: Wiley, 1962).

CHAPTER FOUR

Institutionally Induced Personality Change: A Case Study

The changes wrought by a change-inducing institution vary widely from person to person, depending as they do on a multiplicity of individual as well as institutional factors. Nevertheless, certain kinds of changes may be common to a majority of the individuals who come under the influence of a given type of change-agency. For example, developmental studies at Vassar College[1] found that certain aspects of personality were particularly subject to change between the freshman and senior years. Furthermore, similar directional changes were observed in students from several quite dissimilar colleges, even though the level of their average freshman scores on personality tests varied greatly. Among personality variables, those found most likely to be affected by the college experience were authoritarianism, impulse expression, and masculinity-femininity. Other quite different areas of change might typify "graduates" of other kinds of institutions—for example, psychiatric clinics, penitentiaries, or military training programs.

In order to gain insight into the over-all process of personality change —and at the same time to appreciate more fully the unique character of

[1] This program of research was carried out under the auspices of the Mary Conover Mellon Foundation. For a more complete account, see N. Sanford (ed.), "Personality Development during the College Years," *Journal of Social Issues*, 12:1–75, 1956.

This is a modified version of a case study originally included in a paper entitled "The Freeing and the Acting Out of Impulse in Late Adolescence: Evidence from Two Cases," in R. W. White (ed.), *The Study of Lives* (New York: Atherton Press, 1963).

each individual's developmental experience—let us turn now to the study of an individual case. This is the case of Penny, a subject from the Vassar studies whose test scores, evaluations by interviewers, and self-assessment all point to a significant degree of development during the college years.

PENNY AS A FRESHMAN

The daughter of a conservative, upper-middle-class family of the Chicago area, this subject has previously attended an expensive private preparatory school. She arrives at college well prepared, perhaps over-prepared, academically. She is also well protected socially, already having friends at the college and feeling secure in her social status. A letter of recommendation from the preparatory school says of her:

"Penny is an earnest, dependable, well-balanced, intelligent girl . . . she leads in a quiet way by example, with friendliness and courtesy to all.

". . . a consistently fine academic record. In her work she is accurate, thorough, and perceptive, with unusual ability of commanding detail as well as broad patterns and trends.

"Her outside activities, in addition to the Student Council (Vice-President), consist of membership in English, French, Current Events, and Math Clubs, and she will participate in the French play."

During the initial freshman interview, Penny reveals a good deal about her underlying self as she discusses her attitudes and behavior in many areas of life.

[*Rooming group and friends.*] "Have two roommates; one I knew very well at school; the other from Kansas. Two friends of the girl I knew at school are next door. We are all very compatible. Karla is one of the most considerate people I have ever met. We never lose our tempers with each other. We all come from more or less the same backgrounds, but not necessarily private schools. We are interested in the same things and have good discussions. We just seem to like the same people, and to have the same friends: girls who don't talk about boys and clothes all the time but yet are fun. My roommates and I talk about religion and different views of life, also about art, music, boys, and sex. About politics if some issue comes up—like McCarthy." [*Do together?*] "We play bridge, talk, study, talk about former school, eat, listen to music."

[*Interests, activities, preferences.*] "Bridge, listening to music, reading, talking . . . a good book, reading, eating good food. It does not take much to please me. . . . I like food—steaks and roast beef. I'll eat any hour of the twenty-four. The food here is not as bad as I had heard. It could be better, but it is well balanced. . . ." [*Weekends?*] "I go around and see my friends here. Get my term papers written. Have dates, play bridge, talk."

[*Men.*] "I have been out both with boys I knew from before and on blind dates. The ratio is about one to one. Blind dates have been arranged through girls in the dorm. I like to meet people. It's fun. You can't lose anything; even if you have an awful time, it's just one evening. . . . Boys should be considerate, fun, interesting, intelligent." [*Looks?*] "Clean-cut looking. I don't care if they are not attractive; yet I know I put some emphasis on looks."

[*Academic work.*] "Wanted to go to college so I could learn enough to be stimulated enough to go on being curious, and would make new friendships. I always assumed I would go. I chose this college because I wanted history. I knew they had a good history department here, and I know some girls who like it.

"I was always on the honor roll. I worked but not as hard as some. I was more interested in other things. I didn't mind homework, but was interested in sports, friends, boys. About the eighth grade I got into a clique that was sort of awful. After tenth grade I was on high honor roll, but there was still a lot of extracurricular activity. Some work, especially math, didn't interest me. But I never had time to read all the history I wanted. It was a kind of rat race.

"I expected the work to be challenging and to be more different from school than it is. I expected to meet all types, make new friends, have fun, have my so-called intellectual curiosity stimulated. I was appalled at first by so much freedom, but I like it a lot. I was a little overwhelmed by the size of the place.

"Religion course is very superior. Chemistry I had never had, but I like it. English much the same as school. But the teacher is not as good. French is exactly the same as school. But I knew about the requirements and I can't complain. It's good for me to have chemistry. I'm looking forward to next year.

"I like the academic atmosphere, the good discussions in and out of class. I like the freedom—there is time to do your work and to plan other things. I like all my courses but English. There is plenty of time, though chemistry is a little of a drain—eight hours per week. I love having the library to study in.

"I got 'very good' in a three-hour written, but I don't think I'm superb in English. I don't know about French; I thought we would get modern literature but instead we got *The Iliad*. We don't get very constructive criticism. There are few conferences. In class we get off the track with the unimportant. I love our religion class. There is reading on our own and then discussion. I would rather find out things on my own than have them handed to me.

"Will probably major in history or political science. I wish I was taking them this year. Maybe religion or philosophy."

[*The faculty.*] "I don't feel I know the faculty, but I could if I took the time. I hate to take their time; others have more problems."

[*The future.*] "As for the future, I want to go to Europe, but perhaps in the summers. I want to work for a year or two, but I don't want a career. I would keep on working after marriage—if my husband didn't mind—until we had our children. I want to have outside interests, to keep on learning, and to have interesting things to discuss with my husband."

On a personality rating card for freshmen, faculty advisers chose ten of a possible thirty-six adjectives as being descriptive of Penny: self-confident, considerate, self-reliant, attractive, respected, friendly, reliable, sincere, well-liked, well-mannered.

At the end of the freshman year one faculty adviser commented: "Gives impression of not beginning yet to operate to full capacity. Has possibilities of doing brilliant work, I think. Alert, interested in variety of things, and an awfully nice girl."

The picture of Penny as a freshman which emerges from these many statements gains depth when we consider the following descriptions of herself at earlier stages of development, given during the life history interview:

[*Self as a child.*] "Talkative, but outside that very healthy and normal. In second and third grades I was bossy; but mother used to think I was really sweet. At five or six I got the car rolling. I was a tomboy."

[*Self as an adolescent.*] "Moody. At times I still am. Just get bad moods. I used to sulk when I couldn't get my way. In school I was well-behaved, but I had a good time with boys as well as girls."

[*Sex information and attitudes.*] "Found out about sex mostly from other girls. And from mother; never from father. I began to find out in the sixth grade, and it has been accumulating ever since. Mother gave some facts prior to menstruation. School friends got it earlier. [*Source of sex morality?*] What I think is right; from parents, I suppose. It's just something in me. No, I never go very far. It's not much of a problem with me."

This history suggests that Penny closely resembles the composite freshman presented in Chapter 3. She arrives at college with a good record and strong recommendations; by the standards of her home, school, and peers she is already performing well. In fact, she adheres to those standards almost rigidly and remains closely tied to a college peer group which represents them. Her impulses are highly controlled, her conscience well developed and apparently integrated into her conscious self. It was quite conceivable that this girl might pass through the next four years, as many other students do, acquiring knowledge but not really changing or developing.

However, the record shows that Penny did change—significantly. In order to understand the nature and magnitude of that change, let us look now at Penny as a graduating senior.

PENNY AS A SENIOR

By her last year in college, Penny displayed many evidences of change. She had a set of beliefs that were radically different from those of her parents, a new set of friends, and comfortable, equalitarian relations with members of the faculty. She had been awarded a full fellowship for graduate study in the social sciences, and an interviewer assessed her prospects for satisfactory marital adjustment as excellent. Penny herself was clearly aware of having changed:

"My values have changed a lot. I have got away from always thinking what others would think. I am associated with people I formerly looked down my nose at. I am more permissive in judging other people. I used to be hard on people of different backgrounds, now I am hard on persons who go through college like vegetables."

These changes were evident in her test scores, too, particularly her scores on *authoritarianism*[2] (F scale) and *impulse expression*[3] (IE scale). Her F-scale score dropped from 96 as a freshman to 61 as a senior. These scores may be compared with mean scores of 118 (s.d., 19.6) and 90 (s.d., 17.5) for Vassar freshmen and seniors respectively. At the same time her IE score rose from 37 (freshman mean: 44, s.d., 15.6) to 76 (senior mean: 53, s.d., 16.8). Thus we see that Penny shows the same kind of developmental changes that were observed in Vassar students generally and have been confirmed in later research elsewhere,[4] although the degree of change was greater for Penny than for most students. It may be useful, then, to focus on these two variables as we trace the development in various facets of Penny's personality.

REBELLIOUS INDEPENDENCE. First to be noted in Penny as a senior is a strong element of rebelliousness. This seems to be mainly an expression of striving for independence. At the same time, it can be seen that she puts rebellious actions into the service of what she considers to be an important principle, such as justice for a member of the faculty.

Six faculty members gave Penny an average rating of 4.5 on *Independence*, defined as the ability to function independently without benefit of authority or guidance by the social group. (This may be compared with a mean of 3.2 with a standard deviation of 0.90 for 78 girls so rated.) She ranks third from the top in this group of students. On *Rebelliousness* she is rated 3.0 on the average (group mean: 2.37) and is eleventh from the highest in the group. It is interesting to note that the faculty members were not inclined to hold Penny's rebelliousness against her, for they also rated her 4.17, fourth from the top, on "the degree to which she is in

---

[2] *Authoritarianism* is a syndrome which reveals a special ambivalence toward authority, including both a desire to yield and a desire to submit. Nine major attributes have been identified (of which the first three are always present): extreme urge, however cloaked, to submit to authority; aggressiveness and/or cynicism; concern with power and toughness; self-censorship; superstition; stereotyped thinking and outlook; rigid conventionalism; morbid fascination with sex; and a threat complex.

[3] *Impulse expression* may be defined as the readiness to express emotional impulses or to seek gratification of them in overt action or in conscious feeling and attitude.

[4] These findings are discussed in H. Webster, M. Freedman, and P. Heist, "Personality Changes in College Students," in N. Sanford (ed.), *The American College* (New York: Wiley, 1962).

accord with your concept of the ideal student." The following excerpts from the interviews show something of Penny's strivings for autonomy:

[*What is the most important thing money can give a person?*] "If you don't have to worry about essentials, you are free to do other things. Money is nice at our age if you can be financially independent from parents."

[*Do you expect financial support from parents after graduation?*] "I will be in graduate school and will have a $1400 grant. I don't know what it would cost; I would like a part-time job so I could be independent. [*How about after marriage?*] I would like to be independent, but I could get help from my parents if I had to have it."

Asked about ways in which she had changed since her freshman year, Penny said: "In school our group always thought we were superior— really something. In college there has been some of the same thing, but I have got to know people who are less concerned with external standards. There is no real necessity to conform to the student body."

[*What has been your parents' attitude toward your college career?*] "They think I have been getting some ideas I shouldn't. I am scared about the future; I hate to ask them for help in going to graduate school. They have sent me to school for sixteen years. . . . Daddy and I differ in respect to politics, social questions, and income tax. On integration we are poles apart. I don't want the kind of life they live in Hometown."

[*What changes have there been in your attitudes toward the faculty or your relations with them?*] "I have changed a great deal since last year. Now I am much more apt to say what I think to teachers. I talk more freely and am apt to be more critical."

[*How did this come about?*] "Chiefly through Mr. A."

Mr. A. was a philosophy teacher who made a great impression on Penny and on a considerable number of other girls. He seems to have shown her convincingly that an academic subject really did have something to do with her own central purposes and concerns, and, through revealing himself to his students, that the intellectual life could, after all, be carried on by human beings. He could often be seen about the campus, in rather nonacademic settings, carrying on animated discussions with groups of girls, of whom one was usually Penny. When it became known that his one-year contract was not going to be renewed, she became a leader of a group of students who circulated a petition and fought valiantly for his retention. Her relationship with him seemed to have opened the way to other teachers, and she actually mentioned five others of whom she had seen quite a lot.

One of the teachers who rated Penny on *Independence* and *Rebelliousness* explained some of his difficulties as follows: "A quiet, reserved girl who looked for and found a hero, whom she defended valiantly against imaginary attacks. This involved defiance of authority indeed." He referred to the same set of events when he noted that Penny was both high and low on *Flexibility*—that is to say, openness to new experience and new ideas: "*very* influenceable, but having found a hero reason would not budge her." Such are the trials of youth. To throw oneself into a cause, to stand one's ground against the powers that be, to go according to one's convictions, loyalties, and sense of justice is to get oneself rated as inflexible. And not without good reason, unfortunately. A year later, a year after Mr. A. left the college, we find Penny still sticking to her position. We may well imagine that as a middle-aged housewife she will look back upon this whole episode as a display of youthful enthusiasm, but she may also consider that she got out of the series of events affecting Mr. A. a good conception—new to her—of what it might mean to be a person of integrity.

Some of the preceding material suggests that the *Aggression* which Penny shows—and she shows quite a bit—is not primarily defensive, or a mere release of some unconscious impulse; rather it is usually organized in the service of some larger purpose, such as the defense of another person or the improvement of an existing condition. Her aggression also seems to be differentiated. She can attack someone but at the same time point out his good qualities; she can criticize her parents or disagree radically with them but at the same time say that she owes a lot to them. These are indications that the aggression is under the control of the conscious processes.

Concerning her parents, Penny says: "No matter how much I may reject my parents now, their ethics and standards have been very important." (She says this after explaining how she differs with them on social and political questions and how contemptuous she is of their kind of life.)

In speaking of faculty members, she is hard-hitting but at the same time fair-minded. She rubs her hands gleefully when asked to speak about the faculty members she likes least. But then she proceeds to give a balanced account in each case.

She says, concerning Professor I.: "A generally ineffectual teacher, but I have heard he has never been the same since he had some illness."

Concerning Mrs. N.: "Very ineffectual—but I like her as a person."

Concerning Miss B.: "She tries to railroad things through on you. She browbeats people, but I have never had her in a course, only in conferences."

Concerning an English teacher: "I admire her mind, but she intimidates people. She always scares me; she is sort of cold. I got a lot out of her course."

She says of a language course: "Repetitious and boring"; of an English course: "The teacher was incompetent and couldn't lead discussions"; of another English course: "Useless—no use in taking more than just a month of it. You got the whole thing in that time; the rest of it was busy work"; of a philosophy course: "He read the assignment in class and then would go into trances." These expressions of her inclination to be sharp and critical, in the interest of her conception of what a good course ought to be, should be taken together with the fact that Penny also speaks at great length and with marked intelligence and sensitivity of the numerous good courses she has had. The point to be emphasized here is that she feels free to criticize, because she can control aggression and because she is willing to give people a leg to stand on.

Concerning *Dominance,* and dominance feelings, some of this seems to run through much of what Penny has to tell us, in so far as it expresses her strong sense of herself and of her intellectual power. But there is very little to suggest that she is interested in the kind of power that one might get from swaying an audience. Although often called shy or reticent, Penny is often chosen by her friends and classmates for leadership roles. Using a standardized list of roles, positions, and activities, they rated her 4 or above on "judge in a juvenile court," "leader of a citizens' committee interested in good government," "representative to the state legislature," "warden of a women's prison," "Washington lobbyist for women's rights," "moderator in labor-management disputes." Her friends here are showing admiration for her mental powers and for her capacity to assume responsibility. Other roles that stand out in these ratings accent nurturance; for example, "helping refugees get settled," or "taking care of children." The head of Penny's school wrote, as we have seen, that she led in a quiet way. It seems that she still does. She took the lead in the matter of the petition for her hero, and recently when an old acquaintance had to be excluded on personal grounds from a group of girls, including Penny, who were going to Europe together, Penny had to be the one to break the bad news.

The need for *Recognition* should also be mentioned here. We find no exhibitionism in Penny, but there are indications that she really would like to do something great and to achieve fame. Several of her teachers have pointed out that she sets such a high standard for herself, or has such a grand conception of what she might do, that she undertakes more than she can finish, gets in a "stew," and fails to hand her work in on time. But, on time or not, she must have handed in much good work, for the six faculty raters give her an average of 4.85 on Intellectual Capacity, second from the top, and use strong terms—"a fine mind," "tremendous reserves of ability," "outstanding performance"—to express their appreciation of her qualities and work.

The point to be emphasized here is that Penny's aggression and dominance, her striving for autonomy and recognition, are part of her conscious functioning. There is plenty of passion, but it is reasonably controlled. One might say, in fact, that in some instances the presence of conscious controls favors the expression of strong feelings.

SEXUALITY. What Penny has to say about sex is worth quoting at some length, because it exemplifies, I think, what we might understand by sexuality that is integrated with the conscious self. In the life-history interview Penny was asked where she got sex information and she said,

"Mostly from other girls, movies, books, very little from parents. I was fairly little when I saw a little boy go to the bathroom." Concerning menstruation she says she was fourteen at the time of onset, had been prepared at school, and that her mother said something about it. "I was not shocked. I felt underdeveloped in my breasts and I still do." Asked about lateness of the pubertal events, she said, "I was not really upset—I was not the latest—not a pressing problem. I don't remember very much."

In regard to dating she says: "In the 7th and 8th grades dating was mostly group stuff. There was pairing off and somebody liked somebody for about a week. At boarding school it was a matter of weekend dating of boys I had known at home. Then at freshman year here, there were blind dates, and they didn't work out. In sophomore year I was in the depths of everything. I wouldn't go out—I don't know what was wrong with me. Last year dating was sporadic. Never until this summer have I gone out with one boy a great deal. I have a tendency to pull back from too much involvement. I have had physical inhibitions, maybe a fear of getting hurt, but not now. I don't feel ready for marriage, I don't feel I am mature emotionally."

[*What was your first sex experience?*] "You mean the first time I parked and did more than just kiss goodnight? That was in the 11th or 12th grade—that was the first really erotic experience. I have never gone much beyond that—I have never petted. I don't think I will go to bed with a boy before marriage. I don't condemn those who do, however; there is probably a good reason. People can't help being carried away by their emotions."

[*Do you have dreams or fantasies about boys and men?*] "There are two I have daydreams about—terribly." (She laughs but is not very embarrassed, according to the interviewer.) "Yes, I think of them making love to me."

[*Have your ideas about sex changed at all during college years—how? when? and why?*] "Yes, when I first came here I was quite inhibited. I don't condemn others for intercourse before marriage, but I don't approve for myself. Emotional entanglements are brought on by intercourse before marriage; also the risk is pretty great no matter what you do to minimize it."

[*What are your views on premarital sex experience if the couple is engaged?*] "It would be O.K. under the right circumstances" [for herself]. "I would want to have my hymen stretched first, because it is fairly thick and I wouldn't want it to be a messy or bloody experience. I am not anxious to be hurt, I guess, or to hurt him."

[*What is the value of virginity?*] "I don't think it is valuable, still I would like to be a virgin at marriage. Probably some of it is fear of pregnancy. I have pretty monogamous ideas, I don't demand the same from my husband. He may have had different needs."

[*What do you think of a married person who has an affair?*] "It would crush me terribly if my husband did—but in many cases it is probably understandable, but I just don't believe in it really."

[*In your opinion is infidelity sufficient grounds for divorce?*] "Yes, it is sufficient, but you do have to take into consideration circumstances. For example, the husband may be away in the Navy. There is no hard and fast rule, but I would discount an affair more if it was under unusual circumstances."

[*What do you think of homosexuals?*] "Well, I think it is too bad. I don't condemn them, I think they are sick. I met some this summer. It is hard on one's wife. This fellow was bi-sexual. In some cases it can't be helped. If one approached me, I would be scared to death, but I feel sorry for them."

[*If you were a bachelor girl for a few years after college, would you adopt a different standard of behavior than you now have?*] "I might, I don't know. I guess I would say no now. But sure, if I don't get married I'd be very likely to change my way of living so that I could have the experience."

[*At present do you feel a discrepancy between the sexual needs of your boy friend and yourself?*] "No, I don't, because I feel that we both want the same thing, but as far as getting equally worked up I know I can and do." (The interviewer says she blushes.)

[*What is your impression of your parents' sex life?*] "This is something I have always wondered about. Father is reserved, polite, doesn't like sex jokes. I have a feeling that Mother is pretty frustrated, though I could be wrong."

The interviewer rates Penny 4.0 on "acceptance of sexual expression," 4.0 on "self-estimate of sexual adequacy," and 5 on "interviewer's estimate of sexual adequacy." Other ratings were: 2 on "moralistic, compartmentalized view of sex," 2 on "resentment or fear of male sexuality," and 3 on "husband-wife relationship viewed as dominant-submissive."

A question might be raised about the rating of fear of male sexuality, in view of what Penny says about not wanting a "messy or bloody experience." The interviewer should be permitted to defend himself:

"I think this gal is highly sexed and highly conscious of her sex needs at times. Her discussion of it could interest any man, even though older and fully committed. I think she may be afraid of intercourse, not for reasons given such as its seriousness emotionally, but also because of her thick hymen, common enough in this physical type. If she gets the right male, she will have a hearty need for intercourse. Her deprivation now is reflected in her fair identity with her mother and in her belief that her father does not satisfy her mother sexually."

The interviewer addresses himself to the right question—that is, whether Penny will have satisfying sexual relations in marriage. The four psychologists, including the interviewer, who know her well believe that she will. What impresses them is her conscious acceptance of so many aspects of her sexuality, including its fearful aspects. This means that her fears are fully open to modification through the experience that a young woman of her courage and warm desire seems bound to have.

More problematic in the case of Penny is the matter of dominance-submission in husband-wife relationships. She has dominance feelings, and these might well become stronger. This means that she might be attracted by a relatively passive and ultimately disappointing male. This outcome may be favored also by her strong nurturant feelings. These tendencies seemed to be involved to some extent in Penny's relations with Mr. A. He was a rather boyish type who got into trouble and was kicked around quite a bit, thus perhaps making himself very appealing to this warm-hearted girl. But, as we have seen, there was more to the relationship than this; moreover, it might be possible for Penny to find a boyish type of man who is adequate and able to take care of himself without being aggressive or high-powered. Actually, what she seems mainly to desire is a relation-ship of equality in which sex takes its place among a variety of other mutually appreciated qualities and feelings.

In her long interview on family, children, and the status of women, equalitarianism in husband-wife and male-female relations is a major theme; and we have seen that she has sought and attained equalitarian relationships with male members of the faculty. Most important, it seems, is a genuine relationship with a man as a person, a kind of relationship in which Penny admittedly has been backward with both sexes. She tells us with respect to one of her new friends at college, "She is the first girl that I have ever really enjoyed being with." Just as her school-college friendship group can be regarded as a coming together for mutual pro-tection of status and of an authoritarian type of personality organization, so should we regard her early dates with boys as a matter of "rating and dating." She tells us that her first enjoyable relationship with a young man came only in the summer after her junior year, when she began going out with a young man who worked in the same social agency that she did. We can be reasonably sure that she will require a well-educated and sensitive man, but happily for her, ardent, if not athletic, lovers may be found in this group.

The kind of sexuality that we find in Penny is well calculated to make for higher scores on the IE scale. Since the scale expresses person-ality at the level of attitude, it is not necessary for a subject to have acted, or acted-out, in order to agree with items expressive of liberality and daring. Thus, for example, Penny would certainly agree that "Women should have as much sexual freedom as men," but this does not mean that she would insist upon their taking advantage of this freedom or upon demonstrating that she herself had done so.

The main argument here is that Penny is striving to make sexuality a part of her conscious self and to a very considerable extent has accom-plished this. She has conscious sexual fantasies of an explicit sort, is aware of the emotions that normally accompany sexual feeling, and is prepared to take responsibility for her actions. One might say that Penny is trying to arrange things so that when she gives herself sexually it will be indeed her *self* that she gives. It is this that gives the impression of strong sexuality, for when sex is fully integrated with the conscious self it can be a channel for the expression of a rich assortment of feelings and emotions. Such integration also means, of course, that sex experiences can become a means for the further development of the personality; like other important experiences sex can take its place within an expanding structure of integrated processes. It is because girls in college are usually quite well developed in their self-controlling functions that they find it less difficult than is commonly supposed to inhibit overt sexual behavior. The broader the life-space the less the chances that sex will assume overriding importance. More than this, there is now a large organization of conscious needs and purposes that has become the basis for self-respect and that can be set in opposition to any particular desire.

In this perspective it seems rather too bad that college girls who, like Penny, want to protect their virginity until after they have established their identity are so often made to look and to feel ridiculous. Having no terms in which to describe their developmental objectives, and living in a culture that does not think in such terms, they are easily made to appear either to be bound by childish fears and schoolgirl conventions or to be shrewdly calculating their chances in the marriage market. Of course, they are not helped by the current male approach, according to which those fascinating "older men"—that is, seniors and graduate students—use the psychological and sociological textbooks to support their argument that a girl who "won't give in" must be neurotic or else hopelessly caught in an outmoded tradition of sexual morality. While there is currently some appreciation of the fact that a girl who early becomes identified with a sex role has great difficulty in becoming anything else, it is not so well understood that the girl who suffers this fate tends to lack the broad development of personality which gives passion and meaning to activity, and hence is not very sexy either.

The argument can of course be made that a college senior who has not yet integrated sexual gratification with the self is a bit late. Penny does appear to have been delayed in her development by a strict conscience, as reinforced by her school and her friendship group. On the other hand, if a girl takes it upon herself to build an identity that includes the developmental advances that a college education can bring, and if in the most favorable developmental sequence identity should precede intimacy, then she would appear to be justified in taking her time.

EMOTIONALITY. There are few manifestations of exhibitionism or the desire for excitement in Penny. Emotionality, however, seems to be freely displayed in her relations with people. This is particularly striking in what she says about the complexities of her relationships with the girls from whom she had to break away during the course of her college years. It is also evident in what her friends and some faculty members say about her. One of her teachers, for example, says she is "gentle, kind, affectionate, and warm." Various ones of her friends say she is "kind, understanding, has strong feelings, loyal, responsive"; "dependent on her friends, very helpful, highly emotional"; "genuinely sympathetic, tolerant, demands a lot of her friends." Apparently she is high on dependence as well as on affiliation and nurturance. Her dependence is shown particularly in her fear of being rejected by the friends with whom she came to college. But the tendencies that we see expressed in her relations with people are not impulses but conscious needs. There is little here that would make for a high score on the IE scale. Rather the opposite; for the scale accents narcissism rather than warm relations with other people. Impulsivity does display itself when Penny feels that she has been or is about to be rejected. This is very probably what lies behind the withdrawal and "moodiness" of which she tells us, and behind the "ill temper," and the "bluntness and curtness" of which her friends have sometimes complained.

There is evidence that Penny is sometimes disorganized and apparently irresponsible. Some of her friends say, for example, that she is "not very responsible about paying bills"; that she is "kind of unorganized and worries too much about details"; that "one wouldn't go too far in trusting her responsibility when it came to decision-making."

Her teachers have noted these same tendencies. One of them says, after pointing out that she has tremendous reserves of ability and great critical intelligence: "In my class she was a person who wanted to do a superlative job, but would not always pay the price this demanded in self-discipline and hard, concentrated work—hence she was late with work, undependable, and even sloppy."

Another teacher seems even closer to the mark: "She seemed to lack confidence in her own ability to achieve a standard of performance living up to her high expectations. The written work came through with an outstanding performance, but in group discussion she was often inarticulate and confused."

Here we see some effects of a strong primitive conscience that is not fully integrated with the conscious self. Underlying conflicts involving strivings for perfection, fear of failure, and a desire to leave the field give rise to manifest disjunctivity. Penny's friends see this as irresponsibility. She tends to do so herself, and some of this kind of tendency is expressed in the IE scale.

Much the same state of affairs seems to manifest itself in changeability and difficulty about making decisions. A teacher says: "As her adviser I discovered that she had grave difficulty in making up her mind in choosing courses, etc. Would change her mind every other day for a week or so."

A close friend says: "In the years that we have been in school together it has always been my responsibility to find her a place to live (which, as it turned out, has always been with me and my friends) because she was totally incapable of finding anyone to live with."

Penny has to do the right thing. Not just because her conscience embodies various conventional demands, but because her vision of greatness, her master plan for herself, must include many things that seem wrong by conventional standards. It takes time to make sure that the more adventurous choice will not hurt anybody or arouse her conscience. At the time when her friend thought Penny was most dependent upon her for a choice of a place to live, Penny was actually trying to break away from her and other old friends in favor of a new-found Jewish friend. She undoubtedly hoped that her friend would say something that would enable her to move and at the same time spare her from having to feel guilty. In any event, Penny never has made a clean break with the girls with whom she lived in her freshman year. All that can be said is that she has gained some perspective on this problem.

In the same connection it is interesting to note Penny's time-perspective. In response to the question, "Does life seem long or short?" she said, "Seems pretty long right now. There's lots of time. I don't feel in any great rush."

This seems to suggest that when Penny eventually arrives at a suitable identity it will be a broad and complicated one, a result of her present efforts to be more and more inclusive. It also suggests that her manifest changeability and indecisiveness do not reflect uncertainty at the deepest levels of the personality.

ENDOCATHECTION AND INTRACEPTION.[5] Penny displays both of these tendencies—and their opposites. She is low on fantasy but high on reflection and abstract thought. She says that during periods of her college years she did nothing but sit around and think. This was often the case in her sophomore year, when she suffered an agony of indecision concerning her friends and turned to religion. But when faculty members and interviewers describe her as a "thoughtful girl," they have in mind activity of a more intellectual sort—the sort that leads to good academic work. She dreams very little, barely remembers her dreams, does not know whether she dreams in color or not, does not have nightmares, and can think of no unusual experiences such as ESP. But she says it would be fun to dream if one could, and she does produce some daydreams. Concerning conscious fantasies she says:

"A lot grow out of immediate experience—wanting to impress people—and there are some sexual ones. Some have been morbid and violent, and I used to have one of being raped, or hurting people I don't like. Sometimes I have sexual dreams in the night that wake me up—or after I wake up in the morning. It's a day-dream then."

The main impression is of strong controlling and inhibiting ego proc-

[5] Henry Murray defines these terms in this way: *Endocathection:* Attaching value to thought or emotion for its own sake. A preoccupation with inner activities: feelings, fantasies, generalizations, theoretical reflections, artistic conceptions, religious ideas. Withdrawal from practical life. *Intraception:* The dominance of feelings, fantasies, speculations, aspirations. An imaginative, subjective human outlook. Romantic action. H. Murray, *Explorations in Personality* (New York: Oxford University Press, 1938), p. 148.

esses that would tend to transform quickly anything coming from the unconscious. Apparently, however, she has self-awareness and acceptance in consciousness of things that would cause anxiety in some people. This relative breadth of consciousness is shown in what she says about bringing up of her children: "Sure there will be problems, emotional and otherwise; I always wonder if you will remember how it was when you were a child."

In general, the accent is on intellectualization and efforts at rational mastery rather than on the direct expression of unconscious fantasies.

In this light it is particularly interesting that seven faculty members rated Penny 4.3 (mean = 2.86), and second from the top, on creativity. This is the more striking when one considers that in most studies of creativity the art students walk off with the highest ratings. Penny seems to be participating in the prevailing stereotype when she remarks, "I'd love to have a creative talent but I don't." Probably we should give the faculty members credit for being able to see and to appreciate the use of imagination in social science work, though they are no doubt expressing here their general appreciation of Penny's ability. And certainly we should credit Penny herself with being able to transform her unconscious processes into intellectual products.

There is evidence, then, of endocathection; but there is also evidence of the opposite, for Penny is heavily involved with people and actions, particularly actions of a humanitarian kind. A rater who knew her well would probably try to give a picture of balance on this variable.

In respect to intraception and extraception, the picture is also mixed. Certainly Penny is often determined by diffuse personal feelings, but at the same time she is very often credited by teachers, friends, and interviewers with being a sharp observer who can be sensible and even levelheaded in dealing with many kinds of problems.

RADICAL SENTIMENTS. One factor in Penny's increased IE score is that as a senior she has become definitely antireligious. This may be in part an expression of her rebelliousness and in part an effort to overcome the shame that she still feels because of her display of foxhole religion when she was a sophomore: "In my sophomore year I turned to religion as a big crutch. I just don't have any religious beliefs now. I just don't buy it."

Some of her further statements are interesting.

[*What is your opinion of the statement that religion is the opiate of the masses?*] "I don't think it is too correct historically. I don't think it is along class lines. Religion offers a way out for some people; it can give a feeling of dignity—a feeling that you are as good as anyone else, if not better." (Then she laughs.) "The Puerto Ricans I worked with last summer were really not very religious. They are not troubled by religion. But religion can obscure a lot at times."

[*In your thinking does man's evolutionary development mean he is anything more than an animal who has invented culture?*] "No, there is no great purpose in life. I came to the conclusion there isn't any a few months ago when I was thinking about my thesis. What difference does it make anyway? It doesn't make very much."

This sort of effort at intellectual analysis, and the effort to be somewhat hard-boiled about it, is characteristic of Penny. It, too, makes for a high score on the IE scale.

In respect to sex morality, we have seen that Penny is to be credited with the kind of relativism that is typical of senior women and that helps to differentiate them from freshmen on IE. I am also arguing that she has a kind of acceptance of sexuality, a kind of spirit about the whole thing, that helps to place her higher on the scale than the average senior.

Then, of course, she is well indoctrinated in the liberal, democratic, antiethnocentric political and social views of most college social science teachers today. She says half seriously that "we ought to secede from the South," and quite seriously that in our international relations "we have got to get away from the idea that our way is the only way." The development of this outlook was a foregone conclusion, once she had formed her relationship with Mr. A., gained her new friendships with "the Jewish girls," and separated herself psychologically from the roommates of her freshman year. She regrets, however, the idea that she might have thoughtlessly taken over a whole platform: "At times there is a conformity of liberalism, especially in the classroom. If you know the students well, you know they are not all that liberal."

As pointed out earlier, liberal or radical views in politics do not find expression in the IE scale, but in the present case the spirit of rebellious independence that lies behind such views would make for a higher score.

In view of the preceding, it would be very surprising if Penny was not low on the F scale. Her score of 61 (down from a freshman score of 96) is in the low quartile for the study group of college seniors. Hers is a kind of militant antiauthoritarianism that is quite in keeping with her spirit of rebellious independence.

All of this case material leads us to this conclusion: In Penny's college career the major theme has been her struggle for a new identity. The movement toward freedom of impulse has been a somewhat incidental benefit of this more or less successful and continuing struggle. What has happened to Penny as she passed through four years of college corresponds quite closely to our model of individual change in a change-promoting institution. In her new identity as a senior she is without doubt a more highly developed and better-integrated person.

FACTORS WHICH FAVORED DEVELOPMENT

An institution as complex as a college embraces many parts, which of course exert varying amounts of influence upon the developing individual. Many aspects of Penny's experience at Vassar played a part in her development—faculty members, courses of study, the student society and culture, her friendship group, the general climate of the college—but the crucial factor has undoubtedly been, as she herself states, the relationship with Mr. A. It is probable that she will always think of him as a decisive influence in her life.

This influence was bound up with his position with respect to the rest of the faculty and the administration of the college. Penny responded not only to his personality and intellectual outlook, but also to his situation and behavior as determined by the system in which he was embedded. I do not wish to suggest that in order for a teacher to "reach" his students he must first be in trouble with his colleagues (although this is, indeed, often a help!); teachers may influence students in various ways, appealing to various dispositions in them. The general point here is that interactions between teachers and students depend on the teacher's position and role in his department, in the faculty community, and in the general social structure of the college. These in turn depend upon various formal characteristics of the college, characteristics such as size, standards, and policy with respect to appointments and promotions of faculty.

Mr. A.'s crucial role was to make it possible for her to break away from her original peer group; and breaking away was necessary to her new freedom, because this group had become the major support of her restrictive conscience and her authoritarian position. Only an adult—not a peer or group of peers—and an admired one who represented intellectual values and enlightened conscience could have played this role. No other agency could have stood in effective opposition to the values represented by the early peer group and fully espoused by Penny herself. She needed a figure that was in some part a representative of her conscience but could at the same time nourish her developing confidence in her own intellectual powers.

That the peer group was primarily a representative of conscience seems plain enough from the record. We can well believe Penny when she tells us that one of her new friends was the first girl she ever really enjoyed being with. Her close association with her early friends was not a source of enjoyment but a matter of necessity. The group of freshmen girls to which Penny belonged, who thought they were, as she says, "really something," were constantly telling themselves, in effect, that they were "good," "all right," beyond moral reproach, while those whom they excluded were "bad" or "low." Not to belong to the in-group was to belong to the excluded group, onto which the girls projected their own "badness." It was fear of being rejected that drove Penny into depression and into religion. Yet she was bound to fear rejection, because however tightly she clung to her friends—"depended" on them—she was unconsciously rejecting them in seeking some freedom from the restrictions they represented. She was indeed in a bad spot when Mr. A. came to the rescue.

After the relationship with Mr. A. became firmly established, Penny could make friends with an entirely different group of girls, who now became very important as supporters of her new value system and her new self-conception. She could also establish friendships with other faculty members, who served her in the same way.

By no means all college girls have the inclination or the capacity to break away from a peer group such as that Penny belonged to, and by no means all the students in Mr. A.'s class were affected in the way she was. There was something in Penny already that made her dissatisfied with her situation in her freshman peer group and open to the influence of someone like Mr. A. There is much in the life-history material to suggest, and nothing to contradict, the notion that, although her conscience came mainly from an identification with her mother, Penny was also influenced a great deal by her father. Very likely she received enough from him, both from their love relationship and through identification, to suggest to her that rebellion against her mother might be possible as well as highly desirable. This might well have been the major source of her drive and desire for something beyond what was allowed by her peer group. It would also explain her capacity to go along with Mr. A. when powerful women of the faculty were suggesting that she was being foolish. Probably it was important, then, that the admired teacher should be a man—and one toward whom she could feel affection and nurturance as well as respect.

Be it noted, finally, that there is nothing in the material to suggest that Penny ever sexualized her relationship with Mr. A., or that he, for all his boyishness, ever indicated to the girls that he valued them for anything other than their intellectual and human qualities. Any departure from these restraints by either one of them would, of course, have spoiled the whole drama. Deep and personal though her problems were, Penny managed to work them out at the level of intellectual activity—thereby taking advantage of one of the unique opportunities offered by the college or university to those whom it would change.

Part Three

From a comprehensive view of the person-in-a-social-system, we turn to more detailed consideration of major subsystems: first, personality. If we are to think seriously about changing people—developing their potentialities or improving their functioning—we must understand well their inner structures and the mechanisms through which these may be reached. It is not enough to know one person, like Penny, well, or even to know many people well; we must have a theoretical formulation of personality, empirically based in so far as possible, that holds for people in general. This section, more than any other in this book, focuses on the inside structure of personality and presents specialized theory of its processes. Attention is given first to the conceptualization of elements of personality, then to their organization, and finally to mechanisms by which features of the social environment become incorporated in the developing personality. In Chapter 5, I present my own version of Freud's familiar yet elusive "structural theory," in which he conceived of the personality as made up of the three major systems: id, ego, and superego. Chapter 6 distinguishes between purely formal arrangements of the subsystems of personality (for example, some are central, others peripheral) and dynamic relationships, which are conceived as underlying regularities of functioning—that is, "dynamic structures." This scheme is applied in a consideration of the idea that personality is organized in levels or strata, and we arrive at the conclusion that "the unconscious" is a key concept in a dynamic theory of personality. Chapter 7 is concerned with the ways in which the structures of personality are built up. The unconscious processes of identification and introjection are considered to be of fundamental importance, but attention is given to various different ways in which the social environment affects personality development. It becomes clear, I think, that a serviceable developmental psychology must be broader than classical psychoanalysis, but it seems equally clear that any psychology that does not give due attention to unconscious processes will always be less than adequate.

CHAPTER FIVE

Elements of Personality: Id, Ego, Superego

Personality is always conceived of as a whole embracing parts or elements. Theorists differ in their conceptions of the elements and of how they are organized or patterned. In their search for elements of personality, psychologists have most often started with a general theory of behavior and then transposed to personality whatever units of analysis had been adopted—for example, "habits" for stimulus response theories, "needs" for functionalist theories, and "regions" for Gestalt theories.

Another way to arrive at elements is to start with a conception of the whole personality and then divide it according to its structural articulation. This was the procedure of Freud when he divided the psyche into the three major systems of id, ego, and superego and then propounded theory according to which the nature of the whole was expressed in the interactions among these systems. As we shall see, none of these systems can be defined without reference to the others and to the whole personality.

Of all proposals for the analysis of personality into basic elements none has been more durable than this scheme of Freud's. This seems to have been due partly to the fact that Freud here committed himself to some notions which numerous writers both before and after him have considered to be of fundamental importance, and partly to the fact that after several revisions he left his formulations of the three systems so vague and incomplete that they could continue to evolve in the hands of his followers. But most important is the fact that psychologists and social scientists have many occasions in their practical work to conceive of whole personalities, and for this purpose better concepts than those of Freud have not as yet come along.

Still, to use these terms in contemporary discussion is to risk failure in communication. They are at once too familiar and too esoteric. Every educated man knows the terms and perhaps must believe he knows what they mean; yet conversations with such men will often reveal that in their minds Freud's concepts are mere stereotypes. For most psychologists, on the other hand, id, ego, and superego carry a great deal of meaning, but these concepts are so closely tied in with one man's system that their use might easily imply more of a commitment to that system than one wishes to make or to be perceived as making. Psychologists by and large do not like being confronted with the meaningless question: "Are you or are you not a believer in Freud?" They accept parts and reject parts of Freud's system and would have to write books to explain just where they stand. It seems safe to say that the great majority of personality psychologists of the older generation make a great deal of use of the concepts of id, ego, and superego. Some do so explicitly, giving them place in their everyday speaking and writing; others use the terms more or less facetiously in talk with colleagues ("My superego would not allow me to work in that area"), having established that their research is concerned with "non-Freudian" matters; still others, probably the majority, keep these concepts alive in the backs of their minds, allowing them to guide thought and action in important matters such as the rearing of children or the maintenance of peace (while using more limited, precise, and specialized concepts in their research), and translating them into everyday language when writing or speaking for general scientific or lay audiences.

The present writer belongs to this last group. It has been quite a few years since I have had occasion to use these terms without definition, as if I were speaking only to the "initiated" or believed everyone was initiated. Yet the concepts have been, and still are, basic in my thought and research in the field of personality. As set down here, they represent my own conceptions of the id, the ego, and the superego—not a summary of what Freud wrote on these subjects.

[Freud's "structural theory," concerning the id, the ego, the superego, and their interactions, was developed comparatively late in his career. His first systematic formulation of the theory appeared in 1923, in his little book *The Ego and the Id*. This book is still the basic source for the "structural theory," although Freud expanded and modified his ideas on this subject in later writings (1926, 1932, 1940). Other expositions of the theory may be found in A. Freud (1936), Hartmann, Kris, and Loewenstein (1946), and Arlow and Brenner (1964).

In the present account I attach considerable importance to the growth of the id, while Freud seems to have regarded the id as "constant," both in its contents and in its modes of operation.

My account of the ego is, in general, in line with what has come to be known as psychoanalytic "ego psychology." A number of psychoanalysts, most notably Hartmann (1958, first published in 1939; 1964) and Hartmann, Kris, and Loewenstein (1946), taking as their point of departure Freud's 1923 essay, have stressed the importance of an "autonomous ego" in the development of personality. Freud, in most of his writings from 1923 on, took the position that at the beginning of life the id comprises the "whole of the mind" and that the ego develops out of the id. According to ego psychology, "apparatuses of the ego," the beginnings of abilities such as perception, memory, and inhibition, are independent of the id at birth—"primary autonomy" (Hartmann, 1964, p. xi)—and may develop, under the impact of external stimuli, independently of determinants in the id and of conflicts between id and ego. More than this, there are ego activities which, though they have their beginnings in the id or in id-ego conflicts, become functionally independent of their origins—"secondary autonomy" (Hartmann, 1964, p. xi).

Freud in one of his last publications (1940) considered that there might be an inborn core of ego processes, but he never gave much attention to activities in Hartmann's (1958) "conflict-free ego sphere." I accept and utilize the concepts of primary and secondary autonomy, and I stress far more than Freud did his idea that the ego has the aim of incorporating the id and the superego within itself. More than Freud, I stress the *contents* of the ego, which are conceived as needs that operate according to the ego's ways. This makes possible some integration of Freudian theory with other psychodynamic theories, such as that of Murray (1938, 1959). The operational definition of ego strength is, of course, a post-Freudian development in psychodynamic theory. It has also been since Freud wrote that the concept of the self has achieved prominence in psychodynamic theory; hence Freud did not attempt to relate self and ego as I do here.

These points of emphasis in the present account are, I believe, consistent with modern "ego psychology," but the major concern here is not with this new look in psychoanalytic theory. I am more concerned with retaining for the id an appropriate place in the structural theory, and in personality theory generally, and with the development of the ego in interaction with the id and the superego. I agree with Hartmann (1958, p. 8) that our need is for a general developmental psychology, and that this will require a *rapprochement* between psychoanalysis and nonanalytic psychology. But whereas ego psychology tends to move psychoanalysis closer to psychology, I am for moving psychology closer to psychoanalysis. (One's perspective here seems to depend on how one was brought up. If one was, so to speak, reared on the early Freud, or met with psychoanalysis by way of medicine and discovered nonanalytic views later, then the autonomous ego processes seem new and interesting. If, on the other hand, one was brought up in academic psychology and then came to psychoanalysis, as was the case with me, it is the most characteristic or distinctive

—that is to say, the older—psychoanalytic ideas that seem most seminal.) Ego processes in the conflict-free sphere may have been neglected by psychoanalysts in the past, but they have not been neglected by psychologists nor are they being neglected now. The problem now, as always since Freud appeared on the scene, is how to keep id tendencies and the more primitive processes of the superego fully in the picture. These aspects of personality always tend to be put aside in favor of what is simpler, more observable, more reasonable, and more flattering to man's conception of himself. I should like to cultivate among psychologists, as I would among developing personalities, friendly feelings toward the id. This should favor its incorporation by the ego. Freud remarked, "Where id was, there shall ego be," but he would have been scornful of any shortcuts to this state of affairs. The id is large, complex, and potent; it is the major source of the ego's richness, and its incorporation by the ego is the individual's most important developmental task.

In the case of the superego, my account differs in important respects both from Freud and from contemporary American trends in psychoanalytic theory-making. I have been influenced by the work of Melanie Klein (1948) and hence place special accent on the role of the child's imagination. The concept of *dimensions* of the superego which can be specified at the operational level was never made explicit by Freud.]

In spite of these deviations from Freud, I believe that what follows is essentially Freudian.

THE ID

The id is the aggregate of all the individual's most primitive emotional strivings. These strivings appear to be mainly an expression of man's biological inheritance, but one may not simply equate the id and the biological, because other, non-id, processes also appear to be native and it is desirable for theoretical purposes to consider that some of the id's tendencies have been modified under environmental influences.

Impulses of the id are usually unconscious, but this is not a defining characteristic of them; processes of the ego and of the superego may also be unconscious, and impulses of the id may under special circumstances break through into consciousness.

An id impulse may be defined, independently of its origins and independently of the conscious-unconscious dimension, in terms of its modes of operation. Here the essential thing is striving for immediate reduction of tension, in disregard of consequences for itself or for other impulses. Tension is subjectively painful, the reduction of tension pleasurable; the id operates in accordance with the *pleasure principle*, the organism's general tendency to avoid pain and to seek pleasure.

The organism comes into the world equipped with some mechanisms by which tension may be discharged immediately through motor activity.

But not all tension can be so readily managed. Often the reduction of tension depends upon there being made available some real object—for example, food, breast, mother. With repetitions, objects which have been instrumental in reducing tension become associated in the child's mind with tension reduction, so that later when tension is built up there will be produced an image of the object which is capable of reducing it. Thus an id impulse is not pure energy, with no information; very early in the infant's life, after only a minimum of learning has occurred, such an impulse is guided by a memory image of a satisfying object or circumstance. Thus it is appropriate to speak of an id impulse as a *wish*, and to speak of the process by which the individual seeks to reduce tension merely by producing an image as a *wish fulfillment*. This is the stuff of dreams, fantasies, hallucinations, and delusions. An important characteristic of the id is that it does not distinguish between memory images and perceptions of actual objects but acts toward the former just as if they were present in reality.

Unhappily for the id, wishing does not alter facts. The degree to which tensions may be reduced by the production of wish-fulfilling images, or by reflex activity in the musculature, is severely limited. For survival and reproduction, and for the maintenance and growth of the individual, other, more effective means for reducing tension have to be developed— hence the ego, that structure of the personality which deals with realities.

Although the id does not change with time in its basic modes of operation, it nevertheless develops as the infant grows into the adult. With physical and physiological growth, more physical energy is made available to the id, and it is lent increasing power through the maturation of the motor apparatus. With time, more and more different kinds of objects are utilized in the reduction of tension, and hence through association and memory there is expansion of the domain of wish-fulfilling imagery. At the same time, there is an increase in the strength and variety of stimuli that generate tensions; fresh internal stimuli come with physical and physiological growth, most strikingly perhaps with the bodily changes of puberty, while external stimuli are brought to bear by the training and discipline which are necessary to the child's socialization. More tension, more frustration, more wishes—thus it is that the id of any individual after infancy has content of considerable breadth and complexity. And this content may vary from one individual to another, depending on the course of their upbringing. "Infantile sexuality"—that is, the child's inclination to find pleasure in the stimulation of various zones of the body and from interaction with a diversity of objects (including persons)—and various forms of aggression, rejection, dependence, passivity, rebelliousness, lust for power, and the like may be ascribed to the id, *provided* that these impulses operate in ways that are characteristic of the id. Id impulses are demanding, irrational, asocial, uncontrolled. When frustrated they seek gratification in imagination. In disregard of logic or reason or reality the id creates and usually inhabits a dream world of its own.

Despite their considerable potency id impulses can be controlled by the ego. In childhood, the ego gains and maintains its control mainly by repression—making the impulses unconscious and keeping them so. When repressed, id impulses are cut off from the maturing effects of experience. As we saw in Chapter 2, the development of the ego makes possible a relaxation of repression and the gradual absorption of the id by the ego; nevertheless, in adolescents and most adults some repressed impulses remain and may be recognized by their infantile or childish quality. Repressed impulses sometimes make brief appearances at the fringes of consciousness, and sometimes through "slips" they find some expression in overt action; in these cases they are experienced as foreign or alien to the self.

The id is a system, a whole whose parts are related. Owing to its internal connectedness its energy may be readily displaced from one object to another. And, as we shall see, the whole system may be affected by changes in the ego or superego.

THE EGO

The most essential function of the ego is to bring about reduction of tension when the primitive devices of the id fail to do so. The process in the id that produces a memory image of an object capable of reducing a particular tension was called by Freud the *primary process*. The primary process serves to give direction to the individual's striving, but it can reduce tension but little, if at all. What is required is a plan of action by which an actual object, with which the individual may interact, is discovered or produced. The process by which such plans are devised and carried out is the *secondary process*. This process operates in accordance with the *reality principle*; it takes into account circumstances that exist in the real world and seeks to govern activity in such a way as to attain in the long run a maximum satisfaction of needs.

In order for the secondary process to operate there must be some delay of energy discharge until a suitable object has been found, and this means that the ego must have some capacity to tolerate tension. This, indeed, is the most essential, as it is the distinguishing, characteristic of the ego. Given this capacity, the ego is able to bring into the service of its tension-reducing activities the basic abilities of the organism—perception, memory, thinking, and action. The beginnings of these abilities—potentialities for them—are given through biological inheritance, and to some extent they develop through maturation, but their development is mainly a product of their interactions with the environment. With experience and with training the individual's powers of discrimination become finer, and his store of usable memory images is vastly enlarged—most notably through the acquisition of a language. These developments make possible a great increase in the ability to think, for the individual is now in a position to select from a vast array of external stimuli and internal images those that are relevant to a given problem, and with language at hand he is able to deal with problems vicariously without being forced to try a variety of overt actions. There is improved judgment of the realities of a situation, and an increased ability to make decisions respecting alternative courses of action. At the same time, the individual acquires increased skill in the use of his muscles, and the ability to carry out complex patterns of movement. In short, with experience and training the ego's efforts to deal with the external environment in such a way as to obtain gratification of needs become increasingly intelligent and efficient.

But to reduce tension through accommodation to or mastery of the environment is not the only task of the ego. It must also deal with internal problems. As pointed out earlier, numerous needs or strivings operate in the personality at the same time. In order that each of these may receive its due the ego undertakes to establish schedules and hierarchies of importance. But despite its best efforts, conflicts arise, and the ego has the further task of finding ways to resolve them. The most common type of conflict, and the type that has the most far-reaching implications for the development of personality, is conflict between impulses of the id and the demands of the superego, the primitive conscience that strives for moral perfection. When id impulses are permitted direct gratification, even when there is conscious pleasure in fantasies of gratification, the superego punishes the ego by arousing guilt feelings. The pangs of conscience, as is well known, may be extremely painful. The ego seeks to avoid them, both by managing impulses in ways that are tolerable to the superego and by softening the superego itself—making it more reasonable and tolerant. Here the ego exercises its important integrative or synthesizing functions. Its ultimate aim, actually, is to incorporate the id and the superego within itself, becoming the sole channel for the expression of impulse and taking over the task of maintaining behavior on a suitably high moral level. This state of affairs is approached in the ideally developed individual. But often things do not go very smoothly. Impulses from the id may increase in intensity and threaten to explode into action; this arouses in the ego extreme anxiety lest the superego punish it, with severity to match the primitiveness of the outbreak of the id. In critical situations of this kind —and we have seen that they are common in childhood—the ego resorts to maneuvers that deny, falsify, or distort reality and hence impair development in the long run. These maneuvers, of which repression is an example, are the defensive mechanisms of the ego. Typically, they operate unconsciously.

In a sense, the sense that has been mainly discussed so far, the ego is a collection of mechanisms. It remains to be pointed out that the ego is a system, a structure having a boundary, contents, and organization. The contents of the ego are mainly needs, strivings whose goals have been set in accordance with reality and which proceed in accordance with the ego's way of doing things. The same kind of needs—that is, needs having the same general goal—may appear either in the id or in the ego, or in both. Consider, for example, the need for dominance. In the id there will be striving for immediate and absolute power, and fantasies of omnipotence. The ego's version of this same general need will be a temperate desire to influence people and an integrated set of techniques for attaining to and maintaining positions of leadership. In time the ego comes to embrace a great variety of particular needs, together with the cognitive schemata and action patterns that have been built up as means for satisfying them. These contents of the ego constitute a coherent unity; they are organized according to the principle that in so far as possible each need should have its due.

The ego's success in obtaining satisfaction of needs is what makes possible its control over id impulses. In the beginning, according to Freud's theory, the ego has no energy of its own. But "it commends itself to the id," as an agency for the reduction of tension, and thus energy becomes available to its mechanisms. As the ego develops and becomes more and more effective, the gains to the organism from the activities of the ego become increasingly greater than the gains that can be achieved by the id, and some of the energy inherent in the id is transferred to the ego. After this development has proceeded for a time a stage is reached at which the ego, which may function as a unit, commands more energy than is embodied in a typical id impulse; and hence the id may be confronted by a stronger force. A man who has a job, a home, friends, a place in the community, satisfying interests, is not likely to sacrifice or endanger this pattern of life, or the personality structure which underlies it, through the indulgence of some momentary passion.

The ego structure *is* endangered by each uncontrolled expression of a primitive impulse. Even if the impulse is gratified and there are not painful consequences, the ego's way of proceeding is called into question. More likely, the expression of the impulse will evoke an outraged reaction from parents or other authorities, or from their internal representative, the superego, and these agencies then act as if they would be happy to relieve the ego of all its controlling functions.

By and large, however, and particularly in childhood, external authorities and the superego are helpful to the ego in its task of controlling impulses. These agencies have force aplenty at their disposal and to some extent they represent that reality which is the most essential ally of the ego.

The ego is also lent strength by the fact that it becomes the object of self-esteem. Among the id tendencies which gradually become absorbed by the ego is primary narcissism or elemental self-love. If the ego is to find satisfaction for this need, a reasonable relationship must be developed between self-satisfaction and actual worth, as reality requires. Here the ego is helped immeasurably by the love and approval of parents and others. Almost inevitably, it seems, the ego makes a connection between these rewards and "good"—that is to say, effectively controlling and organizing—behavior; thus its regard for itself is supported, as it is shaped, by the regard of others. The fact that it may take pride in its accomplishments, and experience self-respect when it is functioning well and shame when it is not, is a circumstance highly favorable to the ego's higher activities. It is a condition necessary to the individual's ability to love other people.

"Ego strength" is a variable that has loomed large in empirical studies of personality. Fundamentally, the strength of the ego is a matter of how much energy is available to it—how much energy, if it came to that, could be set in opposition to an id impulse or to demands of the superego; and this depends upon the structure of the ego—that is, the degree of differentiation and elaboration of its mechanisms for reducing tension. The stronger the ego, the more effectively it will perform its functions; hence indices of ego strength are measures of the adequacy of performance in various spheres of activity. Accuracy of perception, objectivity, judgment, common sense, tolerance of ambiguity, self-insight, initiative, persistence, competence in solving problems, tolerance of frustration, flexibility of adaptation, ability to learn from experience, capacity for logical thinking, planning ability and foresight, ability to stick to promises and to carry out resolutions—these and many other measures of performance are indices of the degree of the ego's strength.

We have spoken of self-esteem and self-respect. Is the "self" that is esteemed and respected the same as the ego system, or do we have to deal here with a different concept? I take the position here that the self, as this concept is most commonly used in contemporary psychology, is not the same as the ego. The self as most commonly conceived is a content of awareness, an aspect of human experience. Using the subjective reports of individuals, it has been possible for psychologists to distinguish numerous variables of content and organization in this self of awareness: different features that are ascribed to it, how they are patterned, how this pattern is valued, how consistent it is over time, and so on. Since the ego, as we have seen, contains processes that are unconscious, ego and self are clearly not coextensive. More than this, what enters into the conscious self may have sources other than the ego; the individual may experience, as part of his self, processes belonging to the id or to the superego. The term "inferred self" has sometimes been used to stand for all the processes that underlie the self of experience.

Although self and ego are separate, there is clearly much overlapping of the two. Of the three systems discussed here the ego is closest to consciousness and in closest touch with the external world. When the ego is carrying out some of its major functions, such as resolving or making a decision, the individual has the impression that his self is determining what he will do. Also, tendencies from the id and from the superego which are excluded from the ego are likely to be excluded by the individual from his conception of his self. Nevertheless, by maintaining the distinction that has been made, we may avail ourselves of the explanatory power of the larger conception of ego and at the same time use self as a special explanatory concept. The individual seeks to build up and to maintain a consistent conception of his self; to do this he must behave in a way that is consistent with this conception, and therefore behavior depends to some extent upon the self-conception. The individual may make a distinction in consciousness between his self as it is and his self as he would like it to be. This ideal self may embody many of the positive goals of the ego, and thus have a large influence in determining the directions of behavior.

THE SUPEREGO

The superego is a hypothetical construct invented to explain such phenomena as self-blame, self-abasement, feelings of guilt, depression, suicidal thoughts, anxiety in the absence of actual threats, oversubmissiveness to external authority, night terrors, compulsive strivings to achieve high moral standards. Most essential in this conception is the notion of an agency inside the personality that punishes antisocial actions or thoughts, and that rewards what by the prevailing social code would be called virtuous. The superego is usually more or less directly opposed to the id. Although it does not necessarily seek to inhibit all impulses, it reserves the right to decide which are acceptable or consistent with its aim of maintaining a high level of morality. Needs of the ego are also often opposed by the superego, for what may be suited to reality may nevertheless fail to conform with the superego's standards.

Although the superego is most essentially a punishing or goading force, we may ascribe content and structure to it. Individuals differ with respect to the kinds of needs or drives that the superego seeks most forcibly to suppress, and with respect to the kinds of ideals that it favors. There are also individual variations in the kinds of punishments and pressures that the superego has at its disposal. The content of this agency may be observed to resemble the ideals and values of the social group in which the individual is brought up; to some extent at least the superego's content changes as the social group changes—for example, when a nation goes to war.

There is ample evidence that the child's parents have the major role in transmitting to him the standards of the community. They have the power to reward desirable behavior and to punish the undesirable, and, given the child's natural desire for approval and fear of punishment, the assimilation of what the parents stand for seems to follow readily enough —through simple conditioning and through the child's ability to imagine what his parents would say or do. The motive force at the disposal of the superego is thus supplied by the child's own basic needs; the superego, like the ego, derives its energy from the id.

It is important to note that the superego develops in childhood and that it always has the features of a childish construction. It is less like the ego than like the id, with which it shares the state of being alien to the ego. The superego operates automatically, inflexibly, unreasonably. It does not make fine distinctions, or argue points with the id or the ego; it simply says, with a tone of finality, "No," or "Do this." The parents that are internalized are not the "real" parents but the idealized or omnipotent parents that the childish mind conceives. And, similarly, the child does not adopt as a model the actual behavior of the parents; rather he is guided by his conception of what they would have him do. Although the superego commonly appears in consciousness, as conscience or as an ideal of perfection, it may also operate unconsciously, giving rise to vague anxiety or to behavior that is self-defeating or self-punishing.

As a construction of the child's mind the superego cannot be merely a copy of prevailing ideas and values as represented by the parents. It may often be noted that an individual makes stronger demands upon himself than his parents do, and that he is more severe with himself than external authorities are wont to be. The explanation appears to be that the severity of demandingness of the superego in action depends not alone upon how much energy has been channeled into it, but upon the strength of the impulses which it undertakes to counter (and upon how large a role the ego is able to play in this struggle).

This close relationship between the superego and the id has led some writers to suppose that the rudiments of a superego exist within the personality before there has been any opportunity for the incorporation of parental prohibitions and sanctions. The infant, who has only begun to distinguish between what is inside and what is outside his own body, may have occasion to fear his own impulses. When frustrated and in a mood to tear things up he may suppose that the things he would like to do might very well happen to him. According to this theory, the child who has nightmares in which animals are threatening to eat him up has not necessarily had any experience with devouring animals or even been told about them; all that is required for the generation of this internal punishing agency is that the child's own wish to bite should have become sufficiently intense. This theory seems well designed to explain anxiety and irrational fears in children who have been gently handled; it may also explain why a misbehaving child, whose impulses have got beyond his own control, welcomes the restraining—even the punishing—hand of the adult. Such a child prefers the actual punishment of the more or less reasonable parent to the punishment that he may give himself in his imagination. The presence of this internal punishing force is an additional reason why the child may happily internalize the prohibitions and sanctions that society offers, and thus build up a social superego on the basis of, or in the place of, the archaic one.

The superego may differ from one individual to another not only in the quality of its contents, as already indicated, but also along several dimensions. The dimension of *strength* refers to the amount of energy that is available, to how much force might be set in opposition to strivings of the id or ego. Strength may be inferred from the amount of anxiety that is experienced, from what the ego is forced to do in order to avoid anxiety, or from the severity of the punishments that are administered—

for example, as feelings of guilt. The *breadth* or *strictness* of the superego refers to the number of different kinds of impulsive strivings that will arouse inhibiting or punitive actions and to the variety of positive goals in whose interest pressure is exerted. *Rigidity* is the tendency to act in an *all-or-nothing* manner. The superego is always rigid as compared with the ego, but some superegos are far more rigid than others. A movie actress may for years conduct her life as if she had no conscience at all and then suddenly claim that she has "found God" and begin behaving in an altogether conventionally moral way. The contrast would be with a superego that acts to keep the individual steadily on a more or less moral course, with occasional fallings from grace.

The superego may be more or less *internalized*, in the sense that it can operate without reinforcement by an external authority. In early childhood it often seems that only the parent can prevent the full gratification of certain impulses; a little later the child will inhibit himself, perhaps call himself bad, when the parent is present, but go his own way otherwise; in time, as socialization proceeds, the child can inhibit his impulses without help from the parent's physical presence. Before this final stage is reached, various stages of partial internalization are passed through. Not all adults achieve complete internalization of the superego, and they may be partially characterized by noting the stage at which development ceased. Signs of an immature superego would be "social anxiety"—that is, inordinate worry about what other people might think, relative freedom from self-reproach until one is "found out" and then a severe but short-lived attack of bad conscience, a high degree of susceptibility to pressures from an immediately present social group.

A superego that has been more or less firmly internalized may later be got rid of or rendered virtually ineffective. It may be repressed by the combined forces of the ego and the id and kept in that state by a succession of delinquent or antisocial actions. Or it may be replaced by external authorities. A superego that has been based mainly upon fear and hatred of the parents remains as a pain-inducing foreign body within the personality; the ego may succeed in rendering it inoperative by permitting an external agency to take over its functions, just as the archaic superego is replaced by a social one.

A further index to be considered in the study of the superego is the degree of its *integration with the ego*. When this integration has occurred, the moral precepts of the superego are in keeping with the individual's own best judgment, and they may be supported by the ego's energy. It is sometimes argued that only under this condition can the superego be said to be genuinely internalized. It may be argued that this is the *sine qua non* for dependably moral behavior, yet apparently the superego may be fully inside the personality, and may endure there, without this integration's having occurred. Certainly this seems to be the state of affairs in depression and in those patterns of behavior dominated by compulsion. When integration with the ego has occurred, the superego is not so much internalized and durable as it is well on its way to being absorbed by the ego. Enlightened conscience, the noblest edifice of the personality, is fully in the domain of the ego. The same may be said of character, when this is understood as the ability and the inclination to conduct oneself in accordance with principles.

It was stated that the superego may be repressed. The reference was to the superego as a whole. This agency, like the ego, is an organized totality. In inhibiting or punishing or goading the id or the ego, it acts as a unit, and it is as a unit that it may be repressed, bribed, assuaged, or evaded.

Let us now emphasize that, although the id, the ego, and the super-ego may be distinguished conceptually, they are but elements in a larger system, the personality, and that no one of them is ever functionally independent of the others. Both the ego and the superego derive their energy from the id. The supply of energy is not unlimited; and this means that the strength of one of these agencies varies with the strength of the others. It is particularly important to note that the strength of the ego is not absolute, but relative to the tasks that it has to perform. When it is largely taken up with defensive operations, we cannot expect of it a high level of performance in its dealings with problems set by the external environment.

INTERRELATIONS OF ID, EGO, AND SUPEREGO

The relations among the three systems are intimate and complicated. Each may be in conflict with, and each may be allied with, each of the others. Conflict, and id-ego and ego-superego integrations, have been noted. The alliance of the id and the superego deserves a special word. This alliance may be inferred from cases in which extreme aggression is directed against the ego, as in suicide, or, more commonly, from cases in which primitive aggressive needs appear to gain satisfaction through attacks on people who are considered to be immoral.

Patterns of relationship among the id, the ego, and the superego offer a basis for the formulation of the central core of the personality. But they by no means suffice to describe all of the individual's characteristic ways of interacting with his environment, or all of the ways in which one personality might differ from another.

In their attempts to describe personality, psychologists have most often started with the observation of behavior. Noting consistency of behavior in varying situations, and sticking as close to the facts as possible, they have conceived of traits or dispositions of personality that would account for observed consistency. Many diverse personality characteristics have thus been conceptualized, and there is no reason to believe that the possibilities of this approach have been exhausted. Personality is a vast and intricate structure built up from simple beginnings. An appropriate conception of its developed state might be that of a relatively stable inner core of relatively few basic elements, surrounded by a multiplicity of tendencies that are in closer contact with the environment. It is possible to be reasonably systematic in dealing conceptually with these outward aspects of personality. One approach is to consider that even in his most superficial interactions with the environment the individual's behavior is guided by needs, in whose service a great variety of abilities and objects are utilized. Observing behavior over a period of time, one may readily infer the existence, as personality characteristics, of: (a) needs (motives, strivings); (b) attachments to objects (things, people, ideas) or to activities that consistently satisfy needs, and rejections of objects that frustrate: hence sentiments, interests, positive and negative attitudes, tastes, preferences, fears; (c) modes and styles of overt behavior, and (d) cognitive schema, beliefs, plans that further satisfaction of needs.

This approach may be brought into line with the Freudian scheme in the following way. Most of the needs—with their integrated modes and objects—which operate in immediate contact with the environment are in the ego; they can be understood as more particular ways in which this agency carries out its functions. Things are not always so simple, however. We have seen that both the id and the superego may also be expressed more or less directly in behavior, and, not uncommonly, what we encounter at the surface are resultants from the interactions of the three central systems. The competence of the individual, as displayed for example in academic or scholarly achievement, in leadership, or in effective social relations, should not be regarded as nothing more nor less than an expression of a strong ego; the id and the superego are usually also involved in competence, though now they will have become integrated with the ego. Here as elsewhere, however, we have to recognize that the same, or at least very similar, patterns of behavior may have different sources within the personality. For example, self-assertion may be a straightforward expression of the ego's needs, or it may be an overcompensation for an inner sense of weakness. As the id, the ego, and the superego develop and carry out their functions in interaction one with another, there comes to intervene between the core and the surface of personality a vast aggregate of subsystems and secondary processes. To determine the dynamic sources of surface manifestations requires not only the accurate observation of these but the investigation of large areas of the person by special techniques.

CHAPTER SIX

Formal and Dynamic Structure in Personality

It is common in the literature to speak of the ego, the superego, and the id, and of other psychoanalytic concepts, as "structures" or "underlying structures" of personality. The reference seems to be to predictable constancies with which certain subgroups of functions (for example, the ego's mechanism of defense) operate. Writers not of the psychoanalytic persuasion also use the term "structure"; sometimes they use different concepts to stand for predictable constancies or regularities of functioning in the personality, and sometimes the word "structure" itself is given a different meaning.

This chapter makes a distinction between "dynamic structure," which is illustrated by the Freudian concepts so far considered, and "formal structure," which refers to a different dimension altogether. By maintaining this distinction and using concepts on both dimensions we may hope to increase the supply of analytic tools available to the theorist.

SURFACE AND DEPTH

We may approach this task, in a somewhat indirect way, by examining the ways in which psychologists have sought to deal with the problem of "surface and depth" in personality. The literature abounds with terms

A shortened version of a paper presented as the Presidential address of the Division of Personality and Social Psychology of the American Psychological Association, San Francisco, September 2, 1955.

which have reference to a distinction between the superficial and the deep: the descriptive or objectively observable versus the inferred; phenotypical versus genotypical; the central versus the peripheral; the behavior versus the underlying dynamics. Psychologists, like the literary characterologists before them, have usually conceived of personality as a whole, existing in time and space and having dimensionality; and to suggest this, they have used analogies from geology, oceanography, architecture, horticulture, and anthropology, as well as from geometry and topology. Thus we find references to the surface, the superstructure, the skin or shell or peel, the mask or veil, the fringe, the periphery, as opposed to the subterranean, the submerged, the foundations or underpinnings, the kernel or core or heart, the hidden or mysterious, the center, the central.

Surface and depth, though common in the literature, are nowhere used as technical terms. "Depth psychology," however, is frequently used to refer to psychoanalysis. The terms usually have evaluative connotations. Everyone wants to be deep or to go deep; no one wants to be shallow or superficial. On the other hand, there seems to be some ambivalence in the matter, for there is the danger that if, like the psychoanalysts, one goes down deep, he might come up dirty.

As evidence of the seriousness with which the matter of surface and depth is viewed in contemporary thought I may quote, not from a psychologist, but from the biologist, Bertalanffy. He distinguishes between the "depth personality with its primeval instincts, emotions and appetites" and "the day personality of consciousness," and goes on to say that "the antagonism between the levels of personality is at the bottom of the human tragedy . . . whether the levels of personality can be properly adjusted is the question upon which man's future depends" (1951, p. 37).

What are the levels? How does one distinguish one from another? And how do the levels interact, if indeed they do?

In taking a brief glance at the history of these problems in psychology, we may start with Freud's division of the mind into conscious, preconscious,[1] unconscious. It is interesting to note that this topography, though it was soon to be replaced in the forefront of psychoanalytic thinking by the trichotomy of superego, ego, id, has been assumed by psychoanalytic writers and has never been altered. It has not been seriously challenged by neo-Freudians. Jung, however, did challenge it, as early as 1912, and by adding the concepts of persona[2] and collective unconscious,[3] presented

[1] *Preconscious:* Not present in consciousness at a given moment, but recallable more or less readily when wanted.

[2] *Persona:* The role which a person plays; the mask he puts on not only for others but for himself. It represents his conscious intentions and the requirements of the real situation, not the more deeply rooted components of personality.

[3] *Collective unconscious:* That part of the individual's unconscious which is inherited and which the individual shares with other members of the species. For Jung's discussion of the persona and the collective unconscious, see C. J. Jung, "Two Essays on Analytical Psychology," trans. by R. F. C. Hull in *Collected Works,* Vol. 7, Bollingen Series XX (New York: Pantheon, 1953).

The definitions in the footnotes of this chapter are taken, unless otherwise noted, from H. B. and A. C. English, *A Comprehensive Dictionary of Psychological and Psychoanalytical Terms* (New York: David McKay, 1958).

a topography of more layers or levels than the original. Both of these schemes were very much in the picture when psychoanalysis began to make an impression in the universities.

Murray, whose *Explorations in Personality* was published in 1938, distinguished between manifest (overt, objectified) and latent (covert, subjectified) needs, and sought to obtain independent measures of the two. It was with the latter, particularly, in mind that Morgan and Murray (1935) invented the Thematic Apperception Test (TAT).

Some of the early work with the TAT, in which the attempt was made to relate variables in the subjects' story productions to variables of overt behavior (Sanford, 1943), stands among the first efforts at objective and quantitative study of variables conceived to be operating on different levels. Tomkins (1947) stressed the point that TAT contents may be indices of behavior, of conscious fantasy, or of unconscious motives, and that it is possible through empirical work to discover which indices are to be referred to which level. This way of looking at things was adopted and furthered by Betty Aron in her manual on the TAT (1949).

Frenkel-Brunswik (1940) has consistently stressed the discrepancies between surface behavior and underlying motives and has underlined the enormous complexity of the relationships between these two levels of functioning. In a later monograph (1942) she educed some evidences of alternative surface manifestations of the same motivating force.

When it came to the work on *The Authoritarian Personality* (Adorno, Frenkel-Brunswik, Levinson, and Sanford, 1950), the authors took it for granted that they should have to distinguish the opinions and attitudes that the subject would express publicly from those he would express only to an intimate friend, and that both these groups of phenomena would have to be distinguished from dispositions that the subject could not admit to himself.

This way of thinking about levels has perhaps been developed most fully by Freedman, Leary, Ossorio, and Coffey (1951), who distinguish the public, the conscious, and the private levels of personality and offer operational definitions of variables on each level, in terms of a theory according to which one kind of variable might be related to all the others.

The line of development just indicated, which has been close to the clinic and close to psychoanalysis, is of course but a part of the recent history of thought and research bearing on the general problem of surface and depth. An adequate account would give much attention to the early work of Kurt Lewin, which made phenotype, genotype, peripheral, central, layer, strata, region, household words in psychology; to the writings of Gordon Allport (1937), whose trait psychology makes large use of the distinctions phenotypical versus genotypical, instrumental versus motivational, specific versus general or central or cardinal, pseudo versus genuine, and whose compelling arguments for functional autonomy[4] were at the

[4] *Functional autonomy:* The tendency of a developed motive system to become independent, said to be based originally on a hunger drive, may later become independent of pendent of the primary drive from which it originated; for example, the motive of acquisi-hunger both as to objects sought and as to strength of motive.

same time, but unintentionally, arguments that there were other, presumably deeper, forces that were not functionally autonomous; and to the work of Cattell (1950) who showed that factorial methods could be applied to problems of dynamics as well as to the task of classifying behavior.

One result of all the history to which I am alluding—history which in very considerable part has as its theme what to do about or to or with psychoanalysis—is that there are now nine concepts which have to be considered in a discussion of surface and depth. In contemporary writing, the surface-depth dimension is spoken of as if it were analogous to, or at least an attribute of, each of these concepts.

Since the concepts are very familiar, I need do little more than mention them here:

1. *Availability to consciousness.* The unconscious is almost always regarded as deeper than the preconscious and the conscious. Preconscious processes, presumably, may vary among themselves with respect to their availability to consciousness.

2. *Availability to the motoric.* The inhibited is usually regarded as deeper than that which is freely expressed in action.

3. *Place in a developmental sequence.* In other schools of psychology besides psychoanalysis, that which is laid down, or set up, early in the individual's development is commonly regarded as deeper than that which is established later.

4. *Biological as opposed to learned.* Biological needs, if they are admitted at all, usually are regarded as more basic (that is, deeper) than derived needs; something more or less biological has a place at the bottom of most motivational pyramids.

5. *Neurologically "lower" or "higher."* Bertalanffy, in the paper quoted earlier (1951), speaks of the cortex, "the organ of the day personality," as being "on top" of the palencephalon, "the organ of the depth personality." There is a certain awkwardness here, for what is neurologically more peripheral sometimes has to be regarded as deeper than that which is neurologically central.

6. *The genotypical versus the phenotypical.* It is common to speak of the genotypical, the integrating, or determining, or ruling, or motivating, as deeper than the phenotypical, the integrated, or determined, or ruled, or instrumental. It is also common to speak of the former as central and the latter as peripheral, though it is doubtful that this is justified if one sticks to Lewin's topology.

7. *Outer versus inner.* These terms, of course, are also from topology, but not all writers have a topological model in mind when they speak of those features of the personality which are dependent upon immediate field conditions versus those which are characteristic of the individual in a deeper sense.

8. *Resistance to change.* The fixed or deep-seated is likely to be regarded as deep in a bad sense; the enduring or persistent as deep in a good sense.

9. *Open to observation versus hidden or mysterious.* Since these conditions depend as much upon the observer as upon the subject, they should probably be left out of consideration.

FORMAL STRUCTURE

The time now appears to be ripe for a serious new effort at clarification in this whole area, and to this end I should like to make a few suggestions.

The first suggestion is that we distinguish between formal structure and dynamic structure. Personality can be—and should be first of all—conceived as a whole, having parts which stand in various purely formal relations one to another. We can fill in the several cells or regions with such contents—needs, sentiments, habits, cognitive dispositions—as we find appropriate, and then proceed to consider dynamics, that is, the ways in which these contents interact and the mechanisms by which effects are achieved.

The next suggestion is that *central-peripheral* and *inner-outer* be adopted as concepts referring to formal structure, and that we hold ourselves strictly to this usage.

Central-peripheral would be used in the topological sense, as offered by Kurt Lewin in his later writings (1951). Central, in this sense, means influencing and being influenced by relatively many other parts or regions of the person, and peripheral means the opposite. An aroused need or an instigation to goal activity would be central, while various activities brought into its service would be peripheral. This seems to be a very common instance of a process being central in the sense of influencing; probably it is a little awkward for most of us to think of the same process as being at the same time influenced by various other processes. But it might be profitable to think in that way. For example, a need to raise self-esteem, when it is aroused, will certainly mobilize in its service various action patterns, and thus be influencing; at the same time it is interesting to consider the sensitivity of such a need—how, in its subjective aspect at least, everything that happens, over a wide area, seems to make a difference to it.

By outer I shall mean here simply those layers or regions of the person that are involved in transactions with the external environment; by inner, those which are not. The conception would apply, quite literally, I think, to the case of a man of whom we say that he is so taken up with external matters that he has no time to be himself. Of ourselves we say that we are so involved with the urgent that we have no time for the important. Lewin used this conception of inner-outer and went on to point out how, in topology, a cell might be outer and yet central, inner and yet peripheral. He did not, however, offer many psychological examples of these states of affairs, nor did he or his students, as far as I know, make much use of these conceptions in considering the structure of personality.

According to Lewin's topological theory, inner layers of the person are separated from the environment by surrounding outer layers, so that a process in an inner region cannot reach the outside save by passing through these outer layers. This theory does not seem to fit the facts of observation. Inner needs do not have to pass through outer regions in order to be expressed in behavior. They will be expressed directly, unless they are anchored inside—as in the case of a man who simply prefers to keep his best thoughts to himself—or unless the channels for their expression are blocked, either because these channels are filled with traffic of day-to-day urgency or because a barrier has been erected against the specific need in question. Consider the case of a man whose everyday behavior is more or less dominated by a persona. We need not suppose that his inner needs can find expression only by passing through this outer layer, though no doubt they may influence what goes on there; instead, there are occasions on which the mask falls away and aspects of the inner personality stand directly revealed.

Now, since central-peripheral and inner-outer are independent aspects of structure, we have to consider that both inner and outer processes (contents) may be either central or peripheral. Time is another structural property that has to be taken into account. Personality structures—whether they be central or peripheral, inner or outer—may be momentary, temporary, or enduring.

Now I suggest that we have a scheme, formal and abstract as it is, that is inclusive with respect to the phenomena of personality. We are in a position to take the first step toward describing, in the terms of the same scheme, the phenomena of child development, of neurosis and psychosis, of normal adulthood.

What is something that is inner, peripheral, and enduring? I suggest a tendency that was long ago more or less effectively insulated by repression, and in time has been more or less washed out as other structures have evolved, but which nevertheless remains a potential, capable of becoming central when just the right stimulus comes along. How about outer, central, enduring? The consistent instrumentalities of taking a social role whose requirements are diverse and taxing, and which does not fit the individual very well, so that his inner needs find relatively little opportunity for expression, offer an example.

Inner, central, temporary would be represented rather well, I think, by the case of an individual involved in a developmental crisis. When, for example, an adolescent is taken up with the problem of independence, we find a structure in which very many needs, sentiments, abilities, cognitive readinesses are influenced by, even as they influence, this central core of striving, while other inner needs, even those which will be determining with respect to life goals, recede temporarily into the periphery.

How, according to this scheme, shall we describe the behavior of a brain-damaged patient? This is the extreme case of outer and peripheral, whether temporary or enduring. The individual is at the beck and call of the stimuli that chance to impinge upon him, and the connections among his responses are minimal. R. W. White (1944) said of one such case: "She is unable to stand apart from the immediate prospectus of the situation or to resist the behavior which it invites. . . . What strikes us about [the brain-damaged patient's] behavior is *immediacy* and *specificity*. It is governed by concrete impressions and present circumstances. . . . These immediate impressions exert such a powerful force on the patient that she cannot resist them or detach herself from their influence." This, of course, corresponds to the condition of the infant who has not yet established any devices for the delay of response.

Paranoia, on the other hand, might be thought of as the limiting case of centralism, everything being related, however unreasonably, to everything else, perhaps in a final desperate effort to prevent the dissolution of the boundaries between the personality and the environment.

It seems to me possible that we might achieve, before long, fairly general agreement about some such scheme for the formal description of personality structure. I assume that the conditions of formal structure, to be described with this scheme, call for explanation mainly in terms of psychodynamic hypotheses.

DYNAMIC STRUCTURE

In psychodynamics it is common to distinguish between adaptive and defensive mechanisms. When we say, as we commonly do, that similar behavior may have different determinants, the major classes of determination that we have in mind are: (*a*) determination by conscious, functionally autonomous, ego-integrated motives, and (*b*) determination by motives that are defensive and unconscious. Another interesting exercise would be to ask ourselves whether processes exhibiting, in various combinations, the formal properties previously discussed might not be either conscious or unconscious. It seems that they can be, and this is true whether we define "unconscious" merely as absence of awareness, or in the Freudian sense.

It is clear that we cannot use the terms central or inner to help distinguish our unconscious, defensive motives. As a matter of fact, it seems that, by and large, the greatest centrality is achieved in conscious functioning, when the use of symbols is brought to the highest level of development; and an inner need that is unconscious is not necessarily more inner than one that is conscious.

Now the important point: unconscious motives are not to be distinguished by calling them deep, in the sense of "underneath"—that is, underneath strata which they must pass through in order to reach the surface. There are too many people who would like to get rid of unconscious motives by burying them in this way. The fact is that making a motive (or some of its integrated effects, instrumentalities, or cognitive content) unconscious may be the very device by which that motive is permitted expression in overt behavior. More than this, whereas defensive mechanisms may operate to prevent environmental stimuli from being perceived, they may be powerless to prevent unconscious discrimination, whereby the most primitive, emotional, irrational needs of the persons come under the direct influence of the environment.

A major function of unconsciousness is to keep things separate, to prevent communication among parts which, if the person were functioning adaptively, would belong together.

These considerations are of crucial importance for social psychology. The social psychologist cannot assume that, because he deals with the average, normal adult, he need concern himself only with responses which are under the sway of the higher mental processes. On the contrary, social stimuli, such as propaganda, may make their appeal directly to unconscious forces; indeed the technique of propaganda consists most essentially in finding ways to bypass the higher mental processes in reaching the responsive primitive needs. Similarly, the truly dangerous social or group phenomena, such as riots or totalitarian movements, and the truly intractable ones, such as social structures in institutions and organizations, usually involve the operation of unconscious mechanisms; in the former case such mechanisms have the crucial function of helping to remove ordinary restraints, while in the latter case the social structure may resist change just because it serves the defensive purposes of various individual members of the group. The social psychologist can ill afford not to be conversant with unconscious mental functioning.

Now let us consider a dynamic formulation of the kind that is frequently made in clinical cases. A case from *The Authoritarian Personality* (1950) will do for the present purpose. Here the formulation was that this man's self-assertive behavior was an attempt to overcompensate for an underlying fear of weakness, which in its turn was based upon unconscious, passive, homosexual impulses. These impulses could be understood as responses to, attempts to deal with, fear of the father (that is, castration anxiety)—a fear which was kept alive by aggression against the father and which in fact was mainly a projection of this aggression onto the father. The aggression against the father, which was somewhat special in this case, was constantly provoked by frustration of the need to be loved by the father—a rather distant and forbidding man who made a poor substitute for the mother who had died when the subject was seven. (This case is discussed at greater length in Chapter 10.)

This, of course, is but a fragment of the whole dynamic structure. For example, fear of weakness finds other expressions besides self-assertion and has other sources besides passive homosexuality; and similarly for the various other contents. But it is enough to suggest what distinguishes this kind of dynamic determination from others that are common in personality theory.

It follows from what has just been stated that the formal concepts of central and inner are not helpful, since they may be—and are with justice —applied in cases where the determination is of quite different kinds. We cannot say that we are talking about things that are more central or more inner. Things which lie further back in our chain of determination may relate directly to processes in the outer layer of the personality and have their direct representatives in behavior.

We can, of course—speaking now in terms of dynamics and not in terms of formal structure—call such things as passive homosexuality or castration anxiety "deep" needs, but we will not convey very much to various other psychologists who use precisely these words to describe quite different motivational factors.

Actually, from the dynamic point of view, there is no good reason why we should draw the dynamic structure vertically, with underlying and overlying contents. We could as well draw it horizontally, with the more genotypical elements on the left and the more phenotypical ones on the right.

It is well to remind ourselves that self-assertive behavior might have quite different determination than that illustrated by our case. For example, it might have come into being as a transformation, in accordance with reality, of infantile omnipotence fantasies that blossomed under a long history of gratifications and reached full fruition as a means for promoting various important goals of the person. It would not be difficult to show, in some instances, that a conscious or preconscious tendency to self-assertion was the motivating force behind diverse specific performances carried out over long periods of time; and in these cases many psychologists would not hesitate to call the motive deep.

What I am leading up to is probably obvious by now: *unconscious* is the crucial concept for distinguishing the kind of dynamics illustrated by the case mentioned above. I mean, of course, unconscious in the psycho-analytic sense; a process is unconscious that is prevented from coming into consciousness by other inner forces. For the study of unconscious processes we do not have to rely upon subjective reports. (It should be added at once, however, that since distortion of the symbolic process is of the essence of unconsciousness, it seems slightly ridiculous to ignore what people say.) For those who do not like too much talk, but prefer to take their cues from the more overt kinds of behavior, the way is open to the objective study of unconscious functioning. Dollard and Miller (1950) have performed an important service by translating Freud's description of unconsciousness into the familiar terms of behavior theory.

Behavior that is motivated by unconscious forces is characteristically inflexible and stereotyped, automatic and obligatory, repetitive in disregard of the situation or the consequences of the behavior. Unconscious motives are marked primarily by insatiability and resistance to modification through experience; they tend to be unresponsive to pleasure or pain, rewards or punishments, logic or argument. As indicated earlier, unconsciousness is a failure to make the connections, usually among symbolic processes, that adaptation would normally require.

Resistance to change, though surely a feature of unconscious processes, is not by itself a dependable criterion. Other processes—such as well-thought-out convictions, patterns of role-taking in highly structured social situations, even certain overlearned habits—may be equally resistant to change. The crucial question concerns the conditions of change. Unconscious motives, usually, yield only to special devices for making them conscious; other enduring processes may be modified by new experience, including new argument, changes in the social situation, heroic deconditioning—things which may be just as difficult to arrange as an expansion of the boundaries of consciousness.

Unconscious motives, characteristically, are laid down relatively early in the individual life, but this does not distinguish them from other motives. We may find in the individual adaptive, controlled, and flexible motives which in their essence have been there more or less from the start. In unconscious motives the infantile elements may be said to have suffered early repression and to have been brought over, unmodified, into the present. Of other motives it may be said that, just as early, they become controlled or adapted to reality, and that they have persisted fundamentally unchanged just because of their flexibility.

In sum, then—and now I wish to refer to the list of meanings of surface and depth—with respect to the kind of motives that I have called most interesting and particularly important, one might say that they tend to be deep, inner, hidden, basic, central, integrating, genotypic, resistant to change, and originating early in the life of the individual. But none of these characteristics applies only to this class of motive. One may even argue for their universality in the species or for their relatively heavy admixture of biological elements without approaching very close to their unique character. What does distinguish them is their unconsciousness, and the special dynamics that proceed from this state of affairs.

Some of my colleagues may conclude that I have ceded too much ground to nonpsychoanalytic or even nondynamic psychology. My answer is that it is best to face facts and this, happily, the psychodynamic theorist can afford to do. Although functional autonomy, or something like it, is no doubt here to stay, we do not need to yield an inch on the line that unconscious motives, with all their elaborate transformations and counter-cathexes, are to be found universally in the human personality. We might, however, go so far as to admit with Kubie (1954) that we are dealing here with "neurotic potential"—something which is surely the stuff of which neurosis is made, given the critical external conditions, but which may also be the major motivating force in creative and socially constructive activity. I believe we showed in *The Authoritarian Personality* (1950) that this potential is, in the culture of today, a determinant of social attitudes that are very widespread.

In research on personality the object of investigation is the psychological organization of the individual. We distinguish parts or subsystems and try to understand them in their relations to one another and to the whole system. We rarely succeed in getting a purchase on *all* the parts, but we may certainly aspire to a grip on all the *kinds* of parts. Among the kinds of parts or subsystems are unconscious ones, and no study of personality that claims to be thoroughgoing can leave them out of account.

The detection and estimation of unconscious motives and mechanisms proceed according to the same general logic that holds for the investigation of any other subsystems of personality. We observe consistent trends in behavior and on this basis conceive of regularities of functioning in the personality; we then design experiments to test whether these hypothetical regularities of function express themselves in predictable ways in specified situations.

In spelling out the behavioral indices of personality systems, we make progress both by clarifying our conceptions of these systems, as this chapter has attempted to do, and by sharpening our observations. Faced with the fact that similar patterns of behavior may have different sources, we should ask, "How similar are those patterns?" For example, it seems quite possible that we might learn in time to distinguish, by direct observation, self-assertive behavior that is overcompensatory from self-assertive behavior that is conscious and adaptive. We would thus define two self-assertive variables, prepare a manual describing their common manifestations, and have them independently rated—preferably by different raters. And the same could be done for various other unconscious and conscious motives.

In determining the indices of unconscious factors we shall have more difficulty with criterion measures than with tests or objective instruments. Determined empiricists have long since delivered the challenge that any personality variable, of any kind, for which criteria can be established can be measured by a scale such as the Minnesota Multiphasic Personality Inventory. Paul Meehl (1955) has made it clear that the challenge holds for castration anxiety, repressed sadism, unconscious Oedipus wishes, and what have you. I should like to see this challenge accepted. I should like to see an enormous amount of effort given to the delineation, in more or less normal individuals, by intensive clinical studies, of a wide variety of hypothesized unconscious motivational tendencies. Then, if the empirical test-developer wants to use these as criterion measures, I should be quite happy. And I would predict considerable success for him, though one might doubt whether he would do any better than someone who used indices from projective techniques or selected items according to theory.

In any event, personality research would certainly profit if some of our vast resources for developing empirical tests could be devoted to studies in which the criterion measures are unconscious forces rather than the usual external performances. If enough such measures were developed and were taken together with existing and to-be-obtained measures of other dynamic variables, the delineation of the major dynamic structures of personality would become possible. And when these were, in turn, ordered to our inclusive scheme of formal properties, we would have before us the prospect of an eventual empirical analysis of the total personality.

CHAPTER SEVEN

Identification, Introjection, and Personality Development

Concepts of "identification" and of "introjection," and other related concepts, are relied upon in psychoanalytic theory, as they are in this book, to explain how dynamic structures become set up within the personality. The superego, for example, is usually considered to be largely a derivative of identifications or introjections made during the period when the child is caught up in the Oedipus complex. But we confront a major difficulty here: Freud never really worked out satisfactory conceptions of identification and introjection. Other writers—psychologists and social scientists as well as psychoanalysts—have since used the term "identification" in a number of ways. Much clarification will be necessary before these concepts can become maximally useful.

SOME CONCEPTS OF IDENTIFICATION

The following passage from Tolman (1943) shows something of the extent of our problem; it also calls attention to an interesting bit of history. "Identification was apparently first noted and named by Freud. But this conception became unnecessarily complicated and it was too closely

A contribution to the symposium, "The Identification Concept and the Theory of Personality and Psychopathology" (Joseph Adelson, chairman), at the meeting of the American Psychological Association, Cleveland, 1953; published in *Psychological Review*, 62:106–118, 1955.

bound up with his whole psychoanalytical system. I shall not mean here by identification, therefore, Freud's own concept, but merely a certain general neo-Freudian notion which seems now to be widely accepted by most psychologists and sociologists" (p. 141). Tolman then goes on to mention three different, though related, processes covered by his general neo-Freudian notion: (*a*) "the process wherein an individual tries to copy —to take as his pattern or model—some other older (or in some other way looked-up-to or envied) individual"; (*b*) "the adherence of the individual to any group of which he feels himself a part"; and (*c*) "the acceptance by an individual of a cause" (pp. 141–142).

It may be added that the term "identification" is also commonly used to refer to the phenomena of empathy and of vicarious living, of sympathy and altruism, and that it creeps into our vocabulary when we try to describe closeness, or loyalty, or even conformity or submissiveness, as between two people. Furthermore, we know that the objects of identification, as the term is variously used, are not confined to other people, singly or in groups, but may include animals, machines, inanimate objects, parts or features of people; and that identification may be expressed not alone in overt behavior but in conscious experience, in attitude, and in fantasy.

More than this, identification is used not only to describe a broad area of everyday behavior; it frequently refers to a mechanism or process by which the personality is changed. Mowrer (1953) distinguishes between "developmental identification," in which the child *learns* to perform ego functions like his parents, and "defensive identification," in which the child accepts the standards of his parents as a means for pleasing them and as a means for controlling his own impulses. I suggest, later, that both of the processes referred to by Mowrer are developmental and that neither is properly called identification.

In much psychoanalytic literature "introjection" is the word for that process, or those processes, by which the individual takes over and makes his own the psychological attributes of other people, but we find that "identification" is used interchangeably with, or in place of, "introjection," as well as to stand for a different process. More recently, Freudian psychoanalysts, in turning their attention to everyday social behavior, have not hesitated to use the term identification in much the same way that Tolman does—that is, to stand for certain activities of the conscious ego and for certain common patterns of everyday social behavior. Thus, for example, Alexander (1932) speaks of "the introspective knowledge of one's own emotions which one uses through identification in the understanding of others." Balint (1948) coins the term "genital identification" to stand for that kind of mutual understanding that we find in a mature love relationship. And Reider (1944) leans heavily upon the concept of identification in explaining good morale in organizations of the armed services.

I have a theory about what has happened. The manifest phenomena of identification—that is to say, the kinds of social behavior mentioned above—were observed before Freud, and attempts at their description have gone forward independently of psychoanalysis—as well they might. But psychoanalysis has been in the air, and psychologists like Tolman and Mowrer, with systems of their own, have from time to time borrowed psychoanalytic terms to stand for conscious ego processes, or aspects of animal behavior, which resembled what Freud had in mind only in some loosely analogous way. Psychoanalysts, for their part, as they have become increasingly interested in everyday matters and increasingly concerned about Freud's neglect of ego psychology, have tended to apply to these surface phenomena concepts originally designed for what was primitive, infantile, unconscious. Thus the watering down of Freudian concepts, it must be admitted, is to be ascribed mainly to Freudian psychoanalysts. Apparently, out of a need to show that Freud's concepts were adequate for the whole range of human behavior, there has been a tendency to stretch and dilute them, sometimes almost beyond recognition. We are not misled by Tolman and Mowrer, because, though we expect much of them, we do not expect them to be more psychoanalytic than Freud. From psychoanalysts we expect to hear about psychoanalysis and are unprepared to see an everyday social phenomenon treated as if it were an unconscious process. One might suggest that, as academic psychologists and psychoanalysts have glowered at each other through the years, there has occurred a certain amount of "identification with the enemy," so that increased similarity of the two groups may be noted. Unfortunately, however, new patterns acquired in this way tend not to be integrated with the ego; in so far as they persist, it is as "foreign bodies" within the personality.

A term that can be employed in so many different ways and that, as Tolman says, has been accepted by most psychologists and sociologists, could hardly mean anything very precise. It might be proposed, quite seriously, that we give up the term "identification" altogether. When we are describing social behavior and have the impulse to say "identification," we must in any case specify "what kind"; if we go a step further and say just what we mean, it will almost always turn out that other words are available, and that they are in fact more accurate. And when it comes to explaining behavior we might agree with Knight (1940) that the phenomena ordinarily called identification are "always based on a subtle interaction of both introjective *and* projective mechanisms." In other words, why not agree that identification is not an explanatory concept, and that as a descriptive one it is too vague to be useful? A moratorium on identification would not, as one might suspect, leave the clinical psychologist quite inarticulate. Instead it might well sharpen his observations of behavior and challenge some of his theoretical assumptions.

I have tried this experiment of doing without "identification" in organizing material on therapeutic cases. The result was the discovery that in formulating the dynamics of the case and in writing out the developmental history one could do very nicely without this term. For describing the common social relationships to which the term has been applied, such words as love, friendship, closeness, loyalty, alliance, solidarity, empathy, fellow feeling, kinship, understanding, sympathy, participation, vicarious living, submission, and acceptance seemed fairly adequate. In the consideration of deeper determining factors one could lean, rather heavily to be sure, on introjection, on learning, and on terms describing various kinds of constructive ego functioning. But—and this is for me a very significant fact—when it came to dealing with certain aspects of the changing therapeutic relationship the concept of identification seemed indispensable. (Naturally, what is true of psychotherapy would be true of other interpersonal relationships.)

I do not mean my identification with the patients; I mean their identification with me. Let us grant that living vicariously in one's patients, getting emotional excitement from their recountings of all the daring and fantastic and all-too-human things that they do, and that we do not have time for, can be quite satisfying. The therapist does not need to read novels or watch television. And let us insist that the only helpful understanding of a patient rests upon the therapist's ability to put himself emotionally in that patient's place. Both of these processes, I believe we may hope, depend upon broadness of consciousness, grasp of reality, sureness of self-control; they are of a piece with the ability to love and to experience a sense of kinship with one's fellow man.

When a patient may properly be said to identify with the therapist, on the other hand, we deal with a process that is unconscious and unrealistic, with a patient who is unsure of himself and, for the moment at least, unconcerned about other people; in desperation he adopts a piece of poor economy as a means of escape from a critical situation. I believe that it is stretching the term identification too much to apply it both to what happens in the therapist—when he is functioning well—and to what happens in the patient; such usage may easily tend to obscure both processes.

We are, of course, accustomed to the idea that the same behavior, or very similar patterns of behavior, may have quite different sources. No one can deny the merit of Knight's suggestion that with respect to those phenomena loosely called identification we make a sharp distinction between source and surface, then proceed with the business of explanation. But I am suggesting that phenomena have been grouped under the heading of identification which are not similar even in their most manifest aspects, or at the least that this similarity is insignificant as compared with their differences. The patient's identification with the therapist and the therapist's understanding of and vicarious satisfaction through the patient constitute a case in point. Others will be offered later in this chapter.

I am also going to suggest that these two phenomena have quite different determinants. Disagreeing with Knight, I would argue that the therapist's constructive and enjoyable reactions to the patient have little if anything to do with introjection or projection, beyond sometimes being in some general way analogous to them. I am also going to suggest that identification, in the sense in which I shall define it, is not a category of behavior but a "mechanism." As a "mechanism," it can be distinguished from introjection, and from other processes by which features of the environment are taken into the personality.

PRIMITIVE IDENTIFICATION

In *primitive identification,* as I shall term my concept,[1] the individual may be observed to respond to the behavior of other people or objects by initiating in fantasy or in reality the same behavior himself. This is identification of the self with the object; it is different from empathy, fellow feeling, vicarious living, and the like—those phenomena which Knight has properly called identification of the object with the self.

Primitive identification is unconscious, or at least more or less unconscious. This differentiates it from conscious imitation, and from other processes by which we more or less accept other people's ways of doing things because we find that they serve us well. When we observe primitive identification in our patients we interpret it; and they characteristically become aware of it with a measure of embarrassment.

Most important, perhaps, primitive identification tends to be *identical;* that is to say, the subject strives to behave in a way that is *exactly* like that of the object. We may note the identity, or the attempt at identicalness, in *detail;* if not in many details at least in *concrete* aspects of the object's behavior. This is what permits us to place primitive identification in the same class with those forms of behavior that tend to be rigid, all out, total —with those reactions which are switched in when, in a critical situation, the limits of the individual's adaptive capacities are surpassed. Thus we may usually note a measure of desperation in the subject who identifies in this fashion. I say that this feature of primitive identification is most important because it really provides us with the key to its understanding; it is the touchstone of its dynamic nature. Primitive identification is one of those reactions—adaptive in the short run, maladaptive in the long run —to which the individual, any individual, may be driven by circumstances.

Primitive identification as here understood is unrealistic. Although the subject strives to be exactly like the object in some respect or altogether, it is rare that he can be in any real sense. We may note striking similarities, but we may also note an aspect of caricature. Behavior in primitive identification is likely to be mechanical or otherwise incongruous; since the subject is not being himself, the behavior that we observe is likely to appear as foreign to him. And, finally, the behavior is rarely, if ever, an appropriate means to any end that is in the subject's long-term interest.

In primitive identification, the object of identification is *there,* a part

[1] It would be preferable for the term "identification" to be used by itself to stand for what I am here calling "primitive identification," if we held ourselves to this usage and found other words to describe related and identification-like processes. But this, at the present stage of our history, is clearly impossible. A reasonable course for now would be to conceive of a continuum extending from primitive identification as it is described here to the kind of "taking over" from others through learning that involves the full participation of the developed ego.

of the subject's external situation. Usually the subject, in identifying, not only perceives the object at the time but is, or can be, perceived by the object. Frequently, it is important to him that his identical behavior be perceived by the object, or by other people who have some importance in the general situation.

In turning from manifestations of identification in behavior to a consideration of underlying dynamics, let us examine the case of the patient who identifies with the therapist—that is to say, who exhibits one kind of such identification, the one which we understand as resistance. Probably most therapists can confirm the original observation of Abraham (1927). In describing "a form of neurotic resistance" found predominantly in narcissistic patients, Abraham writes, "In place of making a transference, these patients tend to identify themselves with the physician. Instead of coming into close relation to him they put themselves in his place. They adopt his interests and like to occupy themselves with psychoanalysis as a science, instead of allowing it to act upon them as a method of treatment. They tend to exchange parts, just as a child does when it plays at being father." What seems most apparent in such cases is that the subject tries rather desperately to protect his self-esteem. The phenomenon seems quite comparable to those most striking instances of identification in childhood: the little boy who must act just like father in some particular, the little girl who exhibits some of her mother's patterns of behavior in an incongruous, grown-up manner. This is by no means always play; the child is frequently deadly serious, and we receive a strong impression of his insecurity. It is as if he cannot be the child that he is, as if he cannot tolerate the sense of weakness or smallness or danger which he feels goes with that role, but must hurry and be, or act as if he were, something different.

This is not, in my opinion, the same process as that by which a child, in the usual case, slowly adopts some of the standards and ways of his admired and loved parents—adopts them and holds onto them because they serve his long-term needs or purposes. In this latter instance we are not likely to be struck by the identity of his behavior and that of the parent. What he adopts for himself, in contrast to what he merely borrows, he quickly puts his own stamp upon, and this from a very early age, so that when we compare him and his parents the most that can be noted is a general similarity. If I seem to be saying that the child who *really* identifies with his parents tends not to exhibit signs of identification, this is close to being just what I mean; but I must of course find other terms for the "real" identification, the integration of parental standards and modes of behavior in a stable ego system.

It would appear, then, that one dynamic source of primitive identification is a threat to self-esteem, a strain that is severe enough so that realistic methods for coping with it do not suffice.

Threats to the subject's physical existence or to the physical integrity of the organism may also lead to primitive identification. Apparently the aim of identification in such instances is to acquire a sense of power and hence to feel equal to the threat. (A two-year-old boy of my acquaintance was terrified by a new puppy that was brought into the house, but after a few hours the boy was crawling about making barking noises and threatening to bite people. His fear of the puppy had vanished.) Sometimes, in situations of dire threat, the individual seeks to protect himself not so much by copying the aggressor as by going over to his side, by joining forces with him. This may be a conscious stratagem more or less deliberately or cynically chosen; but sometimes the whole proceeding is largely unconscious, the subject deceiving himself in judging his own interests as well as the motivations and moral justification of his enemy or authority.

In cases of extreme domination, where the existence of the subject as an independent, choosing, decision-making individual is threatened, it seems that he has the alternatives of either taking over the ways of his guard or parent or of having no personality at all. There may be no possible alternative but to submit, but in submitting one may still maintain some sense of self through participating in the personality of the oppressor. Members of ethnic minorities seem often to exhibit this kind of identification with the dominant group. A patient in extended therapy may show a similar reaction at a certain stage of the therapeutic relationship—for example, when dependence on the therapist is intensified by real difficulties and by the necessity of making numerous readjustments.

Primitive identification would appear to be, then, a desperate attempt to deal with a crisis involving the self. We have seen that such a crisis is commonly precipitated by the aggressive or dominant actions of another person or object in the subject's immediate environment, from which no means of escape can be found. At the same time, it is important to note that the crisis may arise out of events that are chiefly internal, in which case the object of identification is likely to be chosen by the subject. An arousal of impulses belonging to a negative identity—for example, feminine impulses in a male—may lead to hasty attempts at identifications having an opposite direction and meaning. Generalized social insecurity, crises in identity like those so frequently endured by new students at boarding school or college, often lead to primitive identification with some of the common ways of a peer group.

It has been stated that when crises of selfhood have sources that are chiefly internal, the object of identification will be chosen by the subject. Now it must be added that some objects are much more likely to be chosen than others, that there are, indeed, "identification evokers"—heroic or sensational figures that seem able to elicit identification in almost anyone. The stronger the stimulus, the less intense the inner crisis needs to be in order for identification to occur. In most people there is probably enough uncertainty of identity or dissatisfaction with the self so that they may be induced to take an ill-advised short cut to improvement. More than this, most clear-cut instances of identification with the dramatic figure are mass phenomena, or at least phenomena involving two or more identifiers. Once identification is made by one or two or three individuals in a group, presumably those in the severest straits with respect to self-esteem, the situation changes; now it becomes difficult to tell whether copying the dramatic figure is induced primarily by *him* or by social pressure. In either case, we have to deal with a regressive attempt either to enhance the self or to protect its existing status.

The present rather critical view of concepts of identification seems a necessary part of an attempt to get the term back into its place, so to speak, partly by reviving some of its traditional meanings. Freud consistently spoke of identification as primitive or regressive. It is only in comparatively recent years, since the onset of the tendency among psychologists and psychoanalysts to "accentuate the positive," that the concept has been given an important place in sound character development, successful psychotherapy, harmonious individual-group relations, and the like. But, since the phenomenon of primitive identification cannot be overlooked, it has become common practice among textbook writers to speak of "good" identifications and "bad" identifications, or of too much or too little. Symonds (1949), for example, lists the "positive" and the "negative" values of identification. Some of the positive values listed—for example, that identification gives a person ambitions and ideals or supplies a basis for sympathy—should, according to the present view, be attributed to processes other than primitive identification. The others—for example, that it may help the individual gain security or strength—should be regarded as "good" only in the sense that they help stave off something worse or represent the best that is possible in the circumstances; as adjustments or adaptations made in an emergency, they serve to hold the fort, as it were, until preparations can be made for a genuine developmental advance.

Identification is undesirable in Symonds' view when it is exaggerated or fantastic or without discrimination. This has been called by other writers *over*identification. But when we are offered an example of the proper amount of identification, it usually turns out to be, not a lesser degree of the same process, but a different process altogether—most commonly, perhaps, the learning of something true or useful from somebody else. The argument here is that we may reduce confusion by using "primitive identification" to stand only for the ultimate maladaptive crisis reaction.

The discussion so far has been concerned solely with behavior in a momentary situation. I have sought to view the phenomenon of primitive identification in field-theoretical terms, the hope being that this may be an aid to experimental attacks on the problem before us. It is commonly assumed, however, that identifications once made tend to persist, that the type of crisis reaction considered here results in lasting changes in the personality. It is a widely accepted theory that "defensive identification," or identification with the feared and frustrating parent of the same sex, is an important source of the superego. The remainder of this chapter will argue, first, that the lasting effects of primitive identification are frequently overestimated; second, that the process by which figures of the environment become models for response readiness in the deeper layers of the personality, as in superego formation, is not identification but introjection; and finally, that there are other processes besides these two by which environmental influences enter into the molding of character.

THE TRANSITORY NATURE OF IDENTIFICATION

If, to take up the first argument, primitive identification is a function of a total situation and is to be understood in field-theoretical terms, then we should expect the identification behavior to change as soon as the situation changes. It seems to me that in the usual case this is just what happens. Identification is evoked by a crisis; when the crisis passes or is mastered, we are able to observe no persisting effects.

It should be borne in mind here that, in the case of the resistant patient, identification with the therapist is a means of keeping him out, of not being influenced by him. I think Abraham is right in likening this behavior to a child's defiance of his parents. In identification with the aggressor the subject does not bring about a basic change in his relations with the threatening figure by his acts of identification, as would be the case should the aggressive pattern become integrated with the ego system; the aggressor remains outside, to be dealt with by repetitions of the same stratagem. The subject who "borrows another personality" in order to achieve a desperately needed identity does not solve his problem in this way; he is defeated either by reality or by psychosis. The adolescent who switches rapidly from one idealized object of identification to another does not finally hit upon one that suits him; he learns finally that he can only be himself. Much consistent behavior that appears to be an expression of an identification with some figure of the past can best be explained, it seems to me, on the basis that a device which proved successful on one occasion is likely to be repeated in an equivalent one. In the authoritarian personality[2] the inclination to identify with figures of authority is, of course, marked, and this is readily traced back to early patterns of identification with parents. But the striking thing is that the authority has not been genuinely internalized, as we know from the fact that it does not operate effectively unless a representative of it is present or close by. We may speak here, as we did in Chapter 5, of an immature or rudimentary superego, and we are not surprised to find that identification with authority figures is the more marked the fewer visible signs there are of a genuinely internalized superego. But actual figures of authority are usually present in reality, and the subject may be observed consistently to rely upon the means he has learned for dealing with them.

To make the best case for the incorporation into the ego system of figures of primitive identification, we should, perhaps, consider those instances in which the conditions of such identification continue for extended

[2] The authoritarian personality is discussed in more detail in Chapter 10. For more complete treatment of the subject, the reader is referred to T. Adorno, E. Frenkel-Brunswik, D. Levinson, and N. Sanford, *The Authoritarian Personality* (New York: Harper, 1950).

periods of time. The concentration camp offers a good example. Bettelheim (1943) observed among prisoners some striking instances of identification with the guards, usually after a man had been an inmate for a long time. Bettelheim, very properly it seems, referred to these phenomena as changes in the personality. The question would be, were these changes maintained after the prisoners were released? I do not know of any studies in which men observed in concentration camps were followed up after release. It seems reasonable to suppose that, just as there were wide individual differences in the tendency to identify with the guards, there would be individual differences in the tendency to persist in the identification after release. Among the factors favoring persistence, first importance might well attach to the presence in the personality of structures deriving from earlier introjection—structures to which the new object became assimilated. But if this were indeed the case, we would no longer be dealing with identification, but with introjection.

Probably one of the main sources of the widely held contemporary view that identification with the feared authority is an important source of the superego is Anna Freud's writing on "identification with the aggressor" (1946). Here it is stated that this kind of identification contributes to superego development, that it represents a stage in the development of the superego. Yet her essay may actually be used to support the present view. For one thing, in those episodes which most clearly exemplify identification with the aggressor or dangerous object—that is, episodes in which the child's identification with the external object is not complicated by the subject's own instinctual needs—Anna Freud says, "it's not clear what became of the threat with which they identified themselves" (p. 122). She makes quite a leap from these episodes from child-analytic practice to the proposition that repetitions of the aggression or danger finally result in the setting up of the threatening agency "inside" the personality. She offers no evidence in favor of this proposition. She does, however, make quite vivid the view that the child "does not wholeheartedly accept this institution," and whereas there seems to be the assumption that later it will, she notes "it is possible that a number of people remain at this stage." In view of our present knowledge of the authoritarian personality, it might be said that a great many people remain at this stage of development; indeed one might question the view that this state of affairs is a stage at all, in the sense that it has a place in a progression toward the full acceptance by the individual of the critical agency. If individuals in whom "identification with the aggressor" is pronounced go on to develop a mature conscience, this is very probably due to the intervention of quite different determinants and not to an extension of this mechanism. In other words, this development would seem to occur in spite of the identification with the aggressor rather than because of it.

Fromm (1947) has seized upon such accounts of superego formation as that given by Anna Freud in her chapter on identification with the aggressor to make his point that the Freudian superego is an authoritarian one. If this account were all we had to go on, Fromm's point would, I think, have to be admitted. In Freud's own writings on superego formation ("On Narcissism," 1934; 1946), however, various other processes are given place; most central, it seems, is the introjection of parental figures as compensation for their loss as love objects. I would suggest that in the contemporary authoritarian personality there is less of the former punitive parent "inside" the personality than either Fromm or Anna Freud seems to imply. But this does not mean that such a personality is empty. There is actually a primitive superego deriving from earlier introjection; it is frequently to escape the onslaughts of this agency that authoritarian personalities seek to align themselves, through primitive identification, with powerful external authorities.

There remains, however, the possibility that an identification initiated in one of our critical situations might become established in time as a means for controlling impulse. It does appear to be true that in authoritarian personalities the most extreme identification with authorities is accompanied by the most intense underlying hostility toward them. It is reasonable to ask whether one of the main functions of the former is not to inhibit or counteract the latter, and whether a device which thus becomes tied to an impulse does not thus gain the status of a fixture in the personality. Indeed, it may be asked whether such a fixture, originally designed to inhibit one impulse, might not be employed to inhibit others as well; in short, whether it does not become, in this way, a part of the superego. I do not wish to exclude such a possibility. But let it be noted that the conditions for this outcome are rather complex; they have to do both with the status of the personality before the crisis that evokes identification, and with processes that operate after its occurrence. As previously suggested, the new figure of identification may be assimilated by earlier introjections. In any case, the new figure is at least a datum of the individual's experience, something to be taken into account in the building of an ego system. But the emphasis here is upon this work of building rather than upon the initiation in a crisis of the unconscious copying reaction.

In sum, primitive identification does not appear to be a very fruitful source of internalized structures in personality. To account for the superego and other internal agencies, we shall have to rely mainly upon introjection and other processes.

THE DYNAMICS OF INTROJECTION

We should not take the too easy course of saying "introjection" whenever it appears that some feature of the environment has somehow found its way into the personality. It is unfortunate that Freud tended to do just this. He seems not to have cared much for Ferenczi's term "introjection"; he did not use it in any strict technical sense but only in a general descriptive way, as when he wrote, "the external restrictions are introjected, so that the superego takes the place of the parental function" (1946, p. 85). This kind of usage naturally has led psychologists to doubt that we need such a fancy word for a process that seems readily described in more familiar, generally accepted terms. R. W. White, in his influential *The Abnormal Personality* (1944), writes, "The concept of *introjection* has been considerably elaborated in psychoanalytic writings. The introjection of parental restrictions, however, is basically a learning process and may even be likened to simple conditioning. The child acts on some impulse, the behavior is punished (or punishment threatened), and this linkage with punishment causes the action to be internally inhibited thereafter" (p. 169). White goes on to explain in similar terms how positive ideals may be inculcated. I think his is an accurate formulation of a very common phenomenon—a matter to which we shall return in a moment—but this phenomenon is not introjection; that is to say, it is not what we shall have to call introjection proper.

For a useful conception of introjection we should go back to the original formulation of Abraham (1927) and to its vigorous following up by his student, Melanie Klein (1948). Here we find the conception of a psychological taking-in that is modeled after oral incorporation. When the object of love or imperious desire is withdrawn or lost, or when its withdrawal or loss seems imminent, the subject may set it up imaginatively inside his personality, where he may, so to speak, have it for good. In infancy, when the boundaries between inside and outside are not yet clearly drawn and when the danger of losing objects upon which there is total dependence is subjectively acute, introjection is probably very common, if not universal. And since the love objects of infancy and early childhood are major sources of frustration, they tend to be hated as well as loved; that is to say, they tend to be loved ambivalently. It seems that frequently the infant, in striving to cope with his aggressive impulses, projects them onto the objects which are central in his scheme of things. Thus the psychological meaning of the introjected objects may depend in considerable part upon what has previously been projected onto them. Although introjection is most characteristically a phenomenon of infancy, it may, its conditions being sufficient, occur at any time of life; in these instances the introjections are referred to, and assimilated by, earlier introjects of the same general significance. In my own experience—and I expect this is common—I have never encountered a case in which introjection loomed large, either as a matter of historical fact or as a phenomenon to be dealt with in the transference, that did not present at the same time a picture of intense oral strivings and oral character traits.

Introjection as here conceived was usually called identification by Freud. The following passage is typical. "If one has lost a love object or has had to give it up, one often compensates oneself by identifying oneself with it; one sets it up again inside one's ego, so that in this case object-choice regresses, as it were, to identification" (1946, p. 86). It is important to note that this is the conception that Freud relies upon in explaining how the superego becomes the heir of the Oedipus complex—that is, identification with parents compensates for their loss as objects. It is true that Freud, most characteristically, I think, referred to these phenomena as *narcissistic*—in contradistinction to *hysterical*—identification. The distinction which he drew in this connection is most important in differentiating between introjection and primitive identification. "The difference, however, between narcissistic and hysterical identification may be perceived in the object-cathexis,[3] which in the first is relinquished, whereas in the latter it persists and exercises an influence, usually confined to certain isolated actions and innervations" ("On Narcissism," 1934, p. 160). This is the basis for the present view that in introjection the object "disappears inside," as it were, there being no longer any relation with an external object but only with aspects of oneself (Freud's narcissistic identification), whereas in primitive identification a continuing relationship with the external object is a distinctive feature (Freud's hysterical identification). Perhaps it should be added that primitive identification is intended to be a broader concept than hysterical identification.

Introjection, like identification, is an unconscious mechanism resorted to in a crisis. But the crisis is at once more severe than, and qualitatively different from, that in which primitive identification is evoked. The danger is perceived to be more extreme, and the capacities for dealing with it are felt to be, as they actually are, far less adequate. For these reasons introjection occurs, most characteristically, in an earlier stage of development than does identification. In order for identification to take place there must exist, at least in rudimentary form, a conception of the self; this is not true of introjection. An essential condition for introjection is lack of clarity regarding the boundaries of the ego. If we ask how one again sets up a lost love object inside one's ego, to refer once more to the preceding quotation from Freud, we obtain our answer by considering that the child at this stage of his development is not clear about what is inside and what is outside. When something that is really inside him is responded to as if it were outside, we speak of *projection*. If something that is outside or was formerly outside is responded to as if it were inside, we speak of *introjection*.

The distinctive feature of the crisis in introjection is frustration in love; there is a loss or deprivation of love, or a real or imagined threat of such a loss. The object that is introjected is always one that has been loved an.bivalently. In the oral and anal stages of development all object relations have this aspect of ambivalence, and it is probably true that all introjections either occur during these stages or have antecedents there.

Of course, the kind of thing I have been trying to describe as introjection does not, so to speak, happen every day. We are talking about a mechanism that comes to the fore particularly in psychosis and in severe

---

[3] *Object cathexis* may be thought of as that state of affairs in which an object (person or some part of a person, for example, the breast) becomes valued positively or negatively because of its relationship to the gratification of the individual's basic erotic strivings.

psychosomatic disturbances. I favor making pretty categorical distinctions between this mechanism on the one hand and primitive identification and normal character development on the other. But I do not favor any such categorical distinction between psychotic and normal people. Better to say that all of us, having been infants, having had oral and anal experiences that were in varying degrees shocking, have varying amounts of psychotic potential, and that it can still be rewarding to study the conditions under which this potential breaks into action.

Abraham made it clear that he considered a superego based on introjection as a "pathologically formed one." Freud, as previously indicated, in describing the superego in the *New Introductory Lectures* (1946), gives the most central role to the self-same processes that Abraham makes so vivid in his study of the manic-depressive psychoses. And for his most vivid description of the superego at work, Freud goes back to the example of melancholia. Some reconciliation of Freud and Abraham may be achieved by recalling that for Freud the superego was, chiefly, one of those lesser evils that loomed so large in his scheme of things; primitive, blind, automatic, unconscious, it was to be got rid of as soon as possible. This is not far from regarding it as something pathological, pathological at least in the sense of being maladaptive, undesirable, not healthy in any normative sense. The superego for Freud was not the same as conscience—at least not usually; it was not the expression of our "higher natures." And Freud does not make the mistake of supposing that the processes by which the mature character is formed are the same as those which operate in superego formation.

OTHER PROCESSES IN CHARACTER DEVELOPMENT

It may seem that we have so restricted identification and introjection that we shall now be hard put to it to explain how so much of the culture, of the parental standards and prohibitions, *does* get firmly established in the personality. I think we need not worry. The processes described by White, previously quoted, cover after all an enormous amount of territory; for many psychologists they are sufficient to account for the whole of character development. Psychoanalysts interested in "developing an ego psychology" should realize that such a psychology has existed for quite a while. The bulk of psychological writing in the field of personality development may properly be put under this heading. Consider, for example, the account by McDougall (1908) of the development of the self-regarding sentiment, an account of conscience that has still to be surpassed, or that by Murphy (1947) of the development of the self, or the description by Newcomb (1950) of learning to take social roles. These writers are describing actual processes that are central to the normal psychology of character development. The fact that they do not accent unconscious processes, or distinctions between conscious and unconscious, that their views were little influenced by psychoanalytic theory, does not for a moment invalidate what they have to say about the particular ego processes upon which they focus. I am not suggesting that our knowledge of normal character development, of constructive interpersonal relations, and the like, is complete, but only that we can restrict primitive identification and introjection in the way that I have indicated without handicapping ourselves in the continuing search.

Now it is possible to see why I suggested that Mowrer's "defensive identification" was actually developmental and not an instance of identification. Accepting parental standards as a means for pleasing the parents and as a means for controlling impulse does not require the operation of any peculiarly psychoanalytic mechanism. The acceptance is by and into the ego system; the whole process may be largely conscious. Standards accepted in this way may contribute heavily to the more or less mature conscience.

I propose, in conclusion, that we do two things: first, that we give more attention to those superego elements that have been based upon introjection; second, that we consider that normal character development can be largely explained, without benefit of either primitive identification or introjection, on the basis of common forms of learning. A child learns which of his actions please and which displease his parents, which win him love and which disapproval; he learns what reactions are effective in inhibiting those impulses which if allowed free rein would lead to catastrophe; he learns how to regard himself in the way others regard him; and in building his ego system and his self-conception he learns what to keep and what to discard.

This conclusion presents me with an intriguing idea. Perhaps there are some psychologists who have not yet given allegiance to (I started to say "become identified with") any of the Freudian, anti-Freudian, or neo-Freudian movements, who still have need to come to terms with Freud and who would rather "be like him" than "have him." Up to now, there have been two major movements: the various neo-Freudians, who believed that Freud went too deep, and the Kleinians, who were equally convinced that he did not go deep enough. One possibility remains, that of going deeper and less deep at the same time. The argument of the new movement would be that Freud was not extreme enough: he stuck too close to the middle of the road. It would not be necessary to say which side of the road one would prefer. If we can make clear and significant distinctions, and learn when to apply which explanatory concept, there is no reason why we cannot continue to make progress in ego psychology even while we continue the exploration of the unconscious.

Part Four

In this section the general approach to inquiry and action set forth in Parts Two and Three is applied to some particular human problems: criminality, neurosis, "the acting out" of impulses, failures in the achievement of sex-role identity, conformity, and lack of creativity. Much use is made of the theoretical ideas presented in Part Three, but at the same time these ideas are expanded and elaborated. The effort is made to show that the study of these problems, with a view to bringing about developmental changes in individuals, is favorable to the generation of theory, and that empirical knowledge may be gained through the use of methods that are suited to the holistic and comprehensive approach such problems require.

Each of the terms just used, in naming the problems, refers to a pattern or patterns of social behavior, and we hypothesize that behind each pattern there is a characteristic dynamic structure of personality. The relationship between the behavior pattern and the personality structure is not, however, one to one. Factors in the social environment of the present interact with conscious and unconscious processes of the personality built up in the past in determining each pattern of behavior. The understanding of these patterns will require close attention to theoretical formulations that have not so far been fully developed—chiefly, the distinction between personality and behavior, the interactions of processes on different levels of the personality, the determinants of fixity and of change in personality, and the interaction of psychodynamic and social factors at each stage of the individual's development.

The order of events in the section has been determined mainly by the consideration that concepts set forth in earlier chapters are utilized in later ones. The discussions of criminality and neurosis are closely tied to the "structural theory" and the theory of unconscious processes offered in Part Three. (The typology of criminals presented in Chapter 8 rests heavily upon the dimensions of the superego as identified in Chapter 5, while the consideration of neurosis in Chapter 9 lays stress upon processes that were made unconscious in childhood.) These matters are fundamental to our understanding of authoritarianism (Chapter 10), while authoritarianism enters prominently into the discussion of "acting out" (Chapter 11), masculinity-femininity (Chapter 12), and creativity and conformity (Chapter 13). The order has been further influenced by the fact that in the earlier chapters of the section we deal with relatively close connections between behavior and underlying personality structure, while in the later ones these connections are relatively loose—and highly complex.

In the over-all organization of the book the present section occupies middle ground between a concern with the inside structuring of personality (Part Three) and the more explicitly social concern of the chapters that follow. Although the emphasis here is upon the personality structures that underlie problematic behavior patterns, these structures are seen to have been largely determined by the social environment of the past. In each problem we deal with an arrest of development, usually one occurring during early periods of the individual's life. We have to be concerned, therefore, both with building the kind of environment for children that will prevent these arrests from occurring and with overcoming the arrests that already exist, so that the affected individual will be freed for further development. In each problem we deal at the same time with behavior that is only partly determined by personality; this means that in each case it is possible to modify behavior by changing the social environment while leaving the personality structures more or less intact. Finally, the studies presented in this section offer considerable support for the point that personality structures are sustained by the social environment of the present and may change as that environment changes. This point becomes a major theme in Part Five.

CHAPTER EIGHT

Personality Factors in Criminality

It is generally agreed today that some of the major determinants of delinquent behavior lie in the social environment, in factors such as poverty, lack of education, broken homes, and demoralized neighborhoods. Any hope that criminals might somehow turn out to be different by nature from the rest of us—and that we might thus be relieved of the responsibility for changing the environmental conditions which promote delinquency—has been repeatedly disappointed. For a time studies sought to demonstrate anatomical or physical differences between criminals and noncriminals, but they have proved unconvincing. Meanwhile evidence of association between environmental factors and delinquent behavior continues to accumulate.

Although knowledge of these social correlates does enable us fairly accurately to predict delinquency in populations, something more is needed if we hope either to correct or to prevent delinquent behavior. It is true that, theoretically, we could expect delinquency rates to drop in response to a broad-scale attack on, say, poverty. In practice, however, we are too rarely able to manipulate these vast forces in an effective way. Even where broad social interventions are attempted, they still must be based soundly on a psychological understanding of the individuals involved. The problem of juvenile delinquency offers an example of the variety of factors

Based on the author's article, "A Psychoanalytic Study of Three Types of Criminals," *Journal of Criminal Psychopathology*, 5:57–68, 1943.

which must be considered. Certainly it shows positive correlations with the environmental factors just discussed. However, delinquent behavior among young people is also expressive of their particular stage of development as individuals. During the teen years they tend to move in gangs and form cultures of their own. To intervene in this situation would require a good understanding both of group processes in adolescent gangs and of dynamic processes within the individual members.

If some understanding of personality theory is useful in controlling criminal behavior in populations, it is indispensable in dealing with the individual offender. Of course, many offenders are psychologically normal —that is, their offense was an accidental or uncharacteristic response to the unique circumstances of the moment. However, in the majority of criminal cases, persistent personality patterns loom large. Recognition of these patterns is fundamental to understanding the offender's career and to planning his management and rehabilitation.

When we examine the adult offender, as we might in a prison setting, it is not difficult to discern in each case characteristic and durable personality structures which have been built up over time and which, over time, have helped to determine criminal behavior. Further, anyone who works with criminals inevitably becomes aware of the recurrence of certain personality types. Some years ago I had the opportunity to become acquainted with numerous penal inmates.[1] When I discovered that without conscious plan I had begun to classify these men into types, I was led into an attempt to make explicit the basis of division, to set down the distinguishing characteristics of each type, and to bring the scheme into relation with existing classifications. Three of the types then distinguished had not been previously described in the literature. It may be useful to review these types here, first, because they have obvious practical value for understanding and managing offenders, and, second, because they serve to illustrate some of the personality processes with which we have been concerned in the preceding section—especially concepts of the different dimensions of the superego.

Criminality, in the psychological sense, is a set of attitudes toward conscience and society. It is something that exists within the individuals, though it commonly leads to offenses against the legal code, it is not restricted to this form of expression. And violations of the law of the land may occur in the absence of criminality (accidental offenses). For the purposes of this discussion the essence of criminality is assumed to lie in the relationship between the personal desires or wishes of the individual on the one hand and the socially derived circumscriptions imposed upon the expression of those desires on the other. In every true criminal, a relationship of this kind endures as an essential feature of the character structure.

By taking into account variations in the quality and the intensity of

[1] These inmates were observed between 1932 and 1935 at the Norfolk Prison Colony, Norfolk, Massachusetts, which was under the progressive administration of Howard Gill. Dr. O. L. Harvey provided helpful suggestions for the development of this typology.

the personal desires and of the social ideals, and by considering the relations between the two, one may distinguish on a common basis four types of criminals:

1. *The presocial.* Those immature and suggestible individuals who vacillate in being subservient either to the ideals of the major society or to the ideals of a minor dissentient group.
2. *The antisocial.* Those who characteristically act according to the ideals of a minor dissentient group.
3. *The asocial.* Those in whom loyalty to social ideals is at a minimum.
4. *The impulsive-addicted.* Those who share the ideal of the major society but periodically give way to uncontrollable impulses.

Criminals of the fourth type will merely be touched upon here. They resemble very closely the "neurotic criminals" distinguished and studied intensively by Alexander and Staub (1931). These writers limit their class of neurotic criminals to those whose criminal behavior has a special symbolic significance—for example, kleptomania, pyromania, and criminality out of a sense of guilt. However, in one sense of the word all four of the present types have neurotic elements. In each case, the criminal tendencies are ingrained in the individual; rather than being appropriate reactions to abnormal situations, they are reactions characteristic of a personality organization that has its origins in early childhood.

Criminals of the present four types may be regarded as *true criminals*, since in all of them we find deficiency or distortion in the social conditioning. They are to be distinguished from the *accidental offenders*, who have adopted the ideals of the major society and are ordinarily law-abiding, but who behave criminally under unusual environmental stress or when toxic conditions or organic mental disease destroy the means by which instinctual impulses are inhibited. Since the present concern is with criminality rather than with crime, accidental offenders may be excluded from the discussion.

THE PRESOCIAL CRIMINAL

We may turn to a consideration of our first type, the *presocial*. This criminal, who vacillates in subordinating his impulses either to the ideals of the larger society or to those of a minor dissentient group, is often described as a weak character. Observers who are impressed by his mild manner and compliant attitude think of him as not really bad, but easily led. Policemen and parole officers write in their reports, not without a certain scornfulness, that he is a sneak thief, a nonvicious offender, a "heeler." Indeed, this individual does seem to lack inner structure, and to take over his ideals from the group of which he is a member at the moment.

In prison, whence he is usually committed for petty thievery either alone or as a minor member of a group, this man is to be recognized by his submissive, deferential, and ingratiating manner, which he exhibits in his relations both with the prison officials and with his fellow inmates. He is adept at currying the favor of the authorities. This he does by verbally repenting his crimes, praising the institution—even informing on his comrades. Common examples, as seen in prison, would be the middle-aged, melancholy Italian or Portuguese who silently accepts every imposition; the cheerfully irresponsible Negro who greets every command or suggestion with a "Yas suh, boss"; the plaintive Irish lad who hopes you will not think ill of him. These men adapt themselves well to prison routine, make tractable inmates, and actually seem to enjoy the ordered regime and freedom from responsibility. Indeed, the behavior of this type of inmate is frequently so conforming, his attitude so cooperative, that he is rewarded with the most desirable jobs and given special privileges. Thus he earns from his fellow inmates the name of Administration Johnny. That he is able to persist in his attitude of cooperation, despite the scorn of the other inmates, is evidence that he is at the moment sincere in his desire to reform. Indeed he often feels that he *has* reformed and is contented while in prison to feel that he has been reinstated as a member of society. For his good behavior in prison he is a likely candidate for parole—that is, if he is a young offender without a long record; but since he lacks the stamina for resisting temptation once he is beyond the surveillance of society's representatives, he is also a likely candidate for recommitment, and this often to the disappointment and chagrin of case workers who believed that the reformation so easily achieved would be permanent.

We may say of offenders of this type that the superego is infantile. The ego also is relatively weak and gives in easily to the relatively strong tendencies from the id. It is as if the process of socialization started in the right direction but was not carried far enough. The individual feels guilty for his crimes once he has been caught, and he is able to inhibit his antisocial impulse so long as a superego prototype is physically present, but when he is left to his own devices or in the company of antisocial companions, the ego is likely to find ways and means for siding with the id.

Some evidence that a rudimentary superego is present derives from the fact that the individual appears to make some effort to come to terms with it. When in the company of society's representatives he is usually quite concerned to justify his offense, and he is adept at rationalization. He points out with feeling that he is not half so bad as the sex offender, the armed robber, or the embezzler whose peculations ran into six figures. Or he may admit his guilt and say that his just punishment will insure his not repeating his crime. Study of the circumstances surrounding his criminal act not infrequently reveals that it followed what was or what the offender interpreted to be an unjust punishment or a loss of love. Convincing himself that his superego had betrayed him or that he could gain nothing by adherence to its demands, he felt entitled to instinctual gratification. These mechanisms, to be sure, are to be found in the normal person, who is rarely free from struggle with his conscience, but they seem to be especially marked in this type of criminal.

There seem to be two types of family pattern which chiefly promote this type of personality organization. First, there is the situation in which the father is weak or inconsequential—perhaps an alcoholic ne'er-do-well—and the mother, typically a harassed, irritable, and dominant woman, takes over all disciplinary matters. The result, apparently, is failure to accept the father's values, and hence arrested superego development. Frequently, it seems, this man does not develop emotionally beyond the stage of a little boy—either a good little boy or a bad little boy, depending upon his status and expectation with respect to the mother's love. Though his sexuality is essentially pregenital, he is frequently married when he reaches the state prison. His relations with his wife are blatantly childish—that is, dependent and ambivalent—and the offense itself is often in part a response to a family quarrel: the offender provoked his wife to nag or neglect him and so provide him with an excuse for his criminal behavior.

The second type of situation in which this personality develops is that in which the father is a strong and aggressive man while the mother is a timid, weak, and frustrated woman who dotes on her son. Here it seems that the fear of the father is so great, and masculine aggressiveness is so effectively disapproved by the mother, that the subject does not incorporate in his own personality the father's values and modes of behavior. Instead, oral-dependent and passive, feminine wishes become directed to the father and father-figures, so that in later life the individual is not only submissive in his relations with aggressive men but actually feels most comfortable when at the beck and call of authoritative figures.

The criminal of the group seems to belong to the erotic libidinal type described by Freud (1932). It is the need to be loved that drives him to fall in with the ideals of the group or the individual that might at the moment offer him support. Thus he is indeed "easily led," for, having no internalized authority whose love he can count upon, he is ready to cast his lot with whoever promises him something. Some of his crimes follow from the fact that he will do anything—the law is no obstacle—to get love; other crimes seem to follow some episodic loss of love and to be either acts of revenge upon the person who denied him, or gratifications of id impulses such as become possible when the individual feels that nothing is to be gained from adherence to the superego. The explanation resorted to by this type of man when his crime followed his feeling of being rejected by an individual or by a community is a standard prison saying: "I had the name; I thought I might as well have the game."

We cannot, of course, equate our presocial type with Freud's erotic type, since some of the impulsive-addicted criminals also seem to belong to this libidinal type. The kleptomaniac, as we know, is often an oral-dependent individual whose crime symbolizes stealing love which he could not get in any other way.

If we were to follow the scheme of Alexander and Staub (1931), we should have to classify these presocial offenders either as neurotic criminals or as accidental criminals. Since, however, the criminal act is not a symbolic one but is rather the direct gratification of an id impulse when the individual's relationships with other people and with his own superego change, we are hardly justified in calling it neurotic in the limited sense of the word. There is perhaps more similarity to the normal individual who characteristically yields to temptation under conditions which render the superego ineffective. However, we are confronted here not merely with occasional lapses into criminality but with a condition of chronic superego infantilism; the criminal actions are far too persistent for us to call them accidental.

A psychoanalysis, probably, would be impossible in those cases where the father was inconsequential; it would be a possible but long and difficult process in those cases where the father was too aggressive and fear prevented the individual from taking over his ways. The only really practical treatment for these offenders is constant surveillance. It is a costly mistake to suppose that the correction of a few major shortcomings of the man's environment will put him permanently on his feet. He will always need a relatively simple life situation, including either membership in a supporting social group or the guardianship of a gentle but firm individual.

THE ANTISOCIAL CRIMINAL

The antisocial criminal, to go on to the next type, has firmly established ideals, but they are the ideals of a dissentient group. Though he expresses himself as against society, he nonetheless acts strictly in accordance with a set of standards. He does not as a rule experience guilt as a result of his crime, but only self-condemnation at allowing himself to be caught. For the deputy or the prison guard this man is a "typical con" or a "tough egg." Indeed his offense typically is armed robbery in the company of one or more companions, and he is not apprehended without a struggle. For his fellow inmates, however, he is a "right guy" who can be counted upon to support fearlessly the code of his group and to oppose the prison authorities at every possible opportunity.

This is the sort of man who gave rise to the conception that there is honor among thieves. Indeed much of the romantic writing about this type of offender—the modern Robin Hood—seems very close to the truth. He is physically courageous, loyal to his fellows, willing to defend the weak against the strong. To a degree rarely matched nowadays by men who adhere to the standards of our major society, he is willing to make sacrifices and to take punishment in defense of his ideals. His spirit is not to be broken by solitary confinement, nor will he compromise himself by accepting any of the privileges which the prison authorities may offer him. Because this man's typical offense is by the usual standard a very serious one—that is, armed robbery—he is likely to arrive at the state prison with, next to the murderer, the longest sentence, and because he is most antagonistic to police authority and has the most courage of his convictions, he is most frequently the object of prison discipline and stands the least chance of being paroled. This is unfortunate, for of all the types of criminals this one is least to be deterred by punishment or the threat of it. The kind of punishment that he usually receives only confirms his convictions that the society with which he is asked to conform is unworthy, and furthermore, for reasons that we shall see, he is the only type of true criminal who ever undergoes a real reformation by means other than psychotherapy.

This type corresponds very closely to the normal criminal of Alexander and Staub. For these writers, the normal criminal is psychologically sound and well organized and is to be distinguished from other normal people only by the fact that the superego is criminal. Though it is likely that such individuals exist—individuals well brought up in a group whose ideals conflict with those of the major society—it is doubtful that Alexander's and Staub's conception will hold for the great majority of our antisocial offenders. It seems, in these cases, that it is not the superego but rather the ego ideal[2] that is criminal. We could of course conceive of the superego as the source of all moral strength in the individual and say that this strength is used to support the criminal ideals. But study of these offenders seems to show that quite apart from the criminal ideals there is a superego content that exists as a foreign body within the personality and which must be dealt with. There is not so much criminality with a conscience as criminality in defiance of conscience. The evidence that a noncriminal superego does exist and exert a profound influence upon the individual's behavior is chiefly from two sources. First, though, as we have said, the antisocial offender does not feel guilty for his crime, he nonetheless seems to be at pains to act in such a way as to assure that he will not feel guilty. He must justify his conduct by exaggerating the evils of the major society; he will spend hours in heated debate to show that "it's the system" that is wrong. Furthermore, he seeks the company of men of similar ideals—ego-ideal prototypes—in order to maintain his conviction; and his career is frequently a succession of increasingly serious offenses, each succeeding one partially determined by a need to be convinced that earlier offenses were right and just.

The second and even more important indication of a noncriminal superego is the evidence of an unconscious need for punishment. Much of the courage and capacity for punishment that these men show would be impossible without a good measure of moral masochism. This type of inmate says with defiance when confronted with prison discipline, "Go

[2] *Ego ideal;* A part of the ego closely related to, but also to be distinguished from, the superego. The ego ideal represents the sum of the ideals adopted from loving, reassuring parents (or parent substitutes, including society and God, so far as these are *positively* valued). From the ego ideal proceed consciously held and actually desired standards of goodness and excellence, standards not of what one ought to be but of what one genuinely wants to be.

ahead and lock me up"; when he is escaping over the wall under fire, "Shoot and be damned"; when he is contemplating future crimes, "I may go to the chair, but I'll take some cops along with me"; when thinking of his long sentence, "You gotta take it on the chin." Thus it appears that he not only hates cops and father-figures but that he also hates something in himself, and that something in himself hates him.

This something in himself that produces violent conflict is the introjected stern father. Almost invariably in these cases the offender's father is found to have been a harsh, brutal man who completely dominated his household. Very frequently he was an immigrant father who struggled against odds to adjust in a strange environment and saw his authority undermined by the inroads of a new culture. In this situation of frustration and unhappiness he vented his feelings on his uncomplaining wife and helpless children.

I may quote from the autobiography of the son of a Greek immigrant, a son who at the age of twenty-one had begun to serve ten to twenty years for armed robbery.

"My first memory has to do with Dad beating Mother. It seems that Mother and Aunt Catherine, who in the meantime had arrived from Greece, were having an argument. I do not recall its exact nature. However, Dad entered the room cursing Mother. He called her a son of a bitch and an old whore, and kicked her in the stomach. I began to cry and felt extremely sorry for Mother, who with her hands pressed to her abdomen had fallen into one of the dining room chairs. . . .

"Dad came home angry one night. Business had fallen off; he was discouraged and was thinking of closing the store. Mother said that it was too bad. If she said anything else, I cannot remember it. Dad swore at her. She ran from the table. Dad kicked back his chair and started for her. She ran out in the hall toward the piazza. Dad ran and kicked her. She cried, 'Don't.' He stood there and cursed. 'You son of a bitch of a whore, you dirty bastard.' I ran and put my hand on his leg and between sobs asked him not to hit Mother. He told me to get away from him and struck at me. I ran up the hall. Poor Mother, heavy with child, stayed on the piazza until he had become quiet and then with a red nose and a drawn, haggard face crept into bed, afraid to speak, afraid to open her mouth for fear that her husband would kick her. Years later, when he would begin to curse, this scene would unfold itself, and I would rise and for every vile epithet he used, call him one in return, while four young children sat and listened."

It is not difficult to see how in such circumstances the young offender conceives an intense hatred of the father, a hatred which is later transferred to the police and figures of authority generally, and how he turns from the home to the neighborhood gang to find social support for his hostile and rebellious impulses. Nor is it difficult to see how this young Oedipus comes to have a sentimental-protective attitude toward women and helpless individuals. They symbolize for him the wronged and mistreated mother. (It may be added here that of all the types of true criminals this antisocial offender reaches the highest degree of psychosexual maturity; though he is inextricably caught in the Oedipus complex he is at least capable of object love. A point that aids in his diagnosis is the fact that he despises sex offenders, whom he conceives as brutal rapists who always select the purest and fairest women.) But it does not do justice to the complexity of this type of case to say that he never knew any but antisocial ideals or even that he achieves at any early age a clean break with the father. It seems better to think of this man's inner situation as an exaggerated form of that which exists in every adolescent boy who reaches the same stage of psychosexual development. This boy, like almost all American boys, comes under the influence of superego prototypes in school, and some acceptance of their influence is a result. Our offender tries to love his father and to be loved by him, and despite the instances of mutual hostility which stand out in the record, introjection of the father does occur. For a long time, usually, there are attempts to placate the resulting harsh superego, and it is only when the superego prototypes have let the subject down and when support is found from membership in an antisocial group that persistent defiance of the superego becomes possible. If the presocial offender previously described belongs to Freud's erotic type, the man we are here concerned with belongs to the compulsive type. Here, of course, he is in company with the normal individual who has a strong superego, well integrated with the ego. But whenever the normal man of strong character says, "I must do this; it is a question of conscience," the antisocial offender says, "I *will* do this, and I hope they lock me up for it."

As we have said, though punishment never has the desired effect upon the antisocial offender, and though he ordinarily makes the most recalcitrant inmate, he nonetheless offers the best prospects for reform. He is capable of the strongest transference to a man who is strong enough to command his respect and who at the same time shows that he understands him. Neither stern discipline, which evokes only open rebellion, nor tender-minded solicitude, which evokes only contempt, will by itself be effective. But a combination of the two can work wonders through its appeal to this offender's sense of loyalty and unwillingness to "let down" someone who has placed confidence in him. His conflict with his father, it seems, not only disposes him to idealize the kind of a man who would never give in to the father, but it also creates for him, by contrast as it were, an image of an ideal father which, when it is approximated in reality, can gain his complete allegiance. Psychoanalysis would certainly be possible, once a transference was achieved, but in this case there would be a question of whether it was necessary.

THE ASOCIAL CRIMINAL

We turn, finally, to a consideration of the *asocial* offender. He stands in marked contrast to the presocial criminal who is subservient to the ideals of the group to which he belongs at the moment, and to the antisocial offender who is more or less permanently loyal to the ideals of a dissentient group. This man is firmly loyal to no ideals whatsoever; he is a law unto himself. Far from being concerned, on the surface at least, with getting the approval of any group, and far from being willing to make sacrifices in the service of any social ideal, his motto is "Look out for number one." For him everything—every social institution, every business enterprise—is a racket, and if he has any ideal guiding image it is that of a perfect racketeer who always "gets his" and is never called a "sucker."

This man may be committed to prison for a variety of offenses, including forgery, armed or unarmed robbery, or murder. Members of the organized rackets who obtain the greatest publicity are usually recruited from this class. Though the antisocial offenders move in groups and are often called gangsters, their romantic adventures are easy to distinguish from the cold, anal-sadistic enterprises of the true professional.

In prison the offender of this type exhibits one of two behavior patterns. He may appear as a vain, exhibitionistic, self-assertive fellow who makes the loudest complaints about the prison regime but backs down when threatened with discipline. His aim, it seems, is to be a "big shot." Whenever inmates are allowed to congregate he is likely to be found in the midst of a group of heelers, regaling them with stories of his life on the outside: his high-powered car, his important acquaintances, the girls he has thrilled. He is nobody's pal and he offers no affection, but, paradoxical though it may seem, this does not prevent him from receiving affection and acclaim. Untroubled by any tendency to put himself in the other person's place, he is able to manipulate his fellows and to gain recognition as a leader. Inmates are likely to call him a "right guy"; his jailers, also slightly awed, remark that he needs "ego deflation."

The other behavior pattern which the man of the asocial type may exhibit is one of proud withdrawal, surly independence, inaccessible spite. A lone wolf in his criminal activities, in prison he tends to keep his own council and thus to earn the reputation of being a "queer guy." He seems either to have repressed his affective tendencies entirely or to be so afraid of being hurt as to be suspicious of all friendly approaches to him.

Though there are of course important differences in the underlying determinants of these two patterns of behavior, at the level of our classification they nonetheless seem to belong together. Both types certainly lack social ideals and are interested only in self-maintenance. At first glance they seem to exemplify the genuine criminal of Alexander and Staub— the hypothetical individual who gratifies his instincts without any restraints whatsoever. This, however, would appear to be an impossible state of affairs in an individual who lives in our culture, and we must seek an explanation in the developmental history. We may say that in both cases there is a weak superego—indeed it is only with difficulty that we find any evidence of superego activity. The ego, on the other hand, is relatively strong, for these individuals are able shrewdly to calculate what is in their best interest and to inhibit or modify id impulses in accordance with the demands of reality. The really determining factor seems to be a preponderance of narcissism.[3] Though it is possible to detect in some of the active, self-assertive individuals we have described an underlying dependence upon the approval of other people (they need this assurance that they are all right), their exhibitionistic manifestations seem more often to be overreactions to earlier blows to self-esteem. Investigation into the history of these individuals will commonly reveal some personal inadequacy which was interpreted as a narcissistic wound and which gave rise to aggressive restriving. In other cases, it is likely that we should find, at the deepest level, oral spoiling, leading to inner narcissistic assurance. His mother perhaps never put him in his place and he became sure that by aggression he could always get what he wanted; only society stood in his way.

In the withdrawn narcissist we may expect to find, as the most important determinant, early love-deprivation of the severest sort. The most vicious offenses are found to be associated with the most tragic childhood experiences. These are the cases, it seems, in which there occur the greatest frequency of broken homes, rejection by the mother, maltreatment and neglect in early childhood, and various other forms of insupport. The individual reacts to this type of situation by saying, as it were, "All right, if you won't take care of me, I'll look after myself." Here, then, there is a secondary narcissism[4] and an underlying need to be loved. Much depends, it seems, upon how early and how severe was the deprivation. One gets the impression that some of these inmates can be reached, that they would like to "break down" and accept an offer of kindness; but in the great majority of cases this type of man is an example of what people seem to mean by a "hardened" criminal. In this case, as in the case of the self-assertive narcissist, punishment seems the most appropriate form of treatment. At the same time, if one's aim is merely to prevent further breaches of the law, this man is far from being a hopeless prospect. It is even conceivable that a more positive program could be devised, perhaps one that would provide extraordinary rewards for conforming behavior. These men will sometimes say with complete determination, "To hell with all this; I am going to find a safe racket."

In devising the present scheme the aim was to bring into dynamic relation factors associated with criminality. (And this aim may be said to have been realized to the degree that the factors so related are the most significant ones.) But a man's criminality, though it may be all that concerns us at a given time, is certainly not all of that man. Each of the present types is, in its essence, a more or less stable pattern of dynamically related factors. Of the individuals who possess one of these patterns, how-

---

[3] *Narcissism:* Pertaining to or inspired by self-love.

[4] *Secondary narcissism:* The withdrawing of psychic energy from objects and investing it in the ego.

ever, no two will exhibit it in precisely the same way. Each type, in other words, is a general framework, broad enough in its outlines to allow for a high degree of variation in its manifestations. Furthermore, to say that a man possesses one of these patterns, and that he manifests it in some particular way, is not to say the last word about him as an individual. He possesses numerous features not included in the patterns—even other patterns of features—with respect to which he may be differentiated from other individuals belonging to the same type. Thus the statement that an offender belongs to one of the present types means that in him this pattern is relatively predominant, not that he possesses this pattern to the complete exclusion of the others. If the distinctions underlying the present scheme are fundamental, as they seem to be, then one should be able, in the great majority of cases, to note the dominant pattern. When this is impossible, when it appears that an individual possesses two or more of the patterns in approximately equal degree, then admittedly he cannot be classified— but at least he is well characterized.

Today, most actions affecting criminals, whether they are in prison or not, are conceived and carried out with populations of offenders in mind. No one supposes that individual treatment for more than a handful of inmates is practicable, and few suppose that it can be effective unless it is coupled with modifications of the environment. If, however, actions directed to populations and groups are to be humane, it will be necessary to remember that these collectivities are made up of individuals, each of whom is at least as complicated as the "types" presented here.

CHAPTER NINE

Psychodynamic and Social Factors in Neurosis

In neurosis, as in certain forms of criminality, we deal with the persistence in the present of motives and ideas that were made unconscious in childhood. This proposition, which is basic to Freud's psychoanalytic theory, has been criticized on the grounds that it overaccents the element of fixity in personality, and underaccents the roles of social factors and events occurring after the period of childhood, in the determination of neurotic and deviant behavior. This chapter states the case for fixity. It attempts to show by means of a case study that traumatic experiences in childhood may have effects that ramify throughout the personality and help to determine an adult's thoughts, feelings, and actions. At the same time, however, it is argued here that even though we retain and utilize this essential component of psychoanalytic theory—which may indeed have been overaccented by Freud and other psychoanalytic writers—we may still give all due attention to social factors and to later as well as early events in the individual life. The task is to assign proper weights to each of these kinds of factors and to understand their interrelations.

Let us turn now to an illustrative case in which both kinds of factors are clearly evident—the case of an obstetrician who seeks psychoanalysis after considering it for ten years. As he says in his first interview, he

This is a slightly modified version of a paper which originally appeared under the title of "Family Impact on Personality: The Point of View of a Psychoanalyst," in J. E. Hulett and R. Stagner (eds.), *Problems in Social Psychology* (Urbana, Ill.: University of Illinois Press, 1954).

thinks it may help him to understand the emotional problems of his patients, or perhaps more important, it may help to prevent him from becoming too involved emotionally with his patients' problems. Still better, since he does not want to avoid caring a great deal about his patients, it may help him control his feelings in such a way that some useful purpose will be served. (He feels a deep sympathy, or one might say empathy, for his patients, and their gratitude is the greatest reward that life has to offer.) More than this, he seeks psychoanalysis because he feels that he is not realizing his full potential. He thinks that he might learn to be more effective, or at least to get over the constant feeling that much has been left undone and that he must do more. In short, he hopes that he may find relief from a pervading sense of insecurity: he must always be somehow on guard and can never quite feel that he is being himself. We learn incidentally as the interview is nearing a close that his mariage is not what it should be and that he is troubled by irritability toward his seven-year-old son.

This man has within the last two years been taken into one of the most lucrative and prestigeful obstetrical practices in the city. This is a triumph for a garment worker's son who was born in the slums—a young man who worked his way through college and who for financial reasons had to delay his entrance into medical school for eight years. It is also an obvious correlate of his felt insecurity, for while he "plays the role" of a very successful physician, he must conceal from his colleagues and patients facts of his background and history (including ten years in a left-wing action group); he must conceal his real opinions and values, even himself. His patients do not know that he is a Jew, though his colleagues do. They found out when, at the close of an intensive investigation on just this point, they asked the direct question, and our man said, "Yes" an answer for which he has repeatedly given himself credit. The colleagues said, "That's all right, since you don't look like one or act like one," and our subject believes that so far he has not let them down. In fact, he tells us, "I have perjured myself a hundred times, saying that when I got to the top I would make everything all right." He adds, "Now I'm honest enough to admit that I like upper-middle-class status—I might even achieve lower-upper—and if one of my kids wanted to marry a lower-class person, I'd be very much upset."

In the second interview the subject tells us something about the nature of his trouble in marriage. He puts it very simply: he cannot get the feeling that he is loved enough by his wife. He can offer no objective basis for this. It is just that he wants her to be happy; he wants her to be appreciative of his efforts to make her happy; he wants to be good and kind and helpful, and he wants approval and gratitude for this. In short, he would like her, by expressions of this kind, to relieve him of guilt feelings. His wife, a highly intelligent woman with achievement aspirations and problems centering on dependence-independence, naturally has difficulty in playing the desired role.

Both his parents were born in the "old country" and came to the

United States in their twenties. The father found a lowly job in a garment factory but was able to save something, and by the time our subject was seven, the father owned his own small shop in the suburbs. In the old country the family had cultural interests and ambitions, and as early as our subject can remember the accent in his family had been upon "middle-class" values. He was quick to win and to keep family approval by being a good student and by being generally unaggressive and well behaved. There is a brother two and one-half years younger, and of all the family members this is the one about whom the subject professes to have the strongest feelings. This brother, always a rebel and nonconformist, has turned out to be the black sheep of the family, and our subject has to deal with the feeling that he should have done more for him. He seems always to have had a bad conscience, too, because of actions with respect to this brother which he has perceived as less than honest or less than loyal. Thus, our subject was held up as a model for the brother, and he continued to accept credit for being a good boy, not fighting, and so forth, long after he knew that he was hiding behind his books, that his brother was beaten by the father for things which he, the subject, would have done had he not been afraid.

An early "memory" concerns the birth of a sister which took place at home when our subject was seven. He remembers the general excitement, his mother's cries, his father's anxiety, the sight of blood. He remembers being sent next door for more hot water, and he remembers his own distress, which was made as acute as possible by the fact that he did not know quite what was going on and was not told until a day later that everything was all right.

The subject remembers his extreme fondness for this infant sister, and he reports that to this day this sister has *him* on a pedestal. He remembers as a boy of ten or twelve baby-sitting in the houses of doctors; he chose his clients carefully so that he would have the chance to examine their medical books. He got jobs as delivery boy for the neighborhood pharmacists—anything that was close to medicine or doctors. One of his idols was the doctor who undertook to explain the evils—physical and mental—of masturbation. As he looks back on his childhood in these early interviews, the subject concludes that he has always liked his father better than his mother.

Now it seems very likely that if one studied in a large sample of men the kind of felt insecurity reported here, one would find it correlated with a variety of social-environmental factors—certainly with membership in an ethnic minority that is discriminated against and with a history of extreme upward mobility on the socioeconomic class scale. Indeed it would not be surprising if the phenomenon we are discussing turned out to be very widespread in our society, sufficiently widespread to suggest the hypothesis that what we see here is the working out in the individual of contradictions inherent in the society itself.

It would seem to go without saying that a therapist who hoped to help a man like the one whose case is before us would need to know something about-such social factors as those just mentioned, and how they applied to the case in question. As a matter of fact, he would have to know something about all this even to converse with this subject at his own level for, as already suggested, the subject is a long-time leftist with more than an academic interest in social ills and social change. Actually, the fact that he is knowledgeable in these matters helps him to agree readily that being a Jew in America has not been and is not a crucial factor in his difficulties. He tells a story in his first interview that seems to indicate that he was refused admittance to a medical school because of its "quota system," but he also tells us that the only reason he did not go on to medical school as soon as he finished college—when he had been admitted—was that he had no money. Thus he readily agrees that his life pattern could be explained better on a class basis than on a basis of minority-group social discrimination. But he does not insist on the importance of the class membership either, because he feels that his reactions in this area have been pretty deliberate and controlled, whereas what he is up against now is something that is rather beyond him.

There is a point of some general importance here. In our studies of the effects of contemporary group memberships upon behavior, some of us, out of our concern for social justice, are likely to oversimplify the significance of caste and class. We are helped along in this by our subjects themselves who naturally would rather attribute their difficulties to external circumstances than admit weaknesses or accept responsibilities in themselves. How often, for example, has Richard Wright's *Black Boy* been used to dramatize the plight of the Negro in America, as if being born a Negro was somehow the cause of the suffering! This is an injustice to artists in general: I have encountered exactly the same kind of suffering that Black Boy endured in a blond Swede from Minnesota who took it upon himself to be an artist. Walter White's case study of Ben Davis, published in *The Progressive,* explained that Davis became a Communist because, as a young lawyer at the time of the Herndon case, he suddenly realized that it was impossible for a Negro to get justice in the South. This is perhaps excellent propaganda, but as social psychology it leaves something to be desired. The most articulate rationalizations of the kind here being considered are perhaps encountered among intellectual or "emancipated" women of the type that go forth under the slogan "It's tough to be a woman in this culture." They use the social-science textbooks to help give themselves comfortable explanations for such things as frigidity, sterility, social irresponsibility, and general skulduggery. These comments are not intended to diminish the importance of social-group and social-role determinants of behavior, but rather to point to one of the difficulties in the way of an accurate appraisal of them. An inner weakness or conflict or source of unhappiness is very likely to be ascribed by the individual to external stresses of the moment, and, since no student of these matters can ever say that he has done all that he should to eliminate these stresses, he has a tendency to fall in a little too soon with this line of reasoning.

But in the present case our subject is evidently not going to be insistent about the contemporary social factors; he is ready to try psychoanalysis. Now someone may suspect that he wants to try psychoanalysis in order not to examine, or to accept the responsibility for changing, his present social situation. There is a point here, too, though it is doubtful that the present case would be the best one to illustrate it. It is generally taken for granted that a man cannot achieve happiness by playing a role that does not suit him or by persisting in a form of self-perjury; there is nothing in psychoanalytic theory to suggest that refuge from social realities might be found in a personal psychoanalysis.

What I am leading up to is this question: What will be the implications for our thinking about personality development if we take the view that in the present case, as in many similar ones, certain crucial determinants have sprung from events which occurred in a particular setting of family life and at a time when particular psychological processes were operating in our subject—namely, the events surrounding the birth of the little sister? I think it will be agreed that the following is a not atypical psychoanalytic formulation.

At the time of the sister's birth, our subject, who had already been displaced from his central position in his mother's affections by his younger brother and who had reason to anticipate a recurrence of this same trauma, harbored aggressive wishes against the mother and perhaps against the unborn child as well. The horror of the occasion of the confinement lay largely in his conviction that his bad wishes were somehow responsible for his mother's suffering and the possibility of her death. This led immediately to the resolve to make amends. How could he ever be good enough to his mother? One thing he could do, maybe, would be to give her all the babies she wanted, and to be very kind to her little daughter. It is the fact that this whole complex was then made unconscious which has permitted it to spread into so many aspects of the personality and which has given the guilt feelings their unmitigable quality. It is as if his many acts of atonement do not get applied to the proper account, and hence his debt remains as great as ever. The act of making a payment is, however, tension-reducing for the moment, so he goes on seeking approval and gratitude from his wife and from his patients. And he goes on being irritated by his son, with whom he is in some sense identified, when this youngster is too aggressive toward his mother.

Naturally we do not get such an outcome as this every time a little sister is born at home without the little boy's being sent to a neighbor's. It depends on what is going on at the time the traumatic event occurs. Among the most significant factors in the present case is the fact that at the age of seven our subject was still involved in the Oedipus complex or, rather, in a particular kind of continuing attempt at its solution. He had not adopted his father's standards and values into his ego system because of ambivalent feelings toward him. Actually, he has adopted more of his mother's attitudes, and far from opposing the father and standing up for his mother, he is submissive toward the former and critical of the latter.

This is the basis for strong homosexual trends in the patient's personality. Of course he is ashamed, now and later, when he sees his brother take punishment for trying to oppose the father; he feels that he should have been a more daring Oedipus.

There is not space here to assemble all the evidence from the analysis of this patient that seems to support this formulation; and even if this were done it is to be doubted that all readers would be convinced. But suppose objective evidence to support all the theoretical propositions offered here were complete, what would be the implications?

One way in which psychologists have handled formulations of this kind has been to say that they may be true for certain neurotics but have no general applicability, that it is a dangerous mistake for psychoanalysts to take a theory of neurosis and write about it as if it were a theory of human nature or of human behavior. The psychologist seems to have a point here. Certainly it is not too difficult to find psychoanalytic writing in which the infantile themes are translated directly into adult social action without too much attention to those instances in which the same infantile events had quite different outcomes or to the numerous other kinds of factors which may have influenced the adult social action in question. In some of these instances, to be sure, the psychoanalytic writer would not have come off too badly if he had remembered to say "in some cases" at the right times and places. Let it be admitted that not all obstetricians owe their choice of a profession to an unconscious desire to help their mothers and give them babies. After all, we have the case of one of our subject's colleagues who, it would appear, has merely carried on his father's business. And certainly there must be other ways in which men with the same kind of childhood situation and the same specific traumata can work out their problems.

But the psychologist who wants to dismiss our subject's case by calling it neurotic is not to be let off so easily. When other questions are at issue, the psychologist is not so ready to make a categorical distinction between normal and abnormal. There seems to be no serious objection to calling *some* of our subject's motivations neurotic, but to do so does not, I believe, really distinguish him from anybody else, since everybody exhibits some motivations of this kind. When intensive studies of normal people, average or superior, are carried out, as was done at the Harvard Psychological Clinic (Murray, 1938), in the OSS assessment work (1948), and at Vassar College (Sanford, 1956), we always find motivations of the kind that have been described here.

Perhaps there *is* a serious objection to calling our subject's motivations for obstetrics "neurotic." The term still has for some people derogatory connotations. Yet we must have a term to stand for those motivations which arise out of infantile traumata, fixation, and repression. "Motives from the deeper layers of the personality" has proved to be fairly inoffensive—perhaps because this expression does not really say what is meant. Murray's "unity theme" (1938) comes close, but this concept actually involves more of a commitment to the crucial importance of infantile experience than even the orthodox analyst would care to make. Perhaps Allport (1937) can help us here. Since the concept of "functionally autonomous motive" was invented, apparently in an effort to get away from, or at least to prevent undue stress upon, precisely what we are here talking about, why not say motives that are *not* functionally autonomous or "functionally nonautonomous" motives? There is only one hitch here. One of the main characteristics of "functionally nonautonomous" motives is their *autonomy,* their autonomy, that is, with respect to everything that motives ought not to be autonomous with respect to—learning, reason, and everyday experience. It has been suggested to me that, since what distinguishes the motives I am talking about is not the way in which they were learned but rather the fact that they are not extinguished as we should expect on the basis of ordinary learning theory, we should call the phenomena in question "nonextinguishing" motives.

But these are precisely the kind of motives that in earlier chapters of this book have been called unconscious. Their "nonextinguishingness" is the most essential feature of unconscious motives. We have no alternative to staying with our chosen term; it may be hoped that with growing recognition of the fact that everybody has unconscious motives the use of this term will not seem derogatory.

Armed with this conception of unconscious motives, we can save the term neurotic for use in reference to sickness or distress of the kind that leads a person to seek help or to have help sought for him. We can now think in quantitative terms: of the degree to which the personality is dominated by unconscious motives, of the strength or amount of the person's resources for dealing with them, of the amount of external stress that confronts him, of the degree to which the social situation offers ready-made arrangements for countering unconscious motives.

Consider for a moment the case of our subject's colleague, the man who took over his father's business. He fits snugly into the medical fraternity, the upper-middle-class business world, the stream-lined, air-conditioned design of Western living. Naturally he has little tolerance for our subject's concern with the patient's "problems," for the "emotional factor," for medical reform, for anything that would interfere with the smooth running of the business. The chances are good that this man is moved by as many unconscious motives as our subject. To prove this, one would only have to change in some more or less radical way the general social situation in which he lives. At any rate, this would be a hypothesis to explain his impassioned resistance to the very idea of change.

Now it may be asked: If this colleague's "adjustment" and peace of mind depend as largely as it seems upon the social set-up in which he lives, might not the same thing be said for our subject? Instead of probing into the deeper layers of his personality, should we not concentrate on changing the social situation in such a way as to make him happier—and his colleague unhappier? Certainly there is no reason to doubt that in a different world our man might be happier. But, whereas it would be easy enough to construct in our imaginations a social situation that the colleague would find intolerable, we cannot imagine any external conditions which by themselves would relieve our subject of the complaints which brought him to psychotherapy. His main struggle now is within himself and with himself, and the grim truth is that he himself has to change. Otherwise, so long as he lived in a family or treated female patients or entered into relations with people who had different standards and values, he would suffer as he does now. More than this, it is impossible to imagine a social system within which problems of the kind here presented would not arise, so long as family life persisted and so long as there was no increase in our knowledge and application of mental hygiene. My utopia, obviously, gives some place to the psychotherapist (or his equivalent), not only because psychotherapy is a rewarding occupation in many ways, but because I am afraid that by the time we reach a state in which people have lost so much freedom, and hence complexity, that they do not have any unconscious conflicts that need to be made conscious, it will be 1984.

The present accent on trauma, fixation, repression, and the persistence of unconscious motives is not intended to imply that other kinds of learning do not occur. For that matter, there could be no objection, I think, to attempts to translate what has been said about unconscious motives into the terms of conventional learning theory—if this will make the phenomena more understandable or more accessible to objective study. The important thing is that the distinctive features of our "failure to unlearn," its critical differences from ordinary, everyday learning phenomena, should not be lost in the shuffle. One might hope that the learning theorist could somehow steep himself in clinical material or do something else to insure that the essential quality of unconscious motives was appreciated.

Attention to such happenings as we have ascribed to our subject—fixation, repression, and so forth—should be a part of the everyday work of the personologist, and the social scientist as well. It could help the latter to remember that most people, though they sometimes behave in remarkably uniform ways under the impact of certain social situations, are still just as complex as the patient discussed here. It might lead him to consider, as one type of hypothesis, that the meaning for an individual of a social group membership, a social role, or a social ideology could depend upon its function within such a personal economy as that found in our subject. It might suggest to him that one way to evaluate a social setting or social program—over and above the degree to which it frustrates or gratifies common human needs—would be in terms of what opportunities are offered (or denied) for transforming unconscious motives in ways that are personally and socially constructive, and for preventing the expression either in consciousness or in behavior of the original infantile tendency.

Psychoanalysis will not steal the show completely. No matter how much insight, how much freedom from childhood fixations, our physician might achieve, he would still have to face the very painful realities of his social situation and to make some very difficult decisions. Indeed one might say that a successful psychoanalysis might well deprive him of mechanisms which he has used to comfort himself and thus lend an additional aspect of grimness to his life situation. Psychoanalysis offers no solution of the great moral and social problems which men must solve with their intelligence; it only hopes to strengthen that intelligence and to help avoid attempts at solution by processes operating mainly below the cerebral cortex.

A stickler for unconscious motives may sometimes emphasize personality factors at the expense of situational factors when his aim is to explain the behavior of adults, but there is certainly less reason for him to do so when the task is to explain why a trauma such as that described should occur. Here, it seems, everybody has a chance. Though, as indicated, I am arguing that the transformations which took place in connection with the birth of the little sister were made possible by processes already going on in our subject, I now want to urge that a complete account would have to give attention to the whole situation in which he was living at the time. That it was necessary to have the baby at home under rather primitive conditions, that the subject was in no way prepared psychologically for the coming of a sister or brother and was not told what was going on, that he was exposed to the dramatic aspects of the event, including the mother's cries, that certain things were expected of the eldest son—all these are things which depend upon the economic condition, the class status, the cultural background of the family. Numerous variables from several disciplines are certainly of immediate relevance here, and our approach to the problem had best be "field-theoretical." We are, of course, used to the idea that "the family carries the culture," that all those deliberate and indeliberate influences which are brought to bear upon the child are determined by the society and by the culture as well as by the personalities of the parents, and that these things are somehow learned or taken over by the child. I am here insisting that the special business of trauma, fixation, and repression—that kind of one-trial learning by which unconscious motives are established—is also profoundly influenced by the society and the culture. True, there is a great deal of biological stuff involved in all this; men and women are reproducing and their young are clinging to the nest. But the question of what is biological and what is social is no different here from what it is in psychology generally.

A word should be said here concerning the question of how we might obtain the objective evidence that is crucial for the kind of formulation made in our case. Psychoanalysis does not need to ask or be granted any special dispensations or concessions in this matter. If there is truth in the formulation about unconscious motives, it will be demonstrated in accordance with the same standards and by means of the same rules of evidence that prevail in psychological science generally. As a matter of fact, psychoanalytic hypotheses have fared rather well when subjected to objective study in recent years. We have, I believe, come quite a long way since the publication of Sears' survey (1943). This progress, it seems to me, has been due not only to clarification of concepts through translation of the psychoanalytic concepts and hypotheses, but to increased understanding of what psychoanalysts are trying to say and above all to improvement in methodology. It has been recognized that reaching the "deep" layers of personality does not depend so much upon investigating a person over a long period of time as upon the way personality has been conceived of in the first place. We do not have to wait until various superficial layers have been removed before we glimpse what lies beneath, but rather, since underlying trends which are relevant are actually operating in any momentary situation, our task is to learn the signs by which they manifest themselves at the surface. In short, we must learn which manifestations are to be referred to which levels. Given this conceptual approach we may believe that clinically oriented, longitudinal studies of children, intensive studies of normal adults, research on psychotherapy, experimental studies of learning, perception, and motivation—all these, carried forward by techniques designed with imagination and psychological insight and by methods of analysis having sufficient scope and subtlety, will in time reveal the true richness and intricacy of personality in society.

We must not suppose, however, that direct evidence of trauma, fixation, repression, and unconscious motives will be very readily forthcoming. To return to the case of our physician, even if there had been numerous workers on the scene at the time—describing the environment, observing and talking with the child, administering projective tests, and so on—it would still have been most difficult to know what was going on inside the mind of that child. The things that the psychoanalyst speaks about most freely and leans upon heavily in his formulations are hypothetical constructs, they will not be directly exposed for all to see, but it may be anticipated that their explanatory power will continue to increase.

In sum, we may say that in order to understand why a trauma that is crucial for neurosis occurs in the first place, why the same particular event or experience may be traumatic in one case but not in another, it is necessary to spell out the interplay of the cultural, social-situational, and psychodynamic factors that were in operation at the time. By the same token, a neurotic pattern is sustained in an adult not only by his awareness of determining factors in himself but by the social situation—social group memberships, commitments to social roles, and so forth—in which he is now enmeshed, a situation that is partly of his own making and partly a consequence of the realities of life.

CHAPTER TEN

The Authoritarian Personality: A Case Study

Another pattern of behavior which involves both individual and social dynamics is *authoritarianism*. Like criminality and neurosis, this complex syndrome apparently has its roots in a peculiar imbalance of power among the id, ego, and superego. Its functioning is largely unconscious and central to a wide variety of overt behavior, such as prejudice, rigid conventionalism, submissiveness to superiors, punitiveness, and other manifestations which will be explored in this chapter. Essentially, authoritarianism is conceived as a failure in development, but it is thought to be fairly common in our society, even among so-called normal people.

While this syndrome is a structure of the individual psychological household, neither its genesis nor its consequences can be separated from the social matrix in which they occur. Wherever this pattern typifies one or more individuals, it is likely to have some effect on the functioning of the social group. The group may in turn modify the individual behavior pattern. Certain conditions in society, such as economic depression with declining confidence in the established order, seem more likely than others to foster authoritarianism in the society's members; similarly, certain roles in society (for example, school teaching or military command) are likely to bring out whatever authoritarian tendencies may lie in the individual.

Adapted from "The Case of Mack," in T. W. Adorno, Else Frenkel-Brunswik, D. Levinson, and N. Sanford, *The Authoritarian Personality*. Copyright 1950 by The American Jewish Committee. Reprinted by permission of Harper & Row, Publishers.

The five-year research which eventually isolated the authoritarian syndrome began in 1944 as a study of anti-Semitism.[1] Our theoretical orientation was mainly Freudian psychoanalytic; it accordingly supposed that persistent social attitudes, like other persistent traits, were somehow organized with the rest of the personality. Early in the study a Likert-type scale was constructed for measuring anti-Semitism (A-S) and later another for measuring ethnocentrism (E). The high correlation between these A-S and E scales (.80) suggested that anti-Semitism was mainly a manifestation of a more generalized hostility to various out-groups and a tendency to glorify the in-group.[2] Furthermore, we suspected that this ethnocentrism was part of a still broader personality pattern which characterized the person who was attracted to fascist or authoritarian ideologies. Our clinical studies had already suggested several personality traits which were likely to be displayed by the prejudiced subjects and not by the unprejudiced:

1. *Conventionalism.* Rigid adherence to conventional middle-class values.
2. *Authoritarian submission.* Submissive, uncritical attitude toward idealized moral authorities of the in-group.
3. *Authoritarian aggression.* Tendency to be on the lookout for and to condemn, reject, and punish people who violate conventional values.
4. *Anti-intraception.* Opposition to the subjective, the imaginative, the tender-minded.
5. *Superstition and stereotypy.* The belief in mystical determinants of the individual's fate; the disposition to think in rigid categories.
6. *Power and toughness.* Preoccupation with the dominance-submission, strong-weak, leader-follower dimension; identification with power figures; exaggerated assertion of strength and toughness.
7. *Destructiveness and cynicism.* Generalized hostility; vilification of the human.
8. *Projectivity.* The disposition to believe that wild and dangerous things go on in the world; the projection outward of unconscious emotional impulses.
9. *Sex.* Ego-alien sexuality; exaggerated concern with sexual "goings on," and punitiveness toward violators of sex mores.

On the hypothesis that the same fundamental needs of the personality lay behind these other traits as behind prejudice, we undertook to develop an instrument which would measure prejudice potential without openly mentioning minorities—the California F scale. The thirty-four items of the final F scale were drawn from interview material, from the literature on Nazism and fascism, and from other sources. For every item

---

[1] The procedures and findings of this study are described in detail in *The Authoritarian Personality.*

[2] Any tendency toward prejudice which is provoked by externally imposed frustrations rather than unconscious needs may be considered as "surface resentment," in contrast to true authoritarianism.

there was a hypothesis stating the nature of its supposed connection with prejudice and its relation to other items in an over-all pattern. All the items of the scale were positive, that is, expressions of the authoritarian position, and were written with a view to inviting the subject to go as far as he would in agreeing with antidemocratic statements; the idea was to appeal to his submissiveness and social imperceptiveness, which were considered to be aspects of the authoritarian syndrome. For example, one of the items stated: "He is indeed contemptible who does not feel an undying love, gratitude, and respect for his parents."

The scale correlated about .75 with anti-Semitism and ethnocentrism in various groups of subjects. It has also demonstrated its validity as a measure of personality, filled as it is with unmistakable expressions of such tendencies as extrapunitiveness, conventionalism, and compartmentalization in thinking. Subsequent research by Eager and Smith (1952), McGee (1954), Barron (1950), and Rosen (1951) has confirmed the capacity of the scale to predict aspects of the F pattern other than prejudice.

Interviews, projective questions,[3] and the Thematic Apperception Test were used in the study of individuals scoring at the extremes on the F scale. These measures revealed other features of personality which were common to subjects with high F scores: a hierarchical conception of human relations, accent on the element of power in such relations, a manipulative attitude toward other people, a readiness to treat property as an extension of the self, self-glorification masking self-contempt, tendency to self-pity, ego-alien dependence, ambivalence toward parents and love objects, undifferentiated conception of the opposite sex, use of sex as a means of achieving status, and moralistic condemnation of the instinctive or earthy. Numerous kinds of social, political, and religious group memberships were also found to be significantly related to authoritarian tendency.

It would be a mistake, however, to think of authoritarianism either as a simple list of traits or, at the other extreme, as a type which might more or less totally embrace a person. Actually, what we are dealing with here is a personality syndrome, a pattern of dynamically related variables which, though it is never precisely the same in any two individuals, exhibits a certain unity and may be thought of as varying in a quantitative way from one individual to another. Among our original subjects it was possible to distinguish certain subvarieties of the extreme authoritarian pattern, depending on the relative dominance of various traits in the over-all syndrome.[4]

So far, we have described only that side of authoritarianism which turns its face outward in the form of observable behavior. What of the hidden side, the dynamic structure that underlies this behavior? A very

---

[3] See Addenda to this chapter for list of questions.

[4] Subtypes of *low* F scorers were also discernable. For typology of both high and low authoritarians, see N. Sanford, "The Approach of the Authoritarian Personality," in J. L. McCary (ed.), *Psychology of Personality* (New York: Logos Press, 1956).

general formulation would be the following: Ambivalent feelings toward in-group authorities (chiefly the parents) lead to intense anxiety about punishment and quite frequently to an inverted Oedipus situation—that is to say, one in which love for the parent of the opposite sex is repressed and submissive love becomes the predominant attitude toward the parent of the same sex. The maintenance of this state of affairs requires rigid defenses, involving a narrowing of consciousness—lack of insight and fear of inner life—and a readiness to project the numerous ego-alien tendencies in the personality. With respect to the genesis of the high F pattern, the interviews revealed numerous differences between our authoritarian and nonauthoritarian subjects in what they said about their childhood situations and their development. The most important determinant, in our view, was authoritarian discipline in the family. But we must be careful. By authoritarian, we do not mean that of a stern father. We mean discipline that is harsh but capricious, that depends more on the emotional needs of the disciplinarian than on any consideration of the needs of the child or of civilization. And for such discipline to produce the authoritarian personality other variables must be present as well.

Let us turn now to a more intensive examination of one case from the original study—the case of Mack, a college sophomore who scored in the high quartile of 167 college students on both the anti-Semitism scale and the F scale. The information from this subject's interview statements and from his responses to projective questions and the Thematic Apperception Test[5] enables us to see the authoritarian syndrome in operation and to trace its development from his early childhood.

INTERVIEW DATA

In the clinical part of his interview, Mack stated:

"Mother was sick in bed a great deal of the time. I remember her reading and singing to us. She devoted her last strength to us kids. I don't have those early recollections of my father. My first recollection of him as a father was one spring morning, when mother passed away. He came back to tell us. Of course, there is such a disparity between his age and mine. He is 77 now. Mother had 3 operations. The third time she left I was very distressed. It was like a premonition. The aunt across the street helped take care of us, when we got sick. Father spent all of his time with us after mother died.

"My sister is 4 years older than I. She has been married about 3½ years. She is a good housewife, has a 2-year-old boy, and is expecting another. I have had very good relations with her, a few arguments, but not like other brothers and sisters I have seen. She took care of the family cooking and took care of me. They called her the little old lady.' That has kept up. She helped put me through school and to buy my clothes. She is an accomplished stenographer and bookkeeper. She loaned me

[5] See Addenda to this chapter for Mack's TAT stories.

money to get started in the East. I have repaid her. No, she has not in-fluenced me much in ideas. She's like myself in that. She doesn't take religion very seriously; she never drinks or smokes, has high ideals. But father was more responsible for that.

"Up to high school I didn't do much thinking about anything. When I entered high school, my sister had left. The four years in high school I spent mostly with my father. When I graduated, he was living with us in ———."

[*What things did you admire especially in your father?*] "Mostly, his attention to us kids was very admirable. He's very honest, so much so that he won't condone charge accounts. He's known throughout the country as a man whose word is as good as his bond. His greatest con-tribution was denying himself pleasures to take care of us kids." [*What disagreements have you had with your father?*] "There haven't been any to any great extent. I had a mind of my own at a very early age. He has too. We've had arguments, but I can't remember any lickings by him. He scolded but usually talked things over. Our arguments were usually about things I wanted that he didn't want me to have—like the .22 rifle I wanted when I was 10, or a bicycle. He had to be very careful about money. He wouldn't let me work—he thought it was beneath me. He was afraid I would hurt myself with the rifle. But he never denied me anything I needed." [*What have been the effects of the age discrepancy?*] "Well, I've had to shift for myself a lot. I would have welcomed instruc-tion that he wasn't able to give me. My first venture socially was in the DeMolay. I was a charter member and later a master counselor. I was vice-president of the student body in high school and president of the student body at business school. He was pleased and encouraged me.

"Bud, my cousin, and I were always together. He is 2 months younger. We played baseball and went hunting, etc. We're still close, though we write seldom. He is in India."

[*What are your most pleasant memories of childhood?*] "Those good times Bud and I had, and with other groups. Skiing and tobogganing. My real pleasures are very simple and always have been. But I like nice equipment, for example, a good rifle. Bud and I had good help from father. He used to spend his winters alone in the mountains, and made his own skis and snowshoes. He showed us how to make them."

[*What did you worry most about as a kid?*] "Well, mostly about being held back by lack of funds. I worried about such things. In the 7th grade, I was the best speller, but I remember a defeat by a girl at the county spelling bee. Often I was just a little under the top. Just like in the service. I went to OCS, and got sick just before getting my com-mission. Usually I tried too hard, like in football. I was not as good an end as I should have been. I dropped passes because I tried too hard and so I was mediocre. Now, when I'm relaxed I have no trouble at all.

"They found I was anemic at the age of 12. I had my first hemorrhage from the stomach when I was 18. It always comes around when I start working too hard."

[*Where did you get your sex instruction?*] "I never had any from my parents, though I did get some suggestions from my aunt; no real instruction. What I know I have picked up from reading. I've listened to men talk, but accepted little of it; I weighed it in the light of what I have read."

[*What was your first sex experience?*] "It was in 1940–41, the aftermath of a New Year's party in Washington. There was liquor. I was always the backward boy. I hope to get married to the girl I'm going with now. She is an awfully nice companion. Most girls are interested only in a good time and want fellows with lots of money to spend. I didn't have the money for giving them a swell time. The girl I'm in love with now lived 9 miles from me. She attended a rival high school. I dated her once in high school. When I got back from the army, I worked in a lumber mill. This girl had graduated from ———— and started teaching. Her uncle is the vice-president of the bank. I talked to him about buying an automobile that she was interested in. I looked it over for her, since I knew something about cars, and told her it was in good condition. I got started going with her that way. I found out that she wasn't interested in money, but was interested in me in spite of my discharge from the army, my poor health and prospects. She's just very good—not beautiful, but a tremendously nice personality. She is French with some Irish in her. She has a nice figure and is very wholesome. When we get married depends on circumstances. It's quite a responsibility. She wants to get married now; she is teaching in ————. I'm under the GI Bill. If I get assurance of four years in college, I might get married this spring. We're well suited; I know she's interested in me, because I have so little to offer. We're both at the proper age. I intend to work part time. I don't like her teaching; I like to support my wife. I've always had that idea. But maybe under the circumstances, that won't be fully possible. She is a good cook, and that is an asset, what with my stomach condition. When I tell her that you approve of our marriage, she will be pleased, but of course I'm always a man to make my own decisions."

ANALYSIS AND INTERPRETATION

ENVIRONMENTAL FORCES AND EVENTS.

Socioeconomic factors. Mack is not very informative with respect to the socioeconomic status of his family—the reason for this is partly because he was not questioned closely enough and partly, as it seems, because he is sometimes tempted to distort the facts. Mack stated on his questionnaire, that the father is a "retired lumberman" with an annual income of $1,000. In the interview we are told that the father has not worked for thirty years (which would mean that he stopped working when he was 47, approximately six years before Mack was born), and that his present income is from "stocks and bonds." At the time he *did* work, the wage, we are told, was $75 a month, hardly enough to have accumulated stocks and bonds the income from which is $1,000 a year. The most plausible hypothesis, it seems, is that Mack is merely guessing at the time since the father retired, that it was actually not so long as thirty years, and that the major portion of the income is from a pension. ("He owned some lumber lands, but he mostly preferred working for other people.") That the father owned his home probably helped to give the family an aspect of stability, but there seems little reason to doubt that Mack was indeed "held back by lack of funds" or that this was a cause for worry.

The status of the family would seem to have been lower middle class, bordering on lower class. There was certainly little upward mobility in the sense of actual social or economic advancement. Whether or not the family was concerned with status is a question. The mother and the aunt appear to have tried to keep the children in Sunday School, but the father, whom Mack regards as his major guide, seems not to have participated in this endeavor. We are told that the father wanted his son to go into business, which is not remarkable; but that he did not want Mack to work as a boy because "he thought it was beneath me" sounds definitely status-minded. It also sounds somewhat dubious. We are led to wonder whether we are not dealing here with the status-mindedness of the son rather than with that of the father. It seems that part of the time Mack would like to gain prestige by giving the impression that his father was a man of parts—a retired lumberman who was "known throughout the country as a man whose word was as good as his bond"—and that part of the time he would attain the same end by showing that he had done well despite the economic handicaps with which he had to contend. A man who retired on $1,000 a year at the age of 47, or when his two children were in infancy—or not yet born—could hardly be described as a go-getter or as a man who was deeply concerned to secure advantages and status for his children. That Mack does not deliberately tell us this may probably be put down as an aspect of his general inability to criticize his father.

Father. Although the father seems not to have been status-driven in the ordinary sense, there is no evidence that he was relaxed or easy-going with respect either to traditional morality or the values of a business community. While Mack undoubtedly exaggerates the virtuous aspects of his father, some of the remarks about his moral strictness have the ring of truth. He "followed the church rules" although he did not go to church, he "drank but little, and never smoked," he was "very honest and strict in his dealings—so honest that he wouldn't condone charge accounts"; even when considerably discounted, these remarks still give a picture of a rigidly moral man or, at the least, of a man who held up this type of standard for his son. That he did so without showing by example that such standards led to satisfying goals—he himself did not work or provide adequately for his family—may well have been the cause for resentment in Mack.

But Mack only hints at this state of affairs. Each time he describes an authoritarian trait or behavior pattern of his father he seems constrained to deny it or to cancel it out by mentioning something of an opposite character: although "he forced some decisions on me," he "allowed me to do as I pleased"; arguments were about "things he didn't want me to have," but "he never denied me anything I needed"; "he scolded but usually talked things over"; "I've had to shift for myself a lot," but "his attention to us kids was very admirable." It is possible, of course, that these statements should be taken at their face value, for such inconsistency as Mack describes is certainly not uncommon among parents. In this case the conclusion would be that our subject had to deal both with authoritarian discipline and with kindly solicitude on the part of his father. This circumstance would not have prevented the discipline from being resented but it would have made open rebellion against it very difficult, if not impossible. With the father in the position of both disciplinarian and love object it would have been necessary for Mack to submit to the discipline in order not to lose the love.

There is reason enough to believe that after the death of the mother Mack's father did have the central role which is here assigned to him, but it is doubtful that Mack got as much from his father as he seems to want us to believe or that the father's dominance was always as easily excused. Mack seems entirely unambiguous when it comes to the matter of his father's distance from himself. Not only does he appear to have been genuinely troubled by the father's advanced age and to feel that this by itself made the latter inaccessible, but the nearest he comes to uttering a complaint against the father is when he refers, repeatedly but as it seems reluctantly, to the old man's retiring nature. It is easy to believe that a man who "used to spend his winters alone in the mountains" was deeply introverted, and it is easy to imagine that after the death of his wife he used to spend a great deal of time brooding at home, rousing himself now and then to issue a categorical command and telling himself occasionally that he ought to take more interest in "the kids." This picture is unlike that found most commonly among the fathers of prejudiced men; one might even go so far as to speculate that Mack's father was himself unprejudiced; but even so, his silence and reserve could have been of decisive importance in impelling Mack in the direction of prejudice. If this father possessed such human qualities as suggested above, they were certainly lost on Mack, who says he "can't understand" his father's withdrawal. It is likely that after the mother's death Mack turned to his father for love and comfort, but there is no evidence that he received it in adequate measure. There is no hint of warmth or demonstrativeness on the father's part; instead he is assigned those empty virtues—moral strictness and kindness—which prejudiced subjects characteristically ascribe to parents with whom they were not on good terms. Silence and distance, no less than meaningless aggression, on a father's part may be a sufficient stimulus for fear and hostility in the son.

In summary, it seems that the nearest we can come to an estimate of what the father was like in reality is to say that he was a defeated man who, in an authoritarian manner, held up conventional moral standards for his son without being able to show by example that adherence to these standards actually led to worthwhile ends; after the death of his wife he seems to have tried to take over some of the maternal functions in his relations with his children but because of his own personality problems he was unable to be understanding or affectionate toward his son.

Cousin Bud. Although very little is known about Bud, the cousin two months younger than our subject, it must be noted that he seems to have supplied more or less constant male companionship for Mack. There is a hint that Bud was the stronger and more assertive of the two boys; Mack was sick much of the time and finally failed in Officer Candidate School because of his stomach condition, while Bud, at the time of our interview, was overseas as a member of the armed services.

Mother. In approaching the question of what Mack's mother was actually like, in her relations with her own son, we face the same difficulty that arose in the case of the father: our subject tends to glorify his parents, and, in assigning traits to them, to express so well his own personality needs that we cannot accept his appraisal at face value. When Mack tells us that his mother was kind and self-sacrificing ("she devoted her last strength to us kids") and that she was morally strict ("she brought us up very strictly in this [church] guidance"), our first thought is that this is what the great majority of our prejudiced subjects—in contrast to the unprejudiced ones—report. The question is whether Mack's mother, and the mothers of most high-scoring men, was actually as he describes her—in which case we should understand the relations of this type of maternal influence to prejudice in the son—or whether the personality needs of the subject are such that he has to describe the mother as he does, even though she may have been quite different in reality.

There seems little reason to doubt that the mother was strict in much the way that Mack describes. She tried to bring up her children according to the moral principles of the Methodist Church and she, no more than the father, could give sex instruction to the subject. This general pattern of strictness seems to have been carried forward by the aunt and by the sister after the mother's death. It can well be imagined that the sister especially, who was cast so prematurely into the role of mother—"the little old lady"—overdid in her attempts to enforce conventional moral standards. But there is no basis for thinking of Mack as a victim of "maternal domination"; the strictness which we may envision here seems no more than what is ordinary among mothers of the lower middle-class.

That Mack may have felt imposed upon by these women, however, is another matter. He may well have felt that the amount of love he received was far from being enough to make up for the restrictions that were placed on him. True, Mack undoubtedly received *some* genuine love from his mother. When he remembers "her reading and singing to us" and notes that he does not have such recollections of his father, when he reports his distress on learning of her death, and when he says—at the conclusion of his TAT session—"there were times when I would have gone to a mother had I had one," it seems clear that he at the least knew what it was to be loved by his mother. But Mack lost this love, and the indications are that it went hard with him. The sense of deprivation and of injustice that this loss may have aroused in him could easily have made later restrictions seem unfair; if at the time of the mother's death Mack harbored some resentment because of her real or imagined strictness, there would be sufficient reason why he, out of guilt feelings, should idealize her.

The mother's illness, which seems to have been a lingering one ("she was sick in bed a great deal of the time" and had three operations), was probably also a significant factor in our subject's development. It could have meant that although he received a certain amount of love, he did not feel secure about it; there must have been many times when he wanted more than she was able to give, and because she was sick in bed he could not be demanding or give vent to the anger which his frustration must have aroused in him.

Mack's illness. Mack's illness as a boy may be regarded both as an event which had important effects upon his later behavior and attitudes and as something which itself may have been, in large part, psychologically determined. That the illness must have been severe and of long standing seems clear from the following: "I have had a lot of sickness; stomach trouble ever since I was 12. I had my first hemorrhage from the stomach when I was 18"; and "I went to OCS and got sick just before getting my commission." An indication of how much this illness has meant to Mack is found in his statement on his questionnaire that "physical weakness, perhaps due to ill health continued over the last four years" is the mood or feeling most disturbing to him.

DEEPER PERSONALITY NEEDS. The concern here is with those needs in Mack's personality which were aroused with particular intensity early in his life and which were later inhibited so that their present activity becomes manifest only in indirect ways. These needs do not form a part of his "better self"; they are not accepted by his ego, and he would conceal them from himself as well as from other people. To appraise these needs, therefore, it is necessary to use special techniques for getting below the surface, to call into play what psychological insight we can, and to rely rather heavily upon inference. The TAT and the projective questions[6] offer some evidence bearing fairly directly upon inhibited trends in the personality; analysis of the interview material with special attention to "giveaways" of hidden motives can provide further understanding. When

[6] See list of projective questions in Addenda to this chapter; cf. *The Authoritarian Personality* (*op. cit.*).

the results of this analysis are integrated with the projective material, and when the conclusions reached are viewed in the light of what is known from psychoanalytic investigation of similar cases,[7] a meaningful formulation of the most important deeper personality needs may be achieved.

Dependence. After a reading of Mack's interview, one might be inclined to say that his dependence—his wish to be taken care of, to have someone to lean upon—is hardly below the surface. He tells us straight out that he missed his mother very much, that he relied upon his sister's care, that there have been times when he has turned to the Bible for comfort; and when he speaks of his approaching marriage it seems plain that he is attracted by the prospect of having someone take care of him. Yet there is sufficient indication that Mack does not really accept his present dependence. It is only under special conditions that the need for love and support comes into the open. The first condition is that this need be made to appear as belonging to the past, as an aspect of his former self that he has, as it were, got over: there *were* times when he would have turned to a mother. The second condition is that the need be justified by the fact of illness. It is as if he felt that being physically ill is beyond one's control and that in this circumstance one cannot be blamed, or accused of being weak, if he accepts help from others. Thus, it is during periods of illness that he likes to turn to the Bible and it is because of his stomach condition that he can tolerate the idea of his wife's working and cooking for him. And even when these conditions are met, Mack does not seem to feel comfortable about being dependent; it is necessary for him to assert that, as a matter of fact, he is, and was, quite independent. This defensive procedure seems to go on unconsciously. Mack is not in the least aware of the bid for sympathy implicit in his recounting of his illnesses and handicaps.

There is, to be sure, nothing particularly remarkable about a young man's having feelings of dependence which he tries to suppress because they do not accord with his ideal of masculinity. But in Mack it seems that we are dealing with dependent impulses which are unusually strong, and which come to the surface in spite of his unusual pains to hold them in check. One might say that one reason he cannot allow himself openly to express these impulses is that they are childish, and that the reason they are so is because they were repressed in childhood and, hence, could not be transformed into more mature forms of expression. It is here that the mother's illness and death would seem to have played a crucial role. As noted above, there is reason to believe that during the early years of his life Mack received considerable love and attention from his mother and

[7] A study of a case very similar to Mack's, based entirely on questionnaire and projective material, has been reported by N. Sanford and H. Conrad, "High and Low Morale as Exemplified in Two Cases," *Character and Personality*, 13:207–27, 1944. See also N. Ackerman and M. Jahoda, *Anti-Semitism and Emotional Disorder* (New York: Harper, 1950); E. Jones, "On Quislingism," *International Journal of Psychoanalysis*, 22:1–6, 1941; N. Sandford, "Identification with the Enemy: Case Study of an American Quisling." *Journal of Personality*, 15:53–58, 1946.

felt close to her. Her illness intensified his need, and her death must have been a severe trauma for him. With the main source of love and comfort thus lost, it is natural that he would make every attempt to repress his longings for dependence. His sister and his aunt were hardly adequate substitutes. And, as has also been noted above, his attempts to get "mother's love" from the father were frustrated by the latter's "distance." Mack's references to his father's devotion and attention can be better understood as expressions of a wish rather than as statements of what the father was like in actuality.

The manifestations of dependence contained in Mack's responses on the TAT seem to have more to do with the father than with the mother. As the examiner points out, the need is for direction and advice rather than for love and understanding, and it appears to be aroused by the fear of rejection. This would seem to reflect certain aspects of Mack's relations with his father, in later childhood, more than it reflects the early tie to the mother. The hypothesis would be that after the mother's death the father became both disciplinarian and love object, and it became necessary for Mack to go strictly according to his father's wishes in order to avoid the danger of a further loss of love. It was not, however, that he expected, or even dared to seek, the kind of warmth and care that he had experienced at his mother's hand. This aspect of the dependence need had been firmly repressed. Both the father-dependence and the mother-dependence conflict at the present time with Mack's ideal of masculinity and can be admitted only when sufficiently rationalized, but it is the mother-dependence that lies deeper and has resulted in the building up of the more elaborate defenses. One way in which this deeper dependence seems to find indirect expression is through the use of symbols. The enjoyment of music and singing in church could have this significance. The same interpretation might be given to several of Mack's responses to the projective questions: his desire to see all of the world, his fascination with natural wonders and with rare jewels and metals. As substitutes for "mother" these cathected objects have the advantage of being sufficiently removed from the human, so that the forces of repression, originally directed against the need for mother, are not brought into play. Mack's dependence upon "things," e.g., food, the Bible, might conceivably be explained in the same way. The special importance of illness, as a condition under which dependence can be admitted and gratified, has already been discussed. It remains only to point out that Mack's stomach ulcer was very probably psychogenic and that in this case it could be regarded, in accordance with generally accepted theory,[8] as an expression par excellence of unconscious dependence.

Hostility against the father. If the attempt to reconstruct the actual behavior of Mack's father was successful, one might say that there was reason enough why our subject should feel hostile toward him. Silence

[8] See, for example, E. Alexander, *et al.*, "The Influence of Psychological Factors upon Gastrotestinal Disturbances; A Symposium," *Psychoanalytic Quarterly*, 3:501–588, 1934.

and distance on the father's part when the son wants to be loved, authoritarian discipline without any demonstration of its purpose—these are stimuli which regularly arouse aggression, and there is no reason to suppose that Mack was an exception. But if Mack has such impulses they must be severely inhibited, for at no time does he allow himself freely to blame or to criticize his father. Indeed, the underlying hostility here hypothesized is very well concealed, and it is only by the maximum use of subtle cues that we become convinced of its existence.

In responding to the projective questions, Mack tells us that "anger" is the emotion which he finds most difficult to control. This is in keeping with his references, in the interview, to his "hot temper" and "stubborn nature." These expressions might be understood in the light of his need to impress us with his masculinity, to present himself as a man who is not to be trifled with. They might be dismissed as the whistling in the dark of a young man who in his overt behavior is—far from being aggressive —rather timid and deferential. But in another response to the projective questions—"murder and rape" are the worst crimes—we are given a hint that aggression might indeed be one of Mack's preoccupations, and when we come to the TAT, evidence that this is true accumulates. Here the analysis seems to reveal "underlying hostile feelings toward the world," "crude aggressive fantasies," and a tendency to "impulsive antisocial acts." A striking figure in the stories is that of a young man "who might do violence if pushed too far." We are given no direct indication of what might be the form of the violence or against whom it might be directed. The responses are like the bare and unqualified "anger" of the projective questions. But in the present light it seems clear that in that instance Mack was doing more than protesting his toughness; he was probably telling us the truth. Not that he frequently becomes angry and gets into trouble; rather, he is afraid he might become angry and release forces which, though not familiar to him, are vaguely imagined to be primitive and chaotic and likely to provoke disastrous retaliation.

What are the reasons for believing that this deep-lying hostility is directed primarily against the father? We have already seen that the father is the central figure in Mack's imagery of his childhood and that the father was the source of major frustrations. The TAT stories contain no instances in which heroes express aggression against father figures, but the TAT analysis contains indications that it is precisely this type of aggression that our subject is most concerned to control. Whereas hostility against women is clearly manifested by TAT heroes and can be regarded as a tendency that is accepted by Mack's ego, the primitive impulsive aggression of which we speak is exhibited only by characters whom the storyteller has been at pains to reject, and it may be regarded, therefore, as ego-alien. This ego-alien aggression is directed against powerful figures, against "oppressors." "The young man looks as if he might commit murder if oppressed." But the heroes do not fight oppression; instead, to quote the TAT analysis, they "identify themselves with the restraining force." Thus, the TAT material favors the hypothesis that underlying aggression against the father has immediately to be countered—disclaimed, redirected, or smothered—because the father is conceived as too strong and dangerous. And in this circumstance the aggression itself is felt to be dangerous.

In this light, a rereading of Mack's interview seems to show clearly the ambivalence of his feelings about his father. It is entirely necessary for Mack that every implied criticism of the father be taken back or counterbalanced by "good" traits; otherwise the hostility might come too much into the open, and with it, images of disastrous consequences. A rather poignant illustration of what Mack is up against is afforded by one of his responses to the projective questions. He gives as one of his two greatest assets, "ability to enjoy people's company." At first glance this might not seem to be much to be proud of, but in Mack's case it represents a real achievement. After telling us, in the interview, of his father's social withdrawal he says, "I looked at my father and saw that I had to do differently," and "I have gone in for social things in spite of a great dread of them." Going in for social things is an expression of rebellion against the father, and hence the "great dread." In no other instance, as far as our material goes, has Mack made so bold; and even here it must have been a comfort to him to know that "he [the father] was pleased and he encouraged me."

Submission, passivity, and homosexuality. With the single not very striking deviation just described, the general picture of Mack's surface attitudes toward his father is one of submission and admiration. And this despite the subject's claim to stubbornness and independence. One might say that his only recourse in the face of what he conceived to be the father's irresistible power was to submit—and then to gain a sense of adequacy by participating psychologically in the father's power. This, in the last analysis, is the homosexual solution of the Oedipus problem.[9] It is not surprising, therefore, to find in Mack's TAT productions clear indications of his fear of homosexual attack. (This is made manifest, primarily, in his treatment of the "hypnotist" picture.)

Even without this piece of direct evidence we would be led to hypothesize repressed homosexuality in order to explain some of the outstanding features of Mack's personality development. The material is replete with manifestations of authoritarian submission. As clear a manifestation as any, perhaps, is the conception of God "as strictly a man, one who would treat us as a father would his son." There would seem to be no doubt that Mack has longed for his father's love—as we should expect in a boy who lost his mother when he was six years old. He tried to replace the imagery of a bad, dangerous father with imagery of a good father who would spend "*all* of his time with us." But Mack is not able to admit this need. Even while *acting* in a submissive and deferential manner he seems to cling to the belief that he is very manly and self-

[9] For further discussion, see: S. Freud, "The Passing of the Oedipus Complex," *Collected Papers,* Vol. 3 (London: Hogarth Press, 1943); E. Jones, *op. cit.;* C. Thompson, "Changing Concepts of Homosexuality in Psychoanalysis," *Psychiatry,* 10:183–190, 1947.

sufficient. The reason for this self-deception, we can well believe, is that, for this subject, to submit to a man and so to gain his love has definite sexual implications. It may be connected with very primitive imagery of passivity and emasculation. One might say that Mack's homosexuality, repressed in childhood in a setting of sadomasochistic relations with the father, has remained on an infantile level; insufficiently sublimated, it cannot find gratification in friendly, equalitarian relations with men but instead determines that most such relations have to be on a dominance-submission basis.

Fear of weakness. It is Mack's repressed homosexuality, very probably, that is mainly responsible for his compelling fear of weakness. If weakness means emasculation, if it means being at the mercy of an irresistibly strong man, then it is not difficult to see why this subject should exert every effort to make himself appear impregnable.

Fear of weakness, and the need to conceal any signs of it, comes almost to the surface in Mack. As we shall see in a moment, it seems to lie immediately behind a number of his most pronounced manifest traits and attitudes. But just because Mack is so concerned to cover up his fear, direct evidence of its existence is not easy to obtain. Perhaps the closest he comes to an open admission is when he writes, in response to the projective question, "What mood or feelings are most disturbing?": "Physical weakness, perhaps due to ill health continued over the last four years." If the weakness is clearly physical and can be excused on the ground of ill health, then it can be fully admitted. But it is not physical weakness alone, but a general sense of inadequacy which seems to be expressed indirectly in Mack's response to the projective question pertaining to greatest assets: "A definite desire to raise myself physically, financially, and socially." Not that a desire to raise oneself is necessarily based upon an underlying sense of inadequacy; the argument that it is so based in Mack's case rests upon what appears to be the extraordinary emphasis that he places upon this desire and upon supporting indications from the TAT. It may be recalled that the analysis of Mack's stories gave considerable emphasis to the "underlying fears and feelings of inadequacy behind the desire to 'be a strong individual' or to 'be like most men.'"

The TAT throws rather direct light upon the sexual aspects of the fear of weakness. The manifest attitudes of contempt and distrust toward women seem clearly to derive from the idea that they will drag a man down or deprive him of his "strong character." It is because women are weak that they are not to be trusted; they are out to exploit the man and to reduce his manliness by involving him in the "sordid" business of sex.

The role of Mack's physical illness, particularly in childhood, in determining the fear of weakness should not be underestimated. We can well imagine that the experiences of illness rearoused the infantile anxiety of helplessness. More than this, the sense of being a "sickly boy" might have put Mack at a disadvantage in his relations with his Cousin Bud, so that homosexual feelings were aroused—with the consequences that have been discussed above. Again, the weaker Mack was in actuality, the stronger would the father appear to him; and it was the idea that the father was too strong and dangerous, we may suppose, that prevented any basic identification with him. This failure in identification would, by itself, be sufficient ground for the fear that he was not quite a man. The mother's illness and death was probably a factor here also. As suggested above, there is some reason to believe that in the early years of his life Mack tended rather strongly to identify with his mother. (His illness may, indeed, have been in some part an identification with her.) He still has his "softer side," as it were. But following her death this identification could hardly have remained as a source of inner security; on the contrary, Mack had had an experience well calculated to promote terrifying ideas of what it might mean to be feminine, and we should expect him to regard any feminine traits within himself primarily as areas of vulnerability.

This consideration of Mack's fear of weakness seems to throw further light on his struggle with dependence. It is very likely that he regards his dependent needs as signs of weakness—the same kind of weakness that has just been discussed—and that this is another reason why he cannot freely admit the existence of these needs. It is as if accepting help or love or comfort from a woman meant being somehow identified with her, and hence open to the dangers with which women have to contend. Accepting help or love or comfort from a man suggests being treated like a woman by that man, and hence threatened with the loss of masculinity. But because in his innermost self Mack would like to be treated in just this way, the sense of weakness is constantly stimulated, and no amount of counteractive striving can entirely dispel it.

DYNAMICS OF SURFACE BEHAVIOR AND ATTITUDES. Given these underlying trends—dependence; hostility against the father; submission, passivity, and homosexuality; and fear of weakness—it is possible to offer reasonable explanations for most of Mack's characteristic traits and attitudes. These surface trends can be understood in large part as derivations or transformations of the deep-lying needs we have discussed. Surface and depth are connected by means of well-known psychological mechanisms.

An abstract formulation of Mack's personality, in its genetic aspects, is sketched in its general outlines in the chart on page 154. Genetically early forces and events appear at the bottom of the chart, and the course of development is followed by reading upward, arrows indicating the directions of determination and the points at which it is applied. No attempt is made to indicate the nature of the causation in the various instances. A rough correspondence between order in the genetic sequence and degree of depth within the contemporary personality structure is assumed, the earliest reaction tendencies being regarded as those which now lie deepest within the personality.

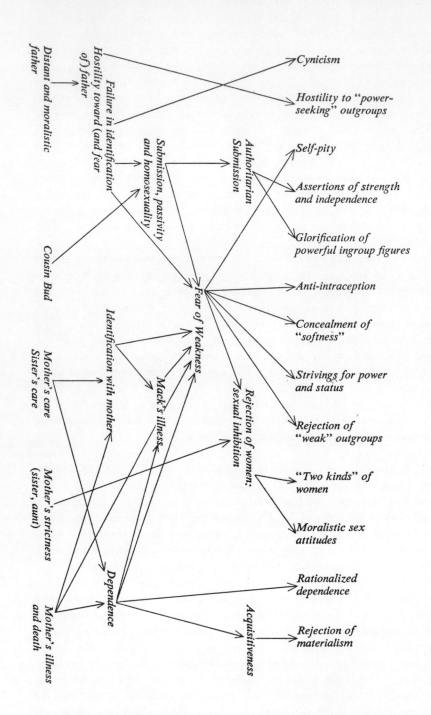

The Genetic Aspects of Mack's Personality

It may be noted at once that fear of weakness occupies the most central position on the chart. Deriving, as we have seen, chiefly from the deep-lying tendencies toward dependence on the one hand and toward submission, passivity, and homosexuality on the other, this fear necessitates several protective devices which lead to a variety of behavior patterns and general attitudes at the surface level. The fear has to be denied, allayed, and if possible overcome. We observe in Mack, therefore, attempts to conceal weakness by verbal denial and by presenting a facade of toughness, to get rid of weakness by projecting it onto other people, chiefly outgroups, and then condemning them on this score, to overcompensate for weakness by strivings for power and status and to allay the sense of weakness by aligning himself with powerful individuals and groups.

Little more need be said, it seems, concerning Mack's straight-out verbal denial of weakness. All through his interview he is at pains to tell us that he is not weak but strong and that if at any time he has appeared to be weak, then this was entirely justified by external circumstances. Of particular importance for Mack's susceptibility to fascist propaganda is the fact that the need to excuse weakness sometimes leads him into distortions of reality; he exaggerates the power and misreads the intentions of out-groups according to the formula: "If I appear to be weak, it is because they are so strong and out to take unfair advantage of me." The mechanism is the same as that which underlies the "persecution complex" so regularly associated with repressed homosexuality, though the conflict in Mack seems much less intense than that found in clinic patients. What we see on the surface here is the self-pity implicit in his thesis that he has done well considering all that he has had to contend with, and his projective thinking about such out-groups as the Jews, the New Deal, and the Washington bureaus. There can be little doubt that the problem with which Mack is struggling here was first presented to him in connection with his childhood relations with his father: "How can I be expected to oppose, to be strong and independent, to become a man, when father is so strong?" That he has been able to transpose the whole complex into the area of group relations saves him from having to oppose any individual or group that is really strong, and at the same time—since his ideas are now shared for various reasons by many other people—to achieve an appearance of "normality" that he would not have were he to concentrate on a single private "enemy."

Mack has made some attempt to conceal weakness by contriving a tough exterior. The leather jacket and the "nice equipment, for example a good rifle," are probably intended as unmistakable signs of masculinity. Mack is unable, however, to behave aggressively,[10] and hence the device of overcompensatory toughness does not serve him as well as it does many prejudiced men. But if he is unable to be physically tough, he can at least

[10] For findings on "passive anti-Semitism," see J. F. Brown, "A Modification of the Rosenzweig Picture-Frustration Test to Study Hostile Interracial Attitudes," *Journal of Psychology*, 24:247–272, 1947.

be tough-minded. His general attitude of anti-intraception can be understood as primarily an attempt to ward off any suggestion of "softness" that might be implicit in a more human way of looking at things.

The most primitive mechanism for dispelling a sense of weakness is the projection: "I am not weak, they are." Mack makes some use of this mechanism, though not in the crudest possible way. It is not so much that he sees weakness where none exists; rather, he thinks of people and groups in rigid categories of weak versus strong, and if any weakness is actually there it is what first strikes his eye, as it were, and he reacts to it in a particular way. His main concern is not to be in any way identified with weakness. Religious people, Jewish refugees, and women may actually be, in one sense or another, weak, but for Mack this is the *main* fact about these groups of people, and he must at all costs set them apart from himself. If one asks why he cannot have pity for weak people but instead actually hates them, the answer is twofold. In the first place, they remind him too much of his own weakness and all the dreadful fear with which it is associated. Second, and probably more important, he believes weak people to be dangerous. When he says that Jews "should not resent" their persecution we can readily infer that he believes they *do* resent it and will seek revenge in time. Women and Negroes, as the TAT analysis made clear, are regarded in this same way. It is to be granted that the strictness of Mack's mother, and later attempts of the sister and the aunt to carry out her policy, helped to teach Mack that women could be aggressive, but there is reason to believe that his notions about the dangerous aspects of "weak" people are based primarily upon a projection. The feeling of being persecuted aroused in him the strongest impulses to violence ("the young man looks like he might commit murder if oppressed") and he imagines that "downtrodden" people are similarly motivated.

Fear of the weak woman, as has been pointed out, would largely explain Mack's sexual backwardness, and this in turn offers sufficient basis for the moralistic sex attitudes expressed on the questionnaire and in the interview. How is the rejection of women to be reconciled with the fact that Mack idealizes his mother and intends to marry a girl with a "tremendously nice personality"? Here it must be considered that Mack actually has two conceptions of women: the "bad," weak, dangerous, exploitive, sexual woman who drags one down, and the good, wholesome, asexual one who gives. It is the former with whom one dares to have sex relations as "the aftermath of a New Year's party"; the latter is described mainly contrasting her with the former; she is not interested primarily in "a good time" or "in spending fellows' money" or in anything "sordid." Undoubtedly the imagery of this "good" woman derives in part from the imagery of the mother "who devoted her last strength to us kids." Certainly Mack would like to recapture some of the love and comfort that he received from his mother, provided this motive on his part can be adequately rationalized. It must be pointed out, however, that his appreciation of his mother seems somewhat overdone, enough so to suggest that his idealization of her is based partly on bad conscience and is an attempt to undo hostility that was directed against her. One cannot be very optimistic about the prospects for Mack's forthcoming marriage. While on the one hand he wants more than any woman can give him, on the other hand he feels it would be weak to ask his wife for anything at all. And this is not to mention the problem of how sex is to be introduced into the picture without spoiling it altogether.

It has already been suggested that Mack's strivings for power and status—his desire to "raise" himself—may be regarded as largely over-compensatory. Indeed, it would be very surprising if some kind of counter-active activity did not have a place among the devices he employs for overcoming the sense of weakness. From this point of view we can understand why it is that the needs for affiliation and recognition when they appear in the TAT are expressed mainly as a desire for having the members of his group look up to him, and why being an officer in the De-Molay and in his class at business school is important to him. The crucial role of the status drive in determining Mack's general ideology was first indicated in the analysis of his remarks concerning vocation and income. There it seemed clear that for him "going up" meant going up in a hierarchy; in his mind the existence of dominant groups and submerged groups was "natural" and, far from being concerned with changing this state of affairs, his aim was to have membership in the groups that were dominant. This is something different from the ordinary, everyday desire to improve one's lot in a sociological sense.

Here again Mack's thinking about group relations seems to be dominated by the rigid categories of "strong" and "weak." In the light of the foregoing personality analysis we may say that, once again, Mack brings to his interpretation of group relations images and attitudes which have remained unchanged since their genesis in the childhood relations with his father. That one was weak and the other strong was then the salient fact, and the persistence of this idea is a part of the fixation upon the traumatic situation of childhood. Since Mack could not conceive of himself as opposing the irresistibly strong father, his attempt at a solution was to convince himself that his father was "good" and so to align himself with him. This corresponds exactly with Mack's present approach to group relations. He does not oppose any group that is, in actuality, strong; instead, he argues that the strong ones are the good ones, and even while admiring and being subservient to them he overcomes weakness through gaining a sense of participation in their power.

This last is, of course, one aspect of the general attitude which we have termed authoritarian submission, and which we have previously seen to be an outstanding feature of Mack's manifest personality. To say that this attitude rests upon an attempt to overcome weakness through identification with power is to mention only one of its major sources. In so far as authoritarian submission is a means for overcoming weakness it stands as a kind of defense against the underlying homosexual submission and passivity; it remains to be pointed out that this surface trend offers at the same time gratification for these very same needs. In glorifying strong groups and individuals—"father figures"—he is expressing the need for a father's love and support and guidance, for a God who is "strictly man, greater than any on this earth, one that would treat us as a father would his son." Whereas most channels for the expression of this need are closed because they pass too close to weakness, it can in certain circumstances come into the open and be gratified—chiefly when the strong man or strong group is *strong enough*, strong enough so that there is a chance for participation in real power and strong enough so that submission can be readily excused. If one should ask why Roosevelt, who was almost universally experienced in this country as a father figure, was not happily accepted and admired by Mack instead of being rejected as a "dictator," the answer would seem to be that he was not strong enough; he "would come off second best in a contest with Winnie," while as for General Marshall, "nobody could alter his position."

Lacking a firmly internalized superego, a result of the failure to achieve a basic identification with the father, Mack looks outside of himself for guidance as to what to do and what not to do, and turns naturally to the authorities that seem strongest and most commonly accepted. He cannot, however, admit that this is the case, but clings to the illusion that he has a stubborn nature and is a man to make his own decisions.

This last suggests that Mack's relations with his authorities are not entirely harmonious, that he is not altogether comfortable with the arrangements that he has made. This is no more than we should expect from a consideration of the sources of his authoritarianism. It springs originally, as we have seen, from hostility toward his father. This hostility led to submission based on fear and, although submission offers other rewards as well, the element of fearful necessity still has an important role in Mack's attitude toward authority. It is this circumstance that gives his adherence to conventional standards the aspect of rigidity; since they have never been fully integrated with the ego, it is necessary to adhere to them strictly lest they be thrown overboard altogether.

Mack's hostility against minority groups and other groups and individuals is almost always justified by him on moral grounds. And the morality to which he appeals is that of the external authorities to which he is subservient. His manifest aggression is, so to speak, in the name of authority. He arranges things so that his conscience and his deepest antisocial impulses operate in collaboration. But if we ask what his conception of the out-group is and why it provokes him so, we are led back to the same sources that gave rise to his conceptions and attitudes concerning in-group authorities. Out-groups are hated for being selfishly and ruthlessly aggressive. (That out-groups are also "weak" may be a logical contradiction, but it is not a psychological one; Mack's thinking about social and political matters is dominated by unconscious processes and, hence, cannot be expected to conform with the rules of logic.) The power-seeking features of the out-group, no less than the admirably strong aspects of the "good" in-group, can be understood as derivatives of the infantile imagery of the father. Since Mack dared not oppose his father but could only submit to him, it became necessary to convince himself that the father was good. But this did not dissipate the original hostility against the father. Nor did Mack attempt to handle it by turning it against himself; one of the outstanding features of his case is the relative absence of self-criticism. What he did was *displace* the hostility onto out-groups; or, better, the frustrating, punishing, persecutory features which had to be denied in the father were seen as originating in out-groups who could then be hated in safety, because they were not strong in actuality, and in good conscience, because the traits ascribed to them were those which the in-group authorities would condemn. Thus each "good" trait that the father is said to have is the opposite of a "bad" trait which belongs to the image of the Jew: while the father's "greatest contribution was denying himself pleasures to take care of us kids," the Jews are not "interested in humanity"; while the father was renowned for his "honesty," one has to be careful of Jewish clothiers. At the same time, when it comes to the one trait in the father which Mack is almost inclined to criticize, that is, social withdrawal, one finds that it too looms large in the imagery of the Jew: they refuse "to mingle and become a part of our people"; "they would rather be alone." If the Jews have thus to bear the brunt of Mack's ambivalent feelings toward his father, there might be some comfort for them in the fact that his feelings toward them are also somewhat ambivalent. It may be recalled that Mack's explanation for what he supposes to be Jewish pressure on Congress and for the fact that Jews have been "fully repaid" for their part in the war effort is that "they are businessmen," and we know that he has nothing but admiration for businessmen, especially those who represent a "concentration of wealth in a certain class," i.e., "the big capitalists." Unfortunately, however, it is very doubtful that the Jews could ever benefit from the positive phase of Mack's ambivalence, for their supposed inability makes them more dangerous to him. The separation of the good father image from the bad is an essential of Mack's personality adjustment and he could no more see "good" in his image of the Jew than he can see "bad" in his father.

As far as our material goes the only outlet for the expression of aggression that Mack has is through his ethnocentrism, that is, through authoritarian aggression against various kinds of out-groups. There is, however, one other manifestation of underlying aggression which may afford some vent for his feelings, and that is cynicism. It seems clear enough now that its major source is the bottled-up resentment with which the present analysis has been so largely concerned. We must understand, however, that in cynicism the destructiveness is directed against the self as well as against the world.[11] Not only is the subject's own aggressiveness projected onto other people, who are then accused of being acquisitive and

[11] For additional findings on cynicism, based on a questionnaire similar to the type employed in this study, see N. Sanford, H. S. Conrad, and K. Franck, "Psychological Determinants of Optimism Regarding the Consequences of the War," *Journal of Psychology*, 22:207–235, 1946.

warlike, but contempt for other people seems to be closely related to contempt for himself. In Mack's case—and this probably holds generally for authoritarian personalities—the self-contempt derives from his sense of weakness, and this, as we have seen, is the aftermath of his surrender to his father. This surrender cannot be wholly excused, and as long as he cannot permit himself to feel aggressive toward those who are actually strong, there will be a nagging reminder that he, in reality, is weak. He tries to free himself from this thought by projecting the contemptibleness onto mankind, and thus there is some basis for saying that he hates others because he hates himself.

To complete the picture it is necessary to return now to the topic of Mack's dependence. The sense of deprivation that followed the loss of his mother, and the growing feelings that because of his weakness people might leave him out or take advantage of him, seem to have generated in him a general attitude of acquisitiveness and, more specifically, a feeling that somebody ought to give him something. The highest praise of mother, father, sister, or fiancée is that they gave or will give to him, and one of the major characteristics of "bad" people is that they are selfish or "not interested in humanity." It is not difficult to infer that his concern with justice is primarily concern with getting something. A man who can speak sentimentally of justice in one breath and almost in the next speak of barring Hitler's victims from this country on the ground that they are "Europe's misfits" is hardly employing the term "justice" in its basic sense. But apparently his acquisitiveness encounters his conventional moral standards and has to be reacted against. He is very careful to assure us that he has "repaid" what he got from others, and he is moralistically temperate in stating his objectives with respect to income. The importance of this conflict about acquisitiveness for Mack's social outlook lies in the fact that it supplies the basis for another accusation against out-groups. They are said to be "materialistic" and "money-minded." This seems to be in part a projection, since out-groups are accused of doing exactly what he and his own group do but would like to deny, and in part a mere complaint about the fact that the world goes its own way without paying much attention to him and his wants.

A remarkable feature of Mack's dependence is that although it has been rendered ego-alien and as an unconscious force leads to the misjudgment and rejection of other people, so much of it still finds expression in behavior. (This has been brought out in the previous discussion of underlying dependence.) This is testimony to his outstanding facility in rationalization, something that is made possible, as it seems, by his unwillingness to look at himself.

This brings us to a place where we must consider Mack's stereotypy, a characteristic of his thinking that is highly pronounced and, clearly, of the greatest significance for his prejudice. In one sense, his stereotyped thinking about social phenomena seems to be related to his general attitude of anti-intraception and to be dependent, in part at least, upon the same underlying conditions. It might be said that one reason why Mack's explanations of social phenomena are so primitive and oversimplified (for example, differences among ethnic groups are categorical and due to differences in blood strain) is that he is unable to make any use of social or psychological theories of determination. This can hardly be due to a lack of intelligence or of information, for an examination of his interview leaves a strong impression that with regard to those factors he is above the average for college students. A stronger argument could be made for the view that his is an educational deficiency, that he simply has not been subjected to instruction about man and society. But this is such a widespread phenomenon in this country that it can hardly be used to explain why Mack stands out from the group. Besides, he could have made some use of the social and psychological viewpoints that are available, but he chose not to. And, for that matter, the fact that anti-intraceptive education is so widespread has itself to be explained, and we can well believe that factors of individual psychology have an important role to play. In Mack's case at least there is a strong suggestion that he cannot reckon with either the sociology or the psychology of other people because he cannot examine the conditions or determinants of his own behavior. Ideas or observations that would be necessary to lend breadth or depth to his view of the world or of himself cannot enter the picture, because they would arouse too much anxiety. It is as if—to put it somewhat dramatically—*he can see only what he has seen before and learn only what he already knows.*

In our consideration of Mack's anti-intraception we were given reason to believe that he has to avoid introspection or attention to human factors in order to maintain his sense of being tough-minded. The fuller analysis of his personality shows that his problem is much more serious: he has to deal with a variety of strong unconscious impulses which are not integrated with the ego and which he feels—not without good cause—might get out of hand. In short, the task of maintaining his repressions imposes a heavy burden upon him. This state of affairs has been described as ego weakness, and Mack's case offers an excellent illustration of this concept. The problems with which he was faced as a child—problems centering around the loss of his mother and the necessity for making an adjustment to the "distant" father—were too much; they were more than the undeveloped ego could handle. Primitive defenses, chiefly repression and countercathexis, were necessary; and since that time, the ego has had to devote so much energy to maintaining these defenses that it could not develop normally. It remains narrow and constricted, in danger of being overwhelmed by emotional impulses from within or authoritative commands from without. Since the inner impulses are more to be feared than the outer authorities, there is rigid adherence to the standards of the latter, but since these authorities are not accepted in any fundamental way, this adherence could be given up altogether in circumstances that made it safe to do so. Since the traumatic experiences of childhood have not been integrated with the ego, the categories with which the child structured the world have persisted, in more or less unmodified form, to dominate contemporary thinking. Since there is little that is truly *inside* the personality, there can be little tolerance of inner conflict and little self-criticism; instead there is an attitude of hostile watchfulness toward a world that is largely alien.

THERAPEUTIC CONSIDERATIONS

Sooner or later, as we examine the case of Mack and the problem of authoritarianism in general, we must confront the question: What can we do about it? It would be a sad state of affairs indeed if one were forced to conclude that the only thing that could be done would be to give intensive psychotherapy to all people in whom authoritarianism in personality was highly developed. Fortunately, it appears that this syndrome may be heavily influenced by the external field forces. The stress placed here upon personality *structure* has not been intended to suggest something fixed and solid, impregnable to influence from outside. Not only is authoritarianism in personality conceived of as more or less normally distributed; it is further believed that almost anyone is capable of having his authoritarianism evoked by sufficiently strong stimuli. The structure itself exists within a larger dynamic organization of personality, the whole of which is in some kind of interaction with the contemporary environment. Little enough, to be sure, is known about the conditions of change or of fixity in such a structure; but it is safe to assume that it is accessible to study by experimental methods. Christie (1949), for example, has shown that rigidity in problem solution—something which has appeared to be a factor in authoritarian personality structure—increases as a function of experimental frustration.

One may conceive of two opposite approaches to the problem of how to reduce authoritarianism and prejudice; and it may well be that progress will be made in the degree to which these two approaches become integrated. The extreme of the one approach is individual psychotherapy; the extreme of the other would be attempts at manipulating the social situation without an understanding of the people who live in it.

It should be remarked concerning individual psychotherapy on authoritarianism of personality that it is not only impractical but very difficult. The person high on the F scale rarely seeks psychotherapy but rather resists the idea; and once a start has been made, the technical problems are trying. One case (Sanford, 1946) has been reported that is fairly representative of the psychopathic type of high scorer on F. Four years of therapy with this individual produced no satisfactory progress. To establish any kind of relationship that would involve him in the therapy was difficult enough; and, when a relationship was finally established, it was, as one might expect, an authoritarian one. With the therapist in the role of authority and this patient in the role of authoritarian follower, any progress in the analysis was exceedingly difficult; he would either act out his new role or else leave the situation altogether.

The feasibility of steps toward the ultimate control of situations that evoke or inhibit authoritarian behavior is perhaps somewhat more hopeful. Attention will have to be given to every type of social structure, ranging from the small group to the society at large. This is a task in which all of the social sciences might well take part. Unless, however, these studies of the social complex take account of the potentialities and readiness within the individuals involved, the major implications of research on the authoritarian personality will have been lost.

It may be hoped that knowledge gained from the intensive study of individuals can be combined with knowledge of group structure and functioning to form an integration of the opposing approaches mentioned. What group structures, what institutional patterns, what cultural trends appeal to or serve to counteract authoritarian tendencies in personality?

At the present time, group psychotherapy and certain experiments in education seem to offer the best samples of the integration being urged. Freedman and Sweet (1954) have offered evidence that patients with many features of the F pattern actually respond better in certain forms of group psychotherapy than they do in individual therapy. And many workers are exploring the possibilities of bringing into the classroom some of the techniques for involving the subject and for removing resistance that have been developed in connection with individual psychotherapy.

George Stern (1964) cites the experience of a social science instructor who was assigned, without his knowledge, sections of students which were composed solely of either authoritarians or antiauthoritarians. He observed at the outset that the authoritarian students lacked curiosity and initiative. He found it difficult to get them involved in a class discussion, although direct questions indicated that they were well informed on the text, and he was constantly tempted to lecture them. Their behavior was in marked contrast to the questioning, critical attitude of the antiauthoritarians:

"The instructor emphasized that his primary objective was to stimulate the free exchange of ideas, superabundant among the antiauthoritarians but initially nonexistent for the authoritarians. His efforts to get the authoritarians to respond included: (1) continued pressure in the form of direct questions, (2) a refusal to lecture or to provide direct answers, (3) encouragement and acceptance of any response from the students, and (4) insistent adoption of absurdly extreme positions."

Finally in the eighth week of the course, after the instructor had openly "tried to seduce them to totalitarianism," the students were sufficiently aroused that they began to ask interpretive questions and to behave in a manner similar to the antiauthoritarians. The new involvement was eventually reflected in the group's achievement. While other authoritarians had tended to dislike this particular course and to do poorly in it, authoritarians in the experimental section did just as well on the final common objective examination as did the antiauthoritarians. And we may expect that a great deal more development took place than could be measured by that examination.

It is not argued, of course, that such an approach is likely to be effective with extreme cases of authoritarianism. Obviously, however, most people are not extreme but "middle" on the F scale, and one may suppose that they are prepared to move in either direction. For them, education in general seems to have some effect, as is indicated by the fact that scores on the F and E scales tend to drop as amount of education increases. We may recall here the case of Penny, whose F scores dropped from 96 to 61 during her four years at college (see Chapter 4). There is evidence that experience with the psychological and social sciences is particularly effective—as knowledge of authoritarian personality trends would lead one to expect. Awareness of self and of one's relations to social processes works directly against authoritariansm; one might hope that educational offerings having such awareness as their objective would be enormously expanded, as they might easily be.

Lest the dissolution of authoritarianism which we observed in Penny lead us to overconfidence in higher education, we must also note the inability of the same college to effect any reduction in the authoritarianism of another student, Pat, whose case we discuss in Chapter 11. Clearly, this is a field of great difficulties as well as great promise.

The preceding remarks have concerned authoritarianism in the adult personality. The prevention of authoritarianism in children is a different matter. Knowledge of the kind of child training that favors ego development and the internalization of standards is becoming very widespread in the United States, particularly in the middle classes, and a movement toward nonauthoritarian principles and practices is being pushed along by the mass media of communication. The coming of age of another generation may mark an appreciable falling off in the amount of authoritarianism in this country.

ADDENDA

PROJECTIVE QUESTIONS

1. We all have times when we feel below par. What moods or feelings are the most unpleasant or disturbing to you?
2. We all have impulses and desires which are at times hard to control but which we try to keep in check. What desires do you often have difficulty in controlling?
3. What great people, living or dead, do you admire most?
4. There is hardly a person who hasn't said to himself, "If this keeps up, I'll go nuts!" What might drive a person nuts?
5. What do you consider the worst crimes a person could commit?
6. It seems that no matter how careful we are, we all sometimes have embarrassing moments. What experiences make you feel like sinking through the floor?
7. If you knew you had only six months to live, but could do just as you pleased during that period, how would you spend your time?
8. We get a feeling of awe when something seems to us wonderful, or

impressive, or really important. What things would give you the greatest feeling of awe?

MACK'S THEMATIC APPERCEPTION STORIES

Mack was presented a series of pictures depicting different kinds of characters in various situations (Morgan and Murray, 1935; Murray, 1943). He was asked to use his imagination to make up a dramatic story for each picture. In each story, he was instructed to cover what was going on in the present, what the people were thinking and feeling, what had led up to the events in the present, and what would happen in the end. (The TAT was administered and scored by Betty Aron, who also contributed to the interpretation of Mack's stories.)

M 1. This would indicate to me a man in distress and a comforting friend. Some accident may have happened, or a death in the younger man's family. There is a certain dullness to the man's expression, probably from the great shock. [*Are the two men related?*] It's possible, but I can't say; I think they may be just friends. I doubt if it's his father. The efforts of the older man to help the other fellow see the brighter side and get him on a steady course again will be successful. The young fellow is a deeply brooding type and maybe won't be too successful, or at best only temporarily. The young fellow indicates the type of person who might do violence if pushed too far. I think he could easily murder somebody on being oppressed. I think he will never completely get over the shock of the death and it affects him in such a way that it makes him hard to get along with from then on.

M 2. This is a young fellow and his girl. They are all dolled up for the occasion. They are just starting out for the night. The style of his clothing is foreign to me; I never saw that sort of thing before. The girl looks to be about 17 and the man about 21—considerably older. After a show, they go some place and eat. Then he gets the girl home about ten or eleven o'clock. From the age of the girl they would get in at a reasonable hour. [*Are they related?*] No, I don't think they are; they are not the same type. I don't think they are husband and wife; they just go together. The girl has a nice, pleasant personality. He is not so deep, and he has a less full character than the girl. The partial view of the other fellow gives me an idea of another story. This involves the same original setup except that they had their pictures taken at a party. This man stepped up and made a smart remark to make them smile for the picture. That fellow's dress doesn't correspond to the girl's. He looks like he was from another period. It might be the early '30's. Maybe the suit was designed for a gag. They have other dates but they gradually drifted apart.

M 3. My first impression is from what I read in newspapers, you know, about the war. He is saying good-bye to his mother. He is of military age—about 23. His mother is about in her early 50's. He is advising her not to worry. He says he will write and asks her to keep him informed of the folks and his friends. He tries to lead her to believe he will see her again soon—like most men would. He seems to be a strong individual. He is clean-cut. Of course, we always like to hope they will all come back, but I can't help but guess that he will not come back. He was killed in the war. They are very close and yet are not the kind to show a lot of observable affection and make a lot of one another. They used to kid one another, and make fun of one another, and yet if one got in trouble they all came to his rescue. That's the kind of family they were.

M 4. It looks something like a street off the main track in New York City. It's a run-down section of the city. These pictures are cleverly done— they don't tell you anything. [*What preceded this picture?*] Well, it's perhaps on a Saturday or Sunday and this businessman is on his way home. I don't think he is very well, all bundled up like that. I think he must be a tailor. He isn't too well off, but is better off than most of his neighbors. He is a family man. As for the woman, it's difficult to give a motive for her. She has something to sell, is poor, and can just keep her family in food and clothes. There is no relationship between these people. It is just the end of the day and each is going home. Each represents a class—the well-off and the poor. This is just a typical scene.

M 5. Oh, oh! This is apt to be rather sordid. It doesn't represent a family scene to me! It may be a prostitute, and I see the old bottle there. This may be a young American down in the tropics; he is dressed in white because of the temperature. As for the woman, it's difficult to say because of the shadows, but she appears of darker skin. The place has crude furnishings. [*What preceded?*] The natural assumption is that they had sexual intercourse. The fellow is about half drunk and is about to consume more. The fellow looks kind of "hang-dog"; perhaps he regrets his recent act or perhaps his station in life. He is down and out and liquor isn't much of a boon to him. He has sufficient depth of character to take himself out of a place like that and to genuinely regret what he did to the woman. She doesn't enter into the story, except to be the object of his lust. He is a better type than she. He can take care of himself. He finally drags himself out of such surroundings and gradually amounts to something. Do I take too long? I get quite involved in these stories.

M 6. This is a public disturbance, perhaps a strike or a race disturbance. He has some negroid features. He started a riot and has now been separated from the group he organized. The police have frightened him and he expects the worst. He is lodged in the local jail for a time and is scared out of such activities again. Maybe he was the fall guy for the group. Without the crowd influence he was pretty docile.

M 7. These people are related. They are mother and son, since their features correspond. She is about 60 and he about 25. He has just told her something he has done which causes her grief and apprehension. She can't condone it, and is shocked. He's upset too, like he'd rather not have told her but had to. He doesn't look the type to get into trouble. This picture gives me trouble. Well, it's the expressions on their faces. This man was responsible for the death of someone loved by both the mother and the man. It was not a crime, but an auto accident. It was sort of negligence on his part and he feels responsible. His mother turns away at first, then comes back to him and decides to help him. It was this way: this fellow in the picture and a friend went for a ride. There was an accident, and this fellow (in the picture) was driving. He was negligent in some way or another, and caused the death of the person riding with him. He is now telling his mother all about it. Well, he and his mother talk it all over, and she helps him by giving him some good advice. She tells him it could have happened to anyone, and that the thing to do now is to forget it and just go right on living as usual. She tells him it is bad to keep thinking about it. [*Does he?*] Yes, he doesn't let it drag his life down. It finally passes out of his memory.

M 8. Well, this suggests a doctor and his patient. Yet, the gesture gives me the idea it might be a hypnotist at work. I don't know much about the field of hypnosis. The patient is unconscious about the face, but his legs aren't relaxed. Usually such performances are put on on the stage, and this seems to be in a private home. Do people keep their clothes on while receiving hypnotic treatment? [*I'm sure I don't know; let's just use our imagination.*] I guess this is a scene on the stage of a theater. This man is a hypnotist and is directing the performance along the lines that would be funny to the audience. The other fellow was taken from the audience and later joins his friends who ask him a lot of silly questions. The performance ends and all go home.

M 9. These people are Negroes, of course. It's the grandmother and the grandson. I'm not very familiar with Negro features, but they look alike, these two. She is a kindly old lady. She looks toil-worn, and has had a hard life of work. She is dressed well. I guess it's a portrait in the home. Some Negroes carry their fortune on their back. These may be of a higher type and are better educated than most Negroes. She was a slave and was freed, and gradually accumulated some money. They are quiet folks. It may be they are enjoying a musical here. After their picture is taken, they go back to their regular routine lives—he to school and she to helping their children to run their homes and just being generally useful.

M 10. This is Christ on the cross, in the midst of flames or smoke. I can hardly reconcile myself to the fact that this is just a photo. It might be a trick picture. Jesus appears life-sized, and so does the cross, yet I don't know of a church with this sized crucifix. Here is a young boy of 8 or 9. In Sunday school he just received a vivid portrayal of Jesus on the cross by a very fine preacher and is very much impressed. That night he has trouble sleeping soundly and while in a semiconscious state sees this image. He is just coming out of this dream when the image fades. This experience stays with him the rest of his life. I know I can remember a few dreams I had at about that age. [*Do you think they influenced you?*] I think they really did, all my life. This boy wakes up in the morning and tells his parents about it, and retains this memory the rest of his life.

CHAPTER ELEVEN

The Acting-Out of Impulse in Late Adolescence: A Case Study

When one interviews large numbers of female college freshmen as we had occasion to do in connection with the Mellon Foundation studies at Vassar, one finds it easy—perhaps all too easy—to divide them into two groups. On the one hand, there are those who seem primarily to need awakening, broadening, opening to experience. They seem to have arrived at a structuring of personality which is premature and brittle, and one wonders whether much change can occur without experiences that might be shattering. In Chapter 4 we examined a case of this type and discussed the processes by which such a person might be induced to change and develop. On the other hand, we also see students who seem primarily to need self-discipline, organization, integration. They seem already to have attained more freedom than they are quite entitled to, there being a serious question as to whether so much expression of impulse is under adequate control by the ego, to say nothing of the possibility that some of these latter students are "impulse-ridden."

The dimension on which these types of students fall at opposite extremes has been called *impulse expression*, a rather broad dimension which extends from compulsiveness, submissiveness, and passivity at one extreme to impulsiveness, assertiveness, and adventurousness at the other. Impulse expression, while certainly not limited to students, invites particular scru-

A modified version of a case study originally included in "The Freeing and the Acting Out of Impulse in Late Adolescence: Evidence from Two Cases," in R. W. White (ed.), *The Study of Lives* (New York: Atherton Press, 1963).

tiny during the college years because it has been shown to be one of the areas in which the greatest changes are produced by higher education.

In the course of the studies at Vassar (Sanford, Webster, and Freedman, 1957), we developed a scale to measure impulse expression (IE). The final IE scale included 123 items, drawn mostly from the Minnesota Multiphasic Personality Inventory (Hathaway and McKinley, 1943), the California Psychological Inventory (Gough, 1957), and Maslow's Scale for Dominance-Feeling in Women (1940). These items were considered to be expressive of one or another of Murray's "needs and traits" (1938) and could be classified into the following four clusters:

Ascendance. "When I work on a committee I like to take charge of things." "I have often either broken rules—school, club, etc.—or inwardly rebelled against them." "I go out of my way to meet troubles rather than try to escape them."

Sensation. "I like to talk about sex." "When I get bored I like to stir up some excitement." "I get excited very easily."

Endocathection and intraception. "I have very peculiar and strange experiences." "I think I take primarily an aesthetic view of experience." "Some of my friends think that my ideas are impractical if not a bit wild."

Radical sentiments. "We cannot know for sure whether or not there is a god." "Politically I am something of a radical." "I believe women ought to have as much sexual freedom as men."

There has been one study in which scores of the IE scale have been related not merely to measures based on subjects' self-ratings but to an external criterion. In a three-day assessment of fifty women in their early forties, five psychologists independently described the subjects by means of a 600-item adjective check list.[1] These women had been given the IE scale, but the raters had no knowledge of the test scores. The following are some of the adjectives that were associated to a statistically significant degree with high and with low scores on IE:

High scorers: big-boned, impulsive, irrepressible, angular, loud, tall, full of pep, erratic, vigorous, restless, impatient, stylish, uninhibited, excitable, outgoing.

Low scorers: retiring, silent, reliable, inhibited, reserved, stolid, humorless, shy, withdrawn, plain, faint-voiced, meek, painstaking, quiet, weary.

If a subject's responses to all the the items on the IE scale were in the direction of impulse expression, he would obtain a score of 123. In a sample of 906 college women the mean score was 45.9, with a standard deviation of 16.0.[2] Men usually score about 10 points higher than women of the same college level. Various studies have shown that seniors score

[1] An account of this study may be found in R. Jung, Analysis of Psycho-social Development: A Study of Adult, Educated Women, Ph.D. thesis, Harvard University, 1962.

[2] For a full account of the statistics of the IE scale and for reports of various studies involving this instrument, see C. Bereiter, "Descriptions and Analyses of the VAI Scales," Bureau of Educational Research, University of Illinois, Urbana, Ill. Mimeographed.

significantly higher on IE than freshmen; the mean for senior women is usually around 50 and that for freshmen women around 40. In one study involving 175 women who were tested as freshmen and again as seniors, it was found that IE score increased in 89 percent of the cases, decreased in 8 percent, and showed no change in 3 percent.

In interpreting the higher IE scores of seniors, my colleagues and I supposed that a "lifting of repression" or some other kind of liberating, or perhaps strengthening, of basic emotional impulses occurred in college, and that this was sometimes a result of certain educational processes. But we could not speak with much assurance for, although the scale has validity in the ordinary sense of the word, it seemed clear that different subjects obtained extreme scores for different reasons. The scale is of the "self-report" variety, and its items have little subtlety; it expresses personality at the level of conscious attitude. One should expect no one-to-one relations between a pattern of such attitudes and either observable behavior or deeper processes of the personality. It is not clear, then, how changes in the IE scores over time are to be explained.

It seemed to us that high scores on the scale could be obtained either by subjects who were "impulse-ridden" or who "acted out" their impulses, being unable to control them even when they wanted to, or by subjects who were "free," in the sense that they could express their impulses without inducing serious conflicts, either within themselves or with society. Again, subjects with low scores on the IE scale might be integrated and stable but relatively simple in personality structure, or they might be rigidly restrained by fear of external or internal punishing agents.

It may be hoped that the IE scale can eventually be modified, or a supplementary scale developed, to discriminate among these types of extreme scorers.

In a sample of sixty college freshmen, correlations of the IE scale with the E and F scales described in Chapter 10 (Adorno *et al.*, 1950) were found to be —.04 and —.03 respectively (Sanford, 1957). The Social Maturity scale, which was designed to reflect the psychological rather than the ideological aspects of authoritarianism (psychological authoritarianism reversed), correlated only .21 with IE. The absence of any high correlation between the IE scale and measures of authoritarianism means that among high scorers on IE there will be some subjects who are high and some who are low on authoritarianism, and similarly for those who score low on IE. It may be that this is a significant basis for differentiating among subjects who are at one or the other extreme on impulse expression.

In Chapter 4 we discussed Penny, a student who scored in the low quartile of freshmen on IE but who moved into the high quartile by the time she was a senior. She provided an example of the person who can freely express impulses under the control of a strong ego. Now let us turn to another young woman, Pat, a sharply contrasting case. On entering college, her score of 57 on IE was already in the top quartile of freshmen. By the time she graduated, she received the highest IE score in her class—

102, a degree of impulse expression that is rarely exceeded among college women. But as we shall see, the nature of Pat's "freedom" and the dynamics that underlie it are very different from those observed in Penny. She seems rather to be acting out her impulses for purposes of defense.

PAT AS A FRESHMAN

In respect to social and educational background, we may describe Pat in almost identical terms to Penny: She came from an upper-middle-class family, attended for twelve years an expensive private school, and arrived at Vassar well prepared academically and secure socially. A letter of recommendation from her preparatory school said of her:

"Patricia has good stuff in her which college should bring out. She is creative and imaginative, and shows marked qualities of leadership. She will always be active, and as she matures she will be a useful citizen.

"Her interests are legion. She is a member of the dancing club, and is secretary of the senior class.

"I think she will do good work in subjects in which she is interested. She will enjoy college life and I think will contribute much to it."

From Pat's freshman interviews we can detect some of the traits which made her already a high scorer on impulse expression:

[*Rooming group and friends.*] "Three roommates; knew one in school, know one other slightly, met the fourth at graduation time at her school. We get along perfectly, although different one from another. We see each other on vacations; go to parties together. We eat together when not dieting. We bought new furniture and hate to split it up. Will probably room together next year. Lots of girls I've met would make good additions. I never had roommates before. I would like about 10.

"I probably have more friends outside our house than inside it."

[*Interests, activities, preferences.*] "Sports have faded out a bit, except swimming and riding. I love singing; there's a group in our dorm. Usually save riding for summer. I own a horse.

"I play the piano by ear—jazz; I love jazz, New Orleans. Roommate is converting me to progressive; not sure yet but I have an open mind.

"I gave up painting at 13. Had modern dancing in school for 12 years and am taking it here. I love dancing in any form.

"I'll go to any movie, but am particular about what I like and don't like.

"I love travel; have been to Europe, South Carolina, St. Louis. I hope some day to go to Africa. I love reading about it, and about the jungles of South America; love animals.

"I like lobster, snails; almost anything—Italian food, sweets.

"I like Scotch and champagne, but hate gin and beer. I haven't felt it much and rather enjoyed it, but felt guilty.

"The record player is going all the time; the four of us have every type of music. I bought a lot of Calypso. Not much time for books here.

I like morbid—Russian—novels, books on the supernatural, anything on Africa. I like scary books. We have an impressive library but not much time to read it."

[*Weekends.*] "Mondays and Fridays run into weekends; Tuesday, Wednesday, and Thursday I get my mind on my work. I do most of my studying in the middle of the week, and rest or loaf on weekends; it's hard to study then.

"Have used up all my over-nights. Usually go to the City first, then to one of the other [coeducational] schools."

[*Men.*] "I go out with brother's friends; they are so much more serious. Not sure enough yet of one boy. One blind date worked out fine; it was arranged through a roommate. I meet men more at parties in the city than here.

"In a man I like a sense of humor—ability to laugh at himself. He should be thoughtful, unselfish. I can't stand conceit. I like intelligence."

[*Academic work.*] "I picked this college over others mainly because of the art department—I have heard so much about it—and also because of the location.

"I went to the same day school for 12 years. After 12 years you get a feeling of complete security. You know everybody. This year the girls began to get the feeling that this college was only for girls from our school.

"Up to the ninth grade I was very mischievous, a bit of a problem, not really interested in my work, always getting into trouble. I was always interested in athletics. After the ninth grade I got elected to a school office; I wanted that more than anything, so I calmed down. I was actually something of a leader; quite active.

"I didn't expect the feeling of security I now have. I expected a bigger place. Maybe it's just that freshmen are looked after. It seems we're practically tucked into bed.

"The work is challenging all right. It's like school but more of it. I never thought there would be day-to-day work. But I like it, and have been used to it. I'm afraid that if I were given two months to do a paper I would save it 'til the last week.

"Art was at the head of my list of subjects. I always loved it. We had a general course in school, and I never forgot a word. Also, my brother knows a lot about it. French—well, I had to take a language, and French is easiest. Had to take a science, and so I have astronomy. I can use my math, but it is my hardest course. I didn't want to take English, but couldn't figure out how to avoid it. I was told I ought to take it; now, even more than art, it is my favorite course. We have a fantastically good professor. He got half of the class in tears reading *Troilus and Cressida*. He's personally interested in you.

"I'm doing very well in English, well in art, and well in French, but I should work harder. Astronomy is a struggle, and I'm just passing. I like it, but I understand a week later than the others.

"At the beginning of the year I would have said I was going to major in art, absolutely; but now I'm doing so well in English.

"I know my English professor quite well. We have had some long conferences. I see a lot of my astronomy teacher but can't really get to know her. Don't know French teacher at all. Mr. C. is my adviser; I can always think up a few problems for him. I have never had men teachers until this year. I find them more understanding, broad-minded, less opinionated. I'm judging primarily by my English teacher; if I ever had a problem, I would think automatically of going to him.

"About the future I don't know. I want to get a job but won't know what until I have gone further. I'll live away from home, in an apartment with other girls, and eventually will get married. But that can wait; I'm having too much fun; I don't want to settle down. At the same time, I don't want to make bachelorhood permanent."

In the life history interview, Pat tells us something of herself at earlier stages of development:

[*Self as a child.*] "Terribly, terribly mischievous—being sent out of room—at 10 or 11 years. Class clown. Mother was at school almost every day. Was given responsibility at 11: keeping chairs pushed in—improved. Never been shy; but being kept in one school gives security. I always had friends."

[*Self as an adolescent.*] "Began to notice boys, and to forget horses. Ever since I have been interested in boys and athletics."

[*Early sex information and attitudes.*] "Menstruation at 12, close to 13. I looked forward to it. Mother probably had told me something, but older brother (six years older) told me all the details. Also I grew up on a farm. Mother talked, but she was quite 'hearts and flowers' about it. Grandmother never would tell mother anything about sex. Father was also innocent; they both learned together. Mother thought grandmother should have talked more.

"In the eighth grade at school we got crushes on seniors. I cried at every graduation. My sister does the same thing.

"Brother teased me, chased me, tickled me. I used to love it, and never got mad at him. At 13 or 14 brother would often take me and my date out. Mother, father would go to him for advice about me. He can be stricter than parents. He had European morals. He was jealous of any attention to me. I go with his friends now; we give parties together, etc."

At the end of Pat's freshmen year, her faculty advisers chose the following adjectives (from a list of 36) to describe her: energetic, attractive, sympathetic, friendly, sincere, well-liked, responsive, well-mannered, sense of humor.

One adviser made this comment: "A wild, giddy, and mildly silly girl, who is, despite all, exceedingly attractive. She is madly and equally enthusiastic about everything, be it a poem by T. S. Eliot or a weekend off campus. She has thrown herself at college from the first day. She is not merely draining the college life cup; she is gulping it down."

PAT AS A SENIOR

If the material from Pat's freshman interviews exemplifies high impulse expression, the following material should do so even more vividly. At the same time, it may show something of the special quality of her impulse expression. In order to test our hypothesis that her impulses are acted out for purposes of defense, we must search the material for indications of deeper needs and conflicts—some of which we should expect to be unconscious.

The discussion may be organized around the major clusters mentioned earlier: ascendance, sensation, endocathection and intraception, and radical sentiments.

ASCENDANCE. Pat's life as a senior revolves about her work as a drama major and her plans for a career in the theater. She entered college with the idea of majoring in art, but as a sophomore she had something of a triumph on the stage, and this soon lead to other successes and the determination to make a career in the theater. As a drama major she had the lead in two productions and parts in four others. Comedy was her forte. The drama major is demanding by itself; it can become engrossing, and a student can get by without doing much work in other courses. The major also involves a way of life, a certain choice of friends, and characteristic ways of relating to the faculty.

When interviewed in the spring of her senior year, Pat had been accepted in a school of the drama and had elaborate plans for the future, which involved close association with friends from college and capitalization on family connections.

Note some of her remarks about the central place of the drama in her life and about her expectations of the future.

"The drama is everything I've gotten out of this place."

Referring to her first success on the stage: "It was my first contact with a cheering audience. I was on a pink cloud. The first time I knew what it was like to hold a whole roomful of people in the palm of my hand."

[What do you expect to be doing five years from now?] "Heading toward the top in the theater. Heading for marriage."

[Twenty-five years from now?] "Right at the top. Have a family. Have all the financial advantages I've had, security, love. Kids will have an easy life without taking it for granted."

[What is your idea of a good life for you?] "Go into the theater, marry a man in the theater, but not an actor. Reach a certain height in theater so I can take time off without losing status. I'm not even thinking of children now."

[What would you leave behind you when you die?] "A legend."

[Can you visualize life without marriage?] "Yes, everything I wanted in the way of a career and lots of affairs. Be happy in self-responsibility—but would miss close, happy family life."

[*What do you think are your chances at succeeding at acting?*] "I estimate my chances as being very high. Everything has always come my way. I have a very rare kind of talent. I need someone to write for me. I may not get anywhere until I'm older. Slapstick comedy usually involves women of 35. I hope to have Mr. Y.'s help. My family has some connections. Being an impulsive person, I might just get married—but acting is such a part of me I couldn't drop it just like that. I could marry someone who is in the theater. . . . It never occurs to you to think you don't have it. I feel that I have it. The only thing might be my health. I run myself down. I never go to bed."

The interviewer rated Pat on "direction of strivings" as follows: Accomplishment 4, Power 4, Self-development 4, Pleasure 3, Material Gratification 3, Nurturance 2, Conformity 1, Humanitarianism 1.

Although desires for power and for recognition are plainly manifest, there is little or nothing in the material to suggest that Pat wants to be a leader. On the contrary, where her central concern with dramatic art is involved, she feels that she has much to learn. She willingly puts herself in submissive or deferential positions with respect to her teachers and fellow drama majors whom she admires. And such is her concern to be universally liked that she very rarely shows any open or direct aggression. But she is not above making aggressive remarks about people, and when she is thwarted in her central aims—her career and the closely associated solidarity with her drama major friends—she is very willing to use aggressive means to have her way.

"Most professors are understanding if you are a drama major but Mr. Z. expects a paper on time.

"One girl has become very irritating—mostly because she just plain bores me—talks too much—I get terribly annoyed.

"We asked for the four of us to room together senior year. Alie didn't come back—we were told we would have to get another roommate. It was the middle of August. I was livid with rage. It was really a suite for three anyway. I wrote the college. They said we'd have to move. I got my Daddy to write Actually I wrote the letter, and they let us keep the rooms, which we had picked to be near friends."

[*What would be your advice to your sister if she were about to come here to college?*] "It's harder to get in than to flunk out. You don't have to grind every day. The things you can get away with—you can overlook most social rules. I have a car up here. I have permission but anyone could have a car. It's easy to get in after hours—especially in my dorm. You can stay out overnight whenever you want. . . . Try to get away from the campus now and then—if depressed go off for a week."

SENSATION.

Sex. Pat is quite frankly preoccupied with sex. She wishes to be regarded as sexy, uninhibited, and, in this sphere at least, amoral. This has raised some question in the minds of the interviewers concerning the reliability of her statements about what she has done. Interestingly, the two interviewers who were most inclined toward reservation with respect to the extent of her affairs were the two with whom she later said she was inclined to "clam up." But all the interviewers would regard the following as a reasonably accurate summary of the sex history:

"When little, we boys and girls played doctor. It was a favorite pastime around 6 and 7. I had insatiable curiosity. Occasionally some mother would call my mother and complain about me taking some kid into the bushes." [*First sex experience of adolescence?*] "I had planned sex experience by practicing kissing and so forth with a large stuffed animal. First experiences were fumbled because of the boy's awkwardness. Until I was 15. That summer there was a boy—French kissing, mild petting. From then I didn't pet below the waist—'til Fred.

"Beginning with Fred there was intercourse. I was 17 and had known him for six months at the time; had done with him all but sleep. Then a number of fellows thereafter. I assumed fellows would try; and I assume I encouraged them without knowing." [*And now?*] "It preys on my mind just as much, but when I'm working I don't think about it so much. I began to worry, not morally, but I just figure it's unhealthy for all relationships to have one classification—sex; but I figure, too, if I feel this way, isn't it normal to give in? . . . Not so much now, but used to have fascination for pornographic literature—especially if graphic, e.g., if I read of an old man seducing a young girl—I would be revolted but at the same time shaking when I put the book down."

From the following we may infer that Pat likes to think and to talk about sex—perhaps that she cannot help thinking and talking about it—and that she is experienced and knowledgeable in this sphere. We may also get an impression of the strength and variety of her sexual impulses—and of boldness, sensuousness, love of excitement, and body narcissism.

"Sometimes get so wrapped up in drama here and summer stock that I don't see parents for several months. And sex is less important. It used to be the key point in any relationship. It's not so now; drama has made it less important. Perhaps I'm just too tired. As with ballet dancers, a creative outlet may be an alternative to sex. I'm glad I have it; otherwise I would follow impulses. Not that I have moral feelings about sex, but I do have a feeling of caution. If I didn't have the interest in drama, I would go from one affair to another.

"Alan reminds me of my father, a conservative covering but underneath real crazy. He makes friends, everyone likes him. He knows how to put me in my place; has the ability to step on me but compliment me at the same time. He makes me feel so good, but he doesn't spoil me. He's very kind. No sex yet, because it hasn't worked before. I become addicted to sex, and companionship suffers. I'm fearful about this, after affairs with Fred and Charlie went wrong."

[*In what way would you like to change yourself?*] "I would like to decrease my interest in sex. It's almost an obsession. Drama relieves some of it because of so much energy consumed. I used to think I was a nymphomaniac because I couldn't get my mind off it. I couldn't enjoy the company of a boy without thinking of sex. Most of my relationships have been physical. I have to change my emotional state."

An interviewer (Life History Interview) says, "S [Subject] greatly enjoys physical experience with other girls, for example, back-rubbing; more pleasurable than with boys. Sometimes feels guilty about this. Asked what would be reaction if during back-rubbing, etc., the girl made a pass at her. S not sure of reaction. She thinks girls are really more skillful lovers than men, can give more pleasures. A good polymorphous-perverse character."

[*Do you have dreams and fantasies about boys and men, romantic or overt?*] "All the time."

[*Romantic?*] "Very romantic—shipwreck—lots of razors—don't like men with beards."

[*Overt?*] "Oh yes."

"It is difficult to stop when petting." [*Enjoyed?*] "Yes, reached climax easily. Really enjoyed the stages leading up to it." [*Masturbating?*] "No, used to when 13."

"I have wanted to look like Marilyn Monroe ever since I was 10. Disappointed when not getting there fast.

"I was always very pleased if a boy said I was the sexiest thing he had ever known."

[*Do you still feel that way?*] "Somewhat, but not quite so much with M. . . . although it would please me too if he would say that."

There is much evidence that Pat's relations with the male faculty are sexualized. For example, concerning Mr. Y., her favorite teacher: "I'd like nothing better than to go to bed with him. There is something so animal about him . . . he has been the biggest influence in my life."

Apparently this tendency is not uncommon among Pat's friends, for concerning types of girls at her college, she says: "Then there's a terribly intellectual group. It is chic to sound terribly cynical. Get away to the city for a civilized week-end. More interested in faculty than in students. About three-fourths of them would like to go to bed with Mr. Y. I'm in this latter group."

We see in some of Pat's remarks about her sex life the element of dominance feeling, which Maslow (1942) noted as a distinguishing characteristic of college women who had had sex experience. This kind of feeling is well represented in the items of the IE scale.

From the life history interview: "Subject also reports that she gets more pleasure in sex from observing response of the fellow to what she does than from what he does to her."

[*Should husband or wife initiate intercourse?*] "Either one."

[*What is a desirable frequency?*] "Whenever the woman wants it. Can't say; pure matter of desire."

Sentience, excitance, play. As taken up with sex as Pat is, she knows many other ways to have a good time and to gratify her impulses.

"I play the piano by ear. I love music. It's an important part of my life—both classical and jazz.

"I like very much the surrealistic school of painting."

Many of the things Pat likes to do cost money. She describes herself as a "big spender," her allowance of $200 a month going mainly for "clothes, food, in the city, transportation." For the future she wants a "small house in the country and a big apartment in town with a maid and two cars." She says her father is not concerned about her spending money, but he reproaches her for not paying her bills on time. And Pat has a good time with her friends:

"Sally and I have the same habits. Stay up 'til dawn. Neither of us works very hard. She's terribly funny.

"Betty is terribly amusing and most unconventional. Our favorite pastime is living in a world of make-believe.

"Sandy has the most incredible sense of the ridiculous. She's like a big, joking, lovable teddy bear. We are going abroad together. I can see us going broke in the first two weeks."

These girls were among the five friends who were asked to rate Pat (1–5 scale, 5 = high) on a set of sixty-two tasks, positions, or activities. They all gave ratings of 5 on—among other things—

A girl to cheer you up if you're depressed.

A date for your brother.

Someone to break the rules with.

Emotionality, impulsion, change, disjunctivity. Some of Pat's remarks in her interviews seem to reveal a problem of emotional control—and a fondness for extravagant verbal expression.

"I will do anything to avoid an argument. I go to pieces when mad, so I avoid this by leaving the field. When I'm angry, I'm angry. There are no degrees."

[*What girls do you admire the most?*] "Audrey. I admired her mind. I practically worshiped her. I hung on her every word. I was flattered that she liked me.

"Mother is more like me than anyone I ever met—highly emotional, nervous; has given me a terrific amount of independence; let me do a lot. My friends can't believe we argue, can't believe she can make me mad—she is hospitable, lenient, has so much common sense. If she doesn't like something I do, she says, 'You're 21, I can't tell you what to do'; but she nags enough so you finally give up."

Pat's playfulness, emotionality, and impulsiveness, as well as her narcissism, are well described by her friends. Five girls whom she listed as her closest friends were asked: "Please indicate by a few sentences or phrases your general evaluation of Pat and your feelings toward her. Mention her negative as well as positive qualities and your negative as well as positive feelings."

"I like Pat very much because she is fun to be with. She is vivacious, although a trifle dull at times, and is therefore very good company. She is a hard-working, interested, and ambitious drama major for which I admire her. We overlook each other's shortcomings, or laugh them away. We're good college friends. I really don't know if this will continue as steadfastly after college since we will be separated quite a bit geographically."

"She's an extremely warm person with a marvelous sense of humor, and a desire to entertain one person or 50,000. She is easy to talk to and has a very active mind. She's opinionated and rather 'catholic' in her tastes, but she's clever enough not to get stepped on. She's romantic and adventurous and inclined to be impetuous, but her *uncanny* luck never disappoints her. She tends to be irresponsible about 'people and things,' but this is merely due to laziness rather than intentional neglect. She's a very independent person in many respects but is dependent on people for her audience (again one or 50,000). She has an extremely strong personality, very winning, and is very natural with everyone. She is adaptable to many situations, but always remains herself. She's extremely easy to live with as she is rarely annoyed by situations, although, if so, she either leaves or remains silent (which is often more effective). She is also the type of friend who remains loyal without having to constantly keep in touch, and I feel I will always be devoted to her."

"I find Pat extremely loyal, affectionate, charming. I am not sure that she is so to people who aren't very close friends, because I think that she is basically completely self-occupied. I am disappointed when I see her liking someone superficially because they bring her out, but I am not otherwise affected because I have known her too long and have too much affection for her to make value judgments. She is bright, lovable, free, independent, etc."

"I think it is rather apparent that I like Pat very much. However, I don't trust her to get things done—she's sort of scatterbrained but you can forgive her because she's sort of a 'dear' person—even though I think it would be a strain to live with her continually and do what she forgets to do. I don't mean to imply that I don't think a lot of her mind —she's a hard worker and I found her a perceptive and keen person in interpreting dramatic parts, mime studies, books, plays, and people. I honestly suspect that Pat often forgets things she feels are not important for her and applies a very keen mind to the things she is very interested in. She gets away with this as far as I am concerned by being a very kind and interested friend. Therefore, I don't think she would be good in positions she is not interested in."

"I don't know Pat as well as my receiving this form seems to imply. Pat is a girl whom I like to spend time with in my less serious moments. She seems like an honest girl who would be loyal to her close friends, but I have never had occasion to count on her in any important situation. She is not in day-to-day living decisive or quick thinking enough for me to ever have chosen her for a boon companion. I can think of nothing about her which is objectionable; she is easy to get along with, forthright, generous, and generally a nice girl."

It is characteristic of Pat that she takes some of her friends more seriously than they take her and overestimates their good opinion of her. Be it noted, however, that even those who speak with the most reserve testify to her ambition and devotion to the theater and to her kindness and loyalty. But concerning this last there is a sour note; four of her friends are fully aware of Pat's narcissism, and one of them suspects that she is not generally nurturant but reserves her kindness and charm for her friends.

ENDOCATHECTION AND INTRACEPTION. Endocathection, according to Murray, has to do with the importance to the subject of "fantasy, reflection, imagination or abstract thought" as opposed to "practical, concrete, physical or social action" (exocathection). We have seen that action is highly important to Pat. The following excerpts from her interview protocols seem to show that fantasy and imagination loom large in her scheme of things, but not reflection or abstract thought.

Intraception is Murray's term for "the disposition to be determined by diffuse personal feelings and inclinations (intangible subjective facts)." We should let Pat speak for herself.

[Writing?] "I love to. Most of it is done in letters. Most of it is humorous. I'd like to do a humorous book some day. I've kept diaries for four or five months. Then dropped it. I've labored on poetry-writing but it wasn't good."

[Painting?] "No, unfortunately. This is not my field. In school, yes, two themes—a torture chamber, or a cliff with water underneath.

"The supernatural has been a hobby of mine. I'm scared of the dark, of disembodied hands and faces." (Pat then tells a long story of an experience in a Scottish castle. A man in a painting seemed to look at her wherever she stood in the large room in which the painting hung.)

"I've wanted to have a supernatural experience. It fascinates me. But I think it's always evil, so it scares me.

"I like thrillers, and ghost stories."

[What have been the most stressful events or situations in your life?] "Probably most distressful is my fear of the supernatural and of the dark. I don't like to sleep in the dark. It's all right if someone else is in the room, even a dog. A fear of a detached hand, and a reflection in the mirror and the person is not there. This can happen even when the lights are on, e.g., watching TV. I can be frozen with fear. I'm fascinated by spooky stories or plays, or hypnosis. I believe in supernatural experiences even though I have not seen them myself. I believe because there is no proof that they don't exist and yet there are too many stories of their happening. For me there is no such things as a friendly ghost."

[*Dreams?*] "I dream every night—many dreams. There is often a fine line between what I dream at night and my daydreams. Sometimes I think it was a dream but it was really a daydream. I know I'm dreaming while I'm in it." [*Color?*] "Yes, three-fourths of my dreams are in color."

[*Nightmares?*] "I dreamed of a monster a few nights ago. I met him in a dark room—only light was on his face—he was horrible. Janet B. appeared and said, 'You're more afraid of me than of the monster.' The monster turned into a small white marble. When I dropped the marble it broke in half. Then it divided again, until there were about 50 pieces.

"The terror came from anticipating something terrible. When I dream I think I can change things—make a comedy or tragedy—but sometimes I can't control it—then I shut my eyes tight and tell myself to wake up."

[*Recurrent dreams?*] "Dream of a little thing that jumps out, out of a drawer or a little box. The worst sensation is that I don't know what it is. It jumps out, cackles, gets all over me. It feels like I'm in a nest of squirming snakes. For a second I'm in absolute agony. I'm being tickled to death. This wakes me up.

"I enjoy jumping off cliffs or sinking under water. After a second I discover I can breathe, or fly. . . . I usually win if someone is chasing me.

"I seldom try to analyze them."

[*Daydreams?*] "Usually I daydream about some man or other. We're stranded on a desert island—or I may be captured by cannibals, and have to do a primitive dance to save the man.

"Often daydream about taking care of somebody who has been in a horrible accident or is crippled in some horrible way—hospital—I've always been scared of something happening to my legs, so either they or I have lost our legs. I can't control the direction. Sometimes I end up crying." [*What meaning of this?*] "First, the dancing. If I couldn't dance I don't know what I'd do. Second, since I was 13, people have been telling me what nice legs I have."

Pat appears to be thrilled by her dreams and fantasies in much the same way as she is by her impulse-gratifying overt behavior. One might say that her unconscious processes are close to the surface and enter prominently into her experience.

In this connection it should be noted that Pat's teachers, seven of them, rated her, on the average, 4.29 on Creativity (5 is the highest). This may be compared with a mean of 2.86 for all the subjects in the sample of seventy-eight interviewees. In this group of subjects Pat is third from the top. The faculty had not only her work on the stage to go on; she also produced some dramatic writing, mostly skits and other humorous pieces.

But Pat is not very much inclined to inquire into things, to analyze or reflect upon experience, or to seek to master events intellectually. Indeed she seems to be somewhat anti-intellectual—or at least anti-academic.

[*Advice to a sister entering college?*] "Take the subjects she is interested in but not get too wrapped up in theory. . . . You have to spend two years after college unlearning some of your beliefs that are based on books.

"Too much introspection isn't good. So much of what is between people is illogical or irrational, but that doesn't make it any the less strong.

"I can't see being married in college. It's O.K. to be married at this age if you're sure, but then why go to college?"

Some of the fears and nightmarish fantasies Pat reports can apparently be really troublesome, and she seems sometimes to struggle to repress them —and sometimes succeeds. "You forget the horrible things so quickly," she says.

RADICAL SENTIMENTS. Pat has a great many sentiments, tastes, and opinions that are "contrary to those held by the majority of respected citizens," and she has others which are unusual for senior women.

She shows very little feeling or involvement respecting politics, government, or international relations. She has little to say about these topics, but some of her brief remarks are interesting.

[*What is your concept of the ideal society?*] "I can't think there should be absolute equality. Some are of higher ability and they get ahead. Everybody should have some chance. If everybody had the same amount of money, I doubt if anybody would get ahead."

[*If you were President of the United States what changes, if any, would you attempt?*] "Slow the pace of the country. Make it less materialistic."

[*In what ways, if any, do you think the United States will really change in the future?*] "If war, there'll be big changes; total destruction. As country gets older it will relax, be less feverish."

[*Will there be a third World War? Will the United States be invaded?*] "Yes—always has been, always will be." [*United States?*] "Yes."

[*Should an avowed Communist teach here?*] "That's a tricky one. Hard to answer. Yes, in that as a theory communism is interesting. I'd like to hear about it from him. No, because he's dealing with impressionable young girls."

Pat thinks the majority should rule, that the government should intervene to promote economic and social welfare "if it has to," and that to be secure as a nation, we should put our faith in NATO, rather than in the U.N. or strong national defense. She has never engaged in political activity and classifies herself as a political conservative.

Religion seems not to have entered meaningfully into Pat's life. She was required to go to Sunday school until she was thirteen.

"I never had any thought about God except at twelve and thirteen. A friend who was a Catholic got me interested."

She is agnostic, does not believe in life after death, prays "only in moments of panic." Children, however, should be brought up with formal religious training. "When older they will be able to understand it." Asked if she disapproved of any religion, she said "Catholicism bothers me." Her father was brought up a Catholic but "dropped it"; her mother, she said, "believes in God with blind faith."

Pat says she wants to have three children, all boys. "If I get married in the late twenties, I'd want to have them right away. If I marry early, then I'll wait two years. I'll use a diaphragm."

[*Why do you want to have children?*] "Good question. I'd like to have something I produced that was really mine."

[*Can you imagine married life without children?*] "Yes."

[*At what age would you want to have your first child?*] "Twenty-six."

[*What kind of childbirth?*] "I don't want to know about it."

[*Would you treat your children any differently from the way you were brought up?*] "Yes. Self-discipline at an early age. . . . Piano practice, etc. Get into habit of working at an early age. I'd like them to enjoy work. I'd be more lenient about their safety—that is, out-of-doors activity and sports."

[*The husband's role?*] "He should administer the physical punishment. Spanking is necessary. Same role as mother. Handle the financial matters."

[*What problems do you anticipate in raising children?*] "Millions. I'm afraid I'll be inconsistent and take my own moods out on them. I'd try to think before I leaped. I'd apologize. I won't reason with them when they're young. There'll be problems about sex—I may develop a very moral point of view."

Pat does not seem to have a very high opinion of women, and she is willing to accept a lower status for them than for men in society.

[*Anything that women should not do?*] "Should not be crusaders, should not meddle in politics, should not be in administrative posts."
[*Why?*] "Women are so concerned with details and miss the issues."

[*What significant contributions are women making to American life?*] "In the arts—sexes should be equal. In education—teachers. In science—they should do more in science."

[*Ideal position of women in our society?*] "Women should be on equal grounds with men in the above areas—the creative areas. A man runs the family, but it should be 60/40."

[*What do you criticize in a woman?*] "Confidential type; shrill voices; cliques, a group of girls talking a special language; not being able to keep a secret; people insensitive to other people's moods. I prefer a little bitch to over-goodness. I'm bored with the all-good."

[*Do you foresee any change in the status of women in this country?*] "Women are going to become more and more like men. Too bad. I hate to see them lose their sex completely."

[*What do you know about women in other countries?*] "I'd hate to be a Frenchman's wife. I don't like the idea of woman's place in the home, raising kids, etc. I want more out of it."

[*Marry into a different group? Educational level?*] "If he was in the theater." [*Economic?*] "I will marry a poorer person. Expect to." [*Religious?*] "I can't see bringing up kids as Catholics, but if I was in love I would." [*Jew?*] "That's difficult; it depends; the environment is anti-Jewish, but half my friends are Jewish. I would probably stop to think about it. If he was in the theater or arts I'd do it." [*Racial?*] "I wouldn't marry a Negro, but I find them physically attractive." [*Political?*] "As long as he's not a Communist."

Pat's remarks about her sexual experiences and behavior, quoted earlier, are perhaps enough to indicate that she has "radical sentiments" in the area of sexual morality. The following statements, however, are more precisely on the point.

[*What are your views on premarital sex experiences?*] "Morally fine with me. But I advise caution to prevent pregnancy. It's people's own business as far as I'm concerned."

[*What is the value of virginity?*] "No value. No, I don't resent the standard; it doesn't exist for me." [*Parents?*] "They're very idealistic about sex. They are willing to talk freely but they're idealistic about it. They'd be disappointed if they knew about my affairs and I see no reason to disappoint them."

[*What do you think of homosexuals?*] "They don't revolt me. They're rather interesting. Just find it interesting. I can't understand it."

The items classified under Racial Sentiments in the IE scale do not cover as wide a range of values and opinions as do the interviews. Of the twenty-three items so classified, 9 have to do with religion, 7 with sex and 2 with modern art. It can be readily inferred from Pat's remarks that she would respond to all the 18 items in the direction of high IE. Probably it would not be difficult to expand the IE scale by building items around some of the other ideas that Pat expresses. But we should not expect to tap impulse expression in subjects like Pat through the use of items that expressed political radicalism or liberalism, or liberal views in respect to child training, family relations, the roles and status of women, or social group relations. Possibly values and beliefs in these latter areas are independent of IE. Pat reveals here a typical authoritarian outlook, and it would be surprising if she did not have a high score on the F scale for measuring authoritarianism. Her score of 135 is second highest among the group of interviewees. (Average for senior women is usually around 94.) She has come down from a score of 157 as a freshman. (Freshman women have average scores of approximately 114.) But, IE and F are virtually uncorrelated in the larger samples. As we have seen in the case of Penny, high IE may go with very low F-scale scores. Does the F scale, then, help to distinguish between the types of impulse expression found in these two subjects? This is a subtle matter that will well repay further study. There may well be subjects who are high on defensive impulse expression, but very low on authoritarianism.

INTERPRETATION

In Pat, impulse expression seems to be but poorly controlled by the conscious ego. The argument is that either her mechanisms of control are weak so that she expresses more than she likes, or else she is driven by deeper needs of her personality to act out her impulses, or both.

It may be hypothesized that behind her intense desire to be an actress, her narcissism, her sexual behavior and preoccupation, her low ethical standards, and her fears is self-doubt, unconscious self-contempt, and a primitive superego that is alien to her conscious self.

Pat is probably aware of self-doubt, certainly of the rather desperate nature of her need for recognition and assurance. She has told us of the vast importance of an audience, and she is able to tell us more of her need for approval: "It doesn't kill me now to hear someone doesn't like me. That used to kill me. I used to think everyone liked me. You get used to professional jealousy in the theater."

But she would probably object to the idea that her desire to be a comedienne still has a large element of self-contempt in it. She can, however, project this conception onto herself as a child.

[*What were you like as a child?*] "Definitely a hellion, but the kind you get mad at and laugh at the same time; I learned from six on that comedy was my field."

And we may recall what she told us as a freshman about being the "class clown" at the age of ten or eleven.

Perhaps it should have been stated earlier that Pat's attractiveness does not lie in her physical features. Indeed she is at a considerable disadvantage in this respect, being too short and plump by ordinary standards, and it was the opinion of her interviewers that her vivaciousness and winning ways were in part an effort to overcome her limitations.

One might say that in her display of irresponsibility and prodigality, in her inhibition of aggression in personal relationships, and in her willingness to make herself look ridiculous for the sake of a joke, she is saying in effect (to women at least), "Look at me; I am harmless, and I need you to tell me I'm all right."

Low self-esteem, mainly unconscious, might go a long way toward explaining Pat's overt narcissism. It may also be an important source of her sexual behavior. She would not want to say "No" for fear of rejection; and in order to be called sexy for long, or consistently, she would have to act the part. Further, having lost any self-respect that might have been attached to more deliberate control of her sexuality, she would naturally decide that she might as well have the benefits of sexual indulgence. Unconscious self-contempt is a likely source also of Pat's acceptance of a relatively low status for a woman in society, and of herself vis-à-vis her husband. And it can help explain her strivings for social status and the benefits of economic security. It is this last that seems mainly behind her anti-Semitism and anti-Communism. She could not do anything that would threaten her social class membership.

Closely associated with Pat's unconscious idea of herself as "no good" there seems to be the idea of herself as a "bad girl." She, of course, denies any misgivings about her moral standards, but we are justified in doubting that it is pure altruism that makes her not want to tell her parents about her sexual behavior. If she were found out, *then* she would feel guilty, though very probably not before. A hypothesis that can organize much of the material Pat has given us is that her superego is relatively infantile, and pretty well out of communication with her conscious self.

We may note, first, the absence from her interview protocols of anything that might suggest the presence of a superego that is integrated with the ego. This is true not only of the material cited but of her interviews taken as a whole. There is little or no inhibition of impulse through the action of inner moral conviction, little or no inclination to blame herself for moral failures, no sensitivity to moral issues, little or no inclination to act according to moral principle. But there is a superego in the present view, one that is denied, projected, externalized, and permitted to operate consciously under special circumstances.

The absence of any admission of moral conflict and the positiveness with which Pat states her position on complex issues strongly suggests that moral feelings, which would give rise to anxiety and guilt, are being repressed. The same conclusion might be drawn from her dogged optimism and belief that her luck will see her through, and from her special susceptibility to boredom. When Pat says she was bored we may take this to mean that anxiety was about to become conscious—as when she said about women that she was "bored with the all-good." It also appears that she denies guilt and anxiety through her near-delinquent behavior itself; by acting often enough in a way that would ordinarily arouse guilt, she may prove to herself that she may do so with impunity; by acting as if she had no superego she might for the time being at least convince herself that this was true.

Then there is the idea that bad things might happen through the action of agencies outside herself. In dreams and in waking fantasies— particularly in the dark—there are threatening monsters, ghosts, evil supernatural agents, a man in a picture whose eyes follow one's movements; there is imagery of torture chambers, detached hands, crippled people. The interpretation would be that Pat's primitive superego, fashioned of her imaginings concerning the consequences of her own impulses, is projected outward. This state of affairs, originating in childhood, has persisted, due in large part to the absence of stable identifications with parents and the consequent failure to develop a reliable social superego.

Pat may be aware of a connection between her impulses and her fears; at least she acts as if she had this knowledge. She has told us of the compulsive nature of her sexuality and of her desire for better control. The notion that she may have been trying to impress her male interviewers with her sexiness does not diminish the likelihood that she really is troubled by her impulses. In any case, it seems that so strong is her disposition to anxiety, and so slight is her tolerance for it, that she seeks external agents to hold her in check. If she were left to her own devices the fearful projected superego would take over; better to be punished and controlled by real people. Hence the desire for a husband who will dominate her—"step on me," "put me in my place." (Someone who was more like a director than like an actor, we might say.) And hence, when this pattern of interpersonal relationships is generalized, her preference for a hierarchical ordering of society. External agencies of control—the external superego—have the great advantage that they can be got around or ignored when they are not needed. One is tempted to call this arrangement the "private-school girls' complex." Thousands of girls like Pat willingly accept the strict regimes of such places and are even sentimental about them; but far from internalizing the discipline, they support one another in reserving the right to behave as they please when the authorities are out of sight. Pat seems to have made this kind of adaptation to her college.

Finally, we may note that Pat can take a moral stance when the behavior of other people is concerned. One might say that she joins forces with her superego when the object of its restrictive or punitive action is outside herself, particularly when some of her own impulses have been projected into that object. This is what seems to be involved when she tells us how she proposes to bring up her children, or about the threat of a Communist teacher to the "impressionable young girls" at college. In telling of her ideas about child-training, Pat gives fresh evidence that she would like to have better control of herself, and that she wishes she had been better controlled. She would not like her children to be like herself. At the same time, she suggests that naughty behavior in her children would tend to arouse her own anxiety—as if her own deeper impulses had gone into action—and, hence, that firm measures might be required.

But why should Pat, a talented girl whose background offered many advantages, suffer from unconscious self-contempt and from the results of failure to develop a social superego? To answer these questions it would be necessary to make a thoroughgoing study of her life history, which would be beyond the scope of this chapter. We are undertaking to formulate the existing personality organization rather than to trace its development. Yet, if childhood experiences were important, traces of them must be operating now, perhaps as determinants of the unconscious processes that we have hypothesized. There is not space for more life history material, but hints are to be obtained from what has already been presented.

Pat probably sets us on the right track when she tells us that the most stressful events of her life have had to do with her persistent preoccupation with sex and that the greatest influence upon her has been her brother. We may believe her when she says that she was introduced early to genital sexuality and that stimulation of sexual impulses was intense and consistent. There seems to have been no period of let-up from the age of about six on. It is a safe assumption that modes of gratification learned so early and so well are not easily given up, and that much of the overt sexual expression that we observe when Pat is a senior is continuous with her childhood pattern.

Childhood sexuality of the kind that Pat knew could hardly exist without fears of consequences, particularly if parental control is not being brought effectively to bear. The evidence seems to be that Pat's parents, rich but relatively uneducated, were unable to supply consistent discipline or stable patterns worthy of identification. The mother seems to have been generally ineffectual, the father a rigid traditionalist unprepared for life in the modern world. They left much of Pat's upbringing to servants and to her brother. In these circumstances—circumstances very unfavorable to the development of a social superego—we should expect just those kinds of fearful imaginings that Pat has always had to contend with.

The kind of childhood sexuality we are talking about here is not only productive of fears; it is also driven by fears. This is where the brother comes in. He seems to have been not only a kind of seducer when Pat was fourteen—and he was the "chaperon" on double dates—but a companion in her earliest sexual investigations and adventures. Out of the fighting and teasing and tickling came a confusion of feelings toward this brother —love, hostility, fear, and a longing to be like him. Sexual gratification became mixed up with the idea that something bad—that is, mutilation —might happen to the man and that something bad might happen—or had happened—to herself. Recall the dream of dancing "to save the man" and the fantasy of nursing crippled people—and recall the desire for a man strong enough to "step on me." As for happenings to herself, recall the fear of damage to her legs. But this last had to be denied if possible; hence the "insatiable curiosity," the dreams of "a little thing jumping out" and of flying. In short, it seems reasonable to suppose that Pat's early sex experiences left her with a set of misconceptions in which sexual activity was mixed up with aggression and fears of damage to herself and to a male partner. She tried to overcome the threat, or the sense, of damage to herself by trying to be like a boy. (She says she was a tomboy and a "messy child" who didn't care how she looked.) But this did not overcome her deep sense of hopeless sexual inferiority, and this, we may suppose, is a major source of the unconscious self-contempt that we have hypothesized.

We have spoken of the superego and of primitive impulses; it may be well to add a brief discussion of Pat's ego functioning. The general picture of the personality brings to mind the old image of the ego as a battleground where a struggle between the superego and the id is carried on. There is, indeed, much in the case to suggest that we are dealing with what is often called "ego weakness." There seems to be relatively little self-insight, or insight into other people; in fact, self-deception would appear to be expressed in her overoptimism and trust in her luck. She does not wish to look very closely at herself, and she does not require of herself that she be consistent. (In five years she expects to be "heading toward top" in the theater, but she tells us that a comedienne cannot succeed until she is thirty-five.) She is tolerant of irrationality in herself and in others. There is much evidence that she cannot bear consciousness of guilt, or conscious anxiety or depression, but must act in order to ward off these feelings. She has a short time perspective, and a narrowness of interest and outlook. One might say that the personality is highly organized around present interests and plans, but one is forced to be somewhat despairing when he thinks of what it would take to enlarge or to change this structure or of what would happen should present plans fall through.

On the other hand, we ought not to speak of the weakness, or the strength, of the ego without considering the dimensions of the tasks it has to perform. Pat has had to deal with a powerful archaic superego and with fairly riotous impulses. An ego that was largely taken up with protecting itself from these forces could hardly be expected to develop well in all its other functions. In the circumstances, one might say that acting-out has proved to be an effective defensive arrangement. And having found a socially valuable form for this major trend of her personality, Pat has been able to organize an enormous amount of energy and talent. This is an impressive achievement. Perhaps it is not so much "strength," in the sense of ability to cope, that is lacking in Pat's ego as it is "breadth"—that is, the expandedness and complexity of the conscious ego that we ordinarily expect to come with general education at the college level. This last might yet be attained—after she has either had some success in the theater or given up the idea of being a professional actress.

PROBLEMS OF INDUCING CHANGE

It is somewhat discouraging to consider, as we must with Pat's case before us, how difficult it is for some students to change developmentally in college, and how difficult it is for the college to encourage that development. What helps one student may hinder another. For example, in Chapter 4 we saw that abandoning old peer groups for new college friends marked an important step in freeing Penny's impulses. But, while Pat's new associations within the department of dramatic art also probably contributed to her increased IE score, they did so by reinforcing a defensive operation that was already in motion. This can hardly be called development, even though many of the activities that now serve her defensive purposes are more valuable culturally than some of the patterns she exhibited as a freshman.

We may ask whether the college might have done more for Pat. In the matter of skills and knowledge in the area of her specialty a great deal seems to have been accomplished. Yet one can accept Pat fully as she is and still wish that her college education had been broader. Suppose she does not succeed as an actress. (And in this field, where many are called and few are chosen, it must be considered that her chances are slight.) One could wish that her education had been such that she could work contentedly at various jobs in the world of the theater, perhaps as a promoter and organizer of a community theater. Again, while there is no doubt that Pat will continue to be an interesting and entertaining person, it seems too bad that she does not have more scope. If we imagine her presiding over a salon, as well we might, it is a little distressing to think of her being limited to theater talk. It seems possible that, had a different set of educational objectives been conceived for Pat in the first place, she could have been influenced by a number of men, in several different departments, in much the way that she was influenced by Mr. Y.

One may raise a more searching question. Should a college be content to leave the character of a girl like Pat the way it finds it? The most disquieting thing in her case is the high F-scale score and what lies behind it. It is difficult to see how an anti-Semitic girl who depends on social status could get along very well in the world of the theater. More seriously, it is hard to see how Pat can develop further as a person without there being some radical shaking up of the existing personality structure. In a sense, the drama major was a reasonable course for Pat. Here was a girl who was looking for strong external control, and she could hardly be expected to accept such control unless it favored a major purpose of her own. What better arrangement, then, than bringing her under the discipline of a strong director in the theater? We have seen that, within limits, this arrangement worked very well. But it does not appear that the discipline has been carried over to other spheres of life or that Pat's need for strong external controls has been reduced. Must she go through life making sure that she always has a strong hand to rule her, be it a director or a husband?

The problem is a difficult one. We know that authoritarianism in personality can be reduced in college, but it is not clear what can be done with a student who as a freshman is as impulse-ridden as Pat was. Perhaps nothing can be done. And we must respect the opinions of those who think that nothing *should* be done. Yet we seem to have no alternative to trying to increase our knowledge of impulse expression, authoritarianism, and personality development in general, so that the colleges—and, more important, the individual student—will have greater choice in the matter.

CHAPTER TWELVE

Masculinity-Femininity in the Structure of Personality

A disposition toward masculinity or toward femininity, in either sex, may be conceived of as a dynamic structure in the personality which, like authoritarianism and impulse expression, is capable of affecting a wide range of behavior. In clinical work a disposition toward masculinity or toward femininity is frequently of crucial importance. Probably most psychoanalysts would agree that every man who goes through psychoanalysis has to deal with his "feminine side" or "feminine impulses"—and every woman with her "masculine impulses." There is much theory and clinical information concerning the ways in which such impulses are differentiated, transformed, manifested, or countered. Yet these phenomena have rarely been the object of quantitative study.

Empirical scales for measuring masculinity-femininity have continued to improve since Terman and Miles (1936) published their pioneer study, and they have achieved some success in distinguishing "sexual inverts" from normals; yet these scales seem to have shed little new light upon the dynamic organization of masculine and feminine impulses within the personality. Textbooks in the field of personality devote very little space to the topic of masculinity-femininity. There is little or no treatment of tendencies toward masculinity or toward femininity as dynamic factors which interact with other variables of personality. In Cattell's (1946)

An expanded version of a paper read at the International Congress of Psychology in Stockholm, July 1951.

comprehensive survey of factorial studies, variables in the area of masculinity-femininity have a very small place.

This lack of progress has no doubt been due in part to the fact that
clinical workers and psychologists more devoted to quantitative methods
have not worked in the closest cooperation. But more important, probably,
has been the failure to solve certain theoretical problems. Allport wrote in
1937: ". . . yet masculinity-femininity (like neuroticism) is another broad
omnibus conception somewhat lacking in incisiveness. Detailed patterns
are covered up by the scores for 'total' masculinity and 'total' femininity.
. . . The proper interpretation of such an empirical variable is all the more
difficult since cultural expectations for men and for women vary so widely
in different social groups. Not until a much narrower, biologically-rooted
criterion is evolved will it be safe to speak of masculinity-femininity as
representing 'one of a small number of cores around which the structure
of personality gradually takes shape.' In short, a better logic of this variable
is desired before admitting it to the psychograph."

Progress along the lines suggested by Allport has been made since
World War II. Erikson (1958) showed how we might achieve a "biologically-rooted criterion" by demonstrating that boys and girls differed
markedly in the spatial feaures of their play constructions, and by educing
evidence that children express in such constructions their body-feelings
and body-images. Franck (1946) and Franck and Rosen (1949), following
up the work of Erikson and seeking to develop "culture-free" tests of
masculinity-femininity, found that males and females differed in their
preference for paintings designed to represent male and female sex symbols
and in their manner of completing simple drawings. These writers also
reported some evidence that differences within a given sex in performance
on these tests were associated with certain variables of personality.

The authors of *The Authoritarian Personality* (Adorno *et al.*, 1950),
leaning heavily upon psychoanalytic theory, found that such conceptions
as "underlying passivity and receptivity," "ego-alien homosexual tendencies," and "conception of female sex role" permitted them to make
meaningful interpretations of quantitative data. Particularly fruitful, it
seemed, was the notion that similar underlying tendencies to sexual inversion were handled in different ways by different personalities, and that
similar—masculine or feminine—manifestations in behavior might have
different sources within the personality. Renaud (1950) has produced
evidence to show that the significance of score on the Minnesota Multiphasic Personality Inventory M-F Scale depends upon the context of personality variables within which manifest femininity operates. He found
that a group of male overt homosexuals and a group of males reporting
fears of homosexuality obtained very similar mean scores on the masculinity-femininity scale; what distinguished the two groups was mainly
the fact that the homosexuals showed a greater tendency to *act* in response
to anxiety and to act in an antisocial way.

The need which these studies have helped to meet has been for a more differentiated conception of masculinity-femininity, for understanding of the different ways in which central tendencies toward masculinity and toward femininity express themselves in behavior, and for consideration of the personality context within which these tendencies operate. Further investigation of this whole area has been facilitated by the development of a number of tests which measure patterns of behavior that can be referred to different areas and levels of the personality. Among them are these:

The MMPI M-F Scale. This well-known scale was based on the intensive study by S. R. Hathaway (1943) of 17 young men who came to him for therapy in connection with homosexual problems and who showed evidence, such as mannerisms, voice pattern, fat distribution, and so forth, of a general tendency toward "sexual inversion." Test items were adminstered to this group and to a group of 117 consecutively entering selectees at an outfitting center during World War II; those items which differentiated significantly between these two groups were retained and further tested against 108 female airline workers. Items finally retained differentiated the enlisted men from the inverts, and from the women.

M-F Scale of the Strong Interest Blank. This scale comprises 202 items from the Strong Interest Blank (Strong, 1943) which were found in a sample of 603 adults to differentiate men from women.

The Gough M-F Scale. The building of this scale (Gough, 1957) began with the sifting of some 500 items in order to determine empirically which ones showed promise of differentiating males from females. It is important to note that most of these items were written, not with masculinity-femininity in mind, but for use in a study of political participation; hence those which survived successive trials with groups of males and females could be thought of as fairly subtle in the sense that they would have no immediate or obvious connection with M-F. Items known to be predictive of intelligence or high educational status were excluded. This pool of items was administered to successive samples of high school and college groups and reduced to a final set of 58 items, all of which revealed significant differences between males and females. In a special study, the responses of 38 reformatory inmates presenting problems of homosexual behavior were compared with those of 38 nonhomosexual inmates matched for age, education, and I.Q. Thirty-two of the 58 items mentioned above were used in this study; each of them showed a difference in the expected direction, and 13 of them yielded differences that were statistically significant.

The Symbol Preference Test. This procedure was devised by Kate Franck (1946) with the thought that it might reveal differences between males and females that were relatively "culture-free." The test materials are 9 pairs of pictures—more or less abstract designs especially prepared by an artist—representing sex symbols. Each pair of pictures consists of one male and one female symbol; the subject is presented with one pair at a time and asked to state which of the two attracts him more. Franck found that the male symbols were preferred over the female ones by both men and women, and that men showed a stronger preference for female symbols than did women. There is evidence that some subjects choose narcissistically, others on the basis of object relations.

Completion of Drawings. This test, developed by Franck and Rosen (1949), presents the subject with 36 very incomplete drawings, which he is asked to complete in any way that he likes. Completions by males and by females have been found to differ typically; for example, men tend to close the stimulus while women tend to leave it open, and men show expansion from the stimulus outward while women show internal elaboration. These and other differences resemble those which Erikson (1958) found in the spatial features of the play-constructions of boys and girls. Each drawing is scored as masculine or feminine according to objective criteria provided in a scoring manual.

The Welsh Figure Preference Test (1949) includes 100 figures or abstract drawings which represent nothing in particular. The subject is asked to state whether he likes or dislikes each. Some 40 of the figures have been found to differentiate men from women, and together they make up a femininity key.

THE M-F FACTOR IN MEN

In the light of the central place which earlier studies had indicated for masculinity-femininity in the personality, the decision was made to include the M-F tests listed above among the various procedures to be used in the assessment studies at the Institute of Personality Assessment and Research of the University of California. In the project to be reported here, 80 male graduate students (two samples of 40 students each) from fourteen departments of the university were studied to find predictors of superior performance in graduate school. The subjects, in groups of 10, spent weekends at the Institute, where they were subjected to some twenty-three hours of testing, interviewing, and observation.

It was thought possible that one or another of the M-F tests might correlate with ratings by the subject's department on "potential success in his profession," "originality," or "all-around soundness as a person." It was considered somewhat more likely that certain combinations of the M-F measures might be predictive of superior performance in graduate school. It seemed that, at the least, the study of M-F in subjects who were being investigated by a wide variety of other procedures might teach us something about the functioning of this factor in the personality.

Effeminacy was one of some 40 variables that were rated with the use of a 1-5 scale, by the assessment staff of nine psychologists. The reliability coefficients for the ratings of effeminacy were .89 in the first sample of 40 subjects, .66 in the second.

We may first consider the intercorrelations among the several M-F measures: the average coefficient is .26, the range .06 to .45. All the measures appear to have something in common. Since the six tests have been shown to differentiate men from women, and since ratings undoubtedly would do so, we may call this something "femininity." Such a factor within the person would seem to be very general indeed, for a great variety of performances are covered by the measures. In view of the fact that the correlations are not very high, we might also make the interpretation that the common factor with which we are dealing is complex—that is to say, it has various dimensions, some of which are more fully expressed in one measure, others in another.

(It is interesting to note that the Completion of Drawings Test, which was designed specifically to measure an underlying "culture-free" femininity and which had not previously been correlated with other measures of M-F, stands up rather well. Not only does it correlate positively with all the other measures, but it exhibits the highest correlation, .45, with ratings on effeminacy.)

The several M-F measures were next considered in relation to a number of variables which on one hypothesis or another seemed possibly related to masculinity or femininity. Correlations very close to zero were obtained in the case of the F scale for measuring authoritarianism, and in the cases of measures of ability to judge others, of self-insight, and of sociometric status among peers. Femininity proved to be positively associated with verbal fluency as rated by the assessment staff, and with several tests of artistic interest and ability: the artist and the musician scales from the Strong Interest Blank, the artist key of the Welsh Figure Preference Test (a scale made up of the figures which separated artists from nonartists), and the tendency to agree with the university's art department as to the aesthetic merit of colored designs produced by another group of subjects. Femininity proved to be correlated negatively with the personality trait *rigidity* as rated by the staff and measured by a special scale, and negatively with preference for *symmetry* as measured by Welsh's test. As would be expected, femininity is related positively with ectomorphy of physique (Sheldon, 1940) and negatively with mesomorphy as judged by the staff. There was no relation between femininity and endomorphy.

Physical scientists, as it turns out, do not differ significantly with respect to M-F from representatives of other disciplines. Although the assessment staff rated the physical scientists as less effeminate—a likely bias —no other M-F measures show a significant difference between our 43 physical scientists and our 37 other subjects.

We may at this point ask ourselves whether more cannot be learned if we consider the M-F tests, not as different measures of the same thing, but as measures of different aspects of a very complex phenomenon, and if we make use of theory in inquiring what the tests actually do measure, and how they relate to each other and to other variables. Let us return to the personality trait *rigidity*. The highest negative correlation between femininity and rigidity appeared in the case of the Symbol Preference Test. Rigidity is rather strikingly associated with the tendency to prefer male symbols. What does this mean? A partial answer can be obtained, it seems, by noting that the most rigid subjects not only prefer male symbols but tend to complete drawings in a feminine way. In other words, they obtain high feminine scores on the Completion of Drawings Test but low feminine scores on the Symbol Preference Test. To be more complete, the lowest rigidity scores were obtained by subjects scoring high (feminine) on both tests, higher rigidity scores were obtained by subjects scoring low (masculine) on both tests, and the highest rigidity scores were obtained by men scoring high (feminine) on drawing completions but low (masculine) on Symbol Preference. A reasonable explanation would be that the Completion of Drawings Test provides an estimate of deeper-lying femininity—femininity at the level of body feeling—while preference for male symbols represents a striving for masculine identity. Men who obtain high feminine scores on both tests have an attitude of acceptance toward their femininity and are flexible sometimes to the point of irresponsibility. In men with underlying femininity who prefer male symbols, the mechanism of overcompensation may be said to be at work: They maintain their inhibition of passive impulses by concentrating upon manifestations of an opposite significance—something which, we may suppose, favors rigidity as a general mental attitude and as a trait of personality.

The same line of reasoning applies to authoritarianism, which in the present sample of men is correlated .44 with rigidity. The authors of *The Authoritarian Personality* became convinced that one of the main sources of this personality syndrome was ego-alien femininity—that is to say, underlying femininity that had to be countered by whatever defenses the subject had at his disposal. Such femininity was only inferred, however; it was not possible to estimate its intensity by any objective test. It is interesting to note, therefore, that in the present sample, scores on Completion of Drawings behave, in their relations to other measures, very much as if they represented that very femininity which was hypothesized in *The Authoritarian Personality*. The highest scores on authoritarianism— and these are not above the average of the population at large—are obtained by men who score high (femininity) on Completion of Drawings but low on those measures of femininity which involve the expression of feminine interests and artistic sensitivity.

As has been stated, the main concern of our research at the Institute was with the prediction of potential success, of originality, and of all-around soundness. We may consider the contribution to this end of our M-F measures.

The common-sense notion that there is in men some connection between femininity and creativity has persisted for a long time, and it has been lent some support by clinical experience. Quite in keeping with this idea are the presently obtained relationships between the M-F measures and ratings of potential success, of originality, and of soundness by the assessment staff. In general, the correlations are negative with potential success and with soundness, but positive with originality. Here again is the suggestion that the man with originality is somewhat feminine and quite possibly "unsound."

We must consider at once, however, the possibility that the assessment staff may be here participating in a common preconception; their idea of originality may have embraced from the start a certain admittance of overt femininity and a certain tendency toward unsoundness. Their ratings of effeminacy correlate .24 with originality and —.43 with soundness.

The man who actually does original work, according to his instructors' estimate, is nondescript in appearance and behavior with respect to the M-F dimension, and quite sound as a person. Here it must be said that at least three members of the subject's department rated him on potential success, on originality, and on soundness as a person. The reliability of the ratings was around .70. In the whole population of students rated by the departments—close to 400 students—potential success, originality, and soundness intercorrelated about .80.

There is no correlation between the staff's rating of effeminacy and the department's estimate of originality; and originality and soundness, as rated by the departments are, as we see, highly correlated. It follows naturally, then, that the correlation between staff ratings on originality and departmental ratings on originality is low (.17 as compared with .40 for potential success and for soundness).

But this is not to say that femininity does not enter the picture of superior performance as seen by the subject's department. Considering our six M-F measures, the trend of correlation is, once again, negative with potential success, positive with originality, negative with soundness—though the correlations are lower than in the case of the staff ratings on these latter variables.

Here a significant fact emerges. The M-F measures which correlate notably with originality are the three scales and the Welsh Figure Preference Test. The coefficients here are .16 to .45. These are the tests which permit the subjects to express interests, tastes, judgments, and values which in the culture of the United States are more characteristic of women than of men. The two tests which are nonverbal and presumably culture-free— the Symbol Preference Test and the Completion of Drawings Test—show no relation to originality. The same is true to some extent of staff ratings of effeminacy, which were based primarily on manifestations in physique, voice, mannerisms, and the like. It may be added here, too, that the several tests which measure artistic interests and abilities, and which are correlated with verbal tests of M-F, also correlate .22 to .45 with departmental ratings of originality.

This suggests the hypothesis that it is not femininity pure and simple —femininity in some basic sense of being passive or receptive, of feeling like a woman or wanting to act as if one were a woman—that goes with intellectual or artistic aspiration and achievement in men. It is rather *sublimated* femininity. That "hangers-on" in the areas of the arts, letters, and sciences—those with the artistic temperament without the art, those with the urge or inclination without the effective drive—are actually effeminate is a common and probably accurate observation. They have indeed contributed to the common stereotype of the "original" person as colorful, Bohemian, loosely organized, somewhat irresponsible, and so on. How often have we heard it said, with a degree of pleased surprise, that a certain man who had achieved some fame in the arts, letters, or sciences seemed "just like everybody else"? Indeed the man who seems like everybody else on the surface, in the sense of having a masculine identity and enough discipline and organization to present a more or less conventional exterior, may present a truer picture of the really productive person than the Bohemian does. Concerning such a person it might be said that his femininity, rather than being felt or displayed, has been sublimated and so has become one source of the creative urge. At the same time his masculine identity, while not necessarily pronounced, was secure enough so that he could permit himself the indulgence of sublimated femininity.

It seems likely that a purer, unsublimated femininity would be no spur to intellectual productivity but rather would exert an influence in the opposite direction. We should suspect that the individual would either defend himself against it, perhaps by exaggerated masculinity, or that he would display it directly, perhaps by being openly passive and effeminate or overtly homosexual. While these attitudes would not exclude some efforts in the direction of sublimation, they might easily impair the individual's effectiveness.

Considerations such as these strongly suggest that any attempt to relate femininity in men to creativity or productivity should start both with a differentiated conception of femininity and with theory concerning both the interrelations of these feminine tendencies and the context of personality variables within which they operate. Some preliminary explorations of this kind could be carried out with the use of data from the several M-F tests and from other measures used with our sample of 80 subjects.

Concerning the three scales and the Welsh test, it could be supposed that while some high M-F scores were obtained by people with genuine sublimated femininity and enough secure masculine identity to permit themselves "feminine" interests and attitudes, others were obtained by the more openly passive, loosely organized, impulsive, and easy-going individuals whose "feminine" interests and attitudes expressed a true lack of masculinity or a desire to display, for one reason or another, their psychological inversion. Perhaps if we had some way to differentiate such dimensions or aspects of femininity, it might be possible to discover relationships between these variables and superior performance in graduate school.

Let us suppose, as it seems we may, that our two nonverbal tests measure true inversion or unsublimated femininity, while the "femininity" measured by the scales and by the Welsh test embodies both unsublimated femininity and other things, including sublimated femininity and a kind of mature masculinity which incorporates feminine interests and attitudes. If, therefore, we subtract scores on the nonverbal tests from scores on the

M-F scales, we should be left with a measure of trends which according to theory are associated with superior performance. The same holds for those measures of artistic interest and ability which, as we have seen, correlate with originality.

All twelve of the indices derived by this subtraction procedure correlate positively with departmental ratings of potential success and, to a lesser extent, with originality. The M-F tests taken singly, it will be recalled, correlate negatively with potential success but, in the main, positively with originality. To be sure, the correlations are fairly low—about .11 to .30—and only a few are statistically significant. It should be noted, however, that we are dealing with a relatively narrow range of talent— all the students will, barring accidents, actually obtain their doctorates —and that we are dealing with departmental ratings of imperfect reliability.

To be noted also is the fact that these correlations are of about the same order as those obtained with the use of ability tests. For example, the Miller Analogies Test, widely used in America in selection for graduate school, correlated .20 with potential success in the first sample of 40 and was then discarded. For the same sample, our own results were somewhat more impressive; the correlations ranged from .30 to .40, and most were statistically significant. It might be mentioned that the subjects in this sample were selected for their extremeness in the departments' estimate (that is, were rated outstanding or the opposite) and, as it happened, were much more variable in respect to M-F than were those in the second sample. What is perhaps more convincing to a clinical psychologist is the fact that correlation is obvious in the extremes of the distributions and that subjects about whom much is known clinically show quite clearly the pattern under discussion. With fair assurance, then, we may say that there is some relation between sublimated femininity as here conceived and higher ratings on potential success by the subjects' departments.

There is one other pattern of response on the M-F measures which shows some relationship to potential success—a pattern which puts the emphasis on masculinity rather than on femininity. Staff ratings on effeminacy—the opposite of which might be called pronounced masculinity— correlate only .06 with scores on the Franck Symbol Preference Test, with the result that our subjects are nicely distributed among the four quadrants of the scatter diagram. Two of these quadrants are of special interest here. For one we may use the term overcompensatory masculinity, or perhaps supermasculinity, to describe those men who were seen as extremely masculine by the staff and who preferred male symbols. The other we will call mature masculinity, to designate the tendency of the men rated extremely masculine to prefer female symbols. The tendency of extremely effeminate men in the third quadrant to prefer female symbols might be called open femininity or acceptance of passivity, while the tendency of effeminate men in the fourth quadrant to prefer male symbols might be regarded as a striving for structure and control. The highest departmental ratings on potential success are assigned to the mature masculine men, the next highest to the effeminate men who prefer male symbols, the next to the openly feminine men, and the lowest to the "superman." These phenomena can be treated as a single variable: degree of *contrast* between staff ratings on effeminacy and femininity score on the Symbol Preference Test. This variable is significantly correlated with the departments' ratings of potential success. (It may be noted in passing that the effeminate men who prefer male symbols tend to be—like the men with overcompensatory masculinity—markedly rigid. Rigidity is uncorrelated with potential success. There may be a basis here for differentiating between "good" rigidity, or firmness, such as *we* have, and "bad" rigidity, or rigidity proper, such as others have.)

A final word concerning the relations of rated effeminacy and performance on the Drawing Completion Test. Here it is the degree of *correspondence* between the two measures that goes with better ratings on potential success. Whether a man has underlying femininity or underlying masculinity, it is better, it seems, that this be in harmony with the rest of the personality than that there should be conflict about it.

THE M-F FACTOR IN WOMEN

Inasmuch as all of the subjects in the study just described were men, the reader may reasonably inquire whether the findings hold true, in reverse, for women. The answer would seem to be a qualified yes. The studies of student development at Vassar (Sanford, 1956), which included some measures of M-F, indicate that we would not have trouble finding feminine counterparts for the typology that has been presented for males. For example, the by now familiar case of Penny would illustrate a gradual achievement of mature femininity. By contrast, overcompensatory femininity can be seen in the history of another student, who had a strong achievement drive based on a tendency to model herself after a brilliant older brother. This girl had a remarkable high school record and won a fine scholarship to college. But then began a "flight into femininity." In her academic work she stayed on the surface, resisting any intellectual commitments on the ground that her courses were not challenging enough. During the summer following her junior year she married. She returned to college with the sole objective of becoming a teacher so that she could provide some necessary support for her husband's professional training. She appeared for the first interview of her senior year, however, sporting a maternity smock. Plans for the future were quite uncertain now, because pregnancy was a possibility she had not considered.

But, for all the similarities, the problems of men and women in establishing their sexual identities are not really parallel, nor will they be as long as our culture views the two sexes as unequal. Sheriffs and McKee (1957) found that both college women and college men rate women lower than men on desirable traits. The traits that are considered desirable, typically, are the conventional masculine ones, such as adventurousness, determination, calm, realism.

This inequality of prestige may be as great a handicap for men as it is for women. If a girl is cut off from certain kinds of activity, prevented from having experiences, or imbued with some limited conception of what she can become, purely because of her sex, her opportunities for full development are surely reduced. But the case is even more serious for the boy or young man who grows up believing that females are categorically different from, and inferior to, himself. He is effectively prevented from gaining the sort of differentiated conception of women that is necessary to mutually beneficial and productive relations with them. He is at the same time forced to deny or to put aside large aspects of himself—his own biological and psychological feminine dispositions as well as any interest or activity that he believes to be "feminine"—and is thus prevented from becoming a whole person. His situation is essentially the same as that of a person with color prejudice. As James Baldwin, Lillian Smith, and other writers have pointed out, the problem of race relations in the United States is primarily the white man's problem. The victim of discrimination suffers, but he is not torn within himself. His problems are external and real, and if he does not accept his situation or identify himself with his oppressors, he can act with a good chance of achieving some sort of personal triumph. Not so the prejudiced individual; he may be prevented from expressing his prejudices in action, or he may restrain himself, but he can never become fully human without fairly deep internal transformations.

PROSPECTS FOR CHANGE

Earlier in this chapter I mentioned that everyone who undergoes psychoanalysis must to some degree come to grips with his alien impulses —feminine for men, masculine for women. It should be added here that when an individual is suffering from strong, deep-lying conflicts in this area, some form of personal psychotherapy probably represents his best opportunity for help. Fortunately, however, there is evidence that other, broader-scale interventions can also effect measurable changes in this variable. The most promising of these interventions is education.

The personality development which occurs in college seems to promote more mature self-concepts in the area of masculinity and femininity. In the Vassar studies, senior girls were found to score higher—that is, more masculine—than freshmen on two verbal tests of M-F (Webster, 1956). These tests are made up of items which in the United States culture differentiate the sexes—for example, "I prefer a shower to a tub bath." Thus a woman's "femininity score" is based on the degree to which she chooses responses that are given more often by women than by men.

As a Vassar student goes through college, she is not in reality becoming less feminine, but only broader and more flexible. She can imagine herself taking a greater variety of roles without endangering what she regards as her essential femininity. She can face up to her inevitable masculine impulses without rigidly denying them or overcompensating for them. As a consequence, she is able to achieve a sort of belated "sublimation"—a condition which we have seen to be positively correlated with success in male subjects. This, it seems, is all of a piece with the greater liberation of seniors that we see reflected in their higher scores on the Impulse Expression, Developmental Status, and Social Maturity scales. Similar observations have been made of male students. E. K. Strong (1943) noted that, as men and women become more educated, they become more alike in their attitudes and interests.

The kind of development which we are considering here does not represent an additional burden to the crowded college curriculum; the fullest possible development of the individual is already the goal of liberal education. Those who espouse this goal do not speak of goals for women and goals for men. They assume, rather, that development is toward full humanity, a state that is equally accessible to both sexes. Qualities that are most highly valued in a democratic society, qualities such as independence of thought, social responsibility, self-awareness and tolerance, and responsiveness to the manifold aspects of culture, can be developed as well in one sex as in the other. This is not to say that there are no biological sex differences of any importance. Sex differences have some relevance to the means by which the goal is to be attained, but not to the definition of the goal itself.

Gradually, as these educational goals are more fully realized, I believe that we can expect to find more mature sex identifications among young people. There will continue to be conflicts, of course, until more mature conceptions of masculinity and femininity have permeated the society at large. But here, too, a liberal education which establishes sound attitudes in a maximum number of individual members may in the end be our most viable means for inducing the desired cultural change.

CHAPTER THIRTEEN

Creativity and Conformity

By definition, creativity and conformity would appear to be natural enemies. We may even be inclined to think of them as the two poles of some single variable. Yet we find on every side what appear to be contradictions of this view, for much productive and well-rewarded work is being performed by people who do a great deal of conforming. In fact, some capacity to conform seems necessary to the kind of creative work that is valued by society, or at least by certain subsections of it. Creative work even manages to go on under some conditions which severely restrict freedom of thought. Conversely, among people who refuse to conform, we are likely to find many who do not create either.

Much of this apparent confusion can be laid to a rather fuzzy use of the terms *creativity* and *conformity*. What we need is a more differentiated conception of each of these factors, a conception which distinguishes between *creative behavior*—that is, a set of acts that result in novel solutions of problems, new ways of posing or viewing problems, or new ways of connecting ideas—and *creativity* as a generalized disposition of the personality, a disposition, that is, to perform creative acts. And similar distinctions must be made for conforming behavior and conformity as a disposition.

Based on the author's paper, "Creativity and Conformity," in D. W. McKinnon (ed.), *The Creative Person*. Berkeley, Calif.: Institute of Personality Assessment and Research, 1961.

We infer personality from observations of behavior, but we can never say that personality is the same thing as behavior. We cannot even be sure that any given segment of behavior is a direct expression of personality. Personality lies behind behavior and may be regarded as a determinant of it, but rarely if ever is it the only determinant. This is true because behavior always depends in some part upon the situation in which the person finds himself at the moment. In order to make the inference that an individual possesses a given quality of personality, we should first have to observe him in many different situations and conclude that a certain kind of behavior was quite characteristic of him. Even this would not justify the inference of a personality characteristic unless we were sure that during the period of our observations the consistent behavior of the individual was not due to the persistence of some external pressure.

In order to say with certainty, then, that the conforming behavior of any given individual indicated a true disposition of the personality toward conformity, we would have to know the meaning of the behavior to the individual and its connections or lack of connections with various underlying structures in the personality. This would require a fairly intensive study of the particular individual.

With this distinction in mind, we can see that creative behavior (or even creativity in the personality) is not necessarily incompatible with some conforming behavior. But creativity and conformity, as dispositions of the personality, seem to be at opposite poles. It is with these dispositions that this chapter will be primarily concerned.

THE NATURE OF CREATIVITY

Why should creativity be tied to the conformity-nonconformity dimension of personality? I should say that both of these tendencies are related dynamically to the same underlying organization of processes in the personality. We may approach an understanding of this structure by noting first that creativity is associated with many personality dispositions besides nonconformity. MacKinnon and his colleagues at the Institute for Personality Assessment and Research at Berkeley (Barron, 1961; Crutchfield, 1963; Gough, 1961; Helson, 1961) have shown that the most creative people in architecture, literature, mathematics, and engineering science are distinguished from less creative ones by, among other traits, their greater flexibility of thinking, breadth of perspective, openness to experience, freedom of impulse, breadth of interests, autonomy, and integrity.

All these personality trends can be seen as resulting from the expansion and differentiation of the ego—a process which occurs normally in the course of personality development. If this is true, then we should expect all the derivative traits that we have seen to be associated with creativity to increase with age and with education. In our studies at Vassar College (Sanford, 1956) we found that this is precisely what they do. The same characteristics which differentiate between creative and noncreative people also differentiate between college seniors and college freshmen. Apparently, then, the creative person is a relatively highly developed person. Consistent with this idea is the fact that the honorific traits which have been attributed to the creative person are found in association with other desirable things besides creativity. For example, Brown (1962) asked the faculty at Vassar to identify the "ideal students" among the graduating seniors. Being nominated as an ideal student turned out to be associated with the same set of measured traits that differentiated seniors from freshmen—and that differentiate creative people from less creative ones.

It is interesting to note in this connection that the honorific qualities under discussion were found to be most pronounced in seniors who had majored in English, next most pronounced in those who had majored in social science. Mathematics and natural science majors were at the bottom of this rank order.

We are talking, then, about a set of personal qualities that are generally considered desirable and that we use when we try to describe a well-developed personality—the complex and well-integrated personality, the mature personality. of broad perspective and firm inner structure, the person of integrity, and so forth. This is the kind of person who seems to score highest on most of our measures of creativity. This makes sense. It also makes sense to note that this well-developed person is valued in other ways as well, whether or not he is creative.

If the creative person is also a well-developed person, how are we to explain the widely acclaimed artist or musician who is spoiled, difficult, almost infantile in psychological make-up? Or the ten-year-old boy who can solve, like lightning, quite complicated puzzles? It would seem at first thought that such creative behavior must spring from great creativity. Further consideration, however, would suggest that the real force behind these performances is not creativity but *talent*—before which, as Freud said, psychoanalysis lays down its arms. The dictionary defines talent as "any natural ability or power." It is inherent rather than developed. Consequently, talent may exist in a wide variety of psychological households, including some that are not altogether attractive by conventional standards. Sometimes it is found in combination with creativity, making possible the world's Leonardos and Churchills. But it exists long before creativity can be developed, and persists even though creativity is never achieved. Many of the effeminate "hangers-on" in arts or letters, whom we discussed in Chapter 12, probably possess talent, but they have not achieved enough integration of personality to use effectively whatever talent they may have. The noncreative talent may be found in other fields, too. Most of us have known a scientist who attracted attention by a few extraordinary insights in his youth, then quickly found a "safe" administrative role in one of those vast scientific enterprises in which it is impossible to tell who does what.

In assessing creativity, we must specify the area of activity. Clearly one does not need breadth and richness and integration of personality to perform certain kinds of creative acts. Solutions, insights, ideas in mathematics, music, art, and certain areas of natural science may demand talent, but they seem to have little to do with complexity or integrity of personality. (This is not to say, of course, that there are not many truly creative people in these fields.) On the other hand, it is hard to see how a man can create anything in social science or in certain kinds of literature without first having much experience and undergoing much development in his personality. It is also a good idea to differentiate between problem-solving creativity and problem-setting creativity. It is one thing to find answers to questions put by others, something else to wonder creatively about whether the right questions are being asked. Thus there are different kinds of creative acts as well as different kinds of personalities, and the relationships between the two are highly complex. Studies of research workers (Gough and Woodworth, 1960) have shown that different workers have different styles of procedure, different modes of thinking, different goals, and widely different motivations—even though their field is the same.

THE NATURE OF CONFORMITY

In any society there are pressures on the individual to conform with the prevailing ways of the group, and there is certainly no lack of commentary these days on the pressures within our own. We shall give some attention to these pressures later in this chapter. However important these external pressures may be, though, the fact remains that where they are constant, some individuals will conform much more quickly or completely than others. To put this differently, for some people a small amount of pressure is enough to induce conforming behavior, while for others pressure must be extreme before there is any weakening of personal autonomy or integrity. Still other people, as we know, tend to react negatively to conformity pressures, doing the opposite of what authority or the social group seems to demand of them. Some actually seem to go around looking for conformity pressures so that they can demonstrate their capacity to be independent. Here we are talking about variations in a *generalized disposition* to conform or to resist conforming.

In most instances of apparent conformity we have to deal with an interplay of situational and personality factors. For example, in a number of experiments (Asch, 1940; Crutchfield, 1963) people have been asked to make judgments while under the influence of their knowledge of the group's judgment. In such a situation the same, or very similar, conforming behavior by different subjects may have had quite different sources. One man might have been so little involved that he did not care and considered conformity the line of least resistance; another might have wanted to be a good sport and felt that he could afford to be in this situation; another typically might have conformed out of convenience but believed himself to be inwardly nonconforming, while still another might have been fundamentally unsure of himself and thus made his judgments by what others thought.

Evidence for the existence of a generalized disposition to conform has gradually been accumulating. We know that if a subject yields to group pressure in performing one task, he is likely to yield in other tasks as well (Crutchfield, 1963). Subjects with a high conformity score on one test are likely to score high on other measures of conformity. Again, those who yield under group pressure characteristically obtain low scores on verbal scales for measuring independence of judgment (Barron, 1963). The same relationship holds for various other measures, such as those of authoritarianism and of rigidity of thinking, which we will see are dynamically related to conformity.

Conformity in the personality is also related to creativity—negatively, of course. The general tendency to yield under group pressure correlates negatively and significantly with virtually all the numerous measures of originality and creativity that have been tried (MacKinnon, 1961). For example, creative architects have been found to be quite independent people. Sometimes their independence goes beyond independence to rebelliousness, or perhaps to compulsive nonconformity. (It must be noted here that the assessment of independence was made at the same time as the assessment of creativity, so we cannot say with any assurance what is cause and what effect. A display of independence may be related to the architect's current success; he can afford to be independent, one might say. Feeling independent now, and valuing independence, he is naturally inclined to credit himself with having been independent as a child or a young man. This is not to suggest, however, that childhood strivings for independence or a deep personal need for autonomy were not present in the creative architects as important features of the creativity syndrome. Theoretical considerations, indeed, would lead us to expect that they were.) Consistent with this picture is the fact that the more creative architects were relatively low on measures of sociability. Creative mathematicians, we have been shown (Helson, 1961), exhibit the same general picture, the women more clearly than the men, while research scientists show the characteristic tendency toward independence without being particularly low on social orientation (Gough, 1961).

If creativity springs from the normal expansion and differentiation within the personality, what are the origins of conformity? I would argue that in the case of true conformity, and not merely conforming behavior, we have to deal with what has been called an authoritarian personality structure. The most essential feature of this structure, it will be recalled, is a basic conflict between primitive impulses on the one hand and a strict, punitive, but relatively unstable conscience on the other. This conscience is at the bottom of the individual's fear of making mistakes, his alertness to what other people think, and his need of support by external moral authorities. It is the fear of offending this conscience through admitting impulses into consciousness that prevents cognitive flexibility (one might think the wrong thoughts) and openness to experience (one might be led into temptation). A personality that is dominated by this conscience-impulse conflict is bound to be a simple personality—a sort of one-conflict personality, as it were—in which case the view of the world is simple; it will be seen in terms of the same "blacks" or "whites" that predominate in the person's inner structure. In such a personality individuality is more or less crushed between the demands of conscience, with its external supports, and the demands of primitive impulse; interests cannot be sustained because if they are determined by conscience they tend to dry up, while if they are nourished by impulse they are liable at any time to arouse conscience and so to be cut off.

The main points of this argument can be illustrated by a particular case of conscience-impulse conflict which was explored in Chapter 12— the problem of femininity in men. In this case the underlying impulse is to be passive, submissive, pliable, soft. If any reader is made a little uneasy by the mention of this subject, he has at least an inkling of how much anxiety exists in a person in whom such an impulse is strong. It goes against conscience and the prevailing standards of our culture; it goes against self-respect; and of course it is repressed, or made unconscious. But the impulse remains alive, expressing itself in indirect or disguised fashions, and forcing the construction of defenses against it. Some men, as we know, yield to their passive impulses and display them openly; but typically there is a brave struggle against them, with an overcompensatory accent on manliness. This kind of all-out masculinity is anti-intellectual, anti-artistic, anticreative, because activity in any of these spheres might be perceived as a giveaway of the repressed passivity. (In women, an over-accent on femininity has the same general implication.) It is not difficult to see how a person who is caught up in a conflict of the kind we are talking about will be characterized by narrowness of consciousness, rigidity of thought and action, and a tendency to reduce everything to a few simple categories—such as weak versus strong. Thus a big problem for men is how to repress their femininity without cutting off the unconscious sources of creativity. The forces of repression are not nicely discriminating but tend to operate in a total way when anxiety has been aroused.

All this sounds a bit discouraging. Must we, in order to be creative, surrender some of our hard-won manliness? Actually, things are more complicated, and not nearly so bleak, as has so far been suggested. What needs to be pointed out is that the basic conflict which I have described occurs first in childhood; the conscience and the primitive impulses so far discussed are childish constructions. If they persist into adult life, as they sometimes do, it is because repression occurred in childhood and was maintained so that there could not be learning from experience. The man who has the kind of fear of femininity that might block all access to his inner life is guided by extremely primitive and grossly distorted views of what femininity is. Who but a little boy could believe that women in our society are characteristically passive and submissive? Or that these are their most important distinguishing characteristics? Such beliefs are best understood as projections of the boy's own unconscious impulses. But a child can imagine almost anything, and the little boy is somewhat given to imagining that the worst things that can happen to people happen not to himself or to people just like himself, but to women. If repression occurs while the little boy is in the grip of such conceptions, he is likely to be stuck with them.

Happily, repression does not always take place. When it does not, the impulses of childhood are modified according to experience and the demands of reality, or if they are not modified in their essential nature, they may find modes of expression that are harmless or even socially valuable. One way, perhaps the best way, to express impulses that cannot very well be gratified in action is to give them free reign in the imagination. This the child naturally does, if repression does not become necessary, and the more he acquires of language and other symbols of our culture the better able he is to do it. This is the basis for the notion that in creativity the imagination is supplied from a wellspring of emotional impulses.

This discussion clearly implies that in order for a change in the structure to occur, there must be a lifting of repression; something that is unconscious must be made conscious. But there is another way of looking at this whole phenomenon. There is no question that a basic conscience-impulse conflict involves large areas of the personality. The conscious ego may be so taken up with this conflict that it has little energy for anything else. Hence we may note poor performance on all kinds of intellectual tasks. If the conflict has persisted since childhood, we may actually find that the conscious ego has failed to develop in an appropriate way. But, as was suggested in Chapter 2, at any given time not all parts of the ego are involved with the individual's unconscious conflicts. The parts of the ego not so involved could still be expanded and developed through experience. This means that in some cases of inappropriate conformity, or lack of creativity, we may have to deal not with a deep-seated structure in the personality but rather with poor development in the ego—something that may have been due to insufficient stimulation or insufficient experience. For example, a young person's fear of making mistakes may be due to his lack of a sufficiently broad perspective on himself, a state of affairs in which any failure is taken as a threat to his whole self-conception. Again, a pronounced fear of social disapproval may be due largely to the fact that the young person has not had the time or the experience to develop his own standards for judging himself.

What I am arguing here is that whereas the authoritarian structure is highly favorable to conformity and the relative absence of this structure is probably a necessary condition for creativity and independence, a lack of these latter characteristics may have other sources. If it has, the lifting of repression or the dissipation of the authoritarian structure would not by itself bring creativity or independence.

SOCIAL PRESSURES FOR CONFORMITY

Probably all of us are conforming in some ways all the time. This is a natural consequence of living in a society. Every society has distinctive modes and standards, and it manages to secure some measure of conformity with these from most of its members. Living in a society and looking at our fellows, we are hardly aware of this, but if we examine the differences between a typical American and a typical Englishman—or a typical Navajo and a typical Hopi—we quickly become aware of how much people conform with the major patterns of their cultures. Socialization is the name psychologists give to the process by which societies induce children to conform with the mores. We have to admit that socialization is necessary, but when we think of the creativity of the child and how it is knocked out of him by the pressures to behave in prescribed ways at school, we may wonder if such socialization is an unmixed blessing.

In trying to understand the degree of conformity with the norms of a given society, we have to consider how many alternative ways of behaving are possible. In simple, primitive societies there is a great deal of uniformity of behavior just because there are not many different kinds of things that people can do or are called upon to do. In modern, highly industrialized societies—mass societies—there is a great deal of uniformity of behavior because people have to adapt themselves to the prevailing technology and social machinery. In such societies there is a great deal of homogeneity of behavior that is not due to any widespread desire to conform but rather to the fact that being different costs too much effort.

But granting much similarity of behavior among people who live in a given society, the fact remains that they differ importantly among themselves in respect to conforming behavior. Much of this diversity can be ascribed to differences in the quality and intensity of the social pressures under which people live. Nevertheless, everybody belongs to subsocieties and subcultures whose norms command respect, and everybody from time to time finds himself in situations in which conformity is rewarded and nonconformity punished.

An acquaintance of mine, a political scientist, has made a study of all the foreign correspondents and news commentators in this country (see also Kruglak, 1955). There are not very many—probably not more than eighty. He has addressed himself to a question that must have occurred to many of us: Why do all these writers, at any given time, adopt the same slant toward the news? At times it has seemed that all must have been given a directive from on high, but I am told this is not so. The writers are simply conforming.

The first thing a foreign news commentator does when he wakes up in the morning is to read, in the *Washington Post* if possible, what the others are saying. He reads the *Post* at home, and *The New York Times* as soon as he gets to the office. Of course the others are simultaneously reading what *he* has said. We are dealing here with a sort of fraternity. Nobody wants to be off-beat or off-base and so run the risk of disapproval by his peers.

Few correspondents or commentators show any independent thinking unless, like Walter Lippman, they speak from positions of such dignity and status and age that they are virtually unassailable. I used to admire the broadcasts of Howard K. Smith from London during the 1940s and early 1950s, but I noticed that not long after his return to Washington in 1960 he began sounding just like all the other Washington newsmen. Many people asked, "What has happened to Howard K. Smith?" A little later the answer came, as far as I was concerned. I heard Alexander Kendrick from London, and he sounded just the way Howard K. Smith used to sound! Both men were reflecting the climate of opinion that prevailed— generally and among their peers—in whatever city they happened to be living in at the time. Of course, our foreign correspondents and news analysts have enormous influence, limited as we are with respect to the foreign news that we can get hold of; but they soon become prisoners of the climate of opinion that they themselves have created, for they cannot risk their popularity by saying anything controversial or unexpected.

This reminds us of the great material rewards of conformity; jobs, promotions, success depend on a man's "going along." It seems likely, however, that for most people these rewards are less important than the need to have the liking and respect of colleagues and peers. Probably the two kinds of benefits go together at the present time, for if a man's peer-rating goes down, he becomes economically insecure, and if he gets into trouble with the "powers that be," few of his colleagues can afford to defend him publicly.

Lest I seem to be picking on the men of the media, let me add that the state of affairs I have described also prevails in science, though perhaps the pressures are not so great. At any given time, certain scientific ideas, concepts, theories, and methods are "in," while others are "out." Furthermore, this is a matter that is not always rationally determined. The alert and routinely successful scientist will be aware of the fashions and will not allow himself to get too far out of step with them. (In this light it may be suggested that ratings by peers—or the average of peer-ratings— might not be the ideal criterion of creativity. It is hard to know what could be substituted for this criterion in current research work, but in evaluating this work it seems well to remember that many great innovators have been given low ratings by their contemporaries and, for a proper evaluation, have had to wait for the verdict of history.)

We may ask how much pressure to conformity can be tolerated without serious interference with creative work. The answer seems to depend heavily upon whether the discipline of the creator is *consensual* or *dissentual*

(Pinner, 1962). A consensual discipline is one that the man in the street accepts as good, without questioning the competence or motives of its practitioners—for example, physics, chemistry, engineering, agriculture, medicine. A dissentual discipline is one about which the man in the street has his doubts, one that he will reject in favor of his own conventional wisdom—for example, economics or sociology. We should expect different types of personalities to be creative in the two types of disciplines, and we should expect them to be affected differently by pressures toward conformity.

Societies and their institutions resist change and direct their pressures first toward the dissentual disciplines. In times of crisis, the pressure spreads to the dissentual aspects of the consensual disciplines. How far can this go without danger to the survival of societies or their institutions? Apparently it can go quite a long way. Members of the consensual disciplines have shown great capacity to adapt themselves to society's pressures. Even members of the dissentual disciplines manage to conform somewhat. The real damage is to the individual personalities who must adapt, rather than to the institutions or organizations that utilize them.

In recent years government agencies, corporations, or even labor unions, and other institutions of society have learned to accord some degree of freedom to the scientists whose creative work they hope to utilize. But freedom is not freedom unless it is complete. Complete freedom implies that the scientist working for the government might question the policies that he is asked to implement, and the scientist working for a corporation might question whether corporations, as such, are good things. It is easy to see why government or corporations might not consider that it was necessary or wise to encourage such complete freedom of inquiry. But whether or not this freedom can be defended on the ground that it is instrumental to governmental or corporate purposes, it probably will not lack defenders on other grounds. It is an end in itself.

CONCLUSION: THE ENVIRONMENT OF CREATIVITY

The main conclusion from the facts and arguments presented here is that we need to direct more attention, not to the discovery or selection of creative or potentially creative people, but to the question of how to nurture the creative potential in everybody and how to foster an environment that will favor creative work by people in whom the disposition has already been developed.

If the creative person is above all a highly developed person, then it would appear possible for us to produce creative people, or to raise the level of creativity in most people, by educational means. We should begin by making the development of each individual's potential the central purpose of education; and then we should produce the knowledge of personality development that would make it possible to use all the resources of the school system, at all levels, in order more fully to realize this purpose.

Knowledge of personality development can tell us when to provide structure and regime for the child and when to be permissive, when to introduce particular ideas, how to foster the life of the imagination while teaching the child what he must know of reality. Knowing as we do that personality development continues throughout the college years, we should design college programs for nourishing the student's general powers and sensitivities rather than programs for shaping him to the requirements of particular specialties or professions.

Even when we are given high levels of development in the individual and, hence, ample disposition to creativity, we do not get creative work unless conditions are favorable to it. This is a sadly neglected area of "creativity research." Not only do broad societal conditions dictate that the creative man who would gain recognition must not be too far ahead of his time, or devote himself too exclusively to that which is dissentual at a particular time, but the environment for working—usually an institutional setting—may also be of great importance. The needs of the creative worker are not generally understood.

In industrial organizations that rely heavily upon research, there is an almost inevitable tension between the needs of the scientist to follow his own bent and the need of the company for projects that promise an early "pay-off." Even when the scientist becomes genuinely involved in an investigation that has practical implications, his work is likely to be part of a larger project that is managed from above, and he finds it difficult to see any connection between his activity and the final outcome. This is "alienation" in the original meaning of that word. A similar problem exists for the creative person in the lower echelons of a business organization. Although most executives claim to value creative thinking in their employees, the worker who is capable of it is likely to meet repeated frustration. His ideas, by their very creativity, imply change and may be perceived as threatening by his coworkers or even his superiors.

University departments, schools, laboratories, or institutes do not always provide the most favorable environments for creative work, either. There are colleges, for example, in which a creative man's style and habits of work might easily cause him to be labeled as deviant, with the result that he would receive little encouragement for what he wanted to do.

Life in the departments of leading universities today is likely to be highly competitive. This is in contrast to the time before World War II when departments were, usually, human communities in which there was a diversity of roles and functions—critic, teacher, housekeeper, mother to graduate students, writer of papers and books, innovator, and so forth. These were settings in which individuals could express themselves and in which the two or three truly creative people (all that it took to make the department famous) could rely upon colleagues for various kinds of help. Today all department members are expected to be stars, to have built into them before they arrived, or before they were promoted, all that it takes to be productive. They are not expected to be concerned about the conditions of work—although freedom from teaching duties is usually supposed to be a great benefit. It is a reasonable hypothesis that the earlier type of academic community was more favorable to a high order of creative work, though not necessarily to more work, than the high-pressure conditions that prevail today.

Even creative people in literature and the arts are being attracted to positions in the universities, which offer rather obvious financial and social advantages over life in the garret. Solitary work can sometimes be harrowing, but. we can only wonder how much freedom the writer or artist surrenders in exchange for security. It is an open question. In any event, since institutional arrangements are the order of the day, it behooves institutions which recruit creative talent to look toward providing a setting in which these people can continue to be creative.

A research institution, whether it be in an industrial, business, government, or university setting, can be regarded as a productive institution whose product is knowledge—the "knowledge factory" (Kerr, 1963). One may analyze such a structure into such factors as recruitment of personnel, allocation of roles and functions, etc., with primary attention to the question of what arrangements favor a maximum output of knowledge. But these institutions are also change-agencies of the sort described in Chapter 3. They have an impact upon the workers who are recruited, assigned roles, and provided with materials and working conditions, and who eventually leave. We may analyze such institutions with attention to what favors and what hampers the individual worker's development and well-being, and with attention to the relations of gains and losses in this area to the output of knowledge.

Universities and colleges are supposed not only to produce knowledge and nourish scholars but also to develop students. It is often assumed that gains for knowledge and for the scholar necessarily involve losses for the student. This is not necessarily so, but to work out arrangements in institutions of higher learning so that their several functions may be integrated remains a most challenging problem for educational research.

Part Five

In this section we return to a consideration of the topics introduced in Chapters 3 and 4. Our particular concern is again with the *interactions* of the individual and the social and cultural systems in which he develops and has his being, but here we consider in more detail than before the workings of these larger systems themselves. We have first seen that the individual develops under the impact of the social environment; then in Chapters 5 through 13 we have considered how structures built up in the personality are determining of behavior in various kinds of situations. Now we accent the point that even in adults the personality structures themselves exist in a kind of equilibrium with the contemporary social environment and may be changed as that environment changes. The fundamental question is this: How may we arrange the social and cultural systems in which the individual lives so that his well-being, effective functioning, and further development may be maximized?

The section begins with a discussion of culture and of society (or social system), of how the two are to be distinguished, and of some of the conditions and processes of change in each.

Some basic concepts for formulating the individual's embeddedness in the social system, and the social system's embeddedness in him, are offered in Chapter 15. Events at the University of California, Berkeley, during the period of the "loyalty oath controversy" of 1949–52 constitute the empirical data. This chapter was written in 1953; a recent addendum attempts to make some of the concepts more explicit and to indicate their general applicability.

In Chapters 16 and 17 we again consider college students. Although their personalities are already highly structured by the time they enter college, it seems natural enough to speak of their further development as a major aim of the college experience. It may not seem so natural to speak of the further development of faculty members, administrators, patients in mental hospitals, and ordinary citizens, yet in this section the argument is made that developmental change can occur at any age.

The term "social system" refers either to a particular agency or to the whole society. Processes in the particular agency or institution—college, mental hospital, industrial organization—have to be understood in terms of their interaction with forces originating in the larger society. Thus, for example, in considering the behavior and development of young women in college, we have to give attention not only to the stimuli that the college may bring to bear but to the conceptions of women and of women's roles that prevail in the larger society. When we ask what might favor the maximum development of the individual woman, we have to consider, as we do in Chapter 16, not only how she might come to terms with an existing role structure but how that structure itself might be changed.

Whether the focus in this section is on action in the larger society or actions in institutions such as colleges (Chapter 17) or mental hospitals (Chapter 18), the approach is still primarily psychological. It is true that knowledge of what is possible and of how to implement desirable changes in our society and culture derives in large part from sociology and anthropology, from which I have borrowed freely. Yet basic to all such changes is the question of what they might do for individuals, and this whether we are speaking of particular individuals or of groups or of the total population. We must always ask concerning any proposed social action or any intervention in a social system how it might affect the individuals involved, just as we ask concerning the various subsystems of the individual how their development might be furthered by social action.

CHAPTER FOURTEEN

Culture and Society

There are ways in which the concepts of culture and of society are basic to the whole approach of this book. In Chapter 1, I suggested that a change in the legal age limit on the use of alcoholic beverages would involve a change in the ideology of temperance organizations. I might add that unless one believed that a change in the ideology had already taken place or was in progress, so that a proposal for a new law would merely add impetus to an existing natural movement, one would be wise not to make the proposal.

The success of residential centers for poor girls—to borrow another example from Chapter 1—will also depend in the last analysis upon cultural change. There has been difficulty in locating these centers because negative imagery of poor girls exists in the minds of many people in geographical areas that would be desirable in other respects and practically advantageous. It has been possible to make some progress without changing this imagery by appealing to the interests of various groups; but, if residential centers and other programs of "the great society" are to succeed, there will sooner or later have to be widespread acceptance of quite a different view of human potentialities than now prevails. While the ideal of equal opportunity for all and the belief that people who are deserving will take advantage of their opportunities are traditional in American life, current programs for helping people who have lived in poverty seem to be based in a very different conception—namely, that people who have been deprived bear the scars of deprivation and will have to be helped to build up the capacities and attitudes that will enable them to seize the opportunities that come their way. This means, in practice, that the most help will have to be given to those who need it most, rather than to people who seem most likely to respond in the desired way. When this happens, the old distinction between the "deserving" and the "undeserving" poor will have broken down, and new ideals of humanity and justice will take precedence over the traditional one of equal opportunity. This will be a radical change in our culture.

Changes of this same order will have to take place if our young women are to achieve adequate sex identity and meet the requirements of their roles in society, and, at the same time, develop fully as individuals. In Chapter 16, I take up this problem in more depth, arguing that while education can do much to free the individual, the full development of significantly larger numbers of American women will depend on the emergence of new social roles. This, in turn, will depend on changes in our culture, particularly on changed conceptions of what women are like and what they can do.

In sum, where we are interested in affecting in a favorable way as many people as possible, either through legal or social actions or through education, we do well to consider the possibilities of cultural change.

The roots of some human problems, however, do not lie so much in our cultural attitudes as in the more tangible aspects of the American society. For example, if we wish to improve the situation of the largest possible number of people who suffer from mental disorder or cultural deprivation, or who are in danger of being caused thus to suffer, the best strategy would probably be to modify those unfavorable environmental factors that are most widely shared; this means societal change to affect such conditions as racial discrimination, unemployment, and bad housing. This is in keeping with the accent on holism and comprehensiveness, as described in Chapter 1. The idea is to affect those processes that are most determining of other processes, as when, in Chapter 3, we considered possibilities of changing a college as a whole through administrative action but saw also that what happens in particular institutions depends on events, planned or unplanned, in the larger society.

CULTURE AND SOCIETY DIFFERENTIATED

In speaking here of cultural change and of societal change, I imply that the two are not the same; I follow what appears to be common current practice in distinguishing between culture and society. Kroeber and Parsons (1958) are good authorities here. They suggest that the term *culture* be used to stand for "transmitted and created content and patterns of values, ideas, and other symbolic-meaningful systems" while the term "society—or more generally, *social system*—be used to designate the specifically relational system of interaction among individuals and collectivities"

(1958, p. 583). Jaeger and Selznick have further narrowed and, as it seems, clarified the concept of culture in suggesting that "culture consists of everything that is produced by, and is capable of sustaining, shared symbolic experience" (1964, p. 663). According to their view not all of a group's language belongs to its culture. Language may be merely a means of communication, "a technical artifact uninformed by symbolically meaningful experience." Thus, for example, to say "we got drunk" is usually to state a fact, to communicate something, but to say "we had a blast" is to invite participation in a remembered experience of emotional significance. The invention of the latter expression to refer to a drinking bout was a cultural attainment though not, as Jaeger and Selznick would no doubt hasten to point out, one of a very high order. It is the connotative rather than the denotative meaning of a word that favors its being a part of culture.

It is not important for the purposes of this volume that we adhere rigidly to a definition of culture or that we always be clear about whether or not a given element belongs to culture. It *is* important that in speaking of culture we accent the ideal, the symbolic, and the meaningful in shared experience, that we accent in other words its essentially psychological and human character.

It is not important, either, that we have a formal definition of society, or that we specify all of its characteristic structures and processes. It *is* important, however, that we follow Kroeber and Parsons in using *society* synonymously with *social system* or *social structure,* no matter how large or small the system or structure might be. This permits us to think of teenage clubs, general hospitals, and collegiate peer-groups as being, for some purposes, of the same order of phenomena and susceptible to analysis with the use of the same terms. It is important, too, to consider that culture and society have different determinants and are independently variable and that any social system—structure, subsociety—may have a distinctive culture, or at least some aggregate of cultural elements that distinguish it from other systems.

To say that we are interested in changing culture is to assume that some cultures are better than others. When we consider the cultures of, say, a youthful surf-board set, an Ivy League college, a chapter of Alcoholics Anonymous, or a large psychiatric center, common sense calls for some kind of evaluation; and I take the same view. What might be the basis for such a normative conception of culture? To find a basis we must have a theory of the origins and purposes of culture. Following such writers as Redfield (1941), Kroeber and Parsons (1958), and Jaeger and Selznick (1964), we may say that culture arises out of human needs and the requirements of social (Aristotle would say "political") life. It is generated whenever a group of people, small or large, attempts to deal in a human way with their common situation. But be it noted that not all the needs that people have necessarily have a role in the generation of culture, and that people do many things about their needs besides create culture. To get food, to stay alive, to reproduce the species—these needs that man has in common with other animals may be met without benefit of culture, though not without some kind of technology and social organization. In order to get justice, which is a distinctly human desideratum, men may resort to explosive violence rather than to the creation of a set of ideals. It is the distinctly human needs—to find meaning, to resolve inner conflicts, to develop, sustain, and express personality—that have the major, if not the exclusive, role in the generation of culture; and culture is generated when men respond to their needs in a distinctly human way, by using their imaginations, creating symbols, enlarging their experience, making their world personally significant.

A NORMATIVE VIEW OF CULTURE

If the purpose of culture is to do something for man, essentially to make him more human, then we may evaluate particular cultures in terms of how well they do what they are supposed to do. If a group of teenagers, frustrated and dehumanized to the point of desperation, and lacking education that might have developed their imaginative capacities, develop some ritual around their drinking and create the idea of "a blast" to symbolize an expression of their pent-up feelings—this rather than actually exploding in poorly aimed aggressive action—they achieve something culturally. But not as much as might be hoped. A particular teenage culture of which this bit of symbolism was a part might be relatively impoverished, relatively lacking in subtlety and richness, relatively ambiguous and diffused. A person who grew up in such a culture and was not effectively exposed to other influences would embody these characteristics within himself. We may ask more of culture than that.

We have suggested here some of the dimensions in terms of which cultures may be compared. First is simple amount—the number and variety of shared symbols that people may use to make sense of their world and to express their inner needs. A culture may be relatively empty or limited, or relatively full and expanded. Many activities might be either largely meaningless or merely instrumental to some practical purpose, or, at the other extreme, most activities might be endowed through symbolization with meanings that connect them with a wide range of human needs and aspirations. In one culture every artifact from buildings to advertisements for detergents may be designed in such a way as to make it virtually impossible for people to find symbolic value in them; and the roles in its organizations—its hospitals, for example—may be defined in such a rigid way that occupants of those roles could find in them no means for the expression of personality but could only be, as it were, parts of the machinery. Children in this culture might be educated for "reality" by preventing any exposure to myths or fairy tales, and youth might be educated solely for vocations by insisting that everything in the curriculum be of "practical" value. On the other hand, around each of these roles, activities, and other artifacts there might be a wide range of symbols and meanings that made it possible for people to become involved with them in a fully differentiated and developed way.

A culture may be expanded but insufficiently differentiated. There may be many symbols, and the symbol-making function may be valued and relatively unimpaired, yet the world of symbols may be narrow and lacking in subtlety. Consider, for example, a culture in which the male population in general was absorbed in establishing its masculinity and dominance over females. Drinking, particularly *much* drinking, would probably symbolize masculinity and nothing more, but, since many other things also symbolized masculinity, we could not regard the culture as empty or impoverished. Similarly, a culture that was much taken up with the problem of evil would be able, as it were, to see evil everywhere and to use many objects, including people, to represent it. The trouble in both these cultures would be twofold: (1) A given object is not responded to in enough different ways; for example, to let drinking represent masculinity is better than giving it no symbolic value at all, but this is far from realizing the possibilities of alcohol. (2) An object may be responded to only in terms of its symbolic meaning rather than as it really is, with the result that rational activity is interfered with or other values are neglected; for example, if "beatniks" represent evil, and the category is used in a sweeping but yet rigid way—to embrace many people who wear beards or dress with varying degrees of untidiness and who are regarded as all alike—then rational actions respecting alienated youth (Keniston, 1965) become improbable, and life becomes very difficult for the "beatniks."

We deal here with the fact that a great deal of culture is created under conditions of extreme strain, when the need for meaning, for a way to structure the world, is acute. This is not a time for subtlety or for fine distinctions, not a time for attending to all the needs of a person or the interests of various groups of people. Cultural elements created under such conditions tend to persist. If the strained situation of the group continues for a time, the shared symbols or meanings tend to become norms, deviations from which tend to be punished in some way. This can be highly restrictive for an individual who has no alternative to living within the group that has produced this culture. The available symbols may be inadequate for the expression of more than a few of his psychological needs, and the meanings which he feels he must accept may interfere with his finding other meanings and with rational thought itself. The belief system of a fundamentalist church, for example, tends to prevent members of that social system from sharing in many of the insights and meanings that have been contributed by the biological, psychological, and social sciences; the categorical separation of "true believers" and other people narrows the self-conception of the former and limits what might be rewarding relationships between members of the church and other citizens.

Finally, a culture may be relatively lacking in integration. Different cultural elements, created in different problematic situations and supported by the norm-sustaining process in societies, may be unconnected one with another or actually incompatible. The trouble with diffusion or fragmentation in a culture is that people have to live with it or in it, and people want to be more or less consistent and all of a piece. When there is conflict in the culture, for example, between the Protestant Ethic and the belief that everybody must have as much fun as possible, the difficulty for the individual is compounded, for this ambivalence works directly against his tendency to be whole. At the same time, however, if the culture is to be richly diversified, a certain amount of conflict seems inevitable. Indeed there seems to be a certain natural tension between diversity and integration; the more the diversity the greater the task of holding things together. In human beings there is a strain toward the maximization of both diversity and unity. It is in respect to this that "high culture"—literature and the arts—renders its great service to man. Any kind of literature or collective fantasy, movies, TV, etc., is of value because it makes available to the individual a world of imagination in which he can express all kinds of inner needs without fear of disapproval. As his needs become more finely differentiated he requires more subtlety, finer shades of meaning, in his world of symbols. For things to be thus differentiated and at the same time unified requires art. In the last analysis, then, the culture that is best for man—like the man who is best for culture—has aesthetic value. As Jaeger and Selznick (1964) point out, this does not necessarily mean that the best culture is one in which there is a strong literary and artistic "establishment." Such an establishment may be cut off from the main body of the society; it may be a sort of subculture, occupied in supplying meanings "for members only." The best culture would be one in which the objects and forms of ordinary life, things widely available in the society, have not only symbolic value but also aesthetic value, in the sense that they embody much meaning within a unified frame.

It should be added that people are never mere reflections of the culture in which they grow up. No two people assimilate their culture in exactly the same way. One might say that each time an individual learns something in a cultural setting there is a person-culture interaction, and the product—a new content in the individual's psychological household—embodies something of the culture and something of what was already there in the person. Yet there is no denying that culture exerts a powerful influence upon human development; hence, it is highly important that we have a basis, such as that just sketched out, for the critique of culture.

It may be emphasized, too, that we have here a basis for criticism of social structures and technologies; they may be such as to make it virtually impossible for the people involved in them to create any culture at all.

The thing to do about culture—any culture—is to improve it. First attention might well be given to those cultures or cultural elements in our own society which because of their impoverishment or maladaptiveness do little for those who participate in them and cause trouble for other people. Examples would be the culture of a college fraternity in which sex is essentially meaningless—merely a "fun thing" to do—or the culture of a hospital in which socially deviant people are regarded as not worthy of treatment, or an authoritarian cultural trend in which rigid ideas about drugs and drug-users hamper the formation of rational policy concerning the treatment of drug addicts.

CONDITIONS AND PROCESSES OF CHANGE

A basic assumption here is that the culture of a group changes when its objective situation—its social structure or technology—changes; for example, I would accept the view that religious fundamentalism has declined with the advance of urbanization. Social change may, however, lead to cultural impoverishment as well as to cultural enrichment. It certainly appears that in our society advances in technology and industrialization have given rise to trends toward standardization, alienation, and impersonalization which have rendered many long-standing symbols irrelevant or meaningless. Festivals and rituals that served well fifty years ago, for example, have either disappeared or been so transformed through commercialization that their symbolic value has been lost. New culture has been created, of course, but whether the creation keeps pace with the loss is hard to say. In any case, it seems that our society has the task of deliberately arranging conditions that are favorable to the preservation and generation of valuable cultural elements, and to the modification of maladaptive ones. It is possible to think of social actions that have some promise of producing such effects. The suggestion that there be a change in the legal age limit would be aimed directly at the inappropriate drinking culture so often found in groups of young people, or a change in the social structure of a hospital might meet some of the status needs of lower-level staff members and thus open the way to change in some of their ideas about lower-class problem drinkers and people who suffer from drug addiction.

As we consider the possibilities of cultural change, we must recognize that it tends to lag behind social change. Culture becomes assimilated by the personality precisely because it serves important personality needs, including unconscious ones. Once cultural elements have been integrated with the inner needs of most of the members of a group, it begins to appear that in order to change the culture it will be necessary first to change personalities—and we begin to think of the possibilities in the next generation. I do not believe, however, that cultural change through education has to wait for the next generation. Efforts toward general public enlightenment can be useful in the meantime. A major problem here is how to get people's attention, or how to present ideas at a time when people are sufficiently interested, or better, when their cognitive structures are sufficiently shaken up, so that there is some receptivity to new ideas. A combination of educational efforts and direct social actions might be most effective. For example, a change in the legal age limit would, as I have said, have large implications for a great many people; if a change in the law were actually effected and adaptations thus became necessary, *this* would be a good time for special educational efforts aimed at changing beliefs about teenagers and about drinking. But it would not be necessary to change the law in order to initiate vigorous public discussion; it would only be necessary to *propose* such a change. If the proposal were made by someone in a position of power, or if a bill were introduced in a state legislature, temperance organizations and the liquor industry would react —and the fat would be in the fire. This too would be a time when one could have some hope that cultural messages prepared in advance, would be received by people who could benefit from them.

SOCIETAL CHANGE

If we are interested in improving culture, and if culture depends in considerable part upon social conditions, then we must be concerned with societal change. More than this, there are some social conditions, such as poverty, which, quite apart from culture, contribute directly to mental disorder, and there are other conditions, such as poor organization of health services, which stand in the way of effective treatment of affected individuals. These conditions must be attacked directly. Someone interested in improving culture might hope that what was done to reduce the rates of mental disorders was at the same time favorable to culture, but all he could reasonably ask would be that the action not impair cultural development.

At the same time, I assume that there is interaction between society and culture. Culture, embracing some of the shared needs and aspirations of a group, has a dynamic of its own, and this may be made instrumental to desired social change. For example, in an effort to improve the lot of lower-class problem drinkers or to eliminate Skid Row altogether we would do well to appeal, as Myrdal (1944) did, to the egalitarian and humanitarian ideals of American culture.

A wide range of social structures have already been touched upon in this book; still others are to be considered in some detail. They range from the American society as a whole, with its various care-giving institutions and systems, to individual hospitals, prisons, colleges, college fraternities, temperance organizations, industrial organizations, governmental agencies, professional interest groups, school systems, and so on. I have spoken of these structures as *systems*. This term is used in its most general sense, the same sense that applies when we speak of belief systems, physiological systems, or personality systems. A system is a set of related (organized) elements or subsystems separated by some kind of boundary from other systems (some of which embrace it) with which it may engage in transactions. My general approach to the analysis of systems, with a view to intervening in their functioning, was set forth in Chapter 1, mainly in the discussion of holism and comprehensiveness. There is more to be said, in general terms, about the strategy of intervention in social systems.

Power. First of all there is the question of power. I assume that planned change in any social system must be through the people who have positions from which they are able to influence the course of events (Dahrendorf, 1959). Authorities or representatives may be removed—totally or partially, suddenly or gradually—or they may be rejuvenated, or pressure may be brought to bear upon them so that they will change their policies. Particularly important for our purposes is the way in which power is distributed, whether it is dispersed widely among the members of the collectivity—as in highly democratic societies or organizations—or concentrated in a relatively few positions—as in churches, care-giving agencies, industrial organizations, or administrative units of government. When we are interested in changing a law, we must reckon first with the fact that power belongs ultimately to all the people of the nation, state, or community; change must come through law-makers who are the peoples' representatives. These representatives have ways of accumulating power of their own but, since they can be removed from office without great difficulty, they are highly responsive to the interests of various groups in the body politic. The case is different with those organizations whose officials are not elected. Rarely in democratic societies is the power of these officials absolute, and they must—if they are to avoid revolutionary change—give some attention to the needs and interests of those under their command, but the major influences to which they are subject are very different from those that impinge upon representatives of the people. Elected officers are often capable of showing some concern for the society as a whole, but their behavior is necessarily largely determined by consideration of who wants what and how much power is possessed by interest groups. Officials of hierarchal organizations usually know very well what interests they are to serve, and they usually have some power to carry out their responsibilities; with them the question is, most often, *how* may they best do what they have taken it upon themselves to do.

CHANGE THROUGH LEGISLATION

Our consideration of a proposed change in the legal age limitation on alcoholic beverages has shown something of what social change involves in a democratic society. Many groups, including groups having considerable power, would have to be shown that such a change was in line with their interests; pressure would have to be brought to bear upon state legislators, who would weigh these interests against other interests and make a judgment as to whether the time was ripe for a change.

The same considerations hold in the case of proposals for legislative action to improve the lot of drug addicts or lower-class problem drinkers of the kind exemplified in Chapter 18. Who is interested in such legislation? There has been some successful political activity in the interest of one type of problem drinker—the kind of person usually, but not necessarily, of middle-class status—who is widely believed to be capable of benefiting from membership in Alcoholics Anonymous. For example, Alcoholics Anonymous and the National Council on Alcoholism, together with affected individuals, members of their families, and other citizens having some influence, have been able to persuade state legislatures to establish state alcoholism programs—sometimes with the proviso that the director of the program be a member of Alcoholics Anonymous. But no one seems to lobby for the man on Skid Row. Since he, like a great many other problem drinkers, is without political power, someone else will have to take an interest in his needs. But who? I have suggested that through making the conditions of these problem drinkers widely known it is possible to appeal to the equalitarian and humanitarian values that prevail in our society. We should not be sanguine, however, about the prospects for the success of a campaign to get something done at the legislative level for this particular segment of the population. A better strategy, it seems, would be to get actions for this group tied in with interests that already exist and with programs for health, education, and welfare that have already been, or are currently being, set in motion. Those who are concerned with action on alcohol problems must do what they can to ensure that problem drinkers and their families are given their share of attention in whatever program is being accented in the broad field of health, education, and welfare at any particular time in the affairs of the nation, state, or community—for example, medical care for the aged, community mental health, or general aid to the poor. An interest in better treatment for affected individuals will be advanced to the extent that it becomes possible to get problem drinkers included within the populations served by improved care-giving facilities generally; an interest in the prevention of mental disorders will be served by all programs aimed at improving the health and well-being of the whole population.

ORGANIZATIONAL CHANGE

In thinking of ways to induce change in a particular organization such as a hospital or a school, we do well to give attention first to the larger systems to which this organization belongs or to which it looks for financial support. Federal, state, and local departments of health, mental health, education, and so on are usually run by professionals who have been given considerable power to carry out general policies or to work for general objectives. Although particular institutions usually enjoy varying measures of "local autonomy," they can be influenced by federal or state agencies through the use of the funds that they control. The power of federal agencies is great and increasing, and local institutions, with the prospect of federal funds before them, tend to speak more and more softly of their autonomy. With the acceptance by state governments of direct federal aid to education, in connection with the passage of the federal aid to education bills of 1965, one of the last pockets of resistance to federal intervention in local affairs was overrun. Of course, both federal and local officials tell themselves that federal aid does not necessarily mean federal control, and it is true that the federal agencies have usually bent over backward in their concern to avoid any semblance of control and to be aware of local conditions. But the fact remains that money is power, and the basic question is how will the power be used. If a federal agency should announce, for example, that it was going to spend several million dollars a year on the training of personnel for work with problem drinkers, most of the medical schools, schools of public health, and schools of social welfare in this country—and perhaps even some departments of psychology and of sociology—would be shaken. It would not even be necessary for these schools or departments actually to receive funds in order to change; the mere prospect of receiving substantial funds would lead to fresh thinking about curricula, thinking which might be highly beneficial to the training center in question. So also for programs for improved care or for research. Typically the professionals who run these federal agencies, though sensitive to what they take to be the intentions and moods of Congress, are in roles that permit some freedom from narrow political concerns. The question for them is what is best to do—best for the particular purposes they are supposed to promote and best for all concerned. Their greatest need is for knowledge, knowledge of the sort that can be accumulated through action-oriented inquiries.

But particular organizations are far from being playthings of the larger networks in which they have place. They do indeed have autonomy, as is best shown by their success in resisting efforts from outside to change them. They also have some power to change themselves. We are particularly interested in the case of an organization whose leaders, or a group of whose professional members, might desire a certain change but be at a loss to know how to bring it about. A consultant—an expert on organizations—might also be at a loss, at least until he had had a chance to study the structure and functioning of the whole.

Here we confront the complex problems of organizational analysis. We may conceive of organizations like hospitals, clinics, or schools as systems, comprising various subsystems, that are organized in order to achieve specified objectives. It is with objectives in view that roles are defined, staff are recruited to fill the roles, and incentives for required role-performances are supplied. When difficulties in the organization's functioning are encountered, questions must be raised as to whether aims have been clearly stated, whether the occupants of various roles understand what they are supposed to do, whether roles have been defined with sufficient attention to how they might contribute to the attainment of objectives, whether roles are well enough integrated, whether there is adequate communication among various departments, and so on. When change is desired, this is mainly a matter of managing incentives in such a way as to bring about new role-performances.

What makes for the greatest difficulties in organizations is the fact that they are not merely rational arrangements for getting work done but also collectivities of people, who have various psychological needs and enter into various kinds of relationships one with another. These relationships, which involve such interests as friendship, status, and prestige, together constitute the informal structure of the organization. This structure is also made up of roles, and it is organized around goals which are often only implicitly stated and which may or may not be in line with official objectives. The informal structure may generate its own belief system—which may favor or hamper officially planned activities. All this means that when attempts are made to change role-performances in the formal structure of the organization, attention has to be given to the implications of the change for the informal structure; it also means that the incentives which may be used to bring about desired role-performances need not be limited to the obvious, such as more pay, but may appeal to any one of a wide range of human needs: the needs for respect, status, challenge, association, and so on.

There usually is tension between the formal and the informal structures of an organization. Organizations, typically, value efficiency, and this is ordinarily to be attained through narrow definitions of roles—definitions that permit only a minimum of expression of personality needs. More than this, organizations tend to react to crises by making their role structures even more rigid—and are then confronted with a general lowering of morale. On the other hand, individuals who work in organizations over relatively long periods of time usually find ways to express some of their personality needs in their role-performances. They vest interest in their roles and so resist organizational change. When this happens, it begins to appear that in order to change the organization it will first be necessary either to change the people in it or to recruit new personnel for key positions. When role definitions are narrow and the personality needs expressed through role-performances are pathological, we may have one of those bureaucratic structures that seems to defy any efforts at change. There is no doubt in such cases that individual personality structures enter importantly into the situation, and that the task of changing the organization is in some ways similar to that of changing personality structure. We should still say, however, that efforts at organizational change should be directed to factors that might affect the organization as a whole rather than be focused upon any particular individual; but such efforts, to be successful, would have to be guided by considerable knowledge of the psychology of personality.

Since every organization, and indeed every continuing group, develops a subculture of its own in which personality needs and organizational or group requirements are accommodated, any intelligent attempt at changing organizational or group behavior must be preceded by careful study of how this accommodation works. The more satisfaction it produces in those members who in fact wield the most influence, the more complex is the task of changing the policies or practices of the organization. On the other hand, the greater the dissatisfaction among the members of the organization, the better the prospects for change. The kind of change that would now be sought would be toward a state of affairs in which activities that gave personal satisfaction and activities that promoted organizational objectives were integrated, in the sense that each favored the other and both were favored by the same conditions.

CHAPTER FIFTEEN

Individual and Social Change in a Community under Pressure

This chapter is concerned with the role of personality in producing social change and with the effects upon the individual of changes in the groups and communities of which he is a part. The large organization or the small community offers some special advantages as a unit for study. The unit is not so large that the necessary observations cannot be made, but is large enough and sufficiently complicated in its structure so that some generalizations derived from its study might hold for the whole society. We must, of course, understand and specify the relations of the small community to the larger society.

The University of California during the period of the so-called loyalty oath controversy lent itself well to this kind of study. Social and political forces present in the nation at large—forces which could not be described or understood without references to history and to the national scene at the time—were brought directly to bear upon the university, resulting in changes in the social structure as sweeping as they were profound. Yet, if one put his mind to it, it was still possible to keep track of individuals. Some, it appeared, had important roles in urging compliance with outside pressure, others in resisting it; all were required to adjust, and this for many involved drastic internal reorganization. These adjustments in in-

An address before the New York State Psychological Association in New York City, January 30, 1953; subsequently published in *Journal of Social Issues*, 9:25–42, 1953.

dividuals led directly to changes in social structure—changes which in their turn required new individual adjustments.

One might wish that some disinterested observers from another university—or, better yet, from another country—might have been on hand to study the social-psychological phenomena which attended the loyalty oath controversy. But apparently there were no such observers in Berkeley in 1949. In the absence of a more detached commentary, I am recounting here the events of those months as they appeared to me. (While this is the report of a participant-observer, I wish to make it clear that I was first of all a participant. My attempts to separate scientific observations from value judgments, therefore, will probably not be wholly successful. Nevertheless, the observations should be useful.)

THE LOYALTY OATH CONTROVERSY, 1949–50

First, let us review briefly the major events of the crisis.

In March 1949, the president of the university recommended to the board of regents that, in view of apparently impending attacks upon the university by groups within the state legislature, all employees of the university be required to sign, in addition to the constitutional oath of loyalty, an oath having special reference to the regents' anti-Communist policy. This recommendation was unanimously adopted by the board.

In June, the academic senate (northern section) met to consider what action to take. Although there appeared to be much unity of feeling in opposition to the special oath, there were many differences of opinion about grounds for opposition and about what was to be done. Finally, a resolution was passed requesting the president to ask the regents that the special oath "be deleted or revised in a manner mutually acceptable to the regents and members of the academic senate." The senate's advisory committee (advisory to the president) was instructed to consult with the president "with a view to working out a solution." No solution was immediately forthcoming; and there followed a period—about a year—of negotiation, dispute, and compromise. During the first five or six months the faculty marshaled its strength and showed increasing firmness, but the regents remained unyielding; and then, under great economic pressure and in the absence of widespread public support, the faculty began a slow retreat from its earlier idealistic position and was finally routed altogether when the regents dismissed forty-five of its members.

The dispute was then taken into the courts, where it remained until November 1952. The final result might be termed a limited victory for academic freedom. But, as so often happens in such cases, so much history had intervened that the final decision had an aspect of anticlimax, if not irrelevance. (The special oath was ruled out, and the dismissed professors were reinstated on the condition that they sign a new oath required of all state employees.)

It needs only to be added that immediately after the defeat of the faculty's political efforts, when they were in a position, so to speak, of having "nothing to lose but their chains," they showed that they were quite unbowed; by their ringing denunciation of the regents' action, by their rejection of the principle of cooperation against conscience, by their practical steps to support their colleagues who had been dismissed, they recaptured the moral position on which they had first taken their stand.

Virtually all of the facts that are needed for the present purpose have been set forth in *The Year of the Oath* by George Stewart (1950) and by others. This chapter may be regarded as an effort to add a few footnotes to that work. Naturally it is impossible to do more than touch upon a few aspects of the whole changing picture. As story material, I am sure the whole thing is old hat. In another sense, however, it is very much alive; for I believe we have here excellent examples of social processes of wide generality and considerable significance. I should like to make one effort to exploit some of this material for social science before it fades altogether from my mind.

The social changes to which the title of this chapter refers include such practical matters as decline in the output of research and in the quality of teaching; such formal organizational matters as changes in routes of communication and in the occupancy of such roles as committee chairmanships; such impersonal social matters as the splitting of the community first into two groups, then into several groups, and finally into numerous splinter groups, or the increased cohesion in some departments and the disruption in others; and finally such changes in the organization of social roles as the decline and disappearance of some leaders and the emergence of others, the breaking up of some friendship groups and the formation of others, changed attitudes toward the president, changed attitudes of students toward professors, and so on. Various social science disciplines have at their disposal the means for describing with some precision states of affairs in all these areas. I am reasonably sure that a systematic study of the California incident in its temporal aspect would yield many hypotheses concerning the conditions of change in these areas; and that in a recurrence of a similar incident it would actually be possible to *predict* changes in formal organization, in role structure, and so on.

As for what happened to individuals, *The Year of the Oath* reports, on the basis of systematic interviewing: worry, depression, fatigue, fear, insomnia, drinking, headache, and indigestion; failure to function well, worsening of relations with colleagues, suspicion, distrust, loss of self-respect. One might say that we were offered a remarkable opportunity to study the dependence of mental health and ill health upon factors in the contemporary social situation. For myself, accustomed to focus mainly on historical determinants of ill health, the experience was an eye-opener.

Unfortunately, it is not possible to go very far into these matters here or with the limited perspective of the psychologist. I have chosen to confine myself to three general topics: first, personality factors as determinants of the individual's role in the production of social change; second, personality factors as determinants of the ways in which other individuals and groups are perceived in a crisis and of the role requirements made upon them; third, some changes in the inner household of the individual resulting from conflict and disruption in the social groups of which he is a member.

PERSONALITY FACTORS AS DETERMINANTS OF ROLE SELECTION

The chapter entitled "Life in the Ivory Tower" in *The Year of the Oath* begins with a rather charming analogy. The academic community at Berkeley is likened to the Indian tribe that used to inhabit the same area, and the onslaught of the university's regents is seen as analogous to the encroachment upon the Indians of the all-powerful Spaniards. The councils in the sweathouse might well have resembled some of those which took place in our faculty club. "Doubtless some of them, uncompromising, counseled resistance, and others pointed out that resistance against such power was mere suicide. Doubtless some advised flight; others, abject submission. . . . If the period of strain was long extended . . . we can only believe that many tribesmen became acutely depressed, that old friends quarreled, that certain renegades went over to the enemy, and that a kind of general disintegration set in. . . ."

This analogy, though subject to revision as we shall see, has the very great merit of regarding the California dispute as but an instance of something that is very general; it invites us to seek the general laws of group conflict and of group change under pressure. More than that, it invites us to consider the role of individual character in determining the course of events, for surely the tribesmen who were advising this or that kind of action were governed largely by their individual personality structures.

The book on *The Authoritarian Personality* (Adorno *et al.,* 1950) was published in the midst of the loyalty oath controversy. A colleague, from the department of speech, who knew this work—and who was evidently mistaking an outward calm for scientific disinterestedness—said to me, "This must be a perfect laboratory set-up for you." Many of us psychologists, in casual conversation, had spoken of the California incident as if the community had suffered an infestation of authoritarian personalities, or as if those authoritarian personalities normally to be found in such a setting, among regents and academicians alike, had somehow got the upper hand. At the same time, however, some reviewers of the book stated that this research represented a "personality approach," in contradistinction to some other kind of approach—presumably a historical or a social or economic one. The question, of course, is how far do factors of personality enter into matters such as the loyalty oath controversy? And granting that they do enter in, how do they take their place within the framework of history and socioeconomic process?

Let us consider, first, some hypotheses concerning the behavior of the regents. It may be that in requiring the special oath they behaved wisely, with a full grasp of the realities of the situation. This hypothesis need not detain us, however, for the fact remains that they acted in such a way as to get large sections of the faculty up in arms; and finding themselves opposed, they resorted to policies and tactics that were unmistakably totalitarian.

It must be pointed out first—and this is the main trouble with Stewart's analogy of the Indian tribe—that the regents were actually a part of the university community. They certainly belonged with the tribe rather than with the Spaniards; strictly speaking, or constitutionally speaking, they were the tribal chiefs. To use another analogy, they were very important members of our "university family." The attack on the university from outside was apparently building up among the Spaniards in the state legislature. The regents and the university administration, acting in their role of tribal chiefs, sought to ward off the attack by appeasement, or even by collaborationist activities. Hence, we never did see in the California dispute that drawing together of the whole community which we expect to see when the enemy is outside and clearly perceived. Instead we saw a deep division within the ranks, such as occurs in modern states whose wars are not only tribal or nationalistic but ideological; everybody, regents and faculty alike, had to be concerned with internal as well as external enemies. More than this, those members of the faculty who wished to fight the external enemy found themselves opposed by established authority, and had thus to engage in activity of a revolutionary sort. George Stewart remarks at another place that if the regents had chosen to lead a fight against the outside enemies of the university, they would have found the faculty behind them to a man. In the actual event, the struggle was essentially a civil one and hence more complicated and disturbing; the emotional implications of such strife go very deep, and divisions within the social group or body politic lead inevitably to divisions within the individual personality. This is a matter to which we shall revert later on.

The attribution of authoritarianism to the regents seems at first glance justified on two grounds: they adopted an attitude of authoritarian submission toward an imagined public opinion—the outside enemy; and they adopted an attitude of authoritarian aggression toward those under their governance. Yet, I believe we should be exceedingly cautious about the assignment of personality determinants of these actions, and we should reject altogether the easy supposition that these authoritarian actions were merely the work of authoritarian personalities.

To dramatize the issue somewhat I should like to suggest that it is very instructive to consider the California dispute from a Marxist point of view. George Stewart's valuable research on the individual members of the board of regents makes it very easy to apply to them the "ruling class" concept. And the whole course of events, from the beginning up to the time of a lower court's decision in favor of the faculty, seemed to be toward a polarity, with the regents, as representatives of established economic power, at one pole and an economically dependent, spiritless,

"proletarianized" group of academic employees at the other. This movement certainly had an appearance of inevitability, and it must be said
that some people on our side seemed ready to adapt themselves to, if not
to help along, this historical arrangement of forces.

The major fault with this version is the consideration that a group of
small businessmen, small farmers, labor leaders, professional men, and
former academicians or university presidents—to approximate George
Stewart's ideal board—would probably have behaved very much as our
regents did. They would now have been men in public life, and in the
prevailing circumstances, they could not have afforded to permit their
anti-Communist valor to become suspect. Moreover, there was no evidence
to suggest that any of the regents consciously attempted to manipulate
things in such a way as to serve immediate economic ends; there were
political motives, to be sure, but here what was to be observed was sensitivity to that public opinion in which they themselves participated even
as they helped to create it.

As the struggle proceeded, the regents, of course, became more and
more totalitarian in their actions. This, I think, is best understood in
field-theoretical terms. They were in a position corresponding somewhat
to that of a teacher before a rebellious and misunderstood class. The more
things threatened to get out of hand the more rigid they became, and the
more rigid they became the greater was the actual danger of an outbreak
somewhere.

This view of the regents' behavior tends to de-emphasize group
membership determinants and to accent the general psychology of response
to social role, to the momentary face-to-face group situation, and to trends
of opinion in the country at large. Further back in the history of the dispute, when threats to the university were building up in the state legislature, the matter would be otherwise, for there, it seemed clear, some
classical authoritarian types could be seen at work. As far as the regents'
behavior is concerned, the most that can be said for authoritarianism in
personality is that it probably gave rise to certain susceptibilities and
readinesses; for example, the stronger the authoritarian disposition in personality, the earlier a regent adopted a rigid attitude toward the rebellious
faculty. If, however, a program for selecting regents or trustees on the
basis of psychological tests were to be adopted, some sort of equivalent of
the F scale for measuring authoritarian trends ought probably to be included in the battery.

When it comes to the faculty and other members of the university
staff, the matter is much the same. Probably few who knew the university
would disagree with George Stewart's statement that "the faculty was
representative of the general population, exhibiting the same range of
political opinion and social outlook." This means that had a scale for
measuring authoritarianism been administered to all university personnel
affected by the oath, a wide range of scores would have been obtained.
And, I suppose, one might have expected a correlation between scale score

and the stage at which the oath was signed. But such a correlation could not have been very high, for a great variety of potent factors, including especially factors other than personal inclination, operated to determine when a given individual would sign the oath. One might say that had the mean F-scale score been high, and dispersion slight, there would have been no controversy in the first place; so large a proportion would have signed at the start that organized opposition would have made no crucial difference.

The point to emphasize is that we are concerned here with a more or less normal distribution of authoritarianism, with a mean probably lower than would be found in the population at large. The question is, how do authoritarian trends in personality exert their influence in such circumstances as we are considering? An attempt at a general formulation would be as follows. In the whole complex of events, situations arise which act as stimuli for the authoritarianism latent in us all; in such circumstances the more authoritarian personalities are the first to respond, and they carry other slightly less authoritarian personalities along with them; then they proceed to help transform the situation in such a way that the stimulus for authoritarian response is greater than it was before. Meanwhile, those who have responded, under strong stimulation, in an authoritarian way find it very difficult to get back to where they were in the first place; a certain commitment has been made, and they find themselves involved in an authoritarian structure. Those who cannot adapt themselves tend to leave the field, and the structure becomes self-perpetuating.

Let us return to the first meeting of the academic senate, in June 1949, when the strong resolution that the special oath be deleted suffered amendment and the advisory committee was instructed to consult with the president with a view to working out a solution. Concerning this meeting George Stewart and his collaborators have this to say: "The faculty makes an important parliamentary mistake, which is to vex them later and perhaps fatally to injure their cause; viz., certain members believe the advisory committee has been entrusted with power to act, while other members believe that the committee has been given power only to *consult* and refer the matter back to the senate"; and, in another place, "If the faculty had firmly asked in June what it asked in September, or in September what it asked in November, the controversy might have ended at that point."

How did it happen that, despite great unity of feeling in support of a clear and firm resolution, the faculty actually emerged from the meeting formally on record as indecisive, willing to consider compromise on principle, and deeply divided? There were, to be sure, technical and accidental factors, such as the unfamiliarity of liberal members—who, as might be expected, had attended too few faculty meetings—with senate rules and parliamentary procedure, but there is strong evidence that the main trouble was psychological. Amid the rousing speeches in defense of democratic rights, there was occasionally heard a voice urging caution: "The regents would not have proposed this if they had not had good reason"; or "We must not declare war on the regents." When it came to the question of just how to proceed, these voices grew more confident: "We must go through regular, established channels." These voices for the most part, it seemed, came from men who were in some sense close to the administration, or who held important administrative posts, or who had done notable work as members of important committees. They were the voices of soundness and conservatism. We must not be hasty with the diagnosis of authoritarian personality trends. There are role determinants to be considered. It seems very likely that some men, in urging caution, were doing no more than fulfilling the requirements of their roles within the university structure, and that in the acceptance of these roles authoritarianism within the personality was of no particular importance. Yet, the occasion was heavily charged with emotion; men were most certainly responding in accordance with reaction systems that went pretty deep. Insofar as there were authoritarian personalities among us, I do not think we need doubt which way they were inclined. But *most* of us listened to the words of caution: we didn't want to do anything foolish; perhaps we didn't want to be identified with those among us who seemed a little too eager to engage in an all-out war against the regents. We wanted to be reasonable. I suppose it is no longer news that totalitarian movements gain their staunchest supporters, in time, from the ranks of the law-abiding citizens. And probably it is in just such situations as this, situations in which various accidental factors could seem to have dictated the choice, that irrevocable steps are taken.

What I am really suggesting, then, is that in situations of this kind we should focus not so much on particular personalities as on *kinds of behavior*. It may be granted that mistaken actions will originate more readily in some personalities than in others, but it is *actions*—their determinants and their consequences—that should command our first attention, for there is the danger that they will be evoked in any of us.

PERSONALITY FACTORS IN THE WAY OTHERS ARE SEEN

One of the major factors making for strain throughout the California controversy was our inability to predict what was going to happen. We rarely had the satisfaction, the ego-supporting experience, of seeing things go according to expectations. We were forever being surprised, taken aback; unable to anticipate happenings, we had to be prepared for anything—which amounted to being fully prepared for nothing. These, of course, are the circumstances of panic. Fear, such as would have been appropriate to real danger, tended to be replaced by anxiety, and, accordingly, the reaction systems of early childhood were aroused and tended more and more to influence our imagery of those about us—the regents, the president, colleagues, students, the general public. The more such imagery came to dominate our perceptions, the less well were we able to predict. A vicious circle was complete.

The regents, of course, were central in all this. Our whole strategy depended essentially on how we sized them up. Now there was—and is —a standing order of the regents that no member of the faculty may communicate directly with a regent; and, since for a very long time the regents had caused no special trouble, they were in the minds of most of us very shadowy figures. As feeling mounted in the June meeting referred to above, the stage was well set for projection. It was apparent from the speeches that were made, that imagery concerning the regents varied widely. At one extreme was imagery of them as wise and benevolent "elder statesmen" who would do nothing but what they, after sober thought, had decided was best for the university. At the other extreme was imagery of them as erstwhile "robber barons," who had now cynically taken on a garb of respectability and public service, while remaining hand-in-glove with the powerful economic interests of the state. The prevailing view, and the one that was to be crucially determining, was that they were at least reasonable men, and that a "mature" approach was not to go off half-cocked but calmly to talk things over with them. If we behaved ourselves, we would be treated with justice—with some sternness perhaps, but certainly with justice.

This imagery of the regents persisted for a long time; it withstood several striking demonstrations that as a group they deviated very considerably from what was imagined. There were, no doubt, a number of men in important faculty positions who had already come to terms with power and were for peace with the regents at any price, but in my opinion their influence would not have been very important were it not for the widespread and deeply rooted feeling that good behavior would be rewarded—that the regents in the end would enact the role of judicious authority. We cannot doubt that men have to be sorely tried before they will undertake to throw off the restraints of constituted authority. The cry "we must put our trust in the good faith of the regents" lasted beyond the time when objective evidence argued to the contrary.

As the regents, by their actions, moved into the unmistakable position of "the enemy," there appeared a tendency to dwell in fantasy upon their overwhelming power and ruthlessness. During some months of the controversy an important question for strategy was how many nonsigners of the oath would the regents fire rather than retreat from their position. *Five hundred* was a more or less official estimate at one time—the estimate of a committee selected to lead the faculty's fight. I think it is fair to say that men—I mean here *men* and not women (who were less prone to this kind of imagery)—who had earlier overestimated the "good father" aspects of the regents were the very ones who tended now to overestimate the ruthless power aspect. The two kinds of imagery are not unrelated. At one meeting a professor, in urging his colleagues to sign the oath and thus accept a compromise proposed by his committee, asserted that the regents would fire five hundred before they would give in *and* that all should put their trust in the good faith of the regents.

For a long time after the start of the controversy, the regents were conceived as a unit. After a number of regents' meetings had been reported in the press, it became apparent that they themselves were sharply divided. Here we seemed to borrow a page from Melanie Klein (1948). We conceived of "bad" regents who would give no quarter at all, and "good" regents who supported the position of the majority of the faculty. It now became possible to hate the "bad" regents and love the "good" regents. This was an aid to internal equilibrium. But the greatest care had to be taken lest in opposing the "bad" regents someone would go too far and alienate the "good" regents.

The analogy—one might almost say the fact—of "the university family" once again seems more fitting than the analogy of the Indians and the Spaniards. The family analogy was employed in a rather striking way by the leader of the "bad" regents. At one stage of the dispute— a fairly late stage—a compromise appeared to have been reached. The arrangement was that the nonsigning professors were to have hearings by the faculty committee on privilege and tenure, whose recommendations for firing or retention were to be followed by the regents. Protesting against this arrangement, the regent whom we shall call Mr. X. angrily exclaimed, "They will tell their brothers, but they won't tell us." This traditionalist had a right to bemoan the fact that insofar as we in America are moving in the direction of totalitarianism, the instrument for enforcing conformity becomes more and more the peer culture rather than traditional authority; but Mr. X. ought to have realized that the major fault lies with him and his kind. Instead of exercising the father role to lead us toward worthy objectives which we all can share, they too often exploit our natural trust, in the interests of power and security for themselves alone.

It would, of course, be wrong to attempt to describe the controversy as mainly a family drama. There were no doubt other determinants, in our culture and in the climate of opinion, of how the regents were perceived. And there was, after all, reality. The present thesis is simply that such emotional undercurrents as I have indicated were always there—to favor misperceptions and to render clear thinking difficult. As pressure mounted and frustration increased, as any way out seemed increasingly remote, as one's identity as a professor was threatened, perceptions of the scene tended increasingly to be influenced by unconscious fantasies.

We find a very similar state of affairs when we come to consider imagery of the president. Abraham Flexner quotes a man whom he describes as a wise philanthropist, head of a great business, and trustee of a university, as saying, "A man may be president of a transcontinental railroad, an international banking corporation, a far-flung business, but the presidency of a great university is an impossible post." Sociology has provided us with a nice understatement of the case: the post involves by its very nature a conflict of roles. One might suggest, again borrowing from sociology, that we have to do here with a "cultural lag." The post seems to have been nicely designed in the beginning for an educator with a philosophy of his own, who could lay down conditions for accepting the post, win the support of his faculty, and push through a program. But the day of the "strong president" seems to be about over. (How many of us could name more than four or five university presidents? The smile is familiar, but I can't remember the name! The situation seems to be somewhat better with the colleges.) Either of the president's roles—appointee and voting member of the regents or chairman of the academic senate—would seem to be enough to all but dominate a strong personality. The university president today seems usually to be enmeshed in a vast machinery; decisions of necessity tend to be purely administrative or political.

And yet the emotional need for a strong president persists. Just as on the national scene the President remains as the vehicle for the hopes and aspirations of the people, despite his steadily decreasing freedom of movement, so with faculties in times of crisis: the need is for a sanctioned leader behind whom all can rally. So I think it was with us anyway. We kept hoping the president would do something; we cherished the illusion that he *was* doing something, long after our better judgment should have told us that we were asking for the impossible. Our hopes went up or down as reports filtered out of the regents' meetings that he had been weak or strong, had stood up well or poorly. There were efforts to exempt him from the skullduggery that was frequently ascribed to "the administration." In short, I think there was a widespread tendency to project onto the president imagery of the "good father." Or, perhaps, somewhat more realistically, on the part of some, that of the "elder brother." The regents, of course, had more or less pre-empted the role of "bad father," but at times when the president appeared to be their ally, he too shared in this projection. I would not exclude the possibility that the president stood, in some of our minds, as a "mother figure." This hypothesis might, as a matter of fact, help explain the persistent hope and belief that the president could somehow intercede with the regents, or take some sort of lead in the struggle for democratic rights. Perhaps our training in American culture was such that it was difficult to believe that mother could get nowhere with father or would not sooner or later speak up for idealism. The precise nature of the imagery would, of course, make little difference; the point is that in our somewhat regressed state, deeper emotional trends influenced the role requirements made upon others and distorted our perceptions of them, thus interfering palpably with the effective pursuit of our purpose.

What "public opinion" is—what "the people" think or will do—is, I suppose, always an excellent screen for projection. In the present instance it was generally assumed that the public would feel little sympathy for our cause, and in a sense this was correct, for within two years the voters of the state were to support a loyalty oath rather overwhelmingly. But this does not mean that we had any special insight into the workings of the public mind, or that many of us were not right for the wrong reasons. In general, I think we committed the unpardonable political error of overestimating popular information and underestimating popular intelligence. For tactical reasons, no effort was made to carry the issue to the public until very late in the day, and then rather gingerly, cautiously, defensively. "Don't make any public statements" became an almost daily warning to nonsigners; there was the implied danger that if they sounded off about democratic rights the people would think they *were* Communists. Yet so complete was our preoccupation with the dispute that we tended unconsciously to assume that others knew about it, too. In my own experience I never encountered anyone outside the academic community who had more than the vaguest notion of what the dispute was about, nor anyone who could not be brought to see, after five minutes of explanation, the justice of our cause. (This is not to say, of course, that he would have voted on our side.)

As members of the academic profession we permit ourselves, from time to time, a certain measure of contempt for other people, not so much for the "mass" of people as for the semieducated—perhaps especially for the alumni—who do most to determine policy in our country. We thus have reason to suppose that the feeling is mutual. And we are well aware, from both subjective and objective evidence, of a traditional hostility toward "teacher." These things, combined with such knowledge as we had about the general climate of opinion, were enough to make us suspect general disapproval. At any rate, once a man had fully identified himself with the opposition to the oath, he felt himself to be in the role of a nonconformist so far as the general public was concerned. The tendency to contempt was now reinforced, for it served as a mechanism of defense.

As evidence that unwarranted assumptions about public disapproval actually injured our cause, I may cite the following: Lawyers on our faculty spoke frequently in our meetings and almost always, it seemed to me, to the effect that we would not stand a chance in court—especially if we stood on constitutional grounds. Now, since our state constitution says clearly that the university shall be kept free of political influence and that there shall be no oath of office other than the long-standing constitutional one, the clear implication was that the court would somehow be guided by a prevalent public opinion. When the appellate court decided for the faculty, and with a clear stand on constitutional ground, the lawyers had no recourse but to say it was a poor decision from a legal point of view. But the damage had been done. The persistent thought that we had no chance in court had a depressing effect upon morale.

I am not saying that an all-out campaign of publicity could have won the day (though I keep thinking of the way the Alien and Sedition Laws were repealed); but it does seem that we worried ourselves more than was necessary with our imagery of the general public, and that we expressed less faith in democracy than is healthy.

It is remarkable how little, in the various discussions of the California dispute, has been said about the students. One might suppose that in a study of a university community, students would have a very important role. Actually, in the California incident student opinion counted not at all. If the student was a teaching or research assistant and so had to sign the oath, he was lost in the shuffle; his, so to speak, was a second-class conscience. Perhaps this is a reflection of the tendency in our culture to prolong adolescence and to regard college students as in no important sense grown up. Our students, like most, were either somewhat radical or generally passive—that is to say, conservative. The best ones—that is, those in whom we could see something of ourselves—were, of course, more on the radical side. They therefore represented those parts of our personality that urged us to do something bold and foolish—and noble. They made us anxious. They had to be held in check, lest they arouse anger in the "bad" regents or timidity in the "good" ones. Naturally, they made many of us wonder whether we were being true to ourselves.

CHANGES IN THE INDIVIDUAL

We may now turn to consider briefly some effects of changes in the community upon the internal structure of the individual. The outstanding fact about a special oath is that it necessarily creates a conflict of conscience, both in those who take it and in those who do not. This was pointed out to us at our first meeting by a European colleague who had witnessed the destruction of the German and Italian universities—very largely with the use of oaths—under Hitler and Mussolini. In our case a number of people signed the oath more or less immediately. There were various reasons. Some regarded it as "just a piece of paper," some sympathized with the regents' action, some—perhaps most—thought with good reason that economic sanctions would be immediate, and some, in the general confusion of that first summer, thought that the academic senate had officially approved the oath. When it became clear that the faculty as an organized body was going to make an issue of it, these men were immediately divided within themselves. On the one hand, there were the demands of loyalty to one's colleagues, and on the other, the need to justify one's action or to uphold the principles that had led to signing the oath. Some warded off guilt feelings by working long and hard to effect the repeal of the oath and by supporting their nonsigning colleagues to the end; others, though working for repeal of the oath, were perhaps overeager for a settlement, and thus too ready to compromise the principles which others were upholding; still others—relatively few, I think—repressed the guilt feelings and grew increasingly impatient with uncompromising colleagues. At least one went over completely to the regents, writing a letter to show his solidarity with them and his rejection of the faculty position.

Nonsigners of the oath appeared to have, during the first months of the controversy, a relatively easier time of it. They had the satisfaction of having taken a conscientious position in defense of traditional principles of freedom, and they had the support not only of their most highly respected colleagues but of the voting majority in the academic senate. But as time went on their position became increasingly difficult. As the academic senate began its retreat, began voting in favor of compromises with the regents, nonsigners began to find themselves not only without the full support of their official body but actually divided among themselves. After the academic senate had voted, when the dispute was about nine months old, to uphold the regents' policy of excluding Communists from positions in the university, thus giving up the principles of "no political test" and "no guilt by association" in the belief that this would end the controversy, those individuals who still felt bound to stand on these principles found themselves in dissent not only from the regents but from the great majority of their own colleagues. Even those who preferred to remain uncompromising with respect to the principle that only teachers may judge the competence of teachers, or who had other good reasons for not signing the oath, found themselves on occasion rather isolated from the larger academic community. At times when some particular strategy or some particular compromise was being urged by the leadership of the senate, the appeal to the nonsigners was on the basis of faculty unity or love of the university—that is, signing the oath at a particular time, it was urged, would spare the university the worst damage. Here then, there was conflict between the demands of individual conscience (or, as some would have it, pride) and the need for conformity with the immediate and highly valued group. In other words, the nonsigner was forced to wonder whether in insisting on the luxury of a clear individual conscience he was not letting his colleagues down.

We might say, then, that both signers and nonsigners suffered from lack of moral support. This is perhaps the point to mention that the distinction between signers and nonsigners should not be overdrawn. Whether or not a person signed the oath, and when, was a function of many factors—not least, economic ones. Hence when it comes to assigning virtue, as you and I would conceive it today, the signer-nonsigner dimension is far from being a complete guide. What mattered most psychologically, it seemed, was whether or not—and the degree to which—a person was allied in spirit with the nonsigners. Almost everybody involved felt the lack of support, and I think we may say that in almost everybody changes in the form of conflict or splitting in an internal agency—the good superego—followed immediately upon, and were determined by, the conflict and splitting in the surrounding community.

We are, of course, accustomed to the idea that the establishment of a superego requires a long series of reinforcements by external agencies;

which reinforcements presumably decrease in importance as the individual matures. Many of us, however, have not been accustomed to paying much attention to the continuing reliance of the more or less mature and enlightened conscience upon external reinforcing agencies. Perhaps in times of relative social stability the phenomenon is not easy to observe; and it is rare that we have the opportunity to observe what happens under social disorganization. In recent years we have been much enlightened, I think, by the observations made within the concentration camps, by Bettelheim (1943) and by others. The author of *Dungeon Democracy* (Burney, 1946), for example, remarks that men whose nations were still fighting in the war stood up better in the concentration camp than men whose nations had gone down through occupation or internal collapse. In the present instance, I think the same processes were at work, though in a situation far less extreme.

But we seem hardly to have accounted in full for the serious internal disturbances that occurred. The split within the faculty community was the more serious for the individual the more exclusively he had come to rely on that community. And such reliance was made necessary for most, it seemed, not only because they were opposing the authority of the regents, but because of the disapproval, real or imagined, of the public at large. It was probably this latter, as much as anything, that threatened one's identity as a professor; if one's professional colleagues were going to be divided and therefore weak where could strength be found? I am afraid that today the first question the typical professor asks himself in a moral crisis is: What are the others going to do?

Can we in this day and age conceive of an individual conscience that is both enlightened and so firmly internalized that it can endure without external support? Can we, without resorting to the concepts of psychopathology? I should doubt it. The Berkeley episode did not provide a crucial test of this question, and let us hope that we never see the experiment undertaken. There were, as we have seen, men and women who held out against the oath despite the power of the regents, the disapproval—real or imagined—of the general public, the impatience of the faculty leadership, and even the solicitous urgings of respected colleagues. But they were not, I think, without external support. They had each other; they had staunch friends outside the university; they had the support—and knowledge of the hopes and expectations—of colleagues at other universities and colleges; they, in many cases, had their wives or husbands, and they had the remembered promptings of admired figures in more remote times and places. Last-ditch nonsigners sometimes joked among themselves about the interesting psychological study they as a group would make. But I am not aware that this needed research was ever undertaken. One hypothesis may be suggested: that they were all in some sense *inner-directed,* to use David Riesman's (1950) term. And another thing: I think most still had roots in some other community or culture than midcentury Berkeley; some had not been at Berkeley long enough to become fully integrated into the university community; others perhaps were just not altogether capable of being integrated. There was also the factor of having other identities besides that of university professor. Finally there was the factor of knowledge, at least a sense of familiarity with what was going on, than which there is no greater supporter of the ego; this, it seems safe to say, was greater on the average, among nonsigners than in the faculty at large. Perhaps it was not so much knowledge as an irresistable impulse to take an analytic view of things. One professor, who has published a statement about the controversy and his position in it, lists among his reasons for not signing the oath his curiosity about what would happen to him.

Since in taking an oath, if one does so seriously and willingly, one gives over part of his individual conscience to those who require the oath, it follows that one is not the same afterward. One has introjected a new object, and it is reasonable to say that that agency, group, or institution is part of conscience. It is not so important any longer to say whether it is inside or outside the individual. The regents, for those who opposed them, were clearly an external persecutor, but since response to them depended on how they were perceived, and how they were perceived depended on what was projected onto them, one might say that the external persecutor was also inside. I need not remind you of the projected father, mother, and sibling imagery, or of the spirited students who had to be responded to as if they were some of our own impulses. As we have just seen, the "good superego," which could make us joyful or depressed depending on whether we felt it was for us or against us, tended more and more as the pressure increased to find residence in external representatives.

Just one more example: *The Year of the Oath* reports many instances of suspicion, founded and unfounded, among the opponents of the oath. This suspicion centered mainly on colleagues or members of the administration who might have "gone over to the enemy," or who might not be doing their part in the struggle, although they appeared to be friends. Now, insofar as a man had tendencies to defection which he could not accept in himself, he would be disposed to see such tendencies in others. Thus, one might say, if there had been no traitors, it might well have been necessary to invent them. But there *were* traitors. As one colleague pointed out, "You can't call it paranoia when one's suspicions are in accordance with the fact." But you can say that the presence of real external traitors made the internal one the more difficult to manage, and that the amount of hostility directed to the external traitor depended in part on the strength of one's internal "bad object."

I still say it is difficult to apply these concepts in the analysis of ordinary human relations in ordinary times. Surely they would never have been thought of had their creators studied only smoothly functioning adult communities. It is in children that the boundaries between the inner and the outer worlds are vague and highly permeable—in children, and in men who have been so reduced by real pressure that modes of reaction appropriate to childhood begin to make their appearance on the scene.

SCIENCE AND COMMUNITY CRISES

A word should be said about the role of social science and of psychology in matters such as the loyalty oath controversy. At one point in the struggle, when the faculty was rather desperately engaged, a colleague proposed a novel strategy. Everybody would sign the oath except two or three "honorary nonsigners" who would be men of great distinction and unquestioned ideological purity. This would rob the regents of numerous attractive victims and offer them, if they held their ground, only the most unpalatable fare.

This strategy was not only very clever; it had a fascinating quality of conspiracy. But it was hooted down by the assembled nonsigners. "Why," they asked, "if we cannot, because of principle, sign the oath for the regents, should we sign it for the sake of this dubious strategy?" Later, of course, many of these same nonsigners were to be forced to accept the principle implicit in this strategy—the principle that it is right to sacrifice a few individual consciences for the good of the group. As I have said, however, this principle was rejected by the faculty in the end.

Now, I wonder whether it was more than an accident that the man who proposed this strategy was a social scientist. I wonder, indeed, if we do not see here a weak spot in the social science outlook, the spot where regression begins when pressure is applied. Social science easily acquires the habit of considering individuals as members of groups; it frequently seems to argue that individuals should lose themselves in groups. How often will it end by casually sacrificing a few individuals for the sake of the group?

Social science is never completely detached from value. It is perfectly proper to ask how social science might be instrumental in the realization of democratic values. But I would suggest that we pay at least as much attention to the values as to the instruments. It is all right for the social scientist to ask how a university might rid itself of a loyalty oath. (It is not all right for social science to lend itself to those who wish to impose one. This would be to say not only that science has nothing to do with value but that science has no interest in humanity.) But suppose we have accepted the task of countering by scientific means the attacks upon the universities. We should strive, it seems to me, to include within our considerations the broadest possible context of values; human affairs being, to say the least, very complex, we as social scientists have to be very careful lest, in our efforts to achieve by the means of science a particular end, we endanger or impair other values which have some necessary, if obscure, relation to our means. Events such as the loyalty oath controversy offer great opportunities for observation *in medias res*, but they do not favor the detachment that is necessary. The next time a situation such as that which prevailed in Berkeley in June 1949 seems about to develop, a team of social scientists, not attached to the university in question and with ample foundation support, should appear on the scene immediately. They would not, of course, be unconcerned about the outcome; but they would view matters in the largest perspective, entertaining a great variety of hypotheses, including outrageous ones. In our situation such scientists might have asked, for example, whether individual liberty might not have been better preserved had there been no organized opposition to the oath at all. Their answer would probably have been in the negative—but there is no certainty.

As for the role of psychology in such a crisis, I believe that it can make a major contribution, not by planning over-all strategy, but by recognizing, and pointing out those instances in which reaction systems brought over from infancy intrude themselves, to interfere with the best-laid plans of normally reasonable men.

ADDENDUM: 1965

It is interesting to recall now, twelve years later, the plea that teams of social scientists be prepared in advance to study crises such as that which came to a head at Berkeley in June 1949. In the fall of 1964 there was another crisis at Berkeley, this time a conflict between students and officials of the university over the question of students' rights of political advocacy. The students who led the revolt referred to their group as the Free Speech Movement, and the mass demonstrations and mass arrests that occurred were headlined in newspapers all over the country. This crisis was a long time brewing. There were many advance warnings of it, including those of the president of the university, writing and speaking in the role of a value-free social scientist (Kerr, 1964); yet no team of social scientists put in an appearance. I can only renew my earlier plea.

It must be said, however, that in 1964 social scientists were quicker than they were in 1949-50 to see the significance of the events—for education and society as well as for social science—and to undertake analysis of them. Within a few months after the 1964 crisis reached its peak, a number of articles about it had been prepared by social scientists who were close to the scene—for example, Becker (in press), Lipset (1965), Glazer and Selznick (1965), and Katz and Sanford (1965). It is also fair to say that the faculty of the university had a better understanding of the events and their implications than in 1949. Perhaps this was due in part to the fact that it was their students rather than themselves who were most directly involved.

Of particular interest here is the similarity of the two crises. Old-timers at Berkeley, recalling the days of the loyalty oath controversy, were saying in 1964, "Here we go again." The cast of characters was the same —students, faculty, administration, regents, state legislature, alumni, the press, and the public; and all played their expected roles. Communication among these groups was poor at the start, as is common in large organizations. The students, prompted by genuine grievances and frustrated in their attempts to get a hearing from responsible authorities, began with oversimplified conceptions of the administration and the regents and overestimations of their power and bad intentions; university authorities and other interested adults, not knowing the students, began with distorted and otherwise mistaken imagery of them: "Communists," "beatniks," "outside agitators," and so on.

As the crisis deepened and passion mounted, the conflict took on more and more of the aspects of a family drama. The authorities—regents, the president, the chancellor, the governor of the state, the police—became bad parents in the eyes of the students (who also, characteristically, hastily found good parents among the adults on the scene). The authorities, being thus perceived and responded to and finding themselves with a genuine revolt on their hands, began to act in accordance with the students' expectations. Some of these authorities, and various other adults who were following the events closely, began reacting to the students as if they represented their own impulses; some felt anxious and called for punishments and rigid controls, while others, always more or less ready for a fight with authority, took pleasure in the activities of the students and did what they could to urge them on.

As it happened, however, not everybody on the board of regents and in the university's administration, and apparently only a minority of the faculty, was caught up in this regressive behavior. Voices of reason, strong voices, were soon heard, and the press, which had begun by participating in and helping to spread the negative imagery of the active students, responded to these voices and began printing more or less accurate accounts of events and even some useful background stories. The regents acted with more wisdom than they did in 1949-50, perhaps because the pressures on them were less in 1964 than they had been during the McCarthy era.

This is an oversimplified account of what was in fact a highly complicated series of events, and I have made no attempt to discuss the merits of the issues. But perhaps there is enough here to support the main point: people bring to the organizations in which they work a wide range of psychological needs over and above such realistic motives as "to get an education," to teach, or to do research. They find in their work and in the social life of the organization the means for satisfying many of these needs and for inhibiting those which cannot be satisfied, because features of the organization serve the same functions as did relationships with other people in the past. Among the needs brought to the situation are unconscious ones such as dependence and hostility, and among the figures from the past who are represented in the organization are the parents and siblings of childhood. These needs and images are always there, ready to help determine responses in particular situations. In ordinary times life is carried on in accordance with the ego's modes of functioning, basic needs being satisfied in socially acceptable ways and figures of the contemporary environment being perceived realistically rather than in accord with images brought over from childhood. But in some circumstances the ego's operations are rendered impotent, as when channels for the expression of grievances are blocked, or when people are prevented from communicating with others who have the power to affect them significantly, or when the organization acts in such a way as directly to arouse primitive impulses, for instance by assuming that students or employees are children. When this happens, primitive modes of adaptation are switched in and what ensues can be understood only by reference to psychodynamic theory.

As I have said, the characters in the 1964 drama were the same as in that of 1949, and all played their expected roles. The plot, however, was different, and in the more recent crisis students occupied the center of the stage. The conflict was less prolonged than in 1949-50, and perhaps for this reason there appeared to be less regression to primitive modes of functioning. (One would have had to be much closer to the Free Speech Movement than I was to know what actually transpired in the inner households of the students.) There was, however, one aspect of the 1964 controversy which may have deep significance for higher education in this country and which, it seems, can be understood as a mixture of appropriate responses to a real situation and strong emotional needs first generated in the family of origin. I refer here to the part played by graduate students in the recent student protests.

THE LEADERS OF THE "STUDENT REVOLUTION"

Most observers agree that the events at Berkeley could not have taken place without the leadership of graduate students. The undergraduate's acquaintance with the university is usually too transitory for him to have much to say about how things ought to be run; usually by the time he has learned the ropes, he is beginning to focus on his life after graduation and is not much disposed to occupy himself with the affairs of his institution. The graduate student, on the other hand, can bring to the undergraduate's cause not only the "authority" of an older person but a wider temporal view of the educational establishment. This last is particularly true if, as was the case in many instances at Berkeley, the graduate student had been an undergraduate at the same institution. The question is, why should graduate students interest themselves in the problems of undergraduates? What could induce them to leave the library or laboratory where we have been accustomed to find them devotedly pursuing their specialties, with primary concern for their future academic careers? Their involvement in general university affairs is something new on the higher educational scene, and the outlook is that it will be with us for some time to come. The following is a partial analysis of what has been happening.

Graduate students in many departments of our universities suffer from the same kinds of pressures and constraints, the same burden of meaningless work, as do undergraduates or even high school students. As departments have grown larger and more professionalized, traditional communities of scholars, embodying graduate students and professors with whom they worked closely, have been disappearing. The graduate student is being put through a series of tests that involve even more serious consequences than do undergraduate tests and is required every minute of his day to think and act within the confines of his profession's requirements. He must in effect surrender himself to his profession. He cannot investigate what he is curious about but only what can be investigated by approved methods. He has not time to explore other fields, or even to get beyond a specialized area of his own field, because whoever is in charge of his work often demands more than can reasonably be done. He cannot ask questions of a sort that might broaden his mind because he cannot afford to display any ignorance. He cannot converse in the language of educated men because this might be interpreted as professional impurity.

Graduate students thus have many occasions to lament their wasted years as undergraduates. In those years they specialized, thinking that in graduate school they would find freedom. Now, when they look back from their new vantage point, they see that they missed, as undergraduates, their best opportunity to pursue their genuine interests and explore new ones. Hence they have a natural inclination to relive their own undergraduate years vicariously through the students who are now entering college—like a mother who wishes she could take the place of her daughter in her adolescent struggles. Or, if they had a good undergraduate experience, they feel sympathy for their younger brothers in the large universities.

In sum, graduate students have been changing sides. Finding the channels into "management" too narrow, the effort to negotiate them too costly in other values, the rewards of belonging to the governing body too remote or otherwise dubious, they have been casting their lot with the "workers."

SOME APPLICATIONS TO ORGANIZATIONAL LIFE IN GENERAL

This state of affairs is a common one in organizational life. When the writer was a graduate student, he was also a psychologist at a state prison colony and shared with other semiprofessionals on the lower levels of that institution's administrative hierarchy much dissatisfaction with the "established authorities"—the top administration and the state authorities—that is to say, the "fathers." This was accompanied by much sympathy for the inmates—the less fortunate "brothers"—and a strong inclination to take their side in some of their conflicts with the administration. The inmates, for their part, saw the young professionals as performers of maternal functions. This seems to be a universal theme in Western societies. Revolutionary situations are prevented from developing by sufficient displays of flexibility and benevolence on the part of the established authorities and the maintenance of channels through which younger men move into the establishment and become fathers themselves.

In institutions such as prisons, hospitals, and schools, the playing out of the Oedipus fantasy—provided it is kept under reasonable control—seems usually to result in benefits for the inmates, patients, or students, who are accorded solicitude that might otherwise be lacking. (Compare this to an authoritarian set-up in which personnel in the middle of the hierarchy are cowed by those above, become identified with them, and take out their frustrations on those at the bottom of the heap.) One might hope that graduate students who now make common cause with undergraduates will retain some of this spirit after they become teachers themselves. If, as they become the "parents," they will remember, without self-contempt, that they were once young themselves, there might be an improvement in undergraduate education.

Industrial, business, and governmental organizations, no less than schools, prisons, and hospitals, offer opportunities for the recapitulation of family life. The young executive whom one meets on an airplane asks, "Who are you with?" thereby revealing that when the question is returned he will name a company that is supplying him with security, identity, status, and group solidarity as well as meeting his purely economic needs. Indeed, it seems that the business or industrial corporation today offers the individual most of the benefits that used to be found in the family of pre-industrial times. A corporation can if it is run well—as well as wise parents would run a family—provide the individual with opportunities to do productive and satisfying work, to have rewarding relationships with other people, and to develop his own personality. If the corporation is badly run, it can create almost as much disturbance for individuals as can those families in which the parents quarrel and separate, or in which there presides a tyrannical father or a weak father and a dominant mother, or in which neither parent has any convictions about what to tell the children.

After an employee has been with a company for a while, his internal systems come to depend for their equilibrium upon the systems of the organization itself. Internal controls find support in external ones, and life goes on more or less in accord with the ego's way of doing things. But let the organization reveal a split in its higher councils or confusion about what employees are supposed to do, or insist on rigid conformity with senseless rules, or make decisions affecting employees without any advance notice or consultation, or insist on competition among people who have grown accustomed to working as a team, or prevent men from seeing the effects of their work, or break down the connection between amount of work and amount of reward—let the organization do such things as this and there will be trouble, revealing how quickly childish fantasy and modes of adaptation come to dominate the scene when strains become too great or when the ego's processes are made inoperative or ineffective.

Harry Levinson *et al.* (1962) has made the point that workers unconsciously view their union with its protection and security provisions as carrying out maternal functions, and management which runs the company as carrying out paternal functions. Seen in this light, there is irony in the fact that unions have been slower than management to recognize the ways in which workers depend upon their organizations for the satisfaction of their psychological as well as their economic needs. Levinson suggests (in a private communication) that it is the failure of organized labor to understand people's psychological needs that leaves it, in a time of affluence and labor-management peace, with a sense of having no place to go. He further suggests that government, too, has neglected its psychology lessons. When a company shuts down, leaving a few thousand people out of work, the problem is likely to be seen as one that calls for retraining on a massive scale, as if each worker were an independent entrepreneur who is out to sell his labor as dearly as possible and whose relations with his company were purely economic. The time may come when companies will not be permitted to close down or move to different cities, but instead will be given government subsidies to assist their reconversion to another manufacturing activity while maintaining relations with their employees.

We may revert now to the problem discussed in the first part of this chapter, where it was indicated that personality characteristics of individuals might help to determine the ways in which roles are taken and thus be a factor in inducing social change. Significantly, it was not possible to find outright villains in the loyalty oath controversy; it appeared that authoritarian behavior was determined more by the situations in which men found themselves than by dispositions of personality, and that, in general, role-occupancy affected personality more than the other way around. So it is with organizations generally today. It is true that we sometimes find an institution presided over by a petty tyrant who succeeds in turning the whole organization into an authoritarian system. Again we may find people in leadership roles who, because of their inability to make decisions or their propensity for making wrong decisions, arouse anxiety in all who are supposed to follow. When these things do occur, conflicts in the individuals can cause conflicts in the organizations. But such circumstances are comparatively rare—much rarer today than they used to be. Organizations have learned to protect themselves from disruptions due to conflicts in individuals by contriving such rigid and all-embracing role requirements that individual personality has little chance to operate—for ill or for good. It was for this reason that, when a few years ago a group of companies were brought to trial and found guilty of price-fixing, blame could not be levied against any particular individual nor could there be found individuals who felt guilty. The point is that members of organizations rarely have the opportunity to act as individuals, but only as occupants of roles, members of committees, and so on.

This has been a familiar state of affairs in industry for a long time;

it came as a rude shock to many people at the time of the 1964 crisis in Berkeley to discover that this is also the state of affairs in our universities. This is the "dehumanization" of the university that was widely lamented at the time. When the students said, "You can't trust anyone over thirty," they meant that they had not encountered any adults in the system who were under any obligation to behave as responsible individuals; what the students were familiar with was role-behavior on the part of officials—and with being themselves treated not as individuals but as aggregates of functions, each of which was to be taken care of by an appropriate agency.

This is the dilemma of the organization today: how to be efficient and avoid the disruptions that may be caused by permitting personality to influence role-behavior without at the same time losing the benefits of leadership and creativity. Role-rigidification is probably an inevitable accompaniment of technological advances. It is also favored by a well-known human failing: our requirement that our leaders never make mistakes— that is, that they be superhuman. It takes a certain amount of courage to imagine that a leader might suffer the same doubts and anxieties as we ourselves do. The only safe course is to make sure that the role dominates his behavior. Large corporations are familiar with the problem and have for a long time been issuing daily calls for leaders and creative scientists. With respect to the last, industrial organizations have been particularly troubled. They cannot do without scientists, and yet it is difficult to know what to do with the good ones that are found. Scientists tend to be independent, and often they have little enthusiasm for the company's purposes; they do not fit well into the role structure.

This problem, as much as any other, has made industrial organizations look to outside consultants for help in dealing with the "human factor." These organizations show an increasing interest in what psychology, psychiatry, and social science can contribute to an understanding of their functioning. They are increasingly aware of the necessity for the human use of human beings. Accordingly they arrange for their managers lectures, seminars, discussion groups, experiences in group dynamics laboratories, and consultations with clinicians. It is somewhat difficult to imagine college and university faculty members and administrators undertaking this sort of thing, but they may be driven to it.

CHAPTER SIXTEEN

Changing Sex Roles, Socialization, and Education

In any society at any given time there is a set of generally prevalent conceptions of what women, as distinguished from men, are like and a set of expectations concerning what the members of each sex should do and be. Individual females and males adapt themselves to these role-conceptions and role-prescriptions with varying degrees of comfort or discomfort. Their adaptation depends, in the first place, on the range and depth of the human needs that may be satisfied through taking the roles as defined, and, in the second place, on varying individual dispositions toward role-behavior, dispositions generated out of biological structures and processes, psychological correlates of these biological variables, and experiences of growing up in a family.

Conforming to any social role, or rebelling against it, is likely to have some effect on the personality of the individual involved. In the case of sex roles, the effect may be profound. More than other social roles, the role of man or woman is intimately involved with one's conception of oneself, it is present from earliest childhood, and it is thrust upon the individual irreversibly without regard for natural inclinations. We may think of the sex roles in a culture as an expression at the societal level of that universal masculinity-femininity (M-F) conflict within the individual which we discussed in Chapter 12. At the same time, the demands of these roles may either relieve or—as is the case in too many societies, including our own—intensify the individual conflict. Of course, the impact of cultural sex roles is not limited to the M-F dimension of personality. Because in most cultures the sex role is the most central role an individual plays, it can promote or hinder full development in various aspects of the personality. As an example, we can readily imagine that in order to fulfill the role-requirements which are generally accepted in feudalistic societies a woman would have to leave large areas of herself undeveloped.

Biological sex differences are used in all societies as a basis for the allocation to roles and statuses. Anthropologists tell us, however, that apart from the functions involved in procreation, there is very wide variation from one culture to another in what is expected of women and of men. These arrangements have usually worked to the disadvantage of women. When we speak today of freedom for women, as distinct from freedom in general, we mean freedom from men.

Contemporary societies define roles for women and men and create ideologies about them in accordance with those societies' situations, stages of development, and directions of change. A student of sex roles in a modern Western society has to take into account durable trends in the ethos, long-range and short-range economic processes with their implications for the needs of production, the nation's international position, and a variety of subcultures and interests that advocate, with varying degrees of success, different sex roles and statuses.

In this chapter I attempt a brief sketch of the scene respecting sex roles in the United States. Then, relying chiefly upon studies of students at Vassar College, I inquire how young women achieve sex identity and adapt themselves to the changing requirements of their roles while seeking to attain wholeness as individuals. From time to time I also point out the implications of all this for young men. Finally, with attention to theory of personality development and to prospects for the United States culture, I offer some suggestions for education at the college level.

THE UNITED STATES SCENE

In the United States the long-term trend, it seems, is toward greater freedom for women and consequent adaptations by men. If we go back one hundred years, we find that, despite the democratic ideology of equality and freedom and despite the widely admired image of the pioneer woman, "respectable" women were severely restricted. Married women had to stay strictly within the confines of the homemaker's role, and single women suffered severely under the prevailing discrimination in education and employment, and in political and social life. Psychological differences between the sexes were exaggerated, and women were generally believed to be intellectually inferior. Then came the Women's Rights Movement, the gradual increase in the number of women obtaining some form of higher education, the gradual admission of women to "female occupations"—which included that of underpaid factory worker—and finally, the vote for women in 1920. World War I was the turning point. Women in huge numbers went to work in the war industries and engaged in various other kinds of activities outside the home. They began to demand and to get the social freedom that was naturally associated with these responsibilities. There was a loosening of traditional standards all along the line. The image of the "flapper" soon came to symbolize the fact that women had sexual desires, as well as a variety of other "natural instincts." By 1920 it was generally agreed that women were the intellectual equals of men, and college teachers, in all subjects except mathematics and the natural sciences, grew accustomed to having the young women in their classes walk off with the highest grades.

The Great Depression had the effect of adding an additional note of realism where work was concerned. In all socioeconomic classes work came to be regarded as a matter of economic necessity, rather than as a matter of appropriateness for one or the other of the sexes. Since that time not even the most privileged young woman has been able to regard work as "unladylike." By the end of the 1930s the entry of a woman into one of the high-level professions was no longer a subject for any special comment. In a 1962 survey of 10,000 graduates of Mount Holyoke College, one of the "Big Seven" women's colleges of the eastern United States, it was found that 40 percent of the class of 1937 went on to obtain graduate degrees (Friedan, 1963). By the late 1930s it was possible to envision a society in which women had true equality. A talented young woman could make plans for entering any profession she chose, and for combining her career with marriage.

World War II was a period of great, and contradictory, changes as far as women's roles were concerned. On the one hand, there was a sharp increase in the proportion of women entering the labor force and a further decline in sex-role differentiation with respect to the kind of work that was done. On the other, there was at the same time a striking drop in the average age at which women married, an increase in the number of children desired, and a decrease in the number of women seeking higher education.

All of these trends continued into, and possibly throughout, the 1950s. In September 1952 my colleagues and I began a study of the students at Vassar College.[1] After two or three years of observation we became convinced that something akin to a "flight into femininity" was common among college women. In 1957 I wrote as follows: "College teachers recall, or imagine, the 'good old days' prior to the First World War; the days when girls who went to college were a pretty special group, out to change the world. They were out to show what women could do; at the least, to prepare themselves for careers that required special train-

[1] Our research was an activity of the College's Mary Conover Mellon Foundation for the Advancement of Education of which the present writer was coordinator. Donald Brown, Mervin Freedman, and Harold Webster, psychologists; John Bushnell, anthropologist; and Richard Jung, sociologist, were members of the research staff. For more complete accounts of the work see Sanford (1956), Bereiter and Freedman (1962), Brown (1962), Bushnell (1962), Freedman (1962, 1963), Webster, Freedman, and Heist (1962).

ing. Figures from the Bureau of Labor Statistics confirm our own observations that a smaller and smaller proportion of college girls today want to prepare themselves for professional work. The marriage age for college women moves steadily lower. In Vassar of 1904 the average age at the time of marriage was 28. This year's seniors, on the average, expect to be married by 23; the freshmen hope to be wives by 22."

In the middle 1950s, leaving college to get married or getting married while continuing as a student was common. Many college women were articulate and determined about their future roles as wives and mothers. At Vassar in 1954 the modal number of children desired by a representative sample of students was four, as compared with the conventional preference for two that had prevailed before World War II. These young women, it seemed, were participating in the dominant mood of the country. To quote again from the 1957 article:

"In the time of the Cold War the crisis has not been great enough to require that all hands pitch in and do useful work. But it has been great enough to place accent on the 'manly virtues' in men and traditional virtues in women. Not only is feminism dead; we have passed into a phase of antifeminism. Clever writers berate women for exercising their new-found rights and privileges. Psychologists and psychiatrists issue grim warnings about mothers' responsibilities to their young children. Thus it is that we have an upsurge of the attitude that one must not appear too bright or too competent, lest this threaten one's ability to take traditional feminine roles."

Betty Friedan (1963) has recently assembled a great deal of evidence to show that the observations we made at Vassar probably held for most college women, and that the general picture drawn was true for the late 1950s as well as for the early and middle years of that decade. "By the end of the nineteen-fifties," she writes, "the average marriage age of women in America dropped to 20, and was still dropping, into the teens. . . . The proportion of women attending college in comparison with men dropped from 47 per cent in 1920 to 35 per cent in 1958" (p. 12).

And reporting on the Mount Holyoke study mentioned above, she writes: ". . . before 1942, most were married at twenty-five or older; after 1942, the marriage age showed a dramatic drop, and the percentage having four or more children showed a dramatic rise. Before 1942, two-thirds or more of the graduates went on to further study; that proportion has steadily declined. Few, in recent classes, have won advanced degrees in the arts, sciences, law, medicine, education, compared to 40 per cent in 1937" (p. 348).

In 1957 Betty Friedan was asked to carry out a questionnaire study of the Smith College class of 1942. "Of the 200 women who answered that questionnaire in 1957, 80 per cent were housewives. . . . Of the 97 per cent of these women who married—usually about three years after college—3 per cent had been divorced. . . . As mothers, 86 per cent planned their children's birth and enjoyed their pregnancies; 70 per cent breastfed their babies from one to nine months. They had more children than their mothers (average 2.94), but only 10 per cent had ever felt 'martyred' as mothers."

Betty Friedan writes of the flight into femininity, or the acceptance by women of "the feminine mystique," as being as much in evidence at the time of her writing, 1963, as it was in the early 1950s or before. There is, however, scattered evidence that the phenomenon reached something of a highwater mark in the middle 1950s and has since leveled off: The proportion of women in the labor force has been increasing and the Department of Labor expects it to continue to increase;[2] the proportion of college students who are women also appears to be increasing now;[3] and the number of college women who desire four or more children seems to have declined since 1954.[4] Although the age at marriage of American women in general may still be dropping, there is no evidence that this is so in the case of college women. College marriages, which became common during and after World War II, are undoubtedly here to stay, but there is no evidence of a rising trend (Hill, 1964).

Finally, there seems to have been a change in the tone and content of the literature on the subject of women's roles. Whereas in the early 1950s it was common for professionals in health, education, and welfare, and in the psychological and social sciences, to promote "the feminine mystique," this is rare today.

In the early and middle 1950s, then, there was a genuine reaction against freedom for women. This was relaxed by the end of that decade, but there are still few signs that the march toward freedom has been resumed, or that the goal of equality is much closer than it was before World War II. Here the striking fact is that the proportion of women seeking and obtaining postgraduate training is small and does not seem to be increasing. The Assistant Secretary of Labor has recently reported, on the basis of a study involving all United States citizens who were 25 to 29 years old in 1960, that 38 percent of the men, but only 10 percent of the women, who had the intellectual capacity for training beyond the baccalaureate degree actually completed a year or more of graduate study (Moynihan, 1964). This is in keeping with the fact that women received only 11 percent of the doctorates awarded during the twelve-month period ending in June 1963. Whereas it seems to be taken for granted that an

---

[2] The Prudential Life Insurance Company (1963) quotes the U. S. Department of Labor estimate that during the 1960s the number of working women will rise at nearly twice the rate for men, and that by 1970 at least two out of every five women aged 20 to 65 will be gainfully employed.

[3] In 1958 the percentage was 35 (Friedan, 1963, p. 12); in 1960, 38 percent of all female high school graduates entered a college-level institution (Moynihan, 1964). In 1963 women received 42 percent of the degrees conferred at the bachelor's and four-year, first-professional level (U. S. Office of Education, 1964).

[4] The decline has been very apparent at Vassar College.

increasing proportion of women will be gainfully employed, and that an increasing proportion will obtain some education beyond high school, this definitely does not mean that there is general acceptance of life styles that might bring them into competition with, or threaten the status of, men. Women graduates of four-year colleges seem to be *deciding* that they do not want graduate or professional education, while girls in the lower and lower-middle classes are still under pressure to accept narrow female sex roles without their having much say in the matter. Project Talent has reported, according to Moynihan (1964), that in 1960 three-fifths of the high school graduates who did not enter college were girls. The discrepancy between boys and girls in respect to college-going is much less in the higher ranges of aptitude than in the lower ranges. Thus, for example, in the top 5 percent, 95 percent of the boys and 92 percent of the girls enter college, compared to 36 percent of the boys and 24 percent of the girls in the 30 to 39 percentile range. Since aptitude of this kind is associated with family income, it seems clear that the most disadvantaged of our citizens, as far as education is concerned, are lower-class girls. These are the girls who are most often exploited sexually and who, of course, swell the ranks of the teen-age married.

At the present time, as for a long time past, we have to deal with cultural as well as individual ambivalence with respect to sex roles. The culture itself presents the young woman with contradictory role prescriptions. She must by all means be glamorous and stunningly attractive to men (which is to be achieved through a narcissistic preoccupation with her physical attributes), but she must be a practical and devoted mother. She must prepare herself for challenging and important work—to be begun after the children have grown up sufficiently—but she must be prepared at all times to accommodate herself to her husband's career plans. She is exhorted to carry on in the feminist tradition but, given a slight change in the national mood, she is told that career women are neurotically driven and unfulfilled. Whatever the prescription, she has only to look about her to find models in older women—models of what to be and what not to be. She has, indeed, a fairly wide range of possible choices. The trouble is that the models themselves are often not sure of their ground. Both the career woman and the woman who devotes herself more or less exclusively to homemaking can readily be thrown on the defensive; and they are easily induced to express hostility and contempt toward each other. Neither role has such universal or unambiguous sanction that it can be taken without any doubt or any wishing that one had chosen the alternative course. Women have incorporated the cultural ambivalence. More than that, neither of these roles, as it has been defined in our society, allows enough expression of the individual's personality needs. It may be that in such a complex society as ours more needs are generated than can find gratification in any social role as presently defined; the taking of a particular role may involve irreversible commitments, to meet which the individual must suppress dispositions toward role-behavior of an inappropriate sort.

THE VASSAR STUDIES

The research which we conducted at Vassar College between 1952 and 1958 yielded much useful data on changes in women's roles. Our findings were based on several measures: a comprehensive group of psychological tests which were given to six entering freshman classes and five senior classes; systematic and fairly intensive interviews with representative groups of students from various classes; and interviews and special procedures which were used to follow a random sample of students from one class—the class of 1958—through their entire college careers. In addition to the study of students, we carried out a three-day assessment of fifty Vassar alumnae from the classes of 1929 through 1935, and administered our tests to groups of alumnae of various classes from 1904 to 1945. Thus it was possible to compare alumnae both to current students and to alumnae of other generations.

The findings at Vassar lend support to the belief that women's conceptions of their roles are changing. For example, comparison of the class of 1904 with later classes, including contemporary ones, shows the declining feminism of which we have spoken; it also shows differences in the selection of women for college then and now. It was our impression when we studied these women in 1954 that the graduates of '04 were more spirited, active, and idealistic than college students of the mid-1950s. Again, comparison of current students with graduates of 1929 to 1935— the group of women studied intensively—gave evidence of a trend toward lessened differentiation. The scheme of educational types that Donald Brown (1956) was able to apply to this alumnae sample seems to hold quite well for current students. We may still distinguish (a) high achievers, (b) over achievers, who work hard and do well without acquiring any serious appreciation of the intellectual life, (c) underachievers, who enjoy college and grow intellectually while there without becoming seriously involved in work, (d) seekers of identity, whose college experience is primarily one of radical adjustment to a social world quite different from the one from which they come, and (e) a group of students characterized primarily by their social activity and orientation toward their peers. But—and this is the important point—today's students do not fit the types so neatly, or exhibit them in so vivid a fashion. In 1930, it seems, people showed a stronger tendency to be one thing or another; today the stronger inclination is to be a balanced or all-around person.

The post-World-War-II movement among college women toward a return to traditional feminine roles seems to reflect a certain cleavage of the generations. Let us consider the case of an alumna from our '29-'35 group who scored very high on "masculinity" and "sex-role conflict." She is a very active, worldly, sophisticated woman, and a rather dissatisfied wife and mother, who was happy to return to the world of work after her youngest child entered school. It is interesting to note the predominant trend in her fantasies, as revealed in the Thematic Apperception Test and in some of her interviews. She wants to belong to, to lose herself in, a large traditional family of an earlier time in which respect for the woman went hand in hand with the heavy demands that were made upon her. She would have been happy and effective as a pioneer wife.

Could it not be that the daughters of such women tend to participate in, and to act out, their mothers' fantasies? This could be a factor contributing to the early marriages, the increased fecundity, and the acceptance of economic dependence upon the family of origin that we observed among college women of the 1950s. It is to be noted that our subjects were mainly of the middle and upper-middle classes. It may well be that young women who now accent emancipation are most often the daughters of immigrants, or of working-class or farm women, who did not participate in the revolutions of the 1920s and 1930s.

ATTITUDES TOWARD SEXUALITY. Because sex and reproduction have always loomed so important in woman's role, it seems appropriate to look for a moment at the changes which have taken place in sexual behavior and women's attitudes toward their own sexuality. Our intensive interviews with forty-eight subjects from the Vassar class of 1958 touched repeatedly on these questions during the senior year. Various aspects of sex were discussed—personal experience, abstract values, social behavior. After four years of interviewing, we had established a close rapport with these students, and we felt no doubt that they were telling us the truth.[5]

Our findings suggest that talk of a "sexual revolution" on the United States college campuses should be discounted. True, we are speaking here of students who graduated in 1958, but current observations at Stanford University and at the University of California, Berkeley, confirm our earlier impressions. Of the women in our samples 20 to 30 percent were nonvirgins at the time of graduation, and of these the overwhelming majority were either engaged to be married or involved in serious relationships. There are very few promiscuous girls. The general picture is in line with that offered in the Kinsey Report (Kinsey and Gebhard, 1953), and the Kinsey group was of the opinion that there had been no great change since the 1920s. Their impression is supported by Bromley and Britten (1938) who reported that 25 percent of a sample of women in college in the 1930s had experienced premarital intercourse.

The mores of college students seem to conform rather well with the ideas and values of the middle class from which most of them come. At the same time, these students participate in the general uncertainty about sexual morality—and about other moral issues—that prevails among educated citizens of the United States. The woman in college who engages in casual affairs or regards sexual intercourse merely as "fun" receives very little support from her culture; hence such behavior either expresses

[5] For a fuller account of the interviewing procedures and of our findings concerning sexual behavior, see Freedman (1965).

a certain amount of individual psychopathology or at least is carried forward at considerable cost in peace of mind.

But if rates of premarital intercourse have not changed radically since the 1920s, there is some reason to believe that the circumstances and meaning of this behavior have changed and that college women approach the area of sex with a different spirit. In the 1920s and 1930s some of the college women who engaged in premarital intercourse were submissive, somewhat masochistic people who could be seduced because they felt they had little else to offer. Today, in the colleges that my colleagues and I have observed, this is extremely rare. Girls who engage in intercourse do so with their eyes open, usually after giving the matter much thought. Our interviews have clearly shown that Vassar students are in little danger of being exploited by men—that indeed, as far as sex relations in the narrow sense are concerned, full equality prevails.

It seems likely, too, that a higher proportion of college women are engaging in necking and petting now than formerly. This goes with increased awareness and frank discussion of sex. Surely a greatly increased proportion of college students are including sexuality in their conscious schemes of things. As our interviewees have made plain, sex experience under the conditions they have laid out for themselves is enjoyable and unaccompanied by feelings of guilt. Homosexuality has declined sharply. At the same time most students try to find a moral basis for what they do.

The whole approach to sex that we find in our subjects would seem to be highly favorable to good sex adjustment in marriage. That such adjustment is indeed the rule for Vassar graduates is indicated by the fact that when 219 graduates of the class of 1957 filled out a questionnaire in connection with their seventh reunion, only one had been divorced. This is consistent with the 3-percent divorce rate found by Betty Friedan (1963) in the Mount Holyoke class of 1942. But does this attainment of adequate sexuality interfere with the development of these young women as whole personalities? Before attempting to answer this question we may consider some additional relevant data.

ATTITUDES TOWARD WOMEN'S ROLES, WORK, MARRIAGE. The young women we have studied do not look with complete favor upon traditional feminine roles. Consider their responses to the question: "What do you criticize in a woman?" Thirty-one percent of our interview sample mentioned unfortunate traits that seem to have no particular sex reference, for example, "intolerant," "snobbish," "selfish." Fourteen percent were critical of activities that do not conform to traditional stereotypes of feminine behavior. Typical of such responses were: "neglecting her children," "overintellectual," "too independent," "not feminine and warm," "dogmatic about her career." Four percent were disposed to condemn "either extreme"—that is, being immersed in either a home or a career to the exclusion of other activities and interests. The majority, however— 51 percent—criticized characteristics that seem to express the "feminine mystique." They were censorious of such things as "marriage as the only goal in life," "reduction of the self to the husband," "leaning on being a woman," "superficial social life," "pettiness and gossip," "not having interests outside of the home and family," "being too tied to the children."

Results of objective testing support the findings of the interview studies. A significant majority of seniors reject the item: "I dislike women who disregard the usual social and moral conventions." This represents a significant change from the responses of the freshmen. A large majority of both freshmen and seniors answer "False" to "I like the sweet 'feminine' type of girl as my friend." A slight majority of freshmen (53 percent) and a larger majority of seniors (63 percent) say "True" to "If I were a housewife and mother, I would also like much outside work or many other activities at the same time." To the item, "Many girls are catty and petty," substantial majorities of both freshmen and seniors respond "True." These attitudes seem to become more pronounced as students go through college; seniors score higher (that is, more masculine) than freshmen on verbal tests of "masculinity-femininity."

Almost all Vassar students expect to be employed after graduation, at least until they marry. Sixty-eight percent of the freshmen and 69 percent of the seniors in our special sample say "True" to the item "I would like a career." What they mean by a career is often a job rather than a profession, but they have in mind work that involves some commitment or important investment of the self. The interviews show that almost every student who responds "False" to "I would like a career" nevertheless plans to work, at least until marriage. By saying "False" she means that she is not particularly concerned to continue her work after marriage or after the arrival of children or to resume it when the children are self-sufficient.

Students are not in conflict about working as unfeminine behavior. They do, however, rather overwhelmingly draw the line at professional work that might tend to bring them into competition with men. We observed that many students scaled down their career aspirations between their freshman and senior years. They shifted to professions or activities which are not so demanding by way of training or preparation and which have less prestige. They seemed to do so partly because of greater realism, greater awareness of the impediments to achieving their original goals, but also because they sensed that men have difficulty in accepting achievement of a high order on the part of women.

Virtually all Vassar students wish to marry—and that within a short time after leaving college. In one survey of a senior class, carried out by Freedman (1964), all the students but one said they wished to marry. Of those who wished to marry, all but two wanted to have children.

Seniors, apparently, have a quite realistic view of their future, for what they expect is highy consistent with what young alumnae are doing. Analysis of 249 questionnaires (almost a total sample) filled out by members of the class of 1957 at the time of their seventh reunion (Davidson,

1964) showed that 81 percent of these young women had worked at paid positions since leaving college. They could not have worked for very long, however, for at the time of the reunion 88 percent were married and living with their husbands. Most were taking care of one or more children, the average number of children per family being 1.4. Of these young women, 52 had earned higher degrees; there were 3 Ph.D.s, 2 M.D.s, 4 LL.B.s, and 43 M.A.s; 16 were still working toward higher degrees. Of those who had worked but stopped, there were 48 teachers, 15 secretaries, 14 researchers, 10 employees of publishers, and 9 social workers. These careers, which many of these women will undoubtedly take up again later, are safely feminine ones. Some of the respondents had continued to work after marriage, for whereas only 28 (12 percent) were single, 59 (23 percent) were still employed.

This, then, is the common pattern of role-taking followed by most alumnae of a selective college and anticipated by young women still in college: to work for a while before getting married; to work at something interesting but not in a field or at a level that will involve competition with men; to plan for some graduate training, preferably in a field that has long been open to women, but to be prepared to interrupt it in favor of marriage; to have children early; to maintain an interest in community affairs; and to plan a return to work, volunteer or paid, when the children no longer need intensive care.

There are deviations from this common pattern. A few of these young women go into the most demanding professions, while more do no paid work at all before marriage. A few continue with their careers after they become wives and mothers. Dispositions of personality enter heavily into the determination of choices of role and, as we know from studies of young alumnae (Freedman, 1962), those who follow the common pattern do so in various different ways, for different reasons, and with different degrees of satisfaction. The great majority of these young alumnae are well satisfied with their lot. They do not show the defensiveness that is so often apparent in women of the older generation. (Unfortunately, we do not have information about people who graduated in the early 1950s.) As will be suggested later, this improved morale may be due to improved education and to cultural change that is now in progress.

We may return now to the question of whether the patterns of sexual behavior and attitude, role-taking, and role-anticipation which we have observed interfere with the development of full individuality in the women students. Our answer must be guarded, for several reasons. For one, the appraisal of personality development during the college years has been a neglected area of psychology, and we cannot claim that the scales we have devised do more than give crude estimates of change in a few aspects of the person. Again, researchers have only begun to explore relationships between developmental changes in personality and the kinds of experiences students have in college; we have to rely here mainly upon clinical studies of individuals.

This much said, I may report our impression that the students who developed best at Vassar participated fully in the prevailing patterns of sexual behavior and attitude. Change in the direction of independence, self-awareness, greater openness to experience, greater breadth of view goes with a *gradual* liberalization of attitude in respect to sex and particularly closely with gains in the direction of making one's sexuality a part of one's conscious self.

Neither premature "freedom," as observed in girls who were having casual affairs, nor sexual "backwardness" was associated with good development. Two of the three "uninhibited" girls in our sample were manifestly troubled and very probably deeply disturbed. (The case of one of these students, Pat, is discussed in some detail in Chapter 11.) Among the students who were most backward sexually some neurotic inhibition was to be found, but for the great majority there was nothing to suggest that development was being impaired or that they might not "catch up" sexually later on. There was nothing to suggest, either, that these were the girls with the greatest potential for achievement.

At Vassar, then, the sexual mores could not be regarded as a barrier to education in the general sense of the term. This is not to say that some of the time spent in dating—in anticipating, preparing for, and reliving it—and in emotional involvements with young men might not have been spent more advantageously in other ways; nor is it to deny that some of our subjects had experiences that favored their defining themselves as sex objects or marriage partners. On balance, however, it seems that their sexual experimentation was valuable to these young women, perhaps chiefly in what it taught them of equality in their interpersonal relations with men. In any event, since colleges are dealing with people who are biologically mature, there is very little that can be done to prevent sexual experimentation. The best course, it would seem, is to turn the state of affairs that actually exists to the advantage of education. I suggest later in this chapter some ways in which this might be done.

It is well to remind ourselves here that our discussion has concerned young women who stay in college to graduate. What about those who drop out in their freshman, sophomore, or junior years? We were not able to discover, by means either of tests or of clinical studies, any consistent differences in personality between students who dropped out and those who graduated. This whole problem is enormously complicated by the fact that students leave college or change colleges for many different reasons, some of them quite beyond the student's control. We do know, however, that some leave college as early as the freshman year in order to get married, and some to enroll in a college where the chances of making a suitable marriage seem greater than at Vassar. Such students present serious problems for the educator.

We should note also that pressures on young women to define themselves in terms of their "femininity" are much greater at state universities, commuter colleges, and some coeducational private colleges than they are at a highly selective woman's college like Vassar.

If we ask now why it is that so few seniors in the best women's colleges wish to undertake the arduous work of preparing themselves for the high-level professions, we must conclude that the main reason is because they see this as conflicting with their desire and intention to marry early and to have children. They have a realistic view of the practical difficulties in the way of combining a career with marriage and are fully aware of the enormous pressure of cultural expectations concerning what a homemaker is supposed to do. It seems also that in the years since World War II the professional career has lost something of its charm. Deep-lying psychological motives for achievement in competition with men seem not as common or as potent as they used to be, and it is easy to criticize the idea that a profession, as defined and practiced in the society of today, is the road to self-fulfillment.

The main pressures toward role-definition and choice of role come from outside the college. We are not likely to see much change in the outlook of women in college until our culture changes, until men become far more capable of equalitarian relations with women, and until the professions are defined in less "masculine" terms and practiced in ways that allow more expression of individuality. It is reasonable, however, for the colleges to encourage young women to consider delaying their commitment to marriage. It seems obvious that parents and the college should view rushing into marriage as a means for achieving an identity, or for solving sexual problems, in the same way that they view other ill-advised and irreversible youthful decisions that put roadblocks in the way of further development. To the ordinary college student the best appeal might be that she cannot be fully human unless she attains full equality with men, particularly with her husband. That equality means obtaining at least as much general education as he does, to guarantee her intellectual competence and companionship. It also means having a reasonable alternative to early marriage and motherhood, and this, in our society, depends heavily on having some marketable skills.

SEX ROLES AND LIBERAL EDUCATION

In Chapter 12 I discussed some of the ways in which a liberal education can help college men and women to resolve conflicts over masculinity-femininity within their personalities. Now I would like to pursue this argument further to show that not only the achievement of a mature sex identity but full development of the entire personality depends on delaying one's commitment to a particular sex role.

This is not to say, of course, that there should be no sex-role differentiation in society. It is rather that the taking of sex roles is a secondary matter, to be governed by the preferences of *developed* individuals.

When education for social roles, including vocational roles, is given priority, individual development is actually impaired, for young people are encouraged to define themselves in terms of what they do rather than in terms of what they are. If this happens in a society that assigns different vocational roles to the sexes, as does ours, there is a clear implication that boys and girls should first define themselves as males and females rather than as human beings.

In the developed individual, performances in social roles are integrated with the personality; they stand as sources of gains for the whole even as they benefit from being able to draw upon all the resources of the person. For example, students who approach sexuality gradually, postponing intercourse until they are psychologically ready, not only attain to a suitable control of their impulses but also avoid the alienation of their sexuality from the rest of their personalities. They create a state of affairs in which sex is the more enjoyable because it is now a channel for the expression of various needs and feelings that have been developed. The same considerations hold for vocational and other social roles. If commitments to such roles are made too early, young people are prevented from having experiences that might develop them; when there is little to the personality besides the role-behavior, the tendency to define the self in terms of the role is strong.

It seems obvious that a girl who becomes a housewife without ever considering other kinds of activities thereby limits herself as a personality. And the same holds for a young man who from his high school days concentrates on a "masculine" profession. What is perhaps not so obvious is that the housewife who feels frustrated at being stuck at home with the children when she might be doing "important" things in the world has mainly her education to blame. It should have given her the resources to avoid boredom, to connect the uninteresting with what *is* interesting, and in the process to improve her work with her children and her home. Her case is not essentially different from that of a man who allows himself to be dominated by the routine aspects of his job because he is unable fully to explore its possibilities or to see it in a context of larger and more interesting processes.

The bored housewife who wants to get a job because she is still in search of identity is likely to be bored with the job, too. The woman who would find identity in a career outside the home is in the same position as a man who would find identity in this way. The trouble in both cases is too much reliance upon external definitions of the self. In the ideal case, where the sense of identity is based upon development in the personality, the man who goes to work every day and the woman who stays home with the children would be able to switch roles without feeling seriously threatened. This is putting the matter strongly, to be sure, but we are clearly approaching a time when there will be no kinds of valuable work that cannot be performed as well by one sex as by the other. At such a time, work-role will be a thin reed upon which to depend for identity. Even now there is little reason, apart from cultural tradition, why the whole matter of who is to do what work could not be settled according to preference and convenience.

The development of the individual personality depends heavily upon the equality of the sexes, in theory and ideology as well as in practice. And the attainment of equality for women depends on personality development in women as well as in men. Higher education can itself go a long way toward developing the kind of self-awareness that would accomplish both these ends. An intellectual understanding of the psychological processes involved in taking a sex role can be made available to every college student, girl or boy. This would be a great help. It would not, of course, be adequate in most cases to "make the unconscious conscious," as the psychotherapist would say, although it has been our experience that four years of liberating education can bring alterations in even the more central structures of the personality. How this may be done more effectively and more often is a pressing problem for research. Inquiry into the matter would probably reveal the great importance of the study of literature, which can familiarize the student with the whole range of human feelings and impulses, and of the study of philosophy, which can challenge the individual's most deeply held values.

The preceding suggestions have to do mainly with the intellectual life of the college. It must be noted, too, that the social organization of the institution may be such as to favor or to hamper the integration of sexuality and sex-role-taking into the personality. It is true that colleges, as compared with all other situations of life in the United States, are bastions of sex equality. It is probable that many young women in college now will never again "have it so good." Even so, sex discrimination is common on our college campuses, and it undoubtedly contributes to the development of sex-linked identities in young men and women. For example, many colleges have different parietal rules for women and for men. All such discriminatory practices should of course be eliminated.

What about the idea of separate colleges for women and for men? On the face of it, this idea seems a glaring example of what I have been complaining about. The matter is not simple, however, for coeducational schools sometimes provide an environment that is extremely unfavorable to a young woman's development. In one coeducational liberal arts college, for example, which exists in a relatively isolated small-town community, the girls are definitely in the role of second-class citizens. Boys are free to go off the campus for dates if they like, whereas the girls, being less mobile, are more or less restricted to the campus. The boys take full advantage of this situation by calling up for dates at the very last moment. Some actually go so far as to require that the girls walk over to their dormitories, rather than vice versa, particularly if the weather is cold! This exploitation of the girls holds in all other spheres of campus life. Of course, the girls are not necessarily hampered thereby in the development of intellectual interests and powers, but it would be surprising if they did not develop a good measure of hostile manipulativeness toward men.

Probably at this stage of our society's development a decision between coeducational and segregated schools ought not to be finally made. Co-education covers much variety in social structure and in approaches to the task of exposing the variables that really make a difference to individual development. The same thing may be said of segregated colleges. Women's colleges will differ significantly, for example, according to the size and potency of the male contingent in the teaching faculty. Such a factor may indeed loom larger than the fact that all the students happen to be girls. It seems not to have occurred to the men's colleges that they might have women on their faculties, so that in their case we do not have to be troubled by a variation in this respect. But such colleges are sufficiently varied in other important respects that it would be very difficult to make generalizations about the relative effectiveness of men's colleges as a group. From our present knowledge it might very well be concluded that co-education versus segregation is not by any means the most important variable among those which are correlated with educational objectives. We probably ought not to eliminate the women's colleges without a more serious attempt to discover some of their unique values and (since they are going to be with us anyway for quite a while) to think of ways and means by which they might best be utilized in the interest of student development.

SOCIAL CHANGE

It is not to be supposed that the reforms suggested here would take hold and be effective in guiding the lives of people unless conditions in society were favorable. The point to be emphasized is that in the United States today conditions *are* favorable to fresh thinking about sex roles and new patterns of role-taking by women. Such are our affluence and our prospects for future affluence that we are able to give more attention to the quality of life and less to its necessities. The prospects are for a con-tinued state of overproduction, as far as material goods are concerned, and for rapid change in the kinds of jobs people are called upon to do. In these circumstances there is no great pressure on women in general to enter the labor force, or on especially talented women to enter one or another of the presently existing professions. The time is fluid—open-ended with respect to sex roles. It is a time, in short, when we are in a position to think seriously about what would be the ideal pattern of sex-role differentiation.

Our society, it appears, will have a continuing need for trained in-telligence, but it may be doubted that training should be limited to the professions as they are now defined. New professions need to be de-veloped. Our greatest tasks at the present time have to do with the de-velopment and improvement of people, with the expansion and enrichment of their lives, with the improvement of their relations one to another, and with the development and maintenance of communities in which these things are possible. We need, both for the sake of the economy and for the sake of individual enjoyment and well-being, a vast expansion in all those activities that cannot be duplicated by machines—activities involving the use of symbols and activities in which people help one another directly. More people must spend more time in educating themselves and others, more time in creating and performing and developing appreciation in the realm of art,[6] more time in looking after the health and welfare of others.

These areas have been neglected by men, and by the professions that men have designed and organized. In the short run, at any rate, women have here an almost unlimited opportunity. Helping professions as presently defined and practiced are not adequate to what I have called our greatest tasks. These professions are too specialized, and they are becoming more so. They tend to focus upon part-functions of individuals and upon subsections and subprocesses of the community. The need is for people who can and will look after whole individuals and whole communities.

Let it be clear that I am not speaking here of "community work" in the traditional meaning of that term; I am not suggesting that women do community work while men become professionals, or that women do any work outside the home without suitable remuneration. I am arguing rather that advances in social-scientific knowledge have made us aware of our need for a whole new array of high-level talent, the efforts of which are focused on the community in the same way that men's efforts are focused on business and the traditional professions. Since these new roles are not yet identified with either sex, there is freedom for women to start out on an equal footing or better.

My conception of action in the community assumes that some women will have to become professional in fields such as city planning, community mental health, school planning, sociology, politics, and so on. But they can be joined by huge numbers of generally educated college graduates who can help to furnish ideas as well as to attain the power necessary to carrying them out. Some of these would need to be high-level generalists who would interest themselves in whole communities and take part in making policy and taking action affecting them. This is a place for our most talented and energetic women, those who are in a position to devote themsevles to study, research, and action in the field of public affairs. And then we need a vast army of generally educated women, "sub-professional," as is sometimes said, who can and will turn their hands to almost anything, who would constitute a sort of "third force," as it were, and who, free of professional constraints, could move into situations where there was special need.

Both groups of generalists would have to be continuously educated—

[6] I do not dwell here on the arts, including writing, in which talented women already have sufficient freedom to work out suitable designs for living.

in situations and by techniques that have not as yet been worked out. One thing seems certain: there would be no great point in their going back to school, to sit among budding professionals learning academic specialties. Instead, they should organize themselves into action groups and insist that the university come to them, through professors who had something to contribute toward solving the genuine problems that were being attacked.

What women as a group need in order to carry out these programs and to attain their own full humanity is *power*—that is to say, political power by which they can influence the course of events in the community, the state, and the nation. Women have long since shown that they have the inclination to take the role of community caretaker and guardian of taste, humanity, and justice. But they have been laughed at, called "clubwomen" or "volunteers," and so rendered impotent. Their defeat has been due to their failure to challenge the assumption that the important decisions will be made by men. Women must get themselves elected to the city council and become its majority. They must use the same strategy on other governmental units. It is hard to see what could prevent their doing this, once it was decided that this was the way to proceed. Once they were in such positions of power, they could see to it that there was no further discrimination against women in other roles.

The social changes that I anticipate are radical and far-reaching in their implications, but they are not likely to come about immediately or to be such that women without higher education can avoid working at many of the same kinds of jobs that they hold today. Most women will continue to work not so much to express their personalities or do good in the world as to sustain themselves and their families and to participate as fully as possible in the benefits of our society and culture. There can be no let-up in efforts to guarantee them equality of opportunity and conditions of work that are suited to their needs.

But for educated women to lay all their bets on finding suitable places within the existing technological system when the system itself needs to be changed—and is already changing—would be a misfortune for the individual women as well as for society. With the advance of technology, work outside the home has become more and more highly organized. More and more of a person's life tends to be dominated by his place within the productive organization. Each individual is asked to adapt himself precisely to the requirements of his role. Any expression of personality is like "noise" in a communication system. Compare this situation with the varied and deeply satisfying life that a generally educated woman can have, and often does have, in the United States today: as companion and sexual partner of her husband, as mother of her children, as the chief sustainer of the intellectual and artistic life of her community (outside of academic institutions), as the guardian of all that is humane within her society.

If women in college today have this vision of their future lives, we should not be surprised if the number obtaining higher degrees declines, and if the demands for general education at the undergraduate level, and for all kinds of continuing education outside of the current academic patterns, continue to increase.

If our society should move in the direction indicated, there would be, at least in the short run, a sharper sex differentiation in the world of work than we have at the present time. Men would feel that their masculine pride was well protected; at the same time, however, they might in increasing numbers begin to discover that there is much more to life than the demonstration of masculinity. They might, indeed, begin to see that women have the best of the bargain and begin to design a society in which men as well as women devoted themselves to family life and became participators in all kinds of intellectual and artistic activities and prime movers in the building of a better society. Men and women—and children—would then do more things together, as they do in well-run colleges and universities and in other Utopias!

CHAPTER SEVENTEEN

Personality Development in College

There seems to be little doubt that some parts of a person can still change after childhood. The multiplication of educational, therapeutic, penal, and other institutions in our society bears witness to a widespread belief that people can indeed change or be changed. Chapter 3 of this book presented a simple model of the process by which change-agencies of this type operate and applied it in a general way to the student-college relationship.

What is not so clear is the exact nature of the change which takes place. Is it really a change in the underlying personality, or merely something more superficial? Here we encounter an old issue in personality theory: that of early or historical versus late or contemporary determination. The former accents the relative fixity or persistence of tendencies established early in the individual life; the latter accents the possibility that important new trends in personality may be set up comparatively late—at least as late as the college years. In Chapter 9 I stated the case for fixity. Now, drawing on our findings from the Vassar studies, I would like to argue for the possibility of change—change, that is, in the central and enduring features of the personality—in college and beyond.

Originally published under the title "Personality Development during the College Years," *Personnel-O-Gram*, proceedings of the 1956 Annual Convention of the American College Personnel Association, Washington, D.C., March 1956; also in a briefer version in *Personnel and Guidance Journal*, 35:74–80, 1956.

EARLY VERSUS LATE DETERMINATION

Psychologists have so far given relatively little attention to developmental changes between the ages of seventeen and twenty-two. The "adolescent studies" that were common in the 1930s seem to have stopped when their subjects were about eighteen, and students of development have now turned their attention largely to old age.[1]

Traditional psychoanalytic thought accents the element of fixity in personality—hence the notion that personality is already formed by the age of eighteen, if not indeed by the age of five. What happens after that is seen as a mere unfolding or expression of what has previously been established. Observed changes in behavior, knowledge, attitude, or opinion, such as those reported in Newcomb's Bennington Study (1943), have been regarded as due not to changes in the structure of personality but rather to the pressures of the contemporary social situation. This view was reflected in Festinger's (1955) comment on the finding of Davidson and Kruglov (1953) that students obtaining low scores on authoritarianism are older and further along in college than those high on authoritarianism. How, he asked, if the F scale for measuring authoritarianism taps some relatively deep and enduring aspects of personality, are we to explain the fact that scores seem to be "so easily affected by environmental experiences"?[2]

There is nothing in clinical studies of adults, either, that would point to the college years as being of critical importance for the development of personality. Until quite recently it would hardly have occurred to the assessor or diagnostician of an adult to inquire very closely about where he went to college or what happened to him there. The investigator would probably have focused, instead, upon early childhood, family background, social class, and contemporary social roles.

An accent on the early determination of personality has some very definite implications for higher education. If we were to take the position that the personality is already well formed by eighteen, it would be reasonable to expect the student to choose his experiences in accordance with motives that are already basic to his personality, and to go about confirming himself as he is. We could be content to see a student choose a college that suits him, take advantage of a system of free electives, select a major in keeping with his established bent—perhaps one that furthers the vocational plan that he has already worked out. The chief job of the college would be to help him acquire the knowledge and skills needed for the

[1] But studies of personality change in the years of middle life have begun to make their appearance. See, for example, Neugarten (1963, 1965), Cumming and Henry (1961), Havighurst (1957), Kelly (1955), Terman and Oden (1959), and Freedman (1962).

[2] In reply to Festinger's question, I would argue that changes in authoritarianism do indeed represent changes in the personality itself, for they involve changes in one of its central structures—the superego. We cannot deny this fundamental fact simply because the changes occurred in response to environmental factors. According to the theory presented in Chapter 6, structures within the personality can be both central and enduring yet "outer"—that is, in close touch with the environment.

successful pursuit of his purposes and perhaps for the satisfaction of the particular needs of his personality. If the personality that is already formed is "neurotic," which is not at all unlikely, then of course the student would need the help of an expert.

The view just stated, which can find abundant support in psychological theory, is in direct conflict with the opinions of many thoughtful educators, who prefer to place major emphasis on the college student's pliability, openness to new experience, and susceptibility to important change. They believe that we cannot be content with teaching students how to realize their values; our major concern, rather, should be with helping them to decide what values to have, always with the thought that they may go in what for them are entirely new directions. We are not to suppose that students learn in accordance with their interests; rather we assume that interest depends on knowledge, that the more a student learns of a subject the more he becomes involved in it, and that in this way new patterns of interest and value may be generated. Instead of permitting students to become confirmed in patterns of motives whose determinants have been childish or accidental or culturally primitive, we should encourage development toward patterns that are valued in our society.

Those who labor to produce changes, as educators do, must believe that changes are possible, and that those which are possible are important. The fact that psychologists, psychoanalysts, and psychiatrists have permitted themselves to be identified with the doctrine of early determination and fixity is, I think, one of the reasons why the psychological sciences have sometimes had hard sledding when they have sought to influence policy in the colleges.

Some clarification, if possible some reconciliation, of these two opposing views of human development is necessary and overdue. Hope lies in the fact that exponents of early determination and fixity have not so much denied the possibility of later change as merely neglected to concern themselves with it. They have, in fact, had in their own field at least one theory of change—making the unconscious conscious—and with it a technique for producing change—psychotherapy. But they have often erred in supposing that knowledge and techniques derived from the clinic could be carried over without much modification to the college situation.

At the same time, exponents of late determination have found themselves rather up against it. College students simply do not change as much as they should; or, better, too many of them apparently do not change at all, going completely through college with the same motives, the same attitudes and values, the same outlook on the world, with which they began. Common assumptions concerning the conditions of change have not been well supported by experience.

The pressing need is for theory concerning the nature and conditions of personality development during the years seventeen to twenty-two, under the impact of those rather complicated social and cultural processes which constitute the college student's world. What kinds of changes, in what areas or processes of the person, may reasonably be expected? What are the factors producing change? And what are the mechanisms by which their effects are wrought?

DEVELOPMENTAL CHANGES

Happily, we are beginning to get the necessary theory, as more people qualified to produce it turn their attention to the area of our concern. Psychotherapists, particularly those who deal with young people, show an increasing tendency to regard the positive effects of their work as *developmental* changes, such as might occur in most people under conditions far less specialized than those of the consulting room. Researchers on personality and mental health, now a large and well-supported group of workers, are directing an increasing amount of attention to the so-called positive aspects of mental health. This leads naturally to a new accent on later rather than earlier stages of development. Most particularly, psychoanalysts and dynamic psychologists have interested themselves in the phenomena of late adolescence and have produced new concepts which, while accenting fresh developments at the college level, do not forsake continuity with the past. I refer particularly to E. H. Erikson (1955), Peter Blos (1946, 1953), and R. W. White (1952).

In these circumstances it is possible to see the beginnings of what a few years ago seemed highly unlikely: a *rapprochement* between those trends in psychology which have been generated in the clinic and the major trends in current academic psychology of higher mental process. The exponents of the latter have argued all along for the importance of contemporary experiences in affecting the organization, or reorganization, of the personality.

R. W. White, in his *Lives in Progress* (1952), has performed a distinctive service by summarizing with lucidity much recent thought about growth trends and processes in late adolescence. In our research under the Mellon program at Vassar, we found much guidance in his writing. White distinguishes and discusses four major "growth trends"[3]: the stabilizing of ego identity, the deepening of interests, the freeing of personal relationships, and the humanizing of values.

Stabilizing of ego identity is a concept which White borrows from Erikson (1955). White defines ego identity as "the self one feels oneself to be." Stabilization is achieved in the degree that the self-conception is based on good ego-functioning, such as would permit the inclusion of deeper, more personal needs and would insure adequate attention to reality.

[3] In Chapter 2 a distinction was made between growth and development, and the distinction has been maintained up to this point. White, however, uses the word growth to stand for what I mean by growth *and* development. His is the most common usage, and in this chapter, where White's work is discussed at length, the maintenance of my distinction would be labored. The reader should bear in mind that where the word growth, by itself, appears in this chapter, either in White's writing or in mine, the reference is to *growth and development*.

With increasing development the ego identity becomes sharper and clearer, more consistent, more autonomous with respect to daily social judgments, freer of transient influences such as temporary successes and failures, and increasingly determined by experience.

Deepening of interests has occurred when "one's own well-being is bound up with the development of an object to its own issue," a point on which White cites John Dewey. Deep interest involves the capability of having one's energies absorbed in the needs and properties of the object. One may lose oneself in one's work and be determined by the demands of an art, a science, a vocation, rather than by personal needs. The interest is autonomous in the sense of being self-sustaining rather than dependent upon persisting patterns of childhood.

Freedom in personal relationships means, essentially, the ability to respond to people as individuals in their own right rather than as mere representatives of the important objects of one's childhood. It means that one does not any longer expect one's teacher to be just like one's father so that the childhood repertory of responses would be appropriate. Hence there is greater range and flexibility of response; one notices more about the object and is less anxious and less defensive. No longer burdened by inappropriate past reactions, one can be more spontaneous, more friendly, more equalitarian.

Humanizing of values involves movement from a literal belief in rules to an attitude of greater relativity and an inclination to see values in relation to their social purpose. It involves learning to see the consequences of precepts and of their violation. There is increasing awareness of the human meaning of values, and increasing ability to bring one's own experiences and one's own motives to bear in promoting a value system. There is movement from traditionally received values to a personally wrought system.

To these four growth trends, I would add a fifth: *general development and strengthening of the ego.* This underlies all of the other trends listed. Stabilization of ego identity clearly implies a certain level of strength and development within the ego; deepening of interests grows out of the individual's ability to incorporate in his ego some of his more persistent and central personality needs; freedom of personal relationships involves essentially the replacement of old defense mechanisms with adaptive devices that spring from the ego and are better attuned to reality; and the humanizing of values is based on the integration of the superego with the ego, which in turn depends on development in the ego itself. The direction of ego growth is toward increased ability to plan realistically, to set goals, to make decisions, and to persist in one's chosen course; toward increasing self-awareness, breadth of consciousness, at-home-ness with one's inner life, awareness of some of the diversity of human values and of the complexity of human experience; toward increasing realism and objectivity and command of feelings.

White speaks of these first four processes as *natural* growth trends.

Erikson, too, in his writings about stages of development, seems to consider them natural; it is by virtue of our being human that we pass through these stages and finally emerge with our ego identity stabilized, our interests deepened, our personal relationships free, our values humanized. It would be easy to start an argument about this. Certainly the evidence that human beings just naturally develop in this way is far from conclusive. It would appear wiser to regard these growth trends as *normative,* to think of them as patterns which are widely and highly valued in our society and which we seek to bring about by means of education, broadly conceived. If they are natural, so much the better for our efforts. Actually, for purposes of research it makes little difference whether the goals of development in which we are interested are natural or not; if we can define them and measure progress toward them, we can study their determining conditions.

It is important to note that, in the discussions of growth trends, no statement is made about the termination of growth. We do not one day get to a place where it can be said that *now* our values are adequately humanized, our interests sufficiently deep. No, these are matters with respect to which most of us can go on improving. This aspect of growth trends is favorable to their study during the college years. We can be sure that students arriving at college are at various places along the way toward the achievement of these developmental goals, and we can be equally sure that none will finish the entire course by the time he graduates.

DEVELOPMENT IN COLLEGE

Many of the commonly stated aims of liberal education can without difficulty be brought under the headings of the five growth trends discussed above. The actual extent and direction of growth, however, is generally assumed to be affected by what happens to the individual student in college. In trying to determine what favors, or hampers, growth we must pay attention to factors arising out of the general culture and social organization of the college community, as well as to the more deliberate policies and practices carried out by the faculty and administration. Three types of influences may be distinguished here:

The over-all culture of the college. As I pointed out in Chapter 3, each college has its own unique culture, in which faculty, administration, and students all participate and which all to some extent internalize.

The various subcultures. A typical college might have a faculty-administration culture plus one major and several minor peer cultures. (In our studies at Vassar, we found an interesting aspect of the peer culture. While the male cultures surrounding Vassar belong logically to the sphere outside the college, the way in which the requirements of these cultures are conceived is so much in the hands of the girls' peer culture that the male cultures are, psychologically, practically inside the college.)

The college society. In this are involved the roles of faculty, administration, and students, and all their attendant definitions and interrelationships.

Not all the forces that are brought to bear upon the college student arise out of the unique culture and society of his college; he is responsive at the same time to diverse aspects of a much wider, more complex social and cultural matrix. It is well to remember that the American college is itself a phenomenon which reflects the culture of this country. Although it not infrequently finds itself at variance with major trends of opinion and value in our society, and often deliberately seeks to divert the student from certain prevalent standards and aspirations, it still continues to turn out graduates whose values, in general, resemble rather closely those that are dominant in the nation as a whole.

These outside forces, too, are of several types:

The American ethos. Whereas the liberal college strives to build in students an ego identity that is relatively independent of external definition, it labors in a culture that places heavy accent on *doing* as the basis for identity. How often one is asked, "What do you *do?*"

The American society. For example, there seems to be much confusion concerning what social role requirements favor or interfere with one's basic identity. Women's roles, discussed in Chapter 15, are particularly ambiguous.

The changing situation of the American society. Compare, for example, American students' preoccupation with the "private sphere," as reported by Gillespie and Allport (1955), with the social and political orientation of Mexican or Egyptian students, whose countries are in a stage of industrial development corresponding to ours of perhaps fifty years ago.[4]

Family, community, and social-class memberships. For the student, stimuli from these quarters are still very much in the picture.

Out of this multiplicity of factors which influence any given student's development in college, only a relatively small number can be predictably controlled by faculty or administration. In view of this it seems remarkable that those students who change at all manage to change in directions that are more or less consistent with the goals of the colleges they attend—and parallel to the growth trends which we discussed earlier. Let us now examine each of these trends more closely and consider how it can be accelerated or retarded by factors in the college environment.

STABILIZING OF EGO IDENTITY. "The sense of ego identity," Erikson writes, ". . . is the accrued confidence that one's ability to maintain inner sameness and continuity (one's ego in the psychological sense) is matched by the sameness and continuity of one's meaning for others" (1955, p. 216). The emphasis, it would appear, belongs on the matching. Inner sameness and continuity can hardly be maintained without some social confirmation,

---

[4] Today, nearly a decade after this paper was originally presented, there is a widespread sense of the development of a new outlook on this point, with students expressing an interest in civil rights, social reform, and the development of their own humanity.

while reliance upon outside judgments to the neglect of personal experience puts the sense of identity at the mercy of the shifting social situation. Stabilization is achieved in the degree that the self-conception is based on the kind of ego-functioning that permits the inclusion of deeper, more personal needs and that at the same time gives adequate attention to reality.

According to theory, anything that increases the likelihood that the sense of self will be based on personal experience rather than on outside judgments favors the stabilization of ego identity. Being placed in social roles that require new responses, having to make decisions concerning what roles one is going to take, learning from experience that some roles are suited and others not suited to one's interests and needs—any situation that brings awareness of one's real preferences and inner continuities helps to establish sound ego identity. So, too, does the condition of being relatively free from circumstances, whether unconscious drives or external pressures, that force one to cling to an earlier inadequate identity.

What shall we make of the fact that, according to our findings at Vassar, seniors show more disturbance with respect to identity than do freshmen?[5] The seniors as a group did indeed express more dissatisfaction with themselves, more apparent vacillation between different patterns, more conscious conflict about what to be. In fact, it appears that, at least among women students, seniors often have to deal with what amounts to an identity crisis; enough inner uncertainty remains that they often feel unprepared for the decisions which now have to be made. Many observers have commented upon the flight into marriage that so often takes place at this time. It appears that the young woman turns to marriage in the hope of attaining a stable identity through intimacy or through a well-defined external pattern. But one cannot enter into a mature affectionate and erotic relationship until after one has attained some sureness about oneself as an independent person. There is some evidence from our sample of Vassar alumnae that marriages undertaken as a means for resolving identity crises did not work out very well.

This is not the whole story, of course. There is more to the matter of sound ego identity than a satisfying and more or less unchanging self-conception. Seniors, in our view, are also striving to include more. They are on the road to becoming richer and more complex personalities; they are striving for stabilization on a higher level. They are thus distinguished from freshmen, whose relative freedom from conflict and uncertainty is

[5] Since this chapter is based on research at a woman's college, most of the discussion has to do with developmental changes in women. Where we are concerned with identity, which is clearly related to sex roles in society, we have to deal with differences between men and women. For example, current observations of male students at Stanford and Berkeley do not indicate that for them the senior year is distinguished by an identity crisis as it is for women. Many senior men wish to postpone full commitment to an occupational role, but it appears that the most critical time for identity usually comes earlier—most often in connection with choice of a major. Where we are concerned with other growth trends, I see no reason to doubt that the propositions offered will, in general, hold for men as well as for women—except where sex is obviously a relevant variable, as it is when we consider students' relations with male or female teachers.

accompanied by a greater narrowness or perhaps rigidity of identity, and a greater dependence upon external definition and support. Seniors have had to give up these kinds of supports without having as yet found adequate replacements.

For many a young woman, the first few years after college are crucial for identity. She must now assume social roles that will be hers for a long time to come. The question is, will she be able to take them without giving up too much of herself? She will not find a pattern that will permit her to include all the identities which were seriously considered, or experimented with, when she was a senior. As a matter of fact, our studies of alumnae twenty to twenty-five years after college indicated that some of these women still had not succeeded in finding expression of certain dispositional patterns which during the college years had been rather important. A more or less suitable self-conception had been achieved by the exclusion of some preferences and aspirations. But these excluded patterns were still very much alive, sometimes prompting implicit assumptions that they would some day be attended to, other times giving rise to guilt and regret or even a nagging sense of self-betrayal. With so many indications that really crucial events occur during the first few years after college, this period should be made the object of special research efforts.

There are many features of the college environment which would appear to be favorable to the development of sound ego identity. It offers an opportunity for a new start in the relative anonymity of the college situation where one can be free of the limiting expectations of the home community. There is the possibility that a sense of belonging to the college culture will replace older, less adequate constructions. College life also presents opportunities for acquiring realistic knowledge of available roles, and for imagining oneself in them—opportunities for experimenting with identities such as serious scholar, glamor girl, or community leader. For women students, feminine identity is favored by experiences with young men and by participation in a student culture that governs procedures for attracting and handling men. Finally, the student is encouraged to give serious consideration to such possible future roles as marriage and career, with their implications for identity.

At the same time the college environment frequently presents circumstances that hamper growth in this area. A schoolgirl identity may be perpetuated through overadjustment to an all too enticing peer culture. There may be pressure to hurry and establish that one is able to attract men and to get engaged. As a result intimacy may be sought ahead of identity, or in place of it, to the detriment of both intimacy and identity. Closely related to this is the felt necessity for remaining uncommitted so that one can move in any one of several directions, as the requirements of marriage may demand. On the other hand, there is sometimes overcommitment or too early commitment to a pattern that is ill suited to one's real needs and preferences. For example, an able student may find herself caught in a major program that she entered more or less by accident, perhaps in a momentary burst of enthusiasm or under the influence of an admired teacher, and from which she cannot now extricate herself for fear of disappointing teachers or parents.

Finally, as was pointed out in Chapter 15, college women often have difficulty in getting a clear conception of what roles an educated woman may take in our society and of how these roles may be related to a basic feminine identity. While colleges are not responsible for this cultural ambiguity, they face the difficult challenge of trying to modify it.

DEEPENING OF INTERESTS. According to theory, growth in this area occurs when there is satisfaction from one's transactions with objects of interest—when problems are solved and challenges met. Interests deepen as one learns through one's own experience of the inexhaustibility of interesting things. These processes, in their turn, depend upon sufficient freedom from anxiety and from the pressures and preoccupations of daily life to give the interest a chance. Growth would seem to be favored by encouragement, by expressions of faith in the student's serious abilities, by treating him as an adult or at least as a promising equal, and by his finding suitable models in the adult world.

The main business of a college is to provide these circumstances and these experiences. It seeks to present objects of interest in an attractive and interesting way, to offer challenges and problems in measured dosages, all in circumstances that allow adequate feelings of security on the part of the student. The college also offers as models people who are very much involved with the "development of the object to its own issue."

There is no doubt that the colleges achieve considerable success in their efforts to bring about deepening of interests. In our experience at Vassar, the great majority of freshmen could readily be placed in one of two groups: first, those who had little or no idea about what they wanted to major in, or what they wanted to do after college; and second, those who had made a definite pseudochoice. The great majority of seniors, on the other hand, showed unmistakable signs of knowing what it was to be genuinely involved in some subject or discipline. Approximately half of them expressed the hope or intention of going to graduate school. (That less than half of these actually went is another story.) Many others had realistic plans for pursuing an interest developed in college. In attitude scales, seniors showed in various ways their stronger adherence to intellectual, aesthetic, and social values, greater maturity of interest, and far less accent upon the superficially social.

But no college will claim that its batting average is as high as it ought to be. Everyone knows college seniors who have enjoyed the social life, made new friends, improved their statuses, but who show no signs of having been seriously affected by anything they studied—that is, studied enough to get by. Again we know college graduates whose lives show no persistence of any interests aroused in college. And what of all those students —30 to 40 percent of freshman classes—who drop out of college before graduation, most of whom do not obtain degrees at any institution?

Clearly there are forces at work in the college environment which hamper as well as develop deep interests. Among them I would be inclined to stress the following: that type of teaching which seeks to overcome student lethargy by pouring on more and more routine work—and which elicits only resistance to learning in the form of routine competence to perform up to the letter of the law; pressure from the adjustment demands of the nonacademic environment; inadequacy in available adult models, or failure on the part of enough adults to take the right kind of personal interest in the student as a potentially serious scholar; imbeddedness in a peer culture that regards serious involvement in work as slightly disreputable.

Quite possibly more fundamental than any of these things is the close relationship between interest and identity. The development of a deep interest is likely to bring a change in the ego identity; and similarly, there seem to be identities, often compulsively maintained, within which deep scholarly or vocational interests simply cannot be permitted to have a place.

Some women students seem contented not to know much or to be able to do much. They just concentrate on being friendly and cooperative, and they conceive of a future in which they will simply go on being this way. It is as if they anticipated and intended to avoid the difficulties of many seniors who do develop deep interests and then become entangled in an explicit conflict over marriage versus career. If these students are not to develop severe cases of other-directedness, they must be trained until they can do something well—in which case they might also become interested. For most young women, the sense of mastery of a subject or a skill is of great importance for that self-confidence which enables them to resist definition of themselves solely in terms of an external role, such as marriage or career. It allows them to wait, and choose, and so find in these social roles self-expression rather than false self-definition.

FREEDOM IN PERSONAL RELATIONS. There is a general theoretical point that growth occurs with an increase in the variety of social experiences that force variation in response. In personal relations unexpected behavior on the part of another person is particularly valuable, for this requires that he be observed and that new patterns of response be tried. Unfortunately, most social learning occurs under conditions of distraction; there is usually enough anxiety so that the tendency to fall back upon earlier responses is strong.

Favoring growth in the college situation are opportunities for new and varied friendships, and for relationships with faculty members which will show that they are not, after all, just like one's parents. There are opportunities, too, for taking adult roles and thus learning, through making the responses, something of what it means to be an adult. Usually the college situation is sufficiently safe that the individual may put out new feelers and sufficiently permissive that the range of feelings can be increased.

But all is not so favorable. It is possible, for example, for a student to find faculty members who will accept, and support by reciprocation, his transferences of infantile patterns, be these dependent, submissive, or erotic. At the same time the peer group may be quite productive of devices for keeping the faculty at a distance, forcing them always to behave like faculty —even to behave all alike—so that little is learned about adultness, either through observation or through forced variation of response. Again, there is likely to be pressure to accept a pattern of dating behavior which practically guarantees that a young man will not be perceived and responded to as an individual in his own right.

In an over-all appraisal, the college does appear to contribute to developing freedom in personal relationships. This is perhaps nowhere better exemplified than in the differences between freshman and senior scores on measures of authoritarianism. The seniors' lower average scores show that as a group not only are they less often restricted to one kind of relationship with adults, but they have less stereotyped conceptions of people in general; they are less likely to make categorical distinctions between youths and adults or between males and females. They also exhibit greater realism in their perceptions and evaluations of their parents.

Another indication of seniors' greater freedom may be found in the Vassar Developmental Scale, which differentiated freshmen from seniors at a high level of reliability in successive samples. The 178 items of this scale seemed to be characterized by one dominating factor—what we called "rebellious independence." In some students the accent was on independence, in others on rebelliousness. The latter, of course, is not fredom, but in college seniors we were inclined to regard it as a sign of progress toward that goal (see Webster, 1956). There were also great individual differences in scores on the developmental scale, with many freshmen scoring higher than the average senior and many seniors scoring lower than the average freshman.

In considering freedom in personal relationships from a clinical point of view, it seemed to us very important to distinguish between students who were primarily adult-oriented and those who were primarily peer-oriented —leaving out of account for the moment the larger middle group who did not exhibit marked tendencies in either direction.

The best examples of classical unfreedom are seen in the adult-oriented group. Here one may sometimes observe quite clear-cut mother-transferences to older women teachers. A student involved in such a relationship will exhibit many signs of immaturity—often including a kind of compulsive devotion to duty that results in consistently good grades. Further observation of these cases, however, will often show that the relationship is serving as a useful means for gaining freedom from a rather overwhelming actual mother; powerful maternal influence, supported by a host of response readinesses brought over from childhood, could hardly be opposed without a strong ally. Since the teacher usually represents more liberal values and a more flexible and enlightened conscience than does the historical mother-image, there is a good chance of educational gain from the relationship. The slower rate of growth on the part of the student who becomes involved in such relationships is by no means an indication that she will not eventually go as far developmentally as her more precocious sister.

Another interesting type of transference is one in which the female student—probably a rather bold and attractive girl—seeks to test whether a male teacher will value her for herself, particularly for her promise as a scholar, rather than for her feminine attributes. Such a relationship is likely to make the teacher a little anxious, but one may hope that he does not shrink from it altogether, for here is one of the most potent sources of academic motivation.

On first acquaintance with a typical peer-oriented student, one might conclude that adults do not enter into her world at all. Closer study, however, soon reveals that she manages them conveniently with one or the other of the two conceptual stereotypes: either they are authorities, disciplinarians to be submitted to or subverted as the occasion requires, or they are benevolent, easily exploited mamas and papas. One of the main functions of peer culture is to maintain this state of affairs, to avoid any real involvement with adults such as would threaten to upset an internal organization and a view of the world which has served well enough in the past. When and how do these students ever achieve freedom in their relations with adults? Many never do. Others can turn from the peer group by the time they are seniors, because membership in the group was only a temporary necessity in order to show their ability to belong; having achieved mastery on this score, they in time exhaust the possibilities of peer culture. Again, the development of a rewarding relationship with a young man may be for some girls the basis for drifting away from the group.

It follows from this conception of the peer group, however, that another way—perhaps the most effective way—in which peer-oriented students can attain freedom in personal relationships is for faculty members to enter importantly into their lives, stirring them up, producing situations that will expose the inappropriateness of old reactions and reveal the difference between these adults and those that have existed in the mind of the peer-oriented student.

HUMANIZING OF VALUES. Development here involves movement from a literal belief in rules to an attitude of greater relativity, to an inclination to see values in relation to their social purpose; it implies an increasing ability to bring to bear one's own experiences and one's own motives in promoting a value system.

It was with respect to the humanizing of values that the quantitative differences between seniors and freshmen at Vassar were most marked. Seniors were clearly more flexible and uncompulsive, more tolerant and impunitive, more rebellious and critical of authority, more unorthodox in religious outlook, more rejecting of traditional feminine roles, more unconventional and nonconforming, more liberal in their views on interpersonal relationships.

What happened, we may suppose, is that old, automatically accepted values were challenged by new, competing ones, inducing conflict and calling for fresh perceptions and thinking. At the same time, wider experience of her own impulses and of empathic reactions to other people confronted the individual student with new phenomena that had to be taken into account.

The college situation offers much to promote these processes of growth. There is exposure to a wide variety of values through teaching, independent study, and actual experience. Traditional values are confronted by more general and more liberal patterns as represented by admired figures—the college as a whole, teachers, and friends, both female and male. The student is required to make ethical decisions but is not altogether without external support. Sexual experimentation, and participation in a community in which sexual experimentation is going on, may lead to questioning of values. Of particular importance is teaching that brings insight into the unconscious sources of compulsively sustained values—for example, teaching that requires students to understand characters in literature before judging them in moral terms.

Although a majority of students do develop more human values in college, this is not true of all. Some seniors are not notably different from the average freshman in this respect. For one thing, the peer culture—if the student does not extricate himself from it—may serve as a powerful support for the historical value system; for another, dependent relations with parents may be maintained throughout the college years, if the parents are clever and persistent enough. Again, an authoritarian conscience may find reinforcement in the college regime itself or in campus authority figures.

There is also some danger that the college setting, while affording an excellent critique of traditional values, will not supply the basis for a new, humanized system. The result may be either more rebellion than is necessary or else tolerance so extreme that it shrinks from any value judgments at all.

In the Vassar studies we found that on most of our tests in this area the scores of alumnae resembled those of freshmen more closely than they resembled those of seniors. On such measures as tolerance, unconventionality, religious liberalism, and the like, it was usual for the seniors to score highest and to be significantly different from the alumnae, who were next highest but not significantly different from the freshmen. This was true both of our assessment sample of alumnae—women twenty to twenty-five years out of college—and of our sample of eighty women from the class of 1904.[6]

[6] It is not true, however, of alumnae four or five years after college; their scores on the measures mentioned here resemble rather closely on the average the scores they obtained as seniors (Freedman, 1962).

These results were not conclusive, owing to shortcomings of sampling and to the possibility that our scale items may have meant different things to alumnae and to college students. Nevertheless, the findings raise some interesting questions. Shall we say that the values of both alumnae and freshmen are closer to those which prevail in our major society and from which the seniors are shaken lose for a time? The women in our assessment sample of alumnae were of about the same age as our freshmen's mothers, and there is not much doubt in our minds that the freshmen, tested the day after they arrived at college, were participating rather fully in the values of home and home community. Shall we say that our alumnae were at one time like our seniors, that four years earlier they had been like our freshmen, and that, having changed in college, they promptly changed back under the influence of the major society, its social roles and responsibilities? Or shall we say that times have changed? Or that the sample of assessed alumnae was unrepresentative?

I would hypothesize that there is a great deal of changing back. If one assumes pliability or some lack of fixity in personality in order to allow for change during the college years, he must, I think, also allow for change during the years that follow. We have no theory to suggest that graduation exercises result in immediate crystallization. Our thought about the college senior is that the range of her potentialities has been considerably increased over the time when she was a freshman, but her fate as a personality will still be heavily influenced by the social roles in which she will soon find herself. I am assuming, of course, that changes in ego identity, interests, personal relationships, and values are indeed changes in personality.

GENERAL DEVELOPMENT AND STRENGTHENING OF THE EGO. Ego functions improve as they are performed with success in increasingly difficult situations. In order to strengthen the ego, tasks calling for a wide variety of ego performances must be assigned the individual, but in situations that are not so difficult or anxiety-provoking that he is forced to fall back on primitive defensive devices. In fact, anything that frees the individual from the necessity of defensive operations favors the development of the ego.

It follows, then, that ego development is hampered both by authoritarian or overprotective regimes and by permissive-chaotic ones. The former do not give the synthesizing functions of the ego a chance for exercise; the latter, through too much stimulation of impulse with consequent anxiety, may put too heavy a strain upon the developing ego.

Colleges offer many opportunities for acquiring skills and techniques, the mastery of which builds self-confidence and favors ego development. Teaching can make a contribution by giving the student a glimpse of the variety and complexity of the social world, by showing how people feel and what it means to be human, by forcing self-awareness through empathy with many kinds of people, real and fictional, by confronting the student with some of the deficiencies of his old, automatically adopted values and thus inducing conflict and requiring decision. Nonacademic aspects of the college environment can encourage ego development by being varied and impelling enough to challenge old values yet protective enough to prevent too much anxiety.

But college is not always a perfect culture for the ego. There are many possibilities for resisting awareness and breadth of experience. There may be authoritarianism in teaching, with rewards for doing precisely what one is told, or authoritarianism in the regime—perhaps in the student government—with its invitation to substitute external control for inner direction. Parents may support the student's old outlook, or the college may give him too much protection against experiences regarded as possibly dangerous. Again, various peer-group devices—tolerance of the superficial C student, "inside dopester" tactics for getting grades, the peer-group value for avoiding issues and not "becoming involved"—all may effectively block ego development.

In spite of these hazards, it would be quite discouraging if our results did not indicate some positive development in ego functioning during the college years. Actually, our test results showed that seniors were well ahead of the freshmen in flexibility of thinking; in capacity to suspend judgment; in tolerance of the uncertain, the indefinite, the merely probable; in skepticism, criticalness, realism.

Interestingly, seniors were less cynical than freshmen in their conceptions of people, far more cynical with respect to institutions and organizations. Seniors showed more self-insight, more inner life, and—let's face it— more "neuroticism." At least, they displayed a greater willingness to admit, even to take a certain satisfaction in admitting, conflicts, worries, doubts, fears, faults, psychosomatic symptoms. Perhaps we are dealing here with response to the situation of being a senior and facing that identity crisis mentioned earlier. Perhaps, for college students, the usual neuroticism scales are not so much measures of durable neurotic structures as they are measures of growing pains. In any event, seniors seemed to show fewer repressive mechanisms of defense.

In considering these five developmental trends,[7] we have to deal with that same curious state of affairs which is so marked in the case of brief psychotherapy: that those who get the most out of it are those who in a sense need it least, who are already farthest along the road to achieving what the therapist would like to bring about.

We have the strong impression that those freshmen who will get the most out of college, in the usual meaning of this expression, are those who

[7] In my discussion of these matters in *The American College* (1962, pp. 271–282) the major developmental trends have been reduced to three: the freeing of impulse, the enlightenment of conscience, and the differentiation and integration of the ego. This discussion is more systematic than that offered here; it is in line with the theory presented in Chapter 5 and it integrates White's conceptions within a larger framework. For me, however, White's conceptions still have charm, and they have the advantage of being close to the data.

already are the most developed in respect to ego identity, interests, personal relationships, values, and general ego-functioning. If we were to undertake to predict success in college on the basis of information collected at the time of application for admission, we would, of course, lean heavily on measures of these growth trends. But, on the other hand, does anyone wish to suggest that young people who are backward in these respects should not be offered the opportunity to grow? We have no choice but to try to discover what conditions determine growth in each area. Possibly, at some future time, after dependable knowledge of these matters has been attained, colleges will offer a variety of educational programs which can be prescribed according to the developmental status of the individual student.

PROSPECTS FOR FUTURE RESEARCH

In this chapter I have indicated some ways in which personality does change in positively valued ways during the college years, and I have suggested some hypotheses concerning the processes and mechanisms by which the student changes through interaction with the complex environment of the college and the larger community.

I believe that research on personality change in college shows great promise. We are approaching territory that is virtually unexplored by the discipline of personality research, and we now have methods and techniques that are ready to hand, having proved their worth in other areas. It is practically impossible to study college students with the use of such concepts and methods without coming up with results that are new and interesting.

But when it comes to research on higher education, research designed to show which policies and practices have which effects on which students, one cannot be quite so sanguine. The difficulties here are enormous. While the basic problems of research design are similar to those encountered in personality research, higher education is much more complex and necessarily requires projects on a vaster scale. It is difficult to design research which demonstrates relationships between personality growth and variables within the college environments. Interview studies have shown that a great many different variables play significant roles. Eventually, however, we may have researches which tell us how these variables act in entire college populations, just as interview studies now tell us of their effect on individual students. In the meantime, we need more interview studies to yield the hypotheses required for more ambitious projects.

In considering the determinants of personality change in students, it was the impression of our research group at Vassar that the over-all culture of the college is more important than any particular factor that can be isolated within it. If this is so, then the same measures of personality change will have to be used in various colleges whose cultures will already have been defined. This will require a project of considerable scope indeed. Still, it need be no larger than some that have been undertaken in military or mental health research. Sooner or later we may expect to hear that such a project has been begun.[8]

Of all the many problems confronting research on higher education, probably none is greater than the establishment of experimental controls. We speak of the college as a change-agency, yet how do we know that the changes in personality which we have observed would not occur to an equal extent in people who do not go to college? No college has so far produced satisfactory scientific evidence that it actually brings about the changes that it hopes, and often claims, to bring about.

Lest we become too skeptical of higher education, it is well to remember that psychological research has not yet produced any evidence that psychotherapy has lasting effects, either. No one is suggesting, however, that either colleges or psychotherapists forthwith cease their activities. Our faith in these institutions as powerful agencies of personality change already has much practical wisdom to support it. But optimum use of their potential and accurate appraisal of their results must await the findings of new research, more extensive and imaginative than any we have yet known. Happily, there are signs that today we may be on the threshold of such research.

[8] As anticipated, several major research projects have been undertaken in the last few years. Some of these are reviewed by the Group for the Advancement of Psychiatry (1962) and King (1964). One study, begun in 1958 under the sponsorship of the Center for the Study of Higher Education at Berkeley, involves twelve different campuses (McConnell and Heist, 1962). Several other studies are now under way, although research reports are not yet completed. They include a mental health project at the University of Florida under the direction of Henry C. Schumacher, M.D.; a developmental study at Massachusetts Institute of Technology under the direction of Benson Snyder, M.D.; the Harvard Student Study under the direction of Stanley H. King; and the Student Development Studies at Stanford University and the University of California, Berkeley, under the direction of the present writer and Joseph Katz. The studies at M.I.T. and Stanford/Berkeley, as well as those sponsored by the Center for the Study of Higher Education, have used scales developed during the Vassar studies described in this book.

CHAPTER EIGHTEEN

The Mental Hospital as a Change-Agency

Early in this book I presented the concept of the social institution as a change-agency, and intervening chapters, particularly those having to do with students in college, have referred repeatedly to the role of such agencies in personality development. Now I would like to introduce an elementary model of the change-process and to apply it to a different type of institution—the mental hospital.

AN ELEMENTARY MODEL OF A CHANGE-AGENCY

In its simplest form (Figure 1) this model shows the entering person A, the emerging person B, and the change-agency through which he passes. It may be seen that, compared to A, B is more expanded, more complex, and more integrated (as indicated by the more permeable barriers between parts). All three of these outcomes are clearly evident in the case of the college student who has received a liberal education. As this chapter will attempt to show, they are also present, though perhaps less dramatically, in the patient who has been successfully treated in a mental hospital. It would be possible, of course, to conceive of an institution whose goals would include only one or two of these three aspects of development.

Within the change-promoting institution are various interrelated sub-systems which either hamper or promote change. The original design of the system is, in most instances, rational. Those who operate it usually have some kind of logic governing what they do, and they apply influences

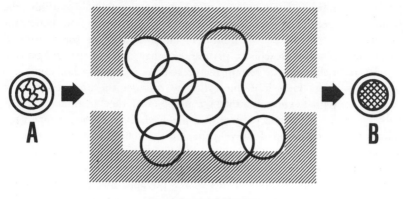

CHANGE-SYSTEM
(*Embracing Subsystems*)

Figure 1. Model of any social system designed to change the person who passes through it.

which, according to some theories, may reasonably be expected to change the person in a desired way. These may be considered *rational processes*. But analysis of an institution after it has been in operation for a time will show that many of its activities no longer have any conceivable relation to its stated objectives. For one thing, all institutions, once they have been set in motion, have to devote time and energy to self-maintenance. For another, institutions change their purposes, and instrumentalities designed for an earlier purpose lose their function; but this does not mean that they will be given up. On the contrary, interest becomes vested in them as they come to serve various individual needs of the institution's members, and hence they persist as *irrational processes* in the system. Small wonder it is, then, that what happens to people who pass through the system is often unanticipated, and actual outcomes cannot be related to procedures that were deliberately undertaken.

The effect of the change-agency on any given individual depends on an interplay of factors: (*a*) factors present within the person, (*b*) factors in his life situation before he entered the change-agency, (*c*) the more or less stable characteristics of the agency itself, be it an institution or an individual professional person, (*d*) the processes of interaction between the change-agency and the individual, and (*e*) forces in the society outside the agency which continue to impinge on the individual. In various combinations, these factors may bring about either change or no change. If there is change, it may be either desirable or undesirable—from various points of view. Even if the change is considered desirable from the point of view of the therapist, educator, or reformer, it may or may not be due to activities he has deliberately undertaken.

This model is intended to be highly abstract and to hold for any kind of institution that has been set up, or has evolved, with the object of changing people in some desired way: schools, training programs, hospitals and clinics, correctional institutions, therapeutic relationships, the family. This permits the comparison of facilities for treating alcoholics, for example, with other kinds of treatment facilities, and the comparison of treatment facilities with schools, prisons, or other kinds of change-agencies.

Let us briefly compare certain features of two-person psychotherapy and college education. Here it is interesting to consider the present model in conjunction with Levinson's (1962) conception of the "treatment career," with its phases of candidacy, becoming involved, the treatment proper, termination, and follow-up. In psychotherapy the subsystems of the change-agency would be the treatment modality employed, the theoretical orientation of the therapist, his training and competence, and his psychosocial characteristics. These features of the therapist and his activities are, of course, central to the psychotherapeutic relationship, but various other factors enter into the determination of what happens.

For one thing, there is the question of how hard it was to get into the system. The opening, we might say, varies in elasticity. If admission is highly selective, this fact alone may have an important bearing on the final outcome—regardless of the competence of the therapist. The patient accepted for treatment by a highly regarded therapist, like the student who has gained admittance to a college of high prestige, may well believe that now everything will be done for him. If the therapist were less acclaimed, the patient might enter therapy with the expectation that he would really have to work, and the outcome might actually be more favorable.

Not only are there parallels between the change-promoting processes of education and of psychotherapy, but there are also parallels in the problems which they face in effecting change. As I mentioned in the preceding chapter, both colleges and therapists have had difficulty in measuring their own effectiveness because of the problem of experimental control. Just as development in college may be due to unplanned actions of the institution or to forces outside the college, so a desired outcome in psychotherapy might be due to some unrecognized activity of the therapist or to events outside the therapeutic situation—events not taken into account in the experimental design of research. There is also some question whether those changes which come about in psychotherapy are enduring or only temporary, just as studies of alumnae at Vassar cast some doubt on the permanence of the personality growth observed in college seniors.

Finally, both types of agencies must face the question of whether it is change itself that they are seeking, or the achievement of some absolute standard. In colleges nowadays there is enormous emphasis upon the latter objective—for example, upon the kind of excellence that insures that a student will be admitted to a good graduate school. Since the major determinants of this excellence are assumed to be already present at the time the student enters college, colleges tend to be very careful about selecting students, less careful about what is done for or to them during their college careers. Few colleges would care to base their reputations upon their ability to change poor students into mediocre ones.

Now the same kinds of choices are, to some extent, open to the psychotherapist. It is one thing to work with patients who are interesting, attractive, possessed of many resources and socially valuable traits, patients who were already practically cured once they had made up their minds to enter psychotherapy. It is something else to work with unpromising characters who might change a great deal but still remain unpromising characters. We can hardly expect psychotherapists to avoid the most promising patients, but let us hope that, like Freud, they accept a variety of those who need their help, including some of the unpromising ones.

Actually, the model of a change-agency holds for any kind of productive institution that undertakes to transform "materials" into "products" with specified qualities. Where we deal with human beings, however, there are various restraints upon what the change-agency can do. Even if we had complete knowledge of the entering person, and knew precisely how any given change might be effected, we would still be hard put to it to decide what changes were most to be desired. Or, if we were certain that some particular change, such as an end to drinking on the part of a patient with alcoholism, was highly desirable, and we thought of actions that would induce this change, we would still have to consider the consequences of these actions for other values—other desired or not-desired states or conditions in the person and in other persons.

We may illustrate some of the ways in which the theoretical model may be applied, prepare the ground for further elaboration, and pose some of the issues that arise in connection with treating people in mental hospitals, by means of a case study.

CHANGING THE PROBLEM DRINKER: A CASE STUDY

Mr. C., a sixty-year-old construction worker, had had a long history of excessive drinking. He had often failed to get work for this reason and had recently been fired for drinking on the job. His wife complained that he was geting drunk more often and becoming more abusive when he did. He appeared to have two patterns of drinking. When he was out of a job, he would go down to the hiring hall, find that nothing was available, then join his friends for a few drinks in a bar; eventually he would come home drunk. At other times he would drink at home while his wife was at work and would be "under the weather" when she returned.

At the insistence of Mrs. C., the family physician committed Mr. C. to a state psychiatric hospital for a ninety-day examination period. His initial interviews revealed that the patient had been a laborer on construction jobs all his working life, as had his father before him. He was not unintelligent. (The psychiatrist reported that Mr. C. could do mental arithmetic faster than he himself could.) But he had had only eight grades of education, while his wife had finished high school. She worked as a salesperson in a small shop, earning more money than her husband and trying hard to maintain middle-class standards of life. When asked whether he had ever considered learning a trade, Mr. C. replied that he had once thought of becoming a butcher, but he would have had to pay $100 for a license. Besides, he discovered that he did not like to kill sheep.

After interviews with the patient and other members of his family, staff members familiar with the case decided on two major avenues of treatment. First, the patient was persuaded to join a therapeutic group of other "alcoholic"[1] patients to gain a more realistic picture of his own drinking. Second, counseling sessions were held with various members of the family, aimed at correcting conditions in Mr. C.'s occupational, social, and family life which appeared to be contributing to his drinking problem. The occupational therapist helped him to learn new skills that were both useful and pleasurable. The social worker made suggestions for expanding and enriching his social relationships. The psychiatrist talked with Mr. and Mrs. C. and their two grown children, individually and in various combinations, in an effort to increase harmony within the family.

After six weeks Mr. C. was discharged, although some communication with the hospital was maintained. When the social worker made a follow-up visit to the patient's home four months later, she found that his drinking, while still continuing, was more controlled, and the general family situation had improved. A number of the changes which she observed could be directly traced to the change-efforts of the hospital staff.

What general terms may be used to describe the changes that took place, or seemed to take place, in Mr. C. while he was in the hospital and during the four-month period following his release? What actions of the hospital staff were effective in bringing about particular changes? Would these activities have been equally effective with other types of patients? For a better understanding of this whole process, let us take a closer look at the mental hospital activities in the light of our model of a change-agency.

THE ENTERING PATIENT (A). Kluckhohn and Murray (1948) have written that every person is in some respects (*a*) like *all* other persons, (*b*) like *no* other person, and (*c*) like *some* other persons. It is important for any change-agency—and perhaps doubly important for the mental hospital —to remember that this applies to every person whom it would change. In saying that the patient in a mental hospital is in some respects like *all* other persons, I mean that the general theory of personality outlined in this book holds for the abnormal as well as for the normal. Whatever his individual problems, Mr. C. was like everybody else in his complexity as

---

[1] There is a great variation in the way the term "alcoholic" is defined by people working in the field of alcohol problems. Some definitions presuppose addiction, by which standard the subject of our case study would probably not qualify. On the other hand, he would certainly be covered by those definitions which use as their criterion disruption of family life or occupation because of drinking. In any event, Mr. C. was admitted to the mental hospital on a diagnosis of alcoholism, so in this chapter the term alcoholic will be used in a general sense to include a variety of types of problem drinkers. This use is not intended, however, to indicate any preference by the author for such a definition.

an individual, in the variety of his needs, and in his responsiveness to the social situation in which he lived. As a result, we would expect changes which occurred as a result of treatment to follow the same principles which govern personality or behavior changes in general.

Mr. C. was also like *some* other people—or, to be more exact, several types of other people. He was like other mental patients to the extent that his problems were rooted in part in personality disorders and were, like all psychogenic disorders, primarily the result of arrested development. He was more like other alcoholic patients than like nonalcoholic patients, and still more like alcoholic patients of his own socioeconomic class. Like a great many lower-class problem drinkers, Mr. C. showed a handicapping lack of competence. He simply did not learn to do things in the areas of work and recreation, and in the realm of the imagination, that a man of his innate capacity might well have learned. Joel Canter (1964) has made similar observations at the Veterans Administration Hospital in Los Angeles. The histories of lower-class alcoholics strongly suggest that they did not learn to take much satisfaction in activities other than drinking. Like Mr. C., who did not bother to learn a trade, many of these men have simply failed to acquire the skills or the interests that would be necessary to a satisfactory life in our complicated society.

Other characteristics of this patient—the fact that he was a family man, that he had had little education, that he was relatively intelligent, that he belonged to the white, Anglo-Saxon, Protestant majority in this country, that he had a rural background but lived in a city—are shared by him with many alcoholic patients. As we shall see, all these characteristics are important in planning his treatment.

It is also important to recognize the ways in which the patient is *not* like certain others. For example, while Mr. C. has some problems in common with all problem drinkers, he is fundamentally quite different from either the typical middle-class, addicted drinker or the homeless drinker on skid row. Any treatment attempt which ignored these differences would surely be doomed to failure.

Another distinction which the hospital must make in assisting alcoholic patients is whether or not they arrive with some motivation for treatment. In the case of Mr. C., there was no such motivation. He expressed amazement and outrage at the commitment action and contended, with the support of his adult son, that his drinking habits had changed little in thirty years. He also refused to admit any truth in his wife's claim that he was noisy, rough, and threatening when drunk. In fact, he was inclined to deny that he had any drinking problem at all, although the psychiatrist noticed that at times he spoke as if he did privately assume that he had at least some problem in this area.

It is interesting to note that Mr. C.'s lack of motivation did not prevent the hospital staff from going ahead with the task of treating him. Their action is in line with a growing body of evidence, such as the findings of Davis and Ditman (1963), that patients who are treated under orders from a court do as well as patients who volunteer for treatment. This is in contrast, however, to common practice at many alcoholic clinics where it is assumed that psychotherapy cannot be successfully undertaken unless the patient seriously desires it.

In identifying a patient as "ill," "alcoholic," "lower-class," and so on, the change-agency must never lose sight of the fact that each patient is unique, like *no* other. It may well be that appreciation of his individuality is the essential common element in all forms of successful treatment.

In saying that a patient is like all others or no others, we are speaking primarily of *what* he is, but this can never be completely separated from *where* he is. The behavior that a person exhibits at the time he enters a change-agency, or during the time he is a candidate for entering one, has to be regarded as due in very considerable part to the general *situation* that he is in at the time. This situation embraces such factors as a family that might be putting pressure on him to accept treatment, his status with respect to employment, the availability of treatment facilities, the beliefs concerning the nature of treatment that are prevalent in his subculture, and various problematic conditions that are consequences of his disorder. In the case of the alcoholic, it seems likely that many of the patterns of behavior that have been said to be characteristic of an "alcoholic personality" can be understood as common responses to the situations that people with drinking problems get themselves into. We assume, ideally, that an assessment of an alcoholic patient will take into account not only the unsatisfactory conditions *in him*—those bounded by the surface of his skin—but also those features of his environment that are helping to determine his behavior. This would appear to be necessary both in order to understand the patient and in order to plan appropriate changes in the situation itself. When we deal with lower-class patients like Mr. C., there is rarely any difficulty about discovering aspects of his situation that cry out for change. With middle-class and upper-middle-class patients, on the other hand, it is common to assume that the external situation may safely be ignored, that even though it may have deteriorated as a consequence of the patient's drinking, he can put it right after he has changed internally. A great deal of disappointment has been occasioned by patients who have spent six months or a year in a private hospital, during which time they remained sober, adapted well, and seemed to respond to intensive psychotherapy, only to return home and after two or three months revert to their old pattern of drinking. It seems likely that closer attention to the external situation, and to the possibilities of modifying it, might avert some disappointment of this kind.

GOALS. When we speak of *outcomes* we mean differences between what the person was like at the time he entered a change-agency and what he is like when he emerges from it. For the alcoholic patient, possible outcomes might include stopping drinking or drinking less, showing improvement in interpersonal relations, or perhaps some change in the structure of his personality. How a change-agency conceives of outcomes and what kinds of outcomes it prefers—that is to say, what kinds of *goals* it sets for itself —depend upon how it conceives of the person who enters treatment as well as upon the values of the institution.

The goals of all change-agencies are either desired changes in behavior or desired changes in personality. We may consider further the fact that it is possible to change behavior without changing the personality. Consider, for example, an alcoholic patient who suffers from dependence and depression. This person might change from a dependence on alcohol to dependence on a person or a social group. This would be an important change in behavior, but it could occur with very little or no change in his personality structure. It is common for psychotherapists to speak of the sober alcoholic who is more difficult to live with than he was while he was drinking.

It is possible also to change the personality without changing overt behavior. A person who has had a great deal of psychotherapy might do the same things that he did before, but for different reasons. For example, he might behave responsibly now because of his own judgment that this is the thing to do, whereas formerly he behaved so out of automatic conformity with social norms. People who undergo intensive psychotherapy frequently report that they feel very different from the way they did before, that they are in fact different, whereas their families and friends insist that they notice no change in behavior. The fact that such people might behave in what appears to be the same way as before does not mean, of course, that psychotherapy did them no good.

Although behavior and personality are different, there is usually some interaction of the two. When we think of change in the behavior of an alcoholic patient, we usually have in mind such things as abstaining, or changing to a more appropriate form of drinking, or drinking as before but changing his social behavior. Many therapies for alcoholics are aimed at putting an end to drinking. Almost everybody agrees that in some alcoholic patients the drinking pattern must be broken up before much else can be done. Often, however, stopping drinking and remaining sober come to be regarded as ends in themselves and, for practical purposes, all that is required. From the point of view being presented here, the fundamental question concerning such changes in behavior is: do they favor or hamper the further development of the individual?

The goals of treatment have to be varied, as varied as are the problems that exist as cause, consequence, or concomitant of the patient's disorder. Nurse (1964), in his research at the Oakland Clinic of the California Division of Alcoholism Rehabilitation, considers criteria of improvement through therapy in the following areas: interpersonal relations, family; interpersonal relations, social; personal responsibility; employment; health; legal status— all these in addition to drinking. This is certainly the wise course to be followed by anyone who does research on the effects of psychotherapy. If he develops measures of change in all these areas, his chances of showing that psychotherapy has some effects are very good, and this indeed was the case in the work reported by Nurse.

Where alcoholic patients are concerned, it seems wise not to aim too high. Lolli (1953) has warned of the dangers of participating in the alcoholic's grandiose fantasies of complete "success." This is not to counsel pessimism, but rather realism, and perhaps a certain relativism with respect to values. From the developmental point of view that has been outlined in this book, one may see that a little change of the right sort may set in motion other processes of change that might lead in time to great improvements in the person's over-all functioning.

Whereas many change-agencies may formulate goals in rather general terms to apply to all who enter, the mental hospital must set up its goals anew for each incoming patient. The treatment goals in the case of Mr. C. were decided upon in a case conference held ten days after he was admitted. By that time five staff members knew him and could contribute to the assessment of the case. The psychiatrist commented that he did not have enough information to formulate the case in psychodynamic terms. He did believe, however, that Mr. C., despite his he-man exterior, had a softer side, perhaps a large feminine component in his make-up, and that he was probably quite dependent upon his better-educated and rather dominant wife. It appeared that his pride had surely been wounded by his increasing difficulty in getting jobs and his having to remain home while his wife worked.

The social worker observed that Mrs. C., too, might have some emotional problems. During the first interview she had seemed upset and uncommunicative. It had not been possible to get a clear picture of her reasons for having Mr. C. committed at this particular time. She had said that his drinking had been getting worse and had dropped hints of some explosive episodes, but no details had been forthcoming. She had only insisted that her husband should not come home until some change had been wrought in him.

On the basis of their combined appraisal of the case, the staff set up its goals for Mr. C. and a plan of treatment designed to bring them about. In the first place, it was agreed that Mr. C. had to overcome his unwillingness to face the truth about his drinking. To accomplish this he was encouraged to join a therapeutic group of alcoholic patients who could point out to him that his denials and rationalizations were familiar "dodges." It is interesting to note at this point that although Mr. C. was admitted to the hospital on a diagnosis of alcoholism, and although reducing his problem-drinking was one of the primary goals of treatment, it actually received much less direct attention than other aspects of his situation. The hospital did not segregate alcoholics on a special ward. No one even suggested that he had to stop drinking. The assumption seemed to be that if he got over his tendency to deceive himself and others, had some harmony restored within his family, found something to do with himself, and was able to obtain emotional support, his drinking would no longer be a problem—that is, that he would get drunk less often, hold his liquor better, not be violent or abusive while under the influence. This is not to say that this is all that can be hoped for in such a case, or that it would even be an appropriate goal for a middle-class patient who was addicted to alcohol. Rather it illustrates how improvement can be sought within the limits of realistic goals. The hospital staff did not decree that Mr. C. become a middle-class man. Although they are middle-class people themselves, mental health workers must allow that there are styles of life different from their own and that individuals have a right freely to choose a life style for themselves.

The focus of treatment, then, was on a variety of other aspects of Mr. C.'s life. The staff agreed that, in an important sense, the family was the patient in this case. Plans were made to interview all members of the family again, separately and in various combinations, to help them see better their own roles in the total situation. There was also consensus on the point that Mr. C. needed, and would continue to need, emotional support outside his family—from friends, community, and the organizations to which he belonged. This presented a problem because Mr. C. and his wife had different sets of acquaintances; he was most comfortable with "the boys" whom he saw at work, in the hiring halls, and in nearby bars, while Mrs. C. had middle-class aspirations and hence acquaintances of a different sort. Perhaps some new directions could be suggested for their social relationships.

There was much discussion of what Mr. C. was to do with himself. It could not be assumed that at his age he was likely to work steadily in construction, but perhaps through occupational therapy some other marketable skill could be discovered or developed. Even more, he needed to develop interests and capacities that would expand his horizons and increase his enjoyment of life.

While the staff agreed that it would be better if Mr. C. could find what he needed in his own community, he might continue to need professional support, at least occasionally, for some time. His case fitted well into the hospital's new program for keeping in touch with patients after their discharge, making it psychologically easy for them to come in again if they felt the need.

Mr. C.'s personality problems, like his drinking, were viewed as only part of a more complex picture. The staff did not assume that he had to overcome his dependency feelings before anything else could be done for him or before he could lead a more satisfying life. His behavior could change, to his advantage and to that of the people around him, without there being any fundamental change in his personality. At the same time, however, action to change behavior could be guided by knowledge of the personality structure.

Those responsible for Mr. C.'s treatment also assumed that some parts of his personality were more susceptible to change than others. This assumption is in keeping with the general theory set forth earlier in this book. However much importance we may attach to unconscious complexes in the determination of disordered behavior, the fact remains that there are always parts of the personality that are not dominated by unconscious processes and hence are open to modification through ordinary experience. Mr. C. could learn; he could acquire new skills, develop new relationships, gain new perspectives. These are changes in personality, for they involve the acquisition of new readinesses for response and the further differentiation of capacities already present. It is important to note that changes of this kind occur in a man of sixty—perhaps not as readily as in a younger person, but they occur—when suitable conditions are present. This helps to explain why various kinds of treatment methods, including ones that make no use of psychodynamic theory, are often of benefit to alcoholic patients. Failure to take account of unconscious processes may sometimes have serious consequences, as when a patient—driven by such processes—behaves in some destructive way before learning can occur, and it may sometimes lead to failure, as when it is assumed that a patient will learn from experience when in fact unconscious processes are preventing him from having the expected experience. But an overaccent on unconscious processes or the belief that they are all-determining may also result in failure, as when it is assumed that a patient who gains some insight into his own functioning will now be able to change his situation in a way that will permit him to live a satisfying life. In the present state of our knowledge we can afford to neglect neither the possibility that unconscious complexes may upset our well-laid plans nor any opportunity for patients to learn what will be useful to them.

Learning from experience, in the sense of acquiring new response patterns, does not, according to psychodynamic theory, alter unconscious structures. But if those parts of the personality that are not dominated by unconscious processes are sufficiently expanded, then there is a change in the relationship of the conscious to the unconscious and hence a difference in the person's over-all functioning. There is also the possibility that this kind of expansion will in time lead to a strengthening of the conscious ego, so that contents that were previously intolerable may now make their appearance upon the conscious scene.

THE CHANGE-PROCESS. We may consider that a patient formally enters the change-system at the time he is admitted to the hospital. He is subsequently exposed to a variety of subsystems which contribute to the ultimate objective of change. Probably the first factor favoring change is the very circumstance of being hospitalized; for a patient with a drinking problem, this is particularly important since it confronts him with the fact that he does indeed have a problem and that it is of serious concern to those close to him.

Another factor is the interaction among patients, which can make them more or less receptive to treatment; in Mr. C.'s case this had a positive effect. He was a friendly man by nature and, when he forgot for a moment his indignation at being committed, his smile was engaging. The general atmosphere in the unit to which he had been assigned was informal, and he soon found a companion to play checkers. After a few days he began to consider that being "put away" was not so bad as he had thought.

The psychotherapeutic group, occupational therapy, interviews with the psychiatrist or social worker—all these form subsystems of the larger change-system which is the mental hospital. Sometimes their functions are independent; sometimes they overlap or supplement one another. As in Mr. C.'s case, their actions are often directed not only to the patient himself but to his family and to a variety of other perceived factors outside the change-agency which might be expected to influence the outcome of treatment attempts.

Although Mr. C. did agree to take part in group therapy, much of what happened to him in the mental hospital could be characterized less as treatment than as education. Many of his problems were a matter not so much of personality as of lack of information, understanding, or imagination on the part of both the patient and other family members. For example, it was discovered that one cause of Mrs. C.'s anxiety over her husband's drinking was the fact that her employer was a total abstainer who often inveighed against "drunks"; she was afraid for her job. After an interview with this man, in which he proved to be a reasonable person and made it clear that he valued Mrs. C. as an employee, it was possible to give her a clearer picture of her own situation and some reassurance.

The problem of social relationships was met by supplying some needed imagination. During a joint interview Mrs. C. had remarked casually that a boyhood friend of her husband's had given up his farm and moved with his wife to town. The social worker suggested that this friend was probably lonesome and could do with some help in getting adjusted to new surroundings. Mr. C. picked up the idea immediately and became quite intrigued with the prospect of "showing Charlie around." Similarly, it was suggested to the couple's daughter that her father might enjoy an opportunity to baby-sit with his grandchildren occasionally.

Occupational therapy is, by its nature, educative. The therapist was able to interest Mr. C. in woodworking and found that he had a talent for it. He learned to make a planter box in a short time and with good workmanship. He promised that when he went home he would buy a small power saw and continue this kind of work.

At first glance, these educational procedures may appear to affect only the patient's overt behavior or his life situation, but they can also affect personality. It is true that when we think of personality change, we usually think of psychodynamic psychotherapy, which aims to change the personality through enabling the individual to gain insight into himself, to admit his unrecognized tendencies into his consciousness so that he might express them in constructive and socially acceptable ways and be less inclined to misjudge himself and the world around him. But development in the personality may be brought about by means other than psychotherapy. The individual is never just a bundle of unconscious complexes, nor is his functioning ever completely dependent upon his unconscious processes. Parts of the person are always open to modification through interaction with the environment. This means that, at any time in the individual's life, development may occur in response to educational procedures, as broadly defined. If individuals acquire new skills, new interests, new capacities for response, new ways of seeing things, they develop as personalities, and changes of this kind can be brought about at any time, even in people who are severely disturbed.

Voth and Mayman (1963), in experiments on the autokinetic phenomenon, have found that some subjects report observing movement of a beam of light while others report no movement.[2] Furthermore, they have shown that variations in this respect are associated with various personal characteristics and psychiatric diagnoses. For example, people who report no movement—and alcoholics tend to fall into this group—are slow to accept a therapist's interpretations of their behavior, but once they accept his proposition, they are likely to act upon it and stick to it in a fairly rigid manner. On the other hand, people who see movement take readily to psychoanalytic interpretations but do not necessarily apply them in their behavior.

People who do not see movement in this situation appear to suffer from a lack of imagination. When crises arise in their lives, they are able to see few possible courses of action; they are disposed to solve their problems through action rather than through some imaginative restructuring of their situation. With some patients, it seems, we must first "open them up"—that is, liberate the unconscious impulses through psychotherapy—and then they will be able to think imaginatively. It may be suggested here that we might attack this lack of imagination directly through education. We might use some of the techniques known to nursery-school and kindergarten teachers for showing individuals that they can, if they put their minds to it and are sufficiently reassured, actually produce fantasies and imaginative plans. Experience has shown that ten-year-old boys can be taught to make up stories about pictures, even though they insisted that this was quite impossible for them and that the activity was in any case more appropriate for girls. It is quite conceivable that if this kind of teaching were directed to unimaginative, stimulus-bound individuals, it might make them more receptive to the ideas that the psychotherapist tries to put across. One might go further, in fact, and suggest that if we were able through teaching to make the life of the imagination available to stimulus-bound people, to render them capable of enjoying reading and

[2] In experiments on the autokinetic phenomenon, the subject is seated in a totally dark room in which only a pinpoint of light is visible directly ahead of him. (He is admitted to the room before the lights are turned off so that he knows that the light is coming from a small aperture in a screen.) Some subjects report seeing the light move randomly and to considerable distances through space, while other subjects report seeing no movement at all.

movies and various forms of play, some of them might not need deep psychotherapy.

In any event, education would still be necessary for most people, as a means of inculcating skills, developing interests, and broadening horizons, even after therapy had freed them so that they could learn from experience. This is not to say that psychotherapy or its equivalent is not a fundamentally important instrument for changing personality and a model for various other change-inducing activities, or that it is not a means *par excellence* for learning about personality. We have to face the fact, however, that it will never be available to more than a small fraction of the people who suffer from mental disorders, and that in most cases it will have to be supplemented by other measures.

THE EMERGING PATIENT (B). By the time Mr. C. left the hospital six weeks after admission, he showed definite signs of a changed attitude toward his alcoholism. According to the leader of the therapeutic group, he was now willing to class himself among the problem drinkers. In his final interview, he spoke jokingly of doing better because he did not want "the boss" to have him "put away" again. Several other aspects of Mr. C.'s life situation had been modified, too, so that there was some reason to hope that his condition would continue to improve.

The goal of the mental hospital, like that of the college, is to set in motion trends of change which will continue to unfold long after the individual has left its immediate influence. The mental hospital, however, shares a common problem with other agencies of change—namely, that of evaluating its own effectiveness. In Chapter 17, I mentioned how difficult it is for either the educator or the psychotherapist to know the kinds and extent of changes he has brought about, what particular planned or unplanned actions caused them, and the degree to which these changes will persist. Unlike most colleges or private therapists, however, many hospitals, including the one in which Mr. C. was a patient, do make an attempt to follow up their cases.

When the social worker from the hospital paid a follow-up visit to the C. home four months after Mr. C. was discharged, she had some reason to feel that the treatment program had indeed wrought favorable changes. The situation was not yet idyllic. Mrs. C. said that she was not altogether happy about her husband's drinking. He had worked only spasmodically since leaving the hospital, spent too much time with the "boys" downtown, and had even involved his friend Charlie in the same pattern. On the other hand, she admitted that there had been no more episodes of violence, and in general she seemed quite relaxed about the matter.

Mr. C. listened to these charges with good nature but was eager to get on to other topics. He had indeed looked up Charlie. Mrs. C. had accompanied him on the first visit and found Charlie's wife, a former schoolteacher, congenial. The two couples began seeing each other with some regularity. Through this couple the C.'s made other new friends in a home for senior citizens on the outskirts of the city. Mr. C. found to his surprise that some of the men, though better educated and better dressed than he, were very happy to talk with him. It also surprised—and considerably amused—Mr. C. to discover that the people in the retirement home regularly had drinks in their quarters before dinner. Mrs. C., who had never drunk except on very special occasions, now joined in as if drinking were the most natural thing in the world. On the day of the social worker's visit, Mr. C. displayed a bottle of wine which he had purchased for a dinner party that evening.

As the occupational therapist had suggested, Mr. C. had bought a power saw and set up a small workshop in the basement. When he presented one of his planters to a friend at the retirement home, other gardeners inquired if they might purchase some for themselves. One of the men even suggested that Mr. C. go into the planter business—a possibility which he was giving some consideration.

The interviews with the couple's son and daughter had apparently been effective, for they had been faithful in coming to see their parents, and the daughter was carrying out a plan which seemed highly constructive. Following the social worker's suggestion, she had made a point of leaving her six-month-old baby and five-year-old daughter with their grandfather on afternoons when she was going out. Mr. C. proved to be an excellent baby-sitter. He was gentle and efficient in taking care of the baby's needs, patient and communicative with the little girl. Not only was he proud of his grandchildren, but he was proud of his skill in managing them.

The social worker left with the impression that the hospital had made some favorable changes in the case of Mr. C. and that the outlook for the future was hopeful. This appraisal might have been quite different if the hospital had been seeking more absolute standards of change, such as total abstinence from drinking or steady employment. Judged by the more general—and I believe more realistic—criteria which the hospital used, however, the social worker's optimism seems justified.

ADAPTATIONS OF THE MODEL

The simple model of a change-agency which was presented in Figure 1 can be modified in various ways to express some of the more complex processes which we have observed in the preceding case study. For example, it may be extended, as in Figure 2, to include additional periods of influence before the individual actually enters the system and after he has left it. Thus, Mr. C.'s "treatment career" (Levinson, 1962) would begin with his wife's first call to the family physician and end with some future time when he has lost all contact or expectation of contact with the hospital.

There is some question of precisely when the interaction with a

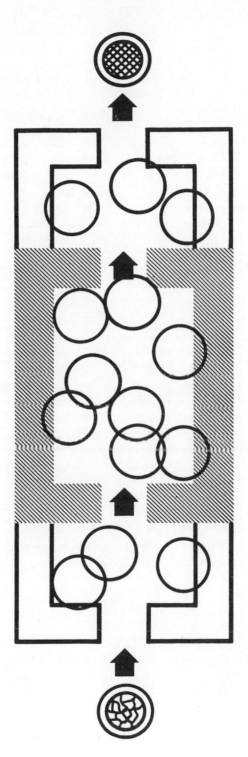

Figure 2.

change-agency begins and when it terminates. In saying that Mr. C.'s treatment career began when his wife called the family physician, we are arguing that at this time both Mr. and Mrs. C. became involved psychologically with the hospital. Thus the study of the ways in which candidates for treatment are actually led, or forced, to enter treatment belongs within the domain of the person's interactions with the change-agency.

Similarly for the terminal phase of a treatment career. We can say that Mr. C. was still within the agency psychologically at the time of the social worker's visit to his home. This is assuming that he had anticipated such a visit, on the basis of what he had been told when he left the hospital, or that he still thought he might talk with someone at the hospital should his troubles revive. This terminal phase of the treatment career will become increasingly important as agencies attach more importance to aftercare. In this case it will, of course, become increasingly difficult to draw a sharp line between the state of being in the agency and the state of being out of it.

In a complex institution such as a hospital some of the subsystems might themselves be considered change-agencies which exist within the larger change-agency. In the case just presented, the psychotherapeutic group, the occupational therapist, and the psychiatrist each interacted individually with Mr. C. and made unique contributions to change in him. Thus we might accurately represent each of these subsystems in the same form as the larger agency. Where there are several such subsystems, their actions may be either successive or overlapping, as indicated in Figure 3.

So far we have pictured the change-agency as surrounded by a solid wall, with only two small openings for admission and discharge of individuals. In practical application this is rarely, if ever, the case. Events in the larger world also affect the individual person who passes through an agency. Mr. C. was not "put away" in a dungeon or on a desert island; his family was still a very important part of his environment, and there were available to him various means of communication with the world beyond the hospital grounds. In an ideal situation professional people not on the hospital staff—such as experts in vocational rehabilitation—would enter the institution to render specialized service. The boundaries of our change-agency, then, should be represented as permeable, as in Figure 4.

The boundaries of the change-agency are also permeable, of course, as far as its own staff is concerned. These professional people have various group memberships and other commitments outside the institution, which can have important effects upon the processes of the change-agency itself. For example, staff members of different professions—psychiatrists, social workers, psychologists, and nurses—usually belong to national or state professional associations. Relations among those associations in the larger world, whether harmonious or conflicting, are likely to be reflected in the relations among their members who work in a given institution; this, in

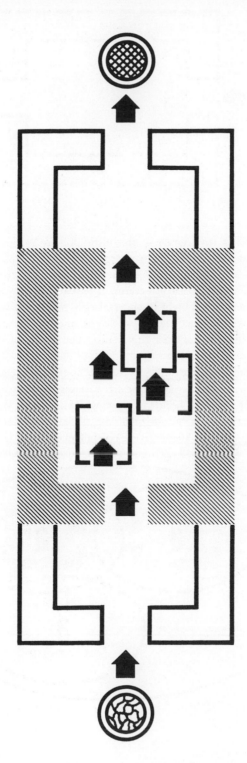

Figure 3.

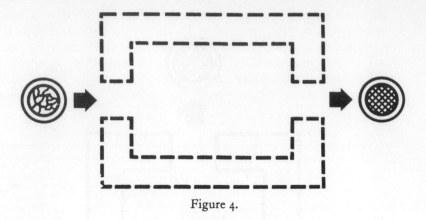

Figure 4.

turn, will affect the morale of the institution as a whole, and hence the well-being of the patients in its charge.

It is to be noted finally that institutions of the sort we are discussing exist within larger social structures. The various institutions, at federal, state, and local levels, which undertake to treat or manage people with, say, drinking problems interact with one another in ways that have important implications for their functioning. Something of this state of affairs is indicated by Figure 5.

We deal here with systems within systems. Agency a may have a place within a state's mental health services, agency a^1 may belong to a community's general health services, while agency a^2 may be a part of a state's correctional system. In each case the larger system is in a position to determine policies and exert heavy influence upon the ways in which

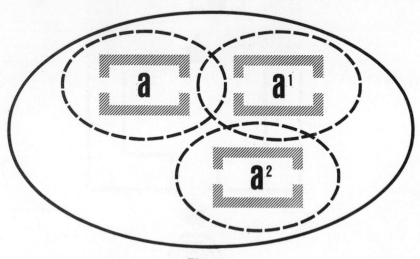

Figure 5.

they are carried out. Again, agencies within the same system or in different systems may collaborate or compete, have different statuses, or be in the role of leader or of follower—circumstances which may exert heavy influence upon the processes of any one agency. All of these agencies and the systems to which they belong exist, of course, within a larger society, whose creations they are and whose manifold processes are crucial determinants of their activities.

My purpose in this chapter has been to show that the same theoretical model holds for colleges, the psychotherapeutic relationship, mental hospitals, and many other kinds of institutions in our society. Thus, even so highly professionalized a situation as psychotherapy probably should be regarded as only a special case of interpersonal relationships; changes in the person which occur in psychotherapy or the mental hospital should be regarded as special cases of change in general.

This kind of approach offers several advantages, both to investigators and to people actively engaged in the operation of change-agencies. For one thing, because of its very generality, the model allows us to cut through the accumulation of rational and irrational processes—the tradition, as it were—of a given institution or type of institution, and to see the fundamental elements of its functioning.

Further, the general applicability of the model enables us to compare institutions, even institutions of quite different natures. As a result, research which focuses on any specific type of change-agency is in a position to contribute knowledge, or at least useful hypotheses, about change-agencies in general. For example, one important area of research might concern the duration of the person's stay within a change-agency and the frequency of his contacts with it. Educators may wonder whether we should have an educational system in which everything is speeded up in order to teach students as much as possible in a limited time or whether education should proceed at a more leisurely pace so that experiences can "sink in" and new insights can be integrated with the student's actual life. In a study of psychotherapy, Lorr (1962) found that the frequency of psychotherapeutic interviews does not make much difference if the over-all time is constant. If the over-all time is a year, probably as much is accomplished with weekly interviews as with twice-weekly. Perhaps educators can learn something from this finding.

Comparative study of change-agencies can not only help us to improve the effectiveness of institutions which now exist, but may also help us to devise some new and still more effective ones. Thus, while we continue to be concerned with developing fresh ideas for the psychotherapeutic relationship, we will do well to look for alternatives to psychotherapy, too. Probably there will never be enough psychotherapists to give help to all the people who want or need it. After all, what we are interested in is changing people, or enabling people to change, or creating conditions under which they can change, in desired directions. As we learn more about the way personality develops and changes within institutions, and more about the processes of the agency which bring change about, we may be able to develop other kinds of instrumentalities which will make more widely available some of the benefits of psychotherapy—and perhaps of other change-agencies as well.

CHAPTER NINETEEN

Social Action to Promote
Individual Development

In this chapter we turn from the change-inducing organization to the larger social scene. Here I wish to argue that legal, administrative, and social actions which affect individuals and groups without involving specific organizational structures should be guided by the same general theory and philosophy that have been applied earlier in this book to the work of organizations such as schools and mental hospitals.

The kinds of actions with which we shall be concerned are usually carried out with a view to preventing mental disorder or promoting mental health; they are usually considered within a framework of preventive psychiatry, or of "community mental health," or of "the public health approach to the prevention of mental disorder." It was pointed out in Chapter 1 that medical models such as these are not entirely adequate. There is need for a more comprehensive developmental model, and we will take further steps toward the construction of such a model here. At the same time, I do not underestimate the value of medical models; the model that will ultimately be most useful must embrace many of the concepts and strategies contributed by the medical specialties already mentioned. Particularly important is the public health approach to the

Parts of this chapter are based on the author's discussion, "The Prevention of Mental Illness," in B. B. Wolman (ed.), *Handbook of Clinical Psychology* (New York: McGraw-Hill, 1965).

prevention of mental disorder. (One might more accurately say *a* public health approach; it is an approach that is widely shared by leaders in public health who are interested in mental disorder and who utilize behavioral science in their work, but not all public health workers accept it.)

In this chapter, then, I undertake first to present this public health approach and to offer examples of how it works out in practice. This supplies a basis for raising some theoretical issues and for discussing the relations of the public health approach to our developmental model.

THE PUBLIC HEALTH APPROACH

"The Final Report of the Joint Commission on Mental Health and Mental Illness states that humane treatment and rehabilitation of the mentally ill is the great unfinished business of the mental health movement. But the great unfinished business really is to do something about the social, psychological and other circumstances leading to this condition."

With the principle stated here by Dr. Dubos (1962) of the Rockefeller Foundation few will disagree. If through prevention individuals and their families can be spared the suffering caused by illness or disorder, and society can be spared the costs of diagnosis, treatment, and care, then it seems clear that prevention is of the most fundamental importance. This would seem to be so even in the case of conditions that are easily recognized and understood and for which the means for successful treatment are ready to hand. But Dr. Dubos has an even stronger case. There is mounting evidence that neither mental disorders nor physical diseases can be controlled—that is, their rates of occurrence in the general population substantially reduced—solely through the diagnosis and treatment of affected individuals. This is a lesson from the past. As McGavran (1963) says: "Contrary to our beliefs generally, there is no evidence that control or eradication of any disease has been accomplished by the approach, procedures, techniques and activities directed at early diagnosis and treatment of disease in individuals." The great health problems—plague, cholera, typhoid, malaria, yellow fever, the dysenteries, hookworm—were not brought under control by treating individuals. Thousands of affected individuals were cured, but rates of infection were not lowered until means were found to change the environment—that is, to remove the infecting agents from the area and to improve the general living conditions of the people.

There is good reason to believe that the case is and will be much the same with noninfectious chronic diseases, mental illness, and the various forms of social maladjustment. This is partly a matter of logistics: with these conditions, as with infectious diseases, there can never be enough therapists to go around; and partly it is a deduction from a theory of causation: for all these conditions there are multiple interacting causative factors, and some of these, since they exist in the environment, cannot be reached by treatment or other actions directed to individuals. The whole argument receives support from the fact that it has not been possible to demonstrate that all the time, effort, and money put into early diagnosis and treatment have actually resulted in any reduction in the rates of occurrence of these conditions.

Traditionally, medicine has been oriented toward helping the individual, particularly the individual who asks for help. And individuals, when they are in trouble or when members of their family are, usually want treatment. They are not disposed to think very much about long-range programs of prevention, nor are they in a position to do much to launch such programs. But disease and disorder in a complex society such as ours are public matters; they affect the productivity and well-being of the whole society and hence call for action by public institutions and agencies. This is the "public health approach" to the control of disease.

Pessimism about the prevention of mental disorders, often voiced in the past, does not seem justified today. For one thing, the public health approach to chronic disease, mental disorder, and behavior problems has not really been tried in practice. It is only in recent years that specialists in public health have been giving a great deal of attention to noninfectious diseases and that social psychiatry has begun to emerge as a specialty in the mental health field. As a result of these developments mental health problems are being viewed in some fresh perspectives. Although these new points of view have yet to prove themselves, it is certainly possible to see today that the "individual approach"—that is, the approach to prevention through diagnosing and treating individuals—cannot provide a complete answer.

Our knowledge of the role of broad social factors in disease—in all kinds of disease, including mental and behavioral disorders—has increased sharply during the last ten or fifteen years and is still increasing rapidly. Today it is possible to see that many of these factors can be modified by social action. At the same time, progress in the biological sciences continues to accelerate. Consider, for example, advances in biochemistry and genetics which make it possible to detect and to alter inborn metabolic errors. Finally, there are signs that our affluent society is at last in a mood for action to improve the lot of the great mass of deprived and disadvantaged citizens who have always suffered the most from all kinds of physical and mental diseases.

The major features of the public health approach are (1) a theory of causation by multiple interacting factors—factors in the *agent* (for example, microorganisms, or a toxic substance), in the *host* (the human organism or organ system), and in the *environment* (the physical and social environment in which both agent and host have their being); and (2) strategies of prevention in which the accent is on rates of occurrence of disease in populations (rather than on the particular affected individual) and the major concern is with aspects of the environment that are widely influential—that is, those which impose strains or provide support for the great mass of people. We may consider these features in turn.

MULTIPLE INTERACTING CAUSES. The theory of complex determination is of very great importance, for there is good reason to believe that adherence to a single-factor theory has held up progress toward prevention for a long time, and is still doing so.

The belief that for each disease there is a single dominating cause is a very old one in medicine, and it received strong support from the successes of public health workers in controlling diseases such as malaria (in which the responsible germ could be eradicated from the environment) and diphtheria (where immunization against the responsible agent was possible). But with other communicable diseases, such as tuberculosis and syphilis, control has proved by no means so simple. Although the responsible microorganisms have been identified and counteracting drugs discovered, these diseases are still very much with us. Following the single-cause logic, one would say that the cause of tuberculosis is the tubercle bacillus. But how are we to explain the fact that, in the United States, out of one hundred people exposed to the bacillus, only three actually contract tuberculosis?

Cassel (1963) has offered a theory of the causation of tuberculosis that illustrates well the interaction of multiple factors. He starts with some observations of Holmes (1956), made in the city of Seattle, Washington. When the city was divided into four economic areas, the rates of tuberculosis were found to be highest in the poorest area, lowest in the richest area. When whites and nonwhites were considered separately, the picture became more complicated. Among nonwhites the highest rates were found in the richest area, while among whites the highest rates were in areas where there was a high proportion of nonwhites in the neighborhood. For both groups, in other words, the highest rates of tuberculosis appeared to be associated with living in an area where there was a minimum of opportunity for satisfying personal contacts with other people.

This same study showed that tuberculosis was associated with frequent changes of job, with being unattached (single, divorced, or widowed), and with living alone in one room. Cassel also cites a British study which found no relation between overcrowding and tuberculosis but noted that rates were almost twice as high for lodgers in families as for members of the families themselves.

In sum, it appears that tuberculosis is most common among "marginal men." But why should this be so? Clearly, not all isolated people develop tuberculosis, even when they are exposed to the bacillus. What other processes are at work? Some light was shed on this question by a study of employees in a TB hospital. A group of employees who had contracted tuberculosis was compared with a matched group who had not. It was found that whereas in the nontuberculous group stressful situations had occurred more or less at random over the years, in the tuberculous group stressful situations had mounted in frequency and intensity over the years, reaching a peak one or two years before the disease was diagnosed. By considering this finding in relation to the preceding, Cassel could argue that tuberculosis is likely to develop when people who have to deal with mounting stress are exposed to the bacillus and have no help or support from society, or from relatives or friends.

But people in this general situation develop other diseases, mental and physical, as well as tuberculosis. There is still the question of why tuberculosis rather than some other ill. One possible explanation was suggested by a study of hospitalized tuberculosis patients which revealed a relationship between hormone balance and recovery from tuberculosis. It was found that there was a relationship between the patient's hormone balance and his emotional state. Low levels of hormone (17-Keto-steroids) were associated with apathy and depression; high levels with anxiety, restlessness, and aggressiveness. If a patient's emotional state changed, so did his hormone balance. Patients whose hormone levels were closest to normal recovered fastest.

Taking all these findings and observations into consideration, Cassel was able to conclude: "Exposure to mounting life stresses in people deprived of emotional support from society will lead to their being overwhelmed with a resulting increase in depression and apathy. Such emotional states may lead to an alteration in hormone balance which increases susceptibility to the tubercle bacillus. If any of these factors are missing, tuberculosis is unlikely to occur." This general approach to an understanding of causation would seem to hold for a variety of conditions—noninfectious chronic diseases, mental disorder, social maladjustment—as well as for infectious diseases. Indeed, if it holds for a disease like tuberculosis, about which much is known, and in which some of the determining factors are readily identified and measured, there is all the more reason why it should hold for the more complicated and obscure mental disorders, or disorders in which psychological factors loom large.

It is to be noted also that factors responsible for the onset of a disease may not be the same as the factors responsible for recovery from it. Two men may develop tuberculosis for essentially the same reasons but one may recover much more rapidly than the other, depending on his inner physical and psychological resources and on the supports offered by his environment.

Reasoning from this very general conception of causation to the possibilities of prevention, one may say that success in removing or sharply reducing any one of the determining factors, or in building up a factor that favors recovery, would reduce the rate of occurrence of the disease in question, and so would some slight success in modifying in a favorable way all the factors involved.

It follows from this that it is not necessary to know precisely how a disease is caused in order to take effective action aimed at its control. A famous example in the public health literature concerns the control of a cholera epidemic in London by the removal of a public water pump. This was long before there was any knowledge of infection by microorganisms. Someone noticed that the frequency of cases varied with the proximity to the pump, so its removal seemed a good action, and it was eventually a sensationally effective one. Similarly, just recognizing an association between socioeconomic marginality and tuberculosis would be enough to indicate that improving the lot of homeless men would reduce rates of this disease, and this without invoking a theory concerning hormone imbalance as a basis for susceptibility to the bacillus. Again, to take an example from the field of mental health, Bowlby and his associates (1951, 1956) did not have to prove that a two-year-old child's separation from his mother for periods of two weeks or longer is a cause of psychopathology in later years; their thesis was persuasive enough that the British Ministry of Health issued a directive permitting and encouraging mothers to visit their children in hospitals for unlimited amounts of time. This administrative action might or might not prevent any specific mental disease, but it might lead to a reduction in the rate of mental illness in general; and, in any case, it seemed a humane thing to do. Obviously, of course, *something* must be known or strongly suspected about the causative factors, and the more that is known the better.

STRATEGIES OF PREVENTION. The public health approach to prevention focuses on rates of occurrence of diseases in populations and then seeks to reduce these rates by actions aimed at causative factors known to be, or thought to be, operating widely in the population in question. The idea is to interrupt the chain of causal events, or to intervene in the system of causation, in such a way as to affect favorably the largest possible proportion of those who are exposed or might be exposed to the disease in question.

Consider, for example, a school system. From the point of view of individual psychodynamics, the proper approach to the prevention of mental illness in childhood would consist in such actions as hiring mentally healthy teachers, teaching them about mental illness and health in children, and training them to recognize signs of disturbance in children and to give psychological first aid. A spokesman for the sociological approach would express grave doubt that these measures would reduce the rate of mental illness among the children in that school system. He would suspect that the causes of disturbances in them lay not only in the personality structures that they brought to school with them but also in the school system itself, that the problematic behavior of teachers and other school personnel sprang not so much from *their* neuroses as from the situation in which they worked, and that, accordingly, proper preventive action would consist in efforts to change the system as a whole, so that conflict was lessened and everybody in it was happier and more productive. A teacher of the writer's acquaintance is sure that a large step in this direction could be taken, in the system in which she works, by putting the school principals on academic tenure.

Considering that in all diseases there is interaction between factors in the *host,* or human organism, and factors in the *environment,* one may readily conceive of four major kinds of intervention. One may (*a*) remove or reduce susceptibilities or (*b*) build strength or resistance in individuals; or one may (*c*) remove or reduce strains or (*d*) build supports in the environment. In the case of tuberculosis, for example, one might seek to maintain or to achieve normal hormonal balance in individuals by removing particular sources of emotional upsets, or one might seek to develop psychological and physical stamina in individuals so that critical situations would be less upsetting to them; or, turning to the environment, one would try to arrange things so that people were not subjected to mounting strains, or were always assured of someone to talk to or to lean upon when they were in trouble.

What was actually done would depend further upon the aim of the preventive activity, whether it was to prevent the development of any signs or symptoms of a disease or disorder (*primary prevention*), or to detect and act with respect to early signs or symptoms in order to prevent a more serious condition (*secondary prevention*). Primary prevention may be *specific*—that is, directed to a particular disease or disorder, or *non-specific*—that is, directed to bringing about changes, either in the host or in the environment, that are presumed to have value over and above their impact on any particular disease or disorder.

In the example of tuberculosis the discussion was focused on non-specific primary prevention. There seems no doubt that improving the psychological functioning of people, reducing the strains under which they have to live, and providing support for them when they are in trouble would reduce the rates of other ills in addition to tuberculosis. Actions of this kind directed particularly to *high-risk* groups of people or segments of the population—in this case, unattached men living in single rooms—who had not yet developed symptoms of the disease would still be non-specific primary prevention. Specific primary prevention would be exemplified by efforts to eradicate the bacillus itself or to prevent its spread or to prevent exposure to it. Secondary prevention of tuberculosis consists in efforts at early diagnosis and treatment. Interestingly enough, efforts of this kind have over the years constituted the main approach to the control of tuberculosis, and rates of this disease have steadily declined; yet there is no evidence that the rate of decline bears any relation to programs of case-finding, medical care, and hospital treatment (McGavran, 1963). Instead, the decline of the disease seems to have been associated with improving economic conditions, which have brought better housing and nutritional status.

SOME PROGRAMS AND PRACTICES

We may achieve some clarification of the concepts of prevention by asking what is to be prevented, in whom, and by what methods.

What is to be prevented? The major aims are to prevent the development of disorders (primary prevention) and to prevent mild disorders from becoming acute or prolonged (secondary prevention).

"Mental disorder" is broadly interpreted to include psychogenic conditions as well as diseases of organic origin—that is, diseases due in very large part to the destruction of brain tissue or to disturbances of the physiological functioning of the brain—and to include not only the psychoses and neuroses but the so-called special phenomena, such as delinquency and alcoholism, with which society has a concern and which affect more people than do the hard-core diseases.

What is to be prevented must also include not merely specific symptoms and patterns of behavior but more general pathological or deviant states. We must allow for the possibility that actions directed toward alcoholism, for example, may in some cases, through failure to deal with a more general underlying condition, lead to the substitution of other, less desirable, manifestations.

Prevention in whom? Primary prevention is almost always directed to *populations of people*—sometimes the whole population of the nation or state. There might be, for example, action to improve the general quality of life, or action to remove some harmful agent that might attack anyone. Efforts at prevention are also directed to *selected groups of individuals*—for instance, people in specially vulnerable age groups: the prenatal population, children, adolescents, old people. People in dangerous situations, "high-risk" groups—for example, people of any age who are economically or socially disadvantaged, or children who have lost a parent, who have a psychotic parent, or whose homes have been broken—are often targets for preventive effort. It is further to be noted that all people, however free from external hazards they may be, go through periods of crisis involving threats to their mental health. At these times there is a place for preventive activity.

Public health programs are also concerned with people of any age who are already in trouble—trouble of a kind that can be diagnosed and that can hopefully be remedied. Here there is, typically, some kind of therapeutic attention to the individual case. This is *secondary prevention.* But people who are already in trouble may also benefit from primary preventive activities directed to the whole population. Indeed, there is as yet no very good way of knowing which people *are* in trouble.

Prevention by what means? Services are often organized with particular kinds of people, or particular problem areas, as a focus of attention. Examples are centers for prenatal care or child guidance clinics. But it is useful to classify preventive activities in more general terms, according to the conditions in individuals and in society that are to be changed. Actions may be directed to populations at large or to selected groups of individuals, to people who are free of symptoms—whether or not they are in dangerous or critical situations—or to people who are in trouble. Various services of institutional units—home, school, church, physicians, social agencies, courts, general hospitals, clinics, prisons, training schools, public health departments, recreational departments, employment agencies, civic organizations, etc.—may engage in these actions singly or in combination.

PRIMARY PREVENTION. Programs of primary prevention may be grouped according to whether they are undertaken by the nation, the state, or private organizations that are national or statewide in scope; by public or private agencies of the local community; or by individuals who have some kind of personal interaction with the people who are the objects of concern.

At the national or state level. Here belong activities by national or state agencies—legislative or administrative—to prevent the development of organic or psychological disorders in the general population or in selected groups of individuals; the activities may be directed to reducing susceptibilities or building strengths in individuals, or to removing hazards or building supports in society. Most often, these programs seek to improve the quality of life for everybody by changing economic and social conditions—for example, reducing unemployment and bad housing.

Not always, of course, are such programs carried forward in the name of mental health, or mental health alone; they are also carried forward in the names of justice and the general welfare. Also, there seems to be increasing understanding of the fact that changes in the economic system, or in the economic well-being of citizens, do not automatically bring improvement in morale or psychological well-being. In order to give everybody a sense of having a fair chance, and a sense of participation in the whole enterprise, it is necessary to look to public morality, to political and social arrangements, and to the system of rewards. Economic benefits to a depressed area, for example, would accomplish little unless something were done to reduce the inhabitants' suspicion of officialdom, or to change the system whereby local leaders or authority figures lined their pockets at the expense of the community.

Also, there is increased understanding of the fact that the conditions of life in modern society are psychologically difficult for many people, including middle-class people, who have economic security, at least at a minimal level. Nearly thirty years ago L. K. Frank (1936) put forward the notion of "society as the patient," and there have since been numerous efforts at "community diagnosis"—that is, efforts to understand how changes in our society and in our national life affect the psychological well-being of people in general. For example, Burgess (1955, p. 14) calls attention to the threats to mental health implicit in the complexity, mechanization, and standardization of living in our society—circumstances which lead to the substitution of impersonal relations among people for personal ones. Analyses of this kind do not usually lead to suggestions for action in particular situations; rather they seek to promote the kind of understanding that helps to make all actions affecting the great mass of people more humane.

More directly aimed at prevention are federal and state programs of education respecting mental illness and mental health. For example, the Children's Bureau has for many years sought to make available to parents current knowledge and ideas regarding child rearing; and the 1950 White House Conference on Children and Youth had effects which, according to Rosen (1961), have "reverberated throughout the past decade," speeding the process by which mental health concepts become part of the professional equipment of workers concerned with children and their families. Similarly, the 1948 White House Conference on Education did much to encourage schools at all levels to take an interest in the healthy personality development of pupils and students.

State departments of health, mental health, and education generally, and increasingly, have educational programs designed to spread the word about mental illness and health among the general public and among members of various professions that have responsibilities for people. Many states require that instruction in hygiene, including aspects of mental hygiene—for example, instruction regarding alcohol and narcotics—be offered in public schools.

Federal and state departments of health often rely upon laws and administrative directives as means for inducing people to take necessary actions to help remove hazards or to immunize themselves. The same approach holds for mental diseases of known organic origin—for example, those due to infections or to nutritional deficiencies.

It is in this area that efforts to control mental disease have met with the most success. Although the number of people affected by mental diseases of organic origin is not nearly so great as that affected by psychogenic conditions, it is still large, and much remains to be done before preventable organic diseases are brought under control. Here psychologists —particularly social psychologists—have an opportunity to play important roles (Rosenstock, 1963). Although a single factor—for example, syphilitic infection—may dominate the system of causation, there is nonetheless a *system* in which psychological and social factors play their parts. In the last analysis the prevention of general paresis will involve understanding and control of abnormal sexual behavior and of attitudes and practices having to do with reporting and accepting treatment for syphilitic infection.

The use of laws to change the behavior of the great mass of people in the interests of prevention raises highly complicated ethical and psychological issues. How far can a government go in making laws to induce people to do "what is good for them" without infringing too much upon individual liberties? How much are people willing to sacrifice in order to increase the likelihood that they or those close to them will be spared some impairment of their mental health? What diverse consequences may flow from a hard-to-enforce law aimed at some particular hazard to health?

The Eighteenth Amendment was thought by some to be a means for controlling the "toxic agent" in alcoholism. But ever since its passage this "prohibition law" and its aftermath have been cited in efforts to show how an unenforceable law, or a law that is based in too narrow a view of the phenomena it is intended to affect, can do more harm than good because of its unanticipated consequences. Certainly the experience of the "prohibition era" in this country generated attitudes and beliefs that have severely hampered rational efforts to deal with the sale and distribution of alcohol. Only in recent years has evidence emerged that national prohibition was not a total failure; and only in recent years have we had the kind of social analysis that can suggest what kinds of legal actions might be expected to modify social practice in constructive ways (Chafetz and Demone, 1962, p. 175 ff.; Jellinek, 1945; McCarthy, 1959).

The view that the passage of a law that affects the interests and behavior of the great mass of the people ought to wait until attitudes and beliefs are such that the law will be universally welcomed and obeyed was challenged by the United States Supreme Court's 1954 decision concerning the desegregation of public schools. This decision took into account evidence, supplied by social scientists, that segregation impaired the mental health of Negro children. The events that followed the decision show what a powerful instrument of cultural change the law can be; they also suggest that there are optimum times and conditions for recourse to sweeping legal remedies. It would appear that the legal action should be in keeping with a cultural trend that is already to be discerned; that there should be enough readiness among the people so that the action will be generally accepted; and that enough resistance to it should remain to allow the action to play an important role in further educating the people and speeding the desired cultural change.

This discussion of primary prevention at the state or national level has so far dealt with actions that affect people in general. There are also, at these levels, legislative or administrative actions aimed at improving the lot of people in special situations of danger. Here belong child-labor laws, and social-welfare legislation generally—for example, provision for special educational facilities for children in "impacted areas," or actions to provide job opportunities or work-study programs for youth of the type discussed in Chapter 1. Psychologists and other social scientists have opportunities here for "community diagnosis," calling attention to groups of people who are in special danger—for example, alienated youth (Keniston, 1962) —or to social practices that are damaging to large segments of the population—for example, the racial segregation of schools. These scientists may also serve as consultants to officials who have responsibility for groups of people in dangerous situations; for example, Lindemann and Caplan (1963) tell the story of how a minimum of psychiatric consultation with Israeli authorities led to highly constructive changes in the ways that immigrants were cared for.

At the community level. As Kahn (1963, p. 62) says, "A local community is in a position to interpose itself between the general social environment and the family or individual." There are from time to time actions by whole communities designed to improve themselves generally and to affect in a positive way all of their families. Here would belong large-scale redevelopment projects or community-wide programs for reducing unemployment, improving intergroup relations, or promoting more gratifying use of leisure. Actions of these kinds, starting with a focus on some particular problem such as juvenile delinquency, may have the effect of improving the morale of the whole community, generating a sense of direction and a sense of pride. From what we know of social factors in mental disorder, such actions might be presumed to reduce rates of morbidity in the community's population.

There are numerous community programs that aim to bring enlightenment respecting mental illness and health to parents and others who have responsibility for the young. Agencies of the community, such as mental health associations, PTAs, and professional organizations, arrange for lectures, discussions, institutes, courses, and uses of the mass media to acquaint parents and others with current knowledge and wisdom affecting the rearing of children. Guidance programs for parents have been set up in clinics, day-care centers, and nursery schools. Brim (1959) has reported on numerous efforts to educate parents for mental health and has pointed out how little is known about the effects of these efforts.

It is also common for mental health specialists working through local organizations and institutions to try to modify the behavior of various professionals who deal with children—for example, pediatricians (Richmond, 1959; Rose and Ross, 1960; Caplan, 1959); obstetricians, nurses, and nursery-school teachers (Brody, 1961; Murphy, 1961; Waldfogel and Gardner, 1961). Then there are community-supported efforts to promote mental health in schools. Here belong efforts to give teachers a fuller understanding of the children they teach (Prescott, 1945; Ojemann, 1956; Allinsmith and Goethals, 1962, pp. 134–55) and efforts to help teachers to understand themselves so that they will be able to provide a more favorable experience for children (Frank, 1962). There are also efforts to influence the curriculum, methods of teaching, and social organization of schools in such a way that individual development, with its implications for mental health, is favored (Biber, 1961). It is in this last area that conflict between educators interested in mental health and educators who emphasize learning of traditional school subjects often becomes acute. Allinsmith and Goethals (1962) report in detail on this matter but are unable to suggest that resolution of the conflict is in sight. Biber (1961), like the present writer (1962), has sought to restate the issues around "life adjustment" versus fundamentalism in education by pointing out that cognitive or intellectual development cannot be separated categorically from the rest of the personality, and by urging that the educational goal should be development of the total individual, rather than either positive mental health or learning of content.

There are also community actions directed to presumably symptom-free people in situations of danger or unusual stress and to people in situations that are likely to be stressful—for example, populations in depressed areas, immigrants or refugees in search of jobs, and middle-class people assembled in housing developments where there is no community.

Glass (1963) offers a good example of this kind of action on the part of military establishments, where efforts have been made to improve the conditions under which men work, live, and fight. He recommends that such efforts be followed by epidemiological work that would note the frequencies with which problems appeared within different units.

Lindemann and Caplan (1963) offer an example of how psychiatric consultation might have improved matters and reduced rates of delinquency in a housing project in the Boston area. They note that the screening procedures for admission to this low-rental housing development made it inevitable that too high a proportion of "unhealthy families" were admitted, and that these had an unfavorable effect upon the healthy families. Consultation by psychiatrists or social scientists with those who had administrative responsibility might very well have led to the working out of a better balance.

Perhaps the best examples of primary prevention directed to people in dangerous situations are the "higher horizons" projects that aim to raise the level of the cultural aspirations of underprivileged youth. In New York City, for example, the program that goes forward under this heading undertakes to speed racial integration, to speed construction of school facilities, to offer more guidance, better teaching, smaller classes in the schools, and by direct action to stimulate the less motivated and more culturally deprived youth (Board of Education of the City of New York, 1960; Wrightstone, 1958). Other cities have instituted "special service schools" designed to give the less privileged children the best in education and counseling. Downing (1959) describes a plan designed to enrich the lives of deprived children by outings and recreational programs and by helping socially isolated families become part of their neighborhoods. Other communities have programs for school drop-outs, for unemployed youth, and for young people who do not fit the educational lockstep.

At the level of personal interaction. In this category belongs intervention by the mental health specialist either through face-to-face relations with the individual involved (direct services) or through close consultation with people such as parents or teachers who have immediate responsibility for the threatened individual (indirect services). Concerning indirect personal interaction, there is a distinction to be made between the activities previously described, in which the effort is made to educate parents or teachers in a general way and to provide generally improved conditions for deprived individuals, and activities in which the mental health specialist works closely with parents or educators in programs designed to meet particular conditions. Pavenstedt (1961), for example, describes a program of special counseling for immature mothers, and Rose (1961) describes a program of counseling for mothers of children with physical abnormalities. Here would belong also Ojemann's (1958, 1961) program for teaching teachers to use educational techniques designed to induce children to adopt a "causal" instead of a judgmental approach to problems.

However, when Ojemann or a specially educated teacher works directly with children in an effort to induce them to think in causal terms, this is direct interaction. The same is true of Seeley's (1959) program of human-relations classes in which students are prepared for forthcoming crises, given reassurance, and made aware of feelings.

This kind of direct approach has been carried furthest by Lindemann and Caplan, and their colleagues (Lindemann, 1944; Lindemann and Dawes, 1952; Klein and Lindemann, 1961; Caplan, 1961). This work is based on what these workers have termed "crisis theory" (Caplan, 1961, pp. 12–14). The essential idea is that people during the course of their development normally reach certain periods of crisis during which they are particularly open to change. Depending upon the quality and intensity of the crisis, the individual may either take a step forward developmentally or fall back upon coping devices that are in the long run maladaptive. The aim of intervention at such periods is to supply the sort of help that would enable the individual to avoid this latter kind of response and to make of the crisis an occasion for a developmental gain. This method is based in psycho-dynamic theory (Lindemann, 1944), but it represents an effort by Linde-mann and Caplan and their colleagues to integrate psychodynamic and public health approaches to prevention. Although the theory of change is an individual psychodynamic theory, the argument is that crises occur very commonly in populations and that a minimum of professional intervention at the right times and places can result in reducing rates of mental illness. A number of different kinds of crises have been studied—for example, entering school (Klein and Ross, 1958), entering college (Silber, Hamburg, and Coelho, 1961), entering professional training (Rosenberg and Fuller, 1957), experiencing loss or death in the family (Lindemann, 1944), and suffering a serious illness (Lindemann).

Few primary preventive activities at any level have been carefully evaluated, and where evaluations have been made, positive results have but rarely been demonstrated. Brim (1959) has pointed up the state of our ignorance concerning the effects of programs of education for child train-ing. With respect to preventive efforts in the schools, the situation is not much better. Ojemann and his colleagues (1955), in one of the few ade-quate studies, were able to produce some evidence of the effectiveness of projects for education in "causal thinking." It is not surprising, in view of the great difficulties, that large-scale programs for changing the social environment in the state or in the community have not been evaluated in ways that would be satisfactory to a psychologist. It must be recognized, however, that programs designed to benefit large groups of people probably never will be evaluated in the way that psychologists are accustomed to evaluate psychotherapeutic procedures or particular educational devices. "Social experiments" do not permit of the same kinds of controls that can be maintained in the laboratory, but humane considerations and good sense still argue that such experiments should be carried out. One may hope those who do the carrying out will recognize the obligation to evaluate and do the best they can in their circumstances.

SECONDARY PREVENTION. The case for secondary prevention—that is, the early diagnosis and treatment of individuals who exhibit some kind of mental disorder—has recently been well put by Kahn (1963), and indeed has been well put by psychologists and psychiatrists over the years. Glass (1963) has reported on how prompt treatment of soldiers at the front seems to have been effective. Waldfogel, Hahn, and Landy (1955) have reported that good results were had with children with school phobias when referral was made early, and Fraiberg (1954) and Bower (1960) have given evidence that children who will have difficulty in learning can be identified in nursery school and that steps to avoid serious difficulty can be taken at that early stage. College psychiatrists—for example, Wedge et al. (1958) and Funkenstein (1959)—have argued convincingly that a relatively small amount of counseling of students in trouble, if it is begun at the right time, can keep the students functioning in the educational sytsem so that the normal educational influences can do their work of building internal strength. Allinsmith and Goethals (1962) have shown that schools are the most natural place for early detection, for first aid, for referral, for rehabilitation and follow-up.

A serious question concerning early detection has to do with the dangers of premature labeling. This can lead children to conceive of themselves as "problems" and then to behave as such, and it can lead people responsible for children to perceive them as disturbed and then to act toward them in ways that encourage their further disturbance. Kahn (1963) has pointed out that "delinquency scales" tend to overpredict delinquency. He urges that, at this stage of our knowledge, scales should be used only in efforts to understand and not to sort out the sheep and the goats. He suggests that dropping out of school is probably a better sign of trouble ahead than is an extreme score on a scale for measuring delinquency. It is perhaps generally true that a preoccupation with early detection can lead to a tendency to find something wrong with everybody, or even to efforts at therapy in cases where doing nothing might have been the treatment of choice.

A fundamental issue that has to be faced by authorities responsible for the mental health of large segments of the population has to do with how the limited resources are to be allocated. There is no question that during the past thirty years the major commitment of resources has been to individual diagnosis and treatment. We are now entering a phase in which primary preventive activities are beginning to participate more fully in budgets for mental health activities. To find and to maintain a proper balance will be a continuing problem for mental health specialists.

Another continuing problem has to do with the coordination of services for people in trouble. There is still competition among agencies for the "good referral," and there is still neglect of people who have "low status" diseases. Further, there is a problem of how to insure that people with mental disorders will be regarded as people and not as "cases" of this or that disease. Troubled people are too often totally defined in terms of their disease or affliction and managed according to procedures that are suited to agencies rather than to the needs of human beings. It will take an enormous amount of social engineering to arrange things so that the troubled individual who needs several kinds of help will be served either by a single broad-purpose agency or by several agencies that can coordinate their efforts, and so that no individual will be pulled apart by conflicts among specialized agencies that either lay claim to his total being or else accept responsibility for only a part of his total problem.

SOME THEORETICAL ISSUES

The public health approach can go quite a long way on the basis of knowledge or hypotheses about the correlations of broad social factors, such as unemployment or bad housing, with mental illness, and on the basis of theory of social structures. Action for mental health would consist in removing or reducing the harmful or hazardous factors, or in intervention at some point in the social structure—within an organization, institution, or community—in such a way as to make for favorable change in the whole.

PSYCHOLOGICAL ASSUMPTIONS AND SOCIAL ACTION. Actions of these kinds, however, always involve, at least implicitly, psychological assumptions or theories—about how people in general will react to an environmental condition, how they are organized as personalities, and how they develop from birth onward.

The British Ministry of Health, in encouraging mothers to visit their children in the hospital, must have assumed that both mothers and children would be happier and less anxious if this were done, and that doctors and nurses could adapt themselves to this change in routine without too much disturbance of their work. But when large-scale social actions are based on wrong psychological assumptions the results can be damaging to large numbers of individuals. In Poland for some years after World War II, the official word was: "We have no delinquency because we have socialism"—this at a time when the police were all but overwhelmed by masses of disturbed and delinquent children, the products of broken homes, poverty, neglect, and general social disorganization. This was not merely official hypocrisy, but an expression of the belief that a far-reaching change in the organization of society would immediately and automatically bring far-reaching changes in people, including children. Again, in England during the same period, large numbers of families were moved from bombed-out areas of the East End of London to clean, comfortable, but rather sterile housing estates in the suburbs around the city. The assumption seems to have been that these former slum dwellers would immediately begin living like middle-class people. They did not; instead they were unhappy, because the women, especially, missed their family and community networks, and because the kitchen, having become small and modern, could no longer be the center of life for the family. Many of these people made their way back to the true communities from whence they came.

In this last instance more appropriate action would have had to be based in knowledge of culture, and of a particular subculture, as well as in knowledge of the general psychological laws according to which cultural values are acquired. Nowadays in this country, specialists who would improve mental health by changing environments are very much aware of cultural factors. This attitude has been favored by public health experience, and of course has been further promoted by the entrance of anthropologists and sociologists into the mental health field. For that matter, it is doubtful that anywhere in the Western world today anyone interested in mental illness or health would seek to apply so doctrinaire a version of the good life as did the British planners of the housing estates. In Mexico, for example, when people are moved by the thousands into new housing developments the closest attention is given to the requirements of family life and to what favors the psychological as well as the physical well-being of people.

The public health approach also makes assumptions about the elements of personality and their organization in individuals. The idea of susceptibility or resistance to disease or to kinds of diseases must have reference to more or less enduring structures in people, structures that are built up over time, predispose the individual to a particular kind of response, and thus help to determine what will happen when stimuli arrive. The public health specialist or the social scientist may or may not believe, as most personality theorists do, that personality functions as a unit and that mental illness or mental health is a condition of the whole person. He may believe—and with good reason—that problematic or deviant behavior can be a response to a momentary stimulus and is open to change without alteration in the structure of the person. But to take preventive actions aimed at particular conditions without giving attention to the complexity of personality, particularly to the interactions of its constituent processes, is to court trouble. Such an action might indeed affect a particular condition in the predicted way, and still do more harm than good if there is no theory to suggest other consequences for other features or functions of the person. For example, segregating slow learners or the gifted and exposing them to special educational procedures in school might result in more appropriate learning of content but lead to a kind of labeling and a self-conception that would be in the long run most unfortunate from the point of view of mental health.

It may also be suggested that attention to personality theory, which deals with the complexity of processes inside the person, is a good safeguard against the extreme forms of collectivism which sometimes emanate from social planners and advocates of large-scale social actions. The frame of mind that permits enthusiasts for social action to concentrate on the group without attention to what goes on inside people would appear to be close to that which can contemplate sacrificing individuals for the good of the group.

Today most specialists who would reduce rates of mental illness by modifying the social environment seem to be aware of these considerations. They are also aware of the great difficulties in the way of persuading people to take measures that might protect their health. Smoking, drinking too much, indulging indiscriminately in sexual relations, driving without seat belts may all be bad for the health, mental as well as physical, but people by and large do not seem to be on the point of changing their ways. Effective actions in areas of this kind will require at least as much knowledge of human motivation as of social processes.

PSYCHODYNAMIC THEORY AND ITS CRITIQUE. Public health workers and social scientists who work in the mental health field have been critical of the individual psychodynamic approach to prevention—an approach that accents the personality-forming events of childhood and sees prevention as primarily a matter of working with individual children who show signs of trouble and with the parents of such children. It is argued that this approach, after years of work and the expenditure of huge sums of money, has not succeeded in reducing rates of admission to mental hospitals; at least there is no evidence that this is the case. This may be because the early treatment was ineffective; children seen in child-guidance clinics went on to become hospital patients anyway. More probably it is because the people who are treated in child-guidance clinics, or treated privately as children, and the people who fill the mental hospitals, are drawn from different populations (Forstenzer, 1961). As is well known from the work of Hollingshead and Redlich (1953) and others (see Rose and Stub, 1955), the highest rates of admission to mental hospitals are found in the lowest economic stratum of society, while there is a strong tendency, pointed out by Albee in his report for the Joint Commission (1959) for child-guidance clinics, and out-patient clinics generally, to turn away or not to have referred to them the people who have the most serious problems. These last, typically, are individuals from the lower economic classes; it is they, rather than individuals who "can benefit from psychotherapy," who from the start are more likely to be destined for the mental hospital. Hence the argument, often forcibly put by social scientists, that the most highly trained specialists in the mental health field—that is, the psychoanalytically oriented psychotherapists—are devoting themselves to the least-ill members of the population affected by mental illness—and are training and otherwise encouraging more people to do the same thing.

This kind of criticism often attributes wrong practices by psychiatrists, clinical psychologists, and social workers to the domination of the mental health field by psychodynamic theories, mainly those of the Freudian variety. There is a strong implication that practice is wrong because the theory is wrong, and that everybody—particularly the mentally ill—would be better off if Freud had not saddled us with his theories about the determination of neurosis in childhood.

This may be doubted. Criticism of mental health practice is one thing, criticism of psychodynamic theories something else. Various psychological theories besides the psychodynamic ones focus on individuals rather than on the mass of people. The way mental health services in this country are organized would seem to depend more on the kind of society we are than on the kind of psychological theory favored by psychiatrists during a particular period.

The rewards for performing two-person psychotherapy with people who are not very sick—and particularly with people who can pay—are by American standards great compared with those for using other kinds of methods with very sick people in public institutions. These rewards are not primarily status and money, though these no doubt have their place; most important is the satisfaction of seeing an individual "improve" or otherwise benefit as a result of therapeutic effort. This satisfaction is of the same kind as that experienced by devoted teachers or counselors of individuals; to observe a favorable change in "the statistics" for a population is not a substitute for it. We should expect what we in fact find: that some professionals of various theoretical points of view, including modern behavioristic ones, prefer to practice individual psychotherapy, and that the role is often chosen before there is commitment to a theoretical position.

No doubt there is interaction between theory and practice. People who are trained for the practice of psychoanalysis, or for psychoanalytically oriented psychotherapy, naturally tend to interpret Freudian theories in ways that lend support to what they do, and their practice often cuts them off from experiences that might broaden their horizons. When they are thus led to take narrow and stereotyped views of neurosis, to overgeneralize from their clinical experience, or to overaccent the role of childhood traumata in personality functioning, they become easy targets for the sociological critics. But these critics, if they are to attack Freudian psychodynamic theories effectively, must do more than suggest that belief in these theories has led to the poor allocation of our mental health resources.

They have, of course, done more. They have attacked the theories directly—both the theory of determination of neurosis in early childhood and the theory of personality change that underlies psychoanalytic psychotherapies. With respect to the determination of mental illness, the social scientists critical of psychoanalysis have argued that broad social and economic factors, such as social disorganization, unemployment, and bad housing, may be more important than emotional crises arising in the context of relationships within the family. But this does not seem to touch the psychodynamic theories themselves, for however much one may be struck by bad cultural and social conditions and feel moved to change them, an explication of their role in psychopathology would still have to make clear the ways in which they affect the individual personality. And here the role of the family as mediator and the role of psychodynamic mechanisms of input and adaptation seem as important as ever.

Nor does the social scientist's accent upon events occurring later in the individual life, rather than upon the events of childhood, lead to any great shaking of the psychodynamic position. It is possible for the psycho-analyst to be quite relaxed about this, agreeing readily that "Later events are important too," for nothing has happened to threaten his view that in every neurotic or psychotic breakdown there was a predisposition laid down in early childhood. This view is not contradicted by evidence that such a breakdown would not have occurred but for severe strains arising in adult life. The psychoanalyst would say that people with neurotic or psychotic predispositions commonly find modes of life that serve their defensive needs or offer enough support so that a more or less adequate existence is possible. Breakdowns come when supports are withdrawn or radical change in the individual's situation renders his defensive operations ineffective. This seems to have happened to thousands of young men when they were inducted into the armed services during World War II.

This is not to say that there are not environmentally determined strains of such severity or of such a character as to cause prolonged emotional disturbance, malfunctioning, or deviant behavior in anyone—regardless of predisposition or resistance. The psychoanalyst would say simply that these disturbances were not manifestations of neurosis in his sense of the term; and the fact that this is so, he would argue, helps to explain why so many people with severe psychological problems get well without benefit of professional help.

INTEGRATION OF PSYCHODYNAMIC AND SOCIAL APPROACHES. Sophisticated critics of psychodynamic theory have warned their colleagues in social science, who have thought they had psychoanalysis on the run, not to throw out the baby with the bath water. It may be suggested to enthusiastic social and situational determinists that they approach this whole baby-bath complex with caution. We are dealing here with differences in emphasis upon one or another aspect of what should be a total theory of causation. In particular cases there will always be a question of whether the situational or the predispositional factors were crucially important, and the psychoanalysts will often turn out to be right.

The psychodynamic theories, then, remain pretty much intact—so far—but when it comes to the question of what to do, the social scientists and the public health specialists have made a point. No psychodynamicist can deny the importance of precipitating factors in mental disease, or of situational events in emotional disturbance. There are enough unnecessary strains and enough failures in support in the lives of enough people in this country to keep an army of preventers busy. And since the strains and lacks of support affect millions, it seems clear that actions that might modify these conditions in whole communities have a better chance of reducing rates of mental illness than does psychotherapy with its very limited applicability.

The second major line of argument against psychoanalysis and the psychodynamic theory has to do with the nature of personality and the processes of personality change. Once again it seems well to separate arguments about practice from arguments about theory. Not only social scientists and public health specialists but many psychologists, psychiatrists, and psychoanalysts have long been aware of the practical limitations of psychotherapy and have sought substitutes for it. The success of such substitutes as group psychotherapy, or even the therapeutic community, does not necessarily imply any criticism of the theory. Nor does the fact that various kinds of psychotherapy other than psychoanalytic ones bring benefits to patients. Actions that induce changes in people and the explanation of those changes are two different things.

The same consideration holds generally for activities designed to effect changes in behavior without pretending to modify the structures of the personality. Certain types of problem drinking, for example, can be regarded as symptoms of underlying disturbances in the personality. Action that leads to the substitution of some other symptom for the problem drinking but involves no change in personality, might be a great benefit both to the alcoholic patient and to people around him.

The crucial theoretical question is how central or all-determining, within the personality, are the unconscious structures laid down in early childhood. There is a tendency sometimes found among psychoanalysts—and often attributed to them by their critics—to suppose that personality formation ·is a matter of building unconscious defenses against instincts, and personality development a matter of undoing, or having undone, these defenses and contriving better ones. Some psychoanalysts and some psychologists sympathetic to psychoanalysis (for example, Hartmann, Kris, and Loewenstein, 1947; White, 1952; and the present writer in earlier chapters of this book), as well as numerous writers of quite different persuasions (for example, Maslow, 1954; Allport, 1961; and Kelly, 1953), have argued, and assembled evidence to show, that this is not the whole story. There are parts of the personality that do not become involved in the child's unconscious complexes, and always there are parts of the personality not dominated by unconscious processes but open to modification through ordinary experience. Significantly, the best evidence for this view has been contributed, not by psychotherapists, who focus on neurotic structures, but by investigators who have seen neurotic or mentally ill people in various settings other than psychotherapy. Most impressive has been evidence from work in mental hospitals that even the most seriously ill patients are still capable of functioning in organized groups and of responding to stimuli which raise or lower self-respect in normal people

(Greenblatt, Levinson, and Williams, 1957; Milbank Memorial Fund, 1958).

The point is of enormous significance, both for the care of the mentally ill and for prevention. It means that much can be done for people in trouble, outside as well as inside mental hospitals, by less highly trained professionals, and even by nonprofessionals, for, on this view of the matter, benefit to troubled people does not flow entirely from changes in their unconscious structure or even from psychological understanding of these structures. And where the concern is with the education and upbringing of children, it means that one makes no mistake when he devotes effort to the development of those parts of the personality that are free or relatively free of involvement with unconscious processes. It does *not* mean that those who have responsibility for troubled children can ignore the unconscious processes determining their symptoms; for although such children can respond to efforts to develop the unimpaired parts of their personalities, some of them will, if not understood, insist in acting out their unconscious motives in ways irreparably destructive to themselves or others. One may hope that with respect to facilities for troubled children we will not always have to choose between those which adhere to rigid stereotypes of Freudian categories and those inspired by a blind optimism concerning what can be achieved by providing a favorable environment.

The final issue concerns the possibilities of modifying unconscious structures of the personality by means other than psychotherapy or its equivalents. Here we may recall the argument stated earlier (Chapter 2) that in individuals with symptoms based on underlying neurotic structures developments in the unimpaired parts of the personality may so change the relationships between what is conscious and what is unconscious that the latter fades into relative insignificance. It has also been argued in this book that unconscious processes are not necessarily cut off from direct influence by social stimuli. A challenging question concerns the interaction of the conscious and the unconscious. The traditional and well-substantiated psychodynamic view is that unconscious processes have a heavy determining effect upon cognition; there is reason to believe that the determination may also be the other way round. This is a frontier area for research—although those who have no truck with concepts of the unconscious will not be intrigued by it.

Once again, this kind of liberalization of the psychodynamic view is consistent with the "new thinking" which supports the activities of social scientists and public health specialists who would reduce rates of mental illness by modifying the social environment. Some supporters of the "new thought" seem to have come by their liberal views too easily. It may be hoped that the practical orientation, and particularly the practical success, of the new breed of mental health workers does not impair investigation into the nature of personality organization and functioning. In the long run, knowledge of these matters will be essential if preventive work is to reach a high level of effectiveness.

THE DEVELOPMENTAL MODEL

It seems clear from the preceding discussion that nonspecific primary prevention is, for all practical purposes, the same thing as action to promote personality development. There would appear to be advantages in deliberately utilizing the latter conception, with its accent on *providing* conditions favorable to *building up* response systems in the individual; this would help to make it clear that various institutions in addition to medical or medically guided ones have important roles to play. The adoption of this approach would not, however, eliminate the necessity for specific preventive activities. Particular hazards in the environment and particular susceptibilities in individuals would still have to be attended to. For example, even if all our young people were well started on the road to personality development, it would still be wise to offer alcohol education in secondary schools and to give special attention to individuals with unusual ways of metabolizing alcohol. Such specific preventive activities should, however, be consistent with the goal of personality development. The point is that all programs of preventive action have to be guided by values—that is, values over and above the simple conviction that mental illness is bad. This follows from the fact that pathological conditions are not isolated in the person (a change in them might induce desirable or undesirable changes in other areas of the person), and from the consideration that actions deemed necessary to prevent an unhealthy condition may affect a person in various ways, some good and some bad.

The mental health specialist faces this issue as soon as he says, as he must, that he wants to be sure his preventive actions do not do more harm than good. The evaluation in such a case cannot possibly be limited to the single dimension of increased or decreased "mental health," for it is unthinkable that all virtues, all desiderata of human development, can be brought under the mental-illness–mental-health rubric. To be convinced of this, one has only to ask what a person who has achieved mental health should do with himself, or whether one would be willing to give up our ideals of individualism if by doing so we could eliminate psychological strains and thus reduce rates of mental illness. It is hard to imagine circumstances in which the goal of reducing or preventing mental illness should take precedence over humanity, or justice, or the fullest possible development of the individual's potential.

Critics of the efforts by psychologists to formulate positive goals for people (too often, unfortunately, under the banner of "positive mental health")—both early critics, such as Kingsley Davis (1938), and late ones, such as Elaine Cumming (1963)—do not belabor the psychologists so much for having values as for having the wrong values—that is to say, values which these sociologists would not put very high in *their* hierarchy. Fundamentally, it seems, writers such as these want more "social conscience" and less "social desirability," or, more seriously, more attention to the welfare of people in general and less to what might be ideal for particular individuals.

In the literature on positive mental health, two conceptions may be differentiated. First, there is the conception of something over and above freedom from illness that stands as resistance to, or relative immunity from, mental illness. There would seem to be a place for this conception, and for research that could specify what such a condition might be. The criticism that positive mental health is indefinable would seem not to apply with any great force here, for to define resistance and to specify it experimentally is presumably no more difficult than to define and to specify susceptibility to illness. The second conception embodies a set of ideals referring to what a person might become. This conception might easily come into conflict with the first one, for it may turn out that qualities—such as insensitivity, for example—which contribute to resistance to illness do not fit into conceptions of the ideal.

Particular conceptions of this second kind are always easy to criticize. Frequently they can be shown to be culture- or class-bound, or to be expressions of particular historical periods. But the search for ideals must go on, and there is no reason why psychologists and social scientists should not take part in the quest. If these scientists are to assist in designing plans for the upbringing and education of children and youth, they must be guided by open-ended conceptions of what people can become. They need commit themselves only tentatively to particular systems of value, while continuing their efforts to improve thinking about values by showing how values are arrived at and what will be the consequences of particular values. Perhaps they can make their greatest contribution by urging—and this flows directly from knowledge they now have—that where human beings are concerned ends and means cannot be separated. In a humanistic approach to prevention, means as well as ends are humanistic. This is to say that long-range programs of discipline or deprivation aimed at the ultimate inculcation of some virtue cannot be supported. What is good for people in the long run is, by and large, good for them *now*, in the immediate situation. Actions that aim to develop people, or to build resistance to mental illness in them, can be evaluated in the momentary situation without waiting for long-range consequences. Such evaluation would take into account the motives, feelings, and behavior of the "helping" parent or professional, as well as the immediate effects of their actions upon the object of their concern. If the helpers are well-motivated and their actions have good effects upon *them*, the chances are that the objects of their efforts will be benefited also.

Part Six

Chapter 20 offers further consideration of some of the issues discussed in Chapter 1, with special attention to the role of the social scientist in society. The chapter begins with an attempt to answer criticisms that have been leveled at social science, mainly by humanistic scholars and philosophers. This leads to a recognition of the fact that social scientists must, and do, proceed in accordance with values of their own. What might be a suitable basis for their value position? It is argued that such a basis may be found in the idea that science itself, properly conceived, is a system of ethics. Some implications of this idea for practice with individuals and groups are then briefly indicated.

CHAPTER TWENTY

Social Science
and Social Practice

Although social psychology, sociology, and anthropology are still relatively undeveloped sciences, they have been shown to possess very considerable social power. For example, since industry has gone in for "human
relations," it has become more difficult for labor organizers to do their
work. Again, the dissemination of knowledge about the social-class structure of the United States has helped to reduce the outward differences
among the classes.

Perhaps because of its increasing potency, the new social science has
in recent years come in for considerable criticism, both from people who
believed their tangible interests to be threatened and from people who have
objected on principle.

The criticisms can be answered, and I shall presently attempt to do so.
But this is not to suggest that the activities of social scientists ought not to
be subjected to continuing scrutiny by the interested public. The newer
social sciences are as yet inadequately professionalized. There is not sufficient definition and understanding by the public, or sometimes on the
part of the social scientist himself, of what these new specialists can and
should do. Where there is power there must be control. The questions of

Most of the first section of this chapter has been taken from the author's paper,
"The New Social Science and Its Critics," *The Humanist,* the American Humanist
Association, Yellow Springs, Ohio, 1957, No. 2. Most of the remainder of the chapter
has been taken from a presidential address before the Society for the Psychological Study
of Social Issues, New York, 1958.

how and by whom the necessary control is to be exercised are ones to which I will return.

The concern here is only with the newer social sciences mentioned above. These are the sciences which study people in their relations with other people. Psychoanalysis—most of it—is included, as part of social psychology. The aim of these sciences, like that of all sciences, is the discovery and dissemination of truth. They go on the assumption that the more truth the better for everybody, and that eventually the truth will make men free. In their applied aspects, all these sciences are concerned with modifying people by means of human interaction, usually verbal interaction. Consulting is not as well defined as research, but it may be said to have a fair amount of sanction in our society.

When the social scientist is acting in the role of *reformer*, or initiator of change—a role that has been recommended in this book—he himself is concerned about objectives, and obviously he is guided by values of his own. It is this role, naturally, which is most in need of clarification and which is most exposed to criticism—both that which is motivated by fear that personal interests may be threatened and that which arises from "ideological" objections. Objections on ideological grounds, which come most often from philosophers, teachers of the humanities, and journalists of the arts, are the most serious and the most telling arguments.

I will pass over what might be called "resistance" to social science— that is, objections based on unconscious motives or other irrational processes—and limit myself to the intellectual or principled criticisms. These can be boiled down to three: that social science is impossible; that it is immoral, in that it violates human individuality; and that it is undemocratic.

The objection that social science is impossible, that it is not really *science*, and that it cannot be scientific because people are too complicated, seems somewhat out of date. It used to be argued that since social science could not measure human tendencies with any precision, it could not predict events; and without prediction there could be no control and, hence, no science. Today, it is the fact that social science *does* have some control of events, enough to make a difference, that has led some of the "realistic" agencies of our society—such as industry and the armed services—to embrace it, and has led in other quarters to viewings with alarm. It is the social scientists themselves who worry most about the difficulties of prediction and control, about how little is really known about social behavior, and about the fact that their disciplines are oversold in certain important segments of our society.

The criticisms of social science on moral grounds have been directed both to its ends and to its means. Truth and freedom as objectives of science are, after all, pretty general; and critics have exercised their right to question intervening or subsidiary objectives—and to question whether the ultimate ends have been pursued consistently. And where the end was acknowledged to be good, it has still been possible for critics to ask whether the means of social science were proper.

With respect to ends, social scientists get it coming and going. Where they have specified goals that men ought to seek, or spoken of what men themselves ought to become, and then have pointed out the means to those ends, they have been accused of totalitarianism. On the other hand, when they have refused to speak about the "positive" or the "integrative" and have confined themselves to the analysis and explication of man's behavior, they have been accused of being soulless creatures bent upon destroying the image of man.

This last accusation must be disposed of at once. To state it as fairly as I can: by accenting man's susceptibility to conditioning and the large influence of his unconscious impulse-life, and by showing the relations of man's higher functions to his lower or more primitive ones, science spreads the impression that man is like a machine or just an animal, and thus encourages people to regard themselves and others as less than human. Well, people do sometimes treat themselves and others as if they were less than human, but there is no evidence that this has anything to do with the rise of science. Actually, there is good reason to believe that this practice was more widespread before the scientific era than it is now. Moreover, it is difficult to see what can be gained by denying any facts about man. He does exhibit machine-like or animal-like proclivities; his nobility lies in his ability to recognize and to overcome such tendencies. And it is precisely the study of such tendencies that promises to be most helpful. The critics sometimes write as if they believed one could not possibly *like* man once one really got to know him; or as if, once his illusions about himself were shattered, he would go to pieces. The stubborn fact is that there is no use in trying to recapture the pre-Copernican or pre-Darwinian conceptions of man. We know too much about him. The only thing now is to know more, particularly about what man has to put up with and what he has to overcome; and thus to achieve a higher compassion.

Social scientists, goaded by such criticism as that just considered, have sometimes tried to set up some positive goals for man. For example, they have tried to define the characteristics of health, or maturity, or good functioning. Not only has this led to the accusation of totalitarianism, but actually, things have sometimes worked out as if the accusation were justified—that is, so great is the need of people for positive guidance that many have adopted the new objectives mechanically and begun behaving as if they were healthy or mature, to the detriment of their individuality and essential humanity.

It is because of its positive value for freedom that social science concentrates so heavily on the restraints upon freedom: both those within the individual—such as unconscious impulses and mechanisms and the workings of conditioning—and those in the social situation. And it is because of this value that social science is very wary about enunciating definite positive goals for man and thus inviting automatic conformity. The values for truth and freedom command many others, and it is because of their adherence to these values that when it comes to most social, political, and moral issues, the social scientists usually turn up on the side of the angels.

Yet, as previously indicated, these values are sufficiently general that when the social scientist works with other people on some particular problem, there is plenty of room for conflict about ends. Thus any individual, group, or institution that enters into a working arrangement with the social scientist will sooner or later have to work out with him adequate clarification of goals. Usually things can be arranged so that no one is too unhappy.

The means of the social scientist—that is, his special knowledge and techniques—are, of course, the basis of such power as he has; they comprise most essentially his specialty, his "mystery," and they are by definition those aspects of his work that are least understood by people who are not social scientists. It is precisely at this point that the principled criticisms are most forcibly directed. The major criticism seems to take one of two forms: (a) that the social scientist "manipulates" people—that is to say, gets them to do things without their full consent by taking them, as it were, unawares and appealing to something lower than their fully conscious selves; and (b) that the social scientist does not respect the uniqueness of each individual personality, but instead, by treating people as if they were nothing more than units in a mass, or by concentrating on particular functions or mechanisms, which are then lifted out of their living context and treated as averages for a group, he contributes to the construction of a false image of man and makes it harder for people to be unique.

It cannot be denied that some social scientists may at one time or another have done some of these things; but it certainly can be denied that the methods of social science in their very nature *require* any manipulation of people or any damage to their uniqueness.

Medicine, of course, has to do those things which the philosophical critic complains about. The patient "places himself in the doctor's hands," permitting him to use anesthetics, drugs, hypnosis—devices which do indeed deprive the individual of his autonomy—on the assumption that the end justifies the means. The physician is able to do his work because he has authority; his privileges and powers have been sanctioned by the public, and no one thinks of depriving him of his authority so long as he adheres to a high professional standard. The intellectual critic of social science would not, we may suppose, object to the use of unhuman means under proper conditions to save his life.

But I cite the instance of medical practice only to indicate that, when the chips are down, even the stanchest defender of our humanity looks upon means not solely from the point of view of how humanistic they are in and of themselves, but with attention to what end is being furthered, what is known about means-end relations, and whether or not the means have social sanction. There is some irony in the fact that social scientists have to listen to so many complaints from these philosophical critics when with respect to the whole matter of therapy the two groups actually stand together. This is the essence of the continuing argument between psychologists and psychiatrists. Psychologists argue that a client who enters psychotherapy in a nonmedical setting is an autonomous person, able more or less to make his own decisions and to govern his own life, and that he is not required to surrender any of this autonomy. Psychiatrists, on the other hand, argue that psychotherapy is for sick people and that whoever undertakes it must be prepared, and have the authority, to assume responsibility for the total well-being of the patient. Psychologists, like the intellectual critics, are out to preserve as much of the individual's autonomy as possible.

Concerning the social scientist who works in an institution with a view to bringing about desirable changes, I can think of no instance in which his methods necessarily entail any manipulation of people or any assaults upon their individuality. There are, of course, circumstances in which he has to be particularly careful to avoid this, as, for example, when he attempts to communicate results of research on the functioning of an institution. Here the social scientist follows the simple rule that scientific knowledge belongs to everybody. He does not, of course, tell everything he thinks he knows as soon as he thinks he knows it; and since considerable time ordinarily elapses between the preliminary gathering of data and the production of demonstrably valid results, people may get the impression that someone is holding out on them. Actually, there is no justification and no necessity for withholding scientific truth from those most likely to be concerned with it. There is no denying that the truth may be painful to some people, for a time, but surely the maintenance of our humanity does not require that for the sake of avoiding temporary pain we foster illusions about ourselves or our situation.

With respect to the value for the unique individual personality, it is necessary to point out that it is impossible to take any planned action affecting groups of people without taking into account their similarities as well as their differences, and that it is impossible to take any planned action with respect to any individual without some conception of his mechanisms and modes of functioning.

Some of the critics, aware of these truths, have themselves sought to avoid any semblance of "manipulating" people by taking no action at all. But this is impossible, unless one virtually withdraws from the human race. In any human relationship, inaction is simply an action of a particular sort, often one with very considerable consequences.

Other critics speak and act as if they believed they were doing all right, with respect to the integrity of the individual personality, so long as they did not know what they were doing; as long as they did nothing deliberately, as it were, and were aware of nothing but good intentions. They should not, of course, be permitted to get away with this. Actually, the most vigorous exponents of uniqueness do not, in their relations with people, behave in any distinctive way; when, for example, they move into administrative roles, as they sometimes do, their stratagems resemble very closely those of most other administrators.

343

In the last analysis, the only way to avoid bad actions with respect to people is to know what will be the consequences of particular actions—in particular individuals or in people in general; and since people can only be reached through their mechanisms or modes of response, these are precisely the things which the philosophic critic, like the social scientist, must learn. Fortunately, such knowledge does not have to be acquired only in school, but is also a product of experience in growing up. This is something with respect to which people differ enormously. For my part, I would feel that my individuality was most likely to receive the attention it deserved when I was being dealt with by people who had a well-developed sensitivity to the needs and mechanisms of others. I should expect to encounter no more of this sensitivity among philosophic critics of social science than among various other kinds of people—for example, truck drivers or headwaiters. This is not to say that education makes no difference; on the contrary, it may make an enormous difference, provided it is education about people rather than about some general philosophical outlook.

The final general criticism is that social science is undemocratic in the sense that it does not look after the interests of everybody. It puts more power in the hands of those who already have the most. The case of the "efficiency expert" is still remembered; or there may be a reference to a paternalistic industry using social-science techniques to keep the workers happy but submissive. In the same category belong the protests against the wide use of social-science techniques for the manipulation of people or the "engineering of consent"—in advertising, public relations, political campaigns, and the like.

This line of criticism has truth and justice on its side, but social science itself is not its proper object. The criticism is properly directed, rather, to our society or to certain large and important trends within it. The social scientist escapes this line of criticism so long as he does not participate in or lend himself to the undemocratic uses of his science.

The question is how the social scientist can avoid participating in misuses of himself and his science. It is sometimes argued that by adhering strictly to the role of researcher, or to that of consultant, he may avoid responsibility for any bad social consequences of his work. It is very much to be doubted that he can thus avoid *all* responsibility. He is not free from considerations of value even when he is performing as a researcher or consultant. Social institutions, like individual human subjects, are very likely to change as a result of being studied, and it is up to the social scientist to insure that such changes are in accordance with considerations of welfare. In the case of consulting, it is a rare social scientist who can claim complete detachment with respect to the ends being sought by his client. These ideas are further developed later in this chapter.

The point here is that since the social investigator *must* be guided by values, and the consultant can hardly avoid being so guided, social scientists are under a heavy obligation to define an ethical position. It is not enough to parry the arguments of humanistic critics. We must find a basis for our position in logic, in the philosophy of science, and in the theory of value. The remainder of this chapter is an effort in that direction.

RESEARCH HAS CONSEQUENCES

There has been growing realization in scientific work of various kinds that the observation of events is itself a determinant of the events being observed; in social psychological work, as well exemplified by Freud's psychoanalytic method of investigation and therapy, there has been increasing attention to the observer as a factor in the determination of the processes under study. When it comes to social research in real-life situations, effects of the research activities themselves can be plainly observed. When we enter an organization as social researchers, exhibit our interest in comparative value systems, and begin talking about means-end relationships, we are bound—so long as we have the slightest status or power—to have an upsetting effect. And the effect will not be limited to those who live under a parochial system and know that science has in the past forced revisions of value systems.

Today, uncertainty about values and about how they are to be arrived at is almost universal. Social scientists are widely believed to be promoting certain kinds of values whether or not they recognize them. The kinds of values that are imputed to us correspond in widely differing degrees to those we actually have, depending upon the extent to which we have clarified our position and upon various dynamic factors in those who do the imputing.

Studying college students by means of questionnaires or interviews affects those students, and this whether or not we do it in accordance with the requirements of our professional ethics. Just studying them has effects.

In the course of the research at Vassar College (described in Chapters 4, 11, 16, and 17) we interviewed a sample of students several times each year throughout their college careers. We have evidence that at the end of that time, but not at the beginning, the interviewed sample differed in personality test scores from students who were not interviewed. This is what one should expect on clinical grounds, and our observations of the subjects, as well as what they themselves said, are in keeping with the test results. The results were in the desired direction. But what would we have done had our interviewees turned out to be more authoritarian, less mature, less confident than their fellows?

Fortunately it is not necessary for the argument to be developed here to show that interviews are a benefit to subjects; it is only necessary to show that the subjects change as a result of being interviewed. The fact that they change at all is enough to call attention to the researcher's responsibility.

The same general considerations hold when it comes to observing students in the mass and then reporting to them one's observations and interpretations. Our observations and analysis of student society and culture were available to the whole college community, including the students, both before and after publication. Students reviewed and discussed this report in their publications and in various informal settings, with us and among themselves. Many of them had to deal with it in one way or another as a class assignment. People cannot read about and discuss their own culture in this way and still go on behaving as they did before; there is a changed perspective and a changed attitude; there is greater awareness and hence greater freedom. If students change, faculty attitudes toward them change—a new process is set in motion. At the same time, faculty members use knowledge about students in their own way.

The communication of research results, an integral part of the purest scientific activity, is at the same time an action that has consequences. Our means for pursuing our objectives are, at the same time, ends—that is, changed attitudes on the part of those who cooperate in the research. By communication I mean, of course, not just reporting results in scientific shorthand, but making things clear; this means taking into account factors of receptivity in those being communicated with.

In the field of higher education it has been clear for some time that survey studies in educational institutions are not enough; the need is for educational experimentation. Since 1956 I have been promoting here and there among educators the idea of an experimental college within a college. It would be designed in accordance with hypotheses growing out of social-science research, and there would be experimental controls. It has been easy to arouse interest in this proposal, and there has been much discussion of its pros and cons. Some objections are practical administrative ones; others grow out of the defeatism and obscurantism that have dogged our colleges and universities ever since they became fully democratic in their administration. Leaving these aside, the remaining objections are of two familiar types: (a) you cannot perform a truly scientific experiment in education because you cannot establish and maintain the necessary controls, and (b) if you do establish the controls and do a proper experiment, you will harm the subjects. Many times I have been told: "The experiment is bound to succeed. Effects would be due to these factors as well as to the social conditions that you propose to set up, so what could you conclude?" I have answered, and quite seriously, "I should conclude that more experimental colleges ought to be set up."

But I would agree with the first objection. Observation of events *does* influence those events. What we have to do, of course, is to study the observer at the same time. I would also agree with the second objection. Passage through an experimental college might indeed have some temporarily upsetting or painful effects on the student—such as being regarded as special or queer or being disadvantaged to some extent upon entry into the job market. So might any educational program have harmful effects, and many of them commonly do. In the present state of our knowledge all higher education is experimental, or perhaps one might better say, wildly adventurous. What more can we do than conceive a program that we believe to be good both in its means and in its ends and then put it into effect?

It is interesting to note that foundation men and educators who are actively engaged in trying to set up experimental colleges do not mean "experimental" in any strict sense of the word—not in the classical "scientific" sense, with its controls, measurements, and so on. It is a matter of "Let's start her up and see if she'll run," the hope being that just the starting up will stimulate educational thinking in wide areas. These men, like a great many scientists, I am afraid, think of science in its operations aspect only, rather than in its attitudinal aspect. The word science makes them think of guinea pigs and Martin Arrowsmith's dilemma, rather than of a great humanistic enterprise which can free those who practice it as well as those upon whom it is practiced.

It is inconceivable that anyone would start an experimental college, or any other kind of educational experiment, in order to demonstrate by harming students that certain things are indeed harmful to students. It is also inconceivable that anyone would need to do this in order to feel that he deserved the name of scientist. One can demonstrate that certain existing practices are harmful, without thinking up new tortures. But the important point is this: Since science, when education is its field of endeavor, has as its main object the development of students as individuals, it could hardly begin by doing something that might be irreparably damaging to that development. I am not saying that the end never justifies the means. I am saying that in science means are also ends, or are inseparable from them. When students volunteer with their eyes open for psychological experiments or experimental colleges, they are already doing what the advancement of knowledge will permit them and others to do more often—namely, participating as free individuals in situations that may broaden experience and enrich the personality.

SOCIAL SCIENTISTS HAVE VALUES

So far, I have been saying that as scientists we must have an ethical system because values are integral to our essential activities whether we are aware of these values or not. Now I would emphasize that, as a matter of fact, our values are showing more or less all the time. It is a plain fact of observation, well known to politicians, foundations, and government officials, that social scientists as a group tend to display a value orientation of a characteristic sort: they are rather overwhelmingly on the liberal or humanistic side of issues. It would be hard to name a subculture whose position with respect to a public question involving values would be more predictable than that of social psychologists. We are constantly getting involved in reformist movements of one sort or another. We are less certain than we used to be about the best ways to promote the general welfare —we have more difficulty in locating the angels, knowing what side *they*

347

are on. But we will nonetheless usually be found lined up against the enemies of freedom and humanity—as soon as we have found out who *they* are.

Why is this? There are, happily, various sources of liberal and humanistic values, but I would argue that for us the main factor has been our training in social science. Granting that an element of susceptibility is important, the essential fact is that if one learns well what is taught in the usual introductory social psychology course, one cannot possibly participate fully in an ethical system that is authoritarian or enthnocentric, or in one that depends in large part upon illusion or narrowness of experience. Once one has been freed of parochial or infantile determinants, there is no going back to them.

Since all societies, including our own, still depend heavily upon, and operate largely in accordance with, ethnocentric value systems, the social scientists are bound to be a little outside. I am not suggesting, however, that we give up our research contracts with the government or that we reduce our efforts to obtain some fair measure of support for social science. What is good for social science is good for the government.

SCIENCE AS VALUE

At this point I want to suggest that the best position for us to take is that science itself is a system of ethics. Like all such systems, the system of science begins with some assumptions: that objective truth exists, that it can be shown through following certain rules of evidence, that universal sharing of the truth is possible and desirable, and that this universality may be arrived at by means other than coercion. The pursuit of truth and its communication are the highest values, and a great many activities and conditions are values because they are essential to the ultimate ones. The ethic derives from its own activity.

The qualities demanded of the scientist are not only skill in method and knowledge of the rules of evidence, but, more importantly, such things as capacity to suspend judgment, independence, originality, unconventionality, tolerance, and appropriate humility. There is, in short, a whole complex of behavior which makes up the scientific attitude or approach.

As far as conditions of society are concerned, science flourishes under that type of democracy that accents freedom of opinion and dissent and respect for the individual. It is against all forms of totalitarianism, mechanization, and regimentation. As Bronowski (1959) has said, it is more human than the machinery of governments or of organizational structures.

It turns out, of course, that values derived in this way are much the same as those which stand high in other great ethical systems. This is indeed fortunate, but it does not mean that science owes anything to these systems. Once its original choice is made, the other values follow logically and in accordance with fact. In the historical development of the ends that are treasured in Western societies, there is reason to believe that science has had a determining role. Bronowski again: "Men have asked for freedom, justice, and respect precisely as science has spread among them" (1959).

The crucial difference between science and other systems of ethics is that science is the only one that can criticize itself and still go on much as before, improved but not shattered. It may have its illusions destroyed and its fundamental knowledge profoundly revised without any serious effects upon its essential position and direction. It can survive psychoanalysis and analysis in the terms of the sociology of knowledge, and values from other systems which have survived such analysis turn out to be precisely those which are integral to the scientific system. Science is not culture-bound, nor is it highly relativistic. What is good is good for everybody. Science is the servant of all mankind, just as it is the creation of all mankind. Thus it constantly enlarges the bounds of human sympathy and favors, even as it forms, human brotherhood. Science is understanding, and hence reconciling and compassionate, without being in any sense soft or neutral.

The ethical systems of other professions, such as business or the military, have become models for whole societies. Why should not the practice of science become such a model—after we have shown, as we can, that joy and beauty have their places in this system? At any rate, anyone who takes it upon himself to be a scientist, and succeeds in living up to its requirements, could view with equanimity his behavior becoming a universal norm.

This whole account distinguishes between the spirit of science and its body, between its attitudinal temper and its methods. It says that the former is the more important, and that if we have it, all we need of the latter will be added unto us. This says something of crucial importance about the scientist as citizen and about the training of scientists.

It says that the roles of scientist and citizen cannot be sharply separated. There are two reasons for this. First, since, as we have seen, the very life of science depends on certain kinds of social conditions, the scientist is bound to take a stand on the side of whatever favors these conditions. Second, and more important, that complex of attitudes which together make up the scientific spirit exists, like all other attitudinal patterns, in individual personalities. If the attitudes are to be sustained, if they are to serve the interests of science, they have to be deeply based and integrated with the rest of the personality. We cannot therefore expect the scientist to give up something of himself, or not really to be himself, just because he finds himself in a different social role. Social science has shown that one of the great ills of modern society is that individuals tend to disappear through allocation of themselves to a great aggregate of social roles and social group memberships, with the result that morality, which exists in individuals, tends to be replaced by group decisions. If the scientist is the first to know this, he should be the last to let it take hold of him. It is not too much to expect of a scientist that he somehow be all of a piece, that he maintain the ideal—if he cannot always maintain the practice—of approaching all important issues in the same spirit of truth-seeking, independence, and tolerance that characterizes his best scientific work.

Concerning the training of scientists, it seems clear that the accent in our country has for some time been upon the method rather than upon the attitude. Indeed, the image of the man dominated by the spirit of science, a man who is thoughtful, serious, eccentric, and quite possibly wise in some matters, seems a bit old-fashioned, if not actually quaint. The modern scientist is likely to strike the observer as practical, efficient, administrative, and, of course, well-heeled. I should like to see a resurrection of the earlier image. Perhaps this would occur if we spent as much time instructing our students, and ourselves, in the attitudinal aspects of science as we spend teaching methods.

SCIENCE *AND* VALUE; SCIENCE *OF* VALUE

The idea of science as a system of ethics might be clarified by considering it in relation to some other ideas. When I say science *as* value I am regarding the two as the same thing. It is no doubt more common to consider them as two different things. If they are two different things, they are either related or not related. There are some moralists and some scientists who claim that science and ethics simply have nothing to do with each other. A more common view is that science and value are different things but are related in some way. We may speak of science *and* value and science *of* value.

With respect to science *and* value the major positions are ethical neutrality and ethical partisanship.

In ethical neutrality there is a clear conception of a difference between fact and value, and the task of the scientist is to make facts available to those who want to use them. This is quite different from ethical blindness, in which the scientist has values without recognizing it, or without recognizing what they are, and from ethical indifference, a type of amoralism which assumes either that there is no way of distinguishing one value from another or that one is as good as another.

Ethical neutrality has much to recommend it. It can show that certain ends are impossible, it can show what means may be employed for certain ends, and it can demonstrate some of the consequences of a given action or policy. How often in practical situations do questions of value—"Ought we to do this or that?"—find answers in factual knowledge or become replaced by other questions. Ethical neutrality is attractively humble and appropriately respectful of other people's right to choose. The trouble with it is that in the last analysis it is impossible. That has been the burden of much of my argument—that we have already made crucial choices and that our means are inseparable from ends. The danger of the neutral position, particularly when it is strongly defended, is that values will creep in unrecognized and turn the position into one of ethical blindness.

Ethical partisanship assumes that the scientist cannot avoid value judgments, and it insists that he state clearly, to himself and others, what his choices are. (We exclude, of course, the case of that particular type of partisan who puts the seeking and communication of truth at the top of the value hierarchy.) The values chosen in ethical partisanship are usually at a high level in the hierarchy—democracy, happiness, health, maturity—and they are usually chosen on the basis of much enlightenment; and then science is seen as instrumental to the indisputably valuable goal. A great advantage of this approach is that it permits its exponent to defend his chosen goal as *a* good without claiming that it is *the* good. Also, the way is open for the scientist to join with other disciplines in the formulation of the major value or values.

The position confronts a major problem in the definition of objectives, such as democracy or health; it also puts an enormous strain upon the objectivity of the scientist. Ethical partisanship flourishes best in times of crisis; it speaks in a voice of urgency: "We must find the means to accomplish our purpose before time runs out." Thus it arouses the partisanship of others. But the great difficulty, and the great danger, is that when the focus is on ends of enormous or momentous value, there is too likely to be carelessness about means. There may be insufficient attention to the incidental or indirect or more ultimate consequences of planned action, or the control of individuals that is necessary to the plan may itself do the very harm that the plan was designed to eliminate.

Science *of* value assumes that since values are held by men, value judging is a mental process that can be studied. Instead of putting science in the service of what is thought to be good, it undertakes the scientific consideration of goodness and badness. This familiar approach has solid achievements to its credit. It has demonstrated that certain things widely thought to be good, like ethnocentrism or a rigid superego, are not good; and that things widely thought to be bad, like some of the less orderly instincts, are not really bad. It has lent the support of science to the great ideals of various ethical systems—for example, justice, truth, beauty, courage, and love. It has undoubtedly improved the quality of value judgments by supplying knowledge of what enters into them, and, not least, it has revealed much about the conditions of moral behavior.

But there is a difference between studying how valuations are made and making them. By treating values as hypotheses, we can learn much about the validity of values, but this does not eliminate altogether the necessity for choice. And there is a logical and a psychological difference between knowing and choosing, however intimately the two may be related. This argument *can* be attacked on pragmatic grounds. To say there is a choice that lies outside the bounds of scientific analysis is to play into the hands of the enemy—those who by virtue of their power, their imbeddedness in authoritarian systems, their revelations, or their intuitions are sure they know what is right. However, in the circumstances of today, there are times when we are better off if we say that we too have chosen and that we have chosen science. This is an act of simple faith, but more than most others, it seems, we stand ready to revise both our knowledge and our evaluations.

Pragmatic considerations aside, we can in no case ignore logic or psychological fact. But in saying that knowledge and choice are different, I am most certainly not saying that we can separate choice from the activities by which knowledge is acquired. This indeed is the core of my argument.

The several ethical positions indicated here are not mutually exclusive in practice. One may hold the position of science *of* value and still be more or less neutral. In the short run, with respect to some sets of objectives, one may announce one's interest in a certain goal and occupy oneself with the investigation of means for its attainment, and one may study evolution by scientific methods. But in the long run, one can be driven out of any of these positions, by logic or reason or by science. One cannot be driven out of the science *as* value position. So we do well to derive our values from this position in the first place. Finally, there is no claim that the scientific ethic covers anything. It covers a great deal—it covers our activities as scientists; it is not up to me to say what it does not cover.

The position that has been outlined here has been honored in practice for a long time, most notably in Freud's psychoanalytic method of investigation and treatment. By the method I mean the whole contractual arrangement according to which both therapist and patient become investigators and objects of careful observation and study; in which the therapist can ask the patient to face the truth because he, the therapist, is willing to try his best to face it in himself; in which investigation and treatment are inseparable aspects of the same humanistic enterprise. This method changed the whole conception of the doctor-patient relationship. In my view, it is the best model for all those human relationships in which an expert in the psychological and social sciences undertakes, in a face-to-face relationship, a scientific approach to the problems of persons or groups.

IMPLICATIONS FOR PRACTICE

Before concluding, let me suggest how this approach has been used in social-scientific work with one type of social group—the large organization. I shall try to show that the position set forth in this chapter can supply a sound ethical basis for much that has been regarded as the best practice in this field. It helps to say why the conditions of work commonly regarded as desirable—independence, financial security, outside-group membership, occupation of a sanctioned professional role—are of such importance, and it can provide a position of strength from which to negotiate in the interests of pure research, long-run objectives, freedom from demands for immediate consultation or practical results.

The position can guide our thinking about what would be ideal. But we have to recognize the gap between the ideal and what is possible in the real world of practice. There is a place for the lone researcher who wants to make some observations and collect some data respecting the processes in his own institution, and there is a place for those social scientists whose duties and commitments largely pertain to helping functions in organization but who wish to exploit the research potential that is implicit in what they do. Indeed, the value of scientific activity in these situations will be the greater the better we are able to see its place within a general scheme.

It follows directly from what has been said that the crowning feature of a scientific approach to organizations is freedom to pursue the truth wherever it may lead. We should obtain, if we can, the right to investigate the organization in *all* its parts and functions. I am thinking here not only of the value at the top of our hierarchy but of what appears to be the nature of organizations. They are organized complexities. We cannot understand a part-function without seeing it in relation to the whole. And if we accept the assignment of aiding the performance of a single function—for example, selection of personnel—without looking into anything else, we may very likely lend support to the organization's defenses. What Freud said about analytic patients holds here almost as well. "If there is a house in the city where the police are forbidden to go, we may be sure that all the local thieves and scoundrels will congregate there." Similarly, if we accept the assignment of consultation in the interests of a subgroup, we are likely to be denied access to other subgroups and so be prevented from obtaining the whole truth.

It is because of the nature of organizations that we may go a long way just by discovering and communicating the truth. All organizations have some implicit and untenable assumptions; all produce some effects that are undesirable and unanticipated; all, we may safely say, are susceptible to some further release of their creative energies. In their nature all organizations are resistant to change. Such is the integration of their role structure that it is often impossible to change one role or function without changing all the others. Individuals who take roles in organizations vest interest in these roles; commonly indeed, the role-behavior is made to serve the defensive purposes of the personality. When this has happened, we may truly say that in order to change the personalities in certain ways it is necessary to change the organization, and that in order to change the organization we must change some personalities. It is because of this dynamic equilibrium in its inner structure that an organization can rarely change save under the influence of forces from outside itself For the same reason, influences from outside, if they are effective at all, are likely to be felt throughout the whole structure.

As organizations are resistant to change, so are they resistant to research. *They* suspect that research is an instrument for inducing change, even though some psychologists may doubt this. Resistance to research, after a research team has entered the organization, is best understood as an aspect of the structure's adaptation to the intruding body. The host prefers changing the intruder to changing itself; at the least, it persists in trying to find out what it is up against. If one understands resistance he can

353

handle it effectively by waiting it out without being too worried, taking the occasion for further clarification of the research approach. But such waiting requires the type of security, financial and other, that I referred to earlier. It also requires, as I am now insisting, some assurance with respect to one's values and with respect to the sanction for his activities. With such assurance one may go further and meet resistance by interpreting it—if, of course, he understands it. Resistance is an expression of the organization's underlying dynamics. To understand it is to understand some of the organization's basic processes, and to interpret it, or even to wait it out while remaining on the scene, is to become an important factor in the determination of the organizational processes.

It is because of the inevitability of resistance, and its crucial place in the investigative-reforming process, that negotiation in advance of actually entering the organization is so important. Resistance can best be met from a previously prepared position, and some of the necessities of organizational life can be won only during the honeymoon period. Advance negotiation is the best safeguard against being forced into the disastrous roles of either authority or Man Friday, or of kindly ineffectuality, from which it is impossible later to extricate oneself. If one chooses to begin by presenting oneself as harmless or agreeable, hoping to win one's way later by helpful performances, one is likely to be disappointed.

This clinical-analytic approach is the one that is most in keeping with the ethical position of science as value. Is this approach enough? This brings us to the major dilemma. Organizations are concerned with finding effective means for achieving their objectives. An educational institution, for example, has to have an educational philosophy and policy and is responsible for its effects upon the lives of its students and for other social consequences of its existence. Science may appropriately concern itself with the demonstration of educational ends-means relationships, using the method of hypothesis-testing, as in the case of the experimental college idea.

Let us assume that the values of science and those of the educational institution are essentially the same, though they may have been arrived at in different ways. (The ethical system of science allows ample room for pluralism as far as educational objectives are concerned.) Now if one is to proceed scientifically, one has to have precise definitions of objectives, and means for measuring attainments. But no matter how liberal the defined objectives may be, they are bound to sound dogmatic and be susceptible to mechanical and rigid implementation. This poses a threat to the basic purpose of an institution of higher learning: to create and maintain conditions under which teachers are free to teach as they please. College and university faculties fear, with some justification, that social science or psychiatry or psychology or, more likely, outside agencies in society may declare for certain objectives and acquire the power efficiently to organize everybody in such a way as to attain them.

This is where the clinical-analytic approach has its most important role to play. Its major task would be to discover and point to whatever was being overlooked in the situation. Its way of maintaining liberality with respect to means would be to concentrate upon specific means-ends relationships, in particular after particular: "If we do this, it must be because we believe such and such, but this other is what in fact happens." Or, "We definitely do not want consequence A, but our activity B seems to be favoring this consequence, so let us try something that is more likely to avoid A."

Formulating general hypotheses and testing them in practice is not a distinguishing activity of science; this is typically the work of those who make and implement policy. The experimental college would not be run by scientists; such a college would be operated by educators who believed that this was the best way to do things (but who could be convinced by experience that it was not). Education already has the social sanction for this kind of activity, and science need not encroach upon its territory. The goal of the scientist here would be to help education become more scientific, not only by offering knowledge but by teaching the values and implications of science.

This brings us back to the values and motives of the scientist—and to the question with which this chapter began: How is the power of social science to be made subject to social control? If the scientist's power is to be effective in the public interest, it must be sanctioned by society. How this is to be done is a question that deserves much public discussion.

One way to solve the problem would be for social scientists to move into roles that have already been sanctioned. For example, a social scientist might become a "line" officer in a business organization or an administrator in a public institution; or, if he desired the most complete sanction for the practice of psychoanalysis, he might earn a medical degree. This kind of thing is common today, and it seems to work fairly well. The only questions are whether such arrangements permit the most efficient use of the social scientist's skills, and whether the costs of establishing the desired sanction might not be exorbitant.

Another way of proceeding would be for people who occupy sanctioned roles to become social scientists. This is being done by managers, administrators, officials, and, particularly, physicians. But once again there is a question of efficiency, of whether it is not too wasteful for people who have trained and become experienced in one specialty to stop and learn another.

It may be best for society to proceed with the institutionalization and legitimization of the social science specialties as professional roles in and of themselves. This indeed seems to be the direction in which the social scientists themselves are heading; they are organizing themselves into associations and devising codes of professional ethics. They must engage in a continuing effort to be quite clear about their roles and functions, their aims and values. This effort will be furthered by adopting the position that science itself is the model, for practice as well as for inquiry.

References

Abraham, K. *Selected Papers*. London: Hogarth Press, 1927.

Adorno, T. W., Frenkel-Brunswik, Else, Levinson, D. J., and Sanford, N. *The Authoritarian Personality*. New York: Harper, 1950.

Albee, G. *Mental Health Manpower Trends*. New York: Basic Books, 1959.

Alexander, F. *The Medical Value of Psychoanalysis*. New York: Norton, 1932.

Alexander, F., and French, T. M. (eds.). *Psychoanalytic Therapy*. New York: Ronald Press, 1946.

Alexander, F., and Staub, H. *The Criminal, the Judge, and the Public*. New York: Macmillan, 1931.

Allinsmith, W., and Goethals, G. W. *The Role of the Schools in Mental Health*. New York: Basic Books, 1962.

Allport, G. W. *Personality: A Psychological Interpretation*. New York: Holt, 1937.

Allport, G. W. *Pattern and Growth in Personality*. New York: Holt, 1961.

Arlow, J. A., and Brenner, C. *Psychoanalytic Concepts and the Structural Theory*. New York: International Universities Press, 1964.

Aron, Betty. *A Manual for Analysis of the Thematic Apperception Test*. Berkeley, Calif.: Willis E. Berg, 1949.

Asch, S. *Effects of Group Pressure upon the Modification and Distortion of Judgments*. Swarthmore College: Progress report on Office of Naval Research Project, Task Order N7onr-38003, 1950.

Balint, M. "On Genital Love." *International Journal of Psycho-Analysis*, 29:34–40, 1948.

Barron, F. "Psychotherapy as a Special Case of Personal Interaction: Prediction of its Course" (doctoral thesis, University of California, Berkeley, 1950).

Barron, F. *Personal Soundness in University Graduate Students.* Berkeley, Calif.: University of California Press, 1954.

Barron, F. "What is Psychological Health?" *California Monthly,* 68:22–25, 1957.

Barron, F. "Creative Vision and Expression in Writing and Painting." In MacKinnon, D. W. (ed.), *The Creative Person.* Berkeley, Calif.: Institute of Personality Assessment and Research, 1961.

Barron, F. *Creativity and Psychological Health.* Princeton, N.J.: Van Nostrand, 1963.

Becker, H. S. "Student Culture in the Changing University." To be published in *Dynamics of Change in a Modern University,* Center for the Study of Liberal Education for Adults, Chicago, Ill.

Bereiter, C., and Freeman, M. B. "Fields of Study and the People in Them." In N. Sanford (ed.), *The American College.* New York: Wiley, 1962.

Bertalanffy, L. von. "Theoretical Models in Biology and Psychology." *Journal of Personality,* 20:24–38, 1951.

Bettelheim, B. "Individual and Mass Behavior in Extreme Situations." *Journal of Abnormal and Social Psychology,* 38:417–25, 1943.

Biber, Barbara. "Integration of Mental Health Principles in the School Setting." In G. Caplan (ed.), *Prevention of Mental Disorders in Children.* New York: Basic Books, 1961.

Blos, P. "Psychological Counseling of College Students," *American Journal of Orthopsychiatry,* 16:571–80, 1946.

Blos, P. "The Contribution of Psychoanalysis to the Treatment of Adolescents." In M. Heiman (ed.), *Psychoanalysis and Social Work.* New York: International Universities Press, 1953.

Board of Education of the City of New York. *Toward Greater Opportunity.* New York, 1960.

Boulding, K. "A General Theory of Growth." In L. von Bertalanffy (ed.), *General Systems Theory.* Los Angeles: Society for General Systems Theory, 1956.

Bower, E. M. *Early Identification of Emotionally Handicapped Children in School.* Springfield, Ill.: Charles C Thomas, 1960.

Bowlby, J. *Maternal Care and Mental Health.* Geneva: World Health Organization, 1951.

Bowlby, J., Ainsworth, Mary, Boston, M., and Rosenbluth, D. "The Effects of Mother-Child Separation: A Follow-up Study." *British Journal of Medical Psychology,* 29:211, 1956.

Bridgman, P. W. *The Logic of Modern Physics.* New York: Macmillan, 1927.

Brierley, Marjorie. "Review of F. Alexander and T. M. French, *Psychoanalytic Therapy.*" *International Journal of Psycho-Analysis,* 32:248–49, 1951.

Brim, O. G., Jr. *Education for Child Rearing.* New York: Russell Sage Foundation, 1959.

Brody, Sylvia. "Preventive Intervention in Current Problems of Early Childhood." In G. Caplan (ed.), *Prevention of Mental Disorders in Children.* New York: Basic Books, 1961.

Bromley, Dorothy D., and Britten, Florence H. *Youth and Sex.* New York: Harper, 1938.

Bronowski, J. *Science and Human Value.* New York: Harper, 1959.

Brown, D. R. "Some Educational Patterns." In N. Sanford (ed.), "Personality Development During the College Years." *Journal of Social Issues,* 12:44–60, 1956.

Brown, D. R. "Personality, College Environments, and Academic Productivity." In N. Sanford (ed.), *The American College.* New York: Wiley, 1962.

Buhler, C. "Maturation and Motivation." *Personality: Symposia on Topical Issues,* 1:184–211, 1951.

Burgess, E. W. "Mental Health in Modern Society." In A. Rose (ed.), *Mental*

Health and Mental Disorder: A Sociological Approach. New York: Norton, 1955.

Burney, C. *Dungeon Democracy.* New York: Duell, Sloan and Pearce, 1946.

Bushnell, J. H. "Student Culture at Vassar." In N. Sanford (ed.), *The American College.* New York: Wiley, 1962.

Canter, J. M. The Role of Motivation in the Rehabilitation of the Domiciled Alcoholic. Unpublished paper presented before the 1964 annual convention of the American Psychological Association, Los Angeles, September 5, 1964.

Caplan, G. "Practical Steps for the Family Physician in the Prevention of Mental Disorder," *The Journal of the American Medical Association,* 170:1497–1506, 1959.

Caplan, G. (ed). *Prevention of Mental Disorders in Children.* New York: Basic Books, 1961.

Cassel, J. C. "Potentialities and Limitations of Epidemiology." In *Key Issues in the Prevention of Alcoholism.* Report of the Northeast Conference, Harrisburg, Pa.: Pennsylvania Department of Health, 1963.

Cattell, R. B. *Description and Measurement of Personality.* New York: Harcourt, 1946.

Cattell, R. B. *Personality.* New York: McGraw-Hill, 1950.

Chafetz, M., and Demone, H. *Alcoholism and Society.* New York: Oxford, 1962.

Christie, R. The Effect of Frustration upon Rigidity in Problem Solution. Doctoral thesis, University of California, Berkeley, 1949.

Crutchfield, R. S. "Independent Thought in a Conformist World." In S. Farber and R. H. L. Wilson (eds.), *Conflict and Creativity.* New York: McGraw-Hill, 1963.

Cumming, Elaine. "Pathways to Prevention." In *Key Issues in the Prevention of Alcoholism.* A Report of the Northeast Conference. Harrisburg, Pa.: Pennsylvania Department of Health, 1963.

Cumming, Elaine, and Henry, W. E. *Growing Old.* New York: Basic Books, 1961.

Dahrendorf, R. *Class and Class Conflict in Industrial Society.* Stanford, California: Stanford University Press, 1959.

Davidson, H. H., and Kruglov, L. P. "Some Background Correlates of Personality and Social Attitudes," *Journal of Social Psychology,* 38:233–40, 1953.

Davidson, Judith S. (ed.). *Vassar 1957.* Class Reunion Bull. Poughkeepsie, N.Y.: Vassar Alumnae Association, 1964.

Davis, K. "Mental Hygiene and the Class Structure." *Psychiatry,* 1:55–65, 1938.

Davis, M., and Ditman, K. "The Effect of Court Referral and Disulfiram on Motivation of Alcoholics." *Quarterly Journal of Studies on Alcohol,* 24:276–79, 1963.

Dollard, J., and Miller, N. E. *Personality and Psychotherapy.* New York: McGraw-Hill, 1950.

Downing, Ruth. "A Cooperative Project of an Elementary School and a Family Agency." *Social Casework,* 25:84, 1959.

Dubos, René. Speech before the National Association for Mental Health. Miami, Florida, 1962.

Eager, J., and Smith, B. "A Note on the Validity of Sanford's Authoritarian-Equalitarian Scale." *Journal of Abnormal and Social Psychology,* 47:265–67, 1952.

Erikson, E. H. "Crises of Normal Development." In C. Kluckhohn, H. Murray, and D. M. Schneider (eds.), *Personality in Nature, Society and Culture.* Rev. Ed. New York: Knopf, 1955.

Erikson, E. H. *Childhood and Society*. New York: Norton, 1955.

Erikson, E. H. "Sex Differences in Play Configurations of Pre-Adolescents." In *Discussions in Child Development,* World Health Organization. Vol. III. New York: International Universities Press, 1958.

Festinger, L. "Social Psychology and Group Processes." In C. P. Stone (ed.), *Annual Review of Psychology.* Stanford, Calif.: Stanford University Press, 1955.

Forstenzer, H. "Problems in Relating Community Programs to State Hospitals." *American Journal of Public Health,* 51:1152, 1961.

Fraiberg, Selma. "Counseling for the Parents of the Very Young Child." *Social Casework,* 35:47, 1954.

Franck, Kate. *Preference for Sex Symbols and Their Personality Correlates. Genetic Psychology Monographs,* Vol. 33, Provincetown, Mass.: The Journal Press, 1946.

Franck, Kate, and Rosen, L. "A Projective Test of Masculinity and Femininity." *Journal of Consulting Psychology,* 13:247–56, 1949.

Frank, L. K. "Society as the Patient." *American Journal of Sociology,* 42:335–44, 1936.

Frank, L. K. Introductory remarks to a panel discussion on ideals and realities in modern education, Bank Street College of Education, New York, 1955 (quoted in W. Allinsmith, and G. W. Goethals, *The Role of the Schools in Mental Health,* New York: Basic Books, 1962).

Freedman, M. B. "The Passage Through College." In N. Sanford (ed.), "Personality Development During the College Years." *Journal of Social Issues,* 12:13–29, 1956.

Freedman, M. B. "Studies of College Alumni." In N. Sanford (ed.), *The American College*. New York: Wiley, 1962.

Freedman, M. B. "Some Theoretical and Practical Implications of a Longitudinal Study of College Women." *Psychiatry,* 26:176–87, 1963.

Freedman, M. B. "The Role of the Educated Woman: An Empirical Study of the Attitudes of the Classes of 1957 and 1958 at Vassar College." In Judith S. Davidson (ed.), *Vassar 1957*. Class Reunion Bull. Poughkeepsie, N.Y.: Vassar Alumnae Association, 1964.

Freedman, M. B. "The Sexual Behavior of American College Women." *Merrill-Palmer Quarterly,* 11:33–48, 1965.

Freedman, M., Leary, T., Ossorio, A., and Coffey, H. "The Interpersonal Dimension of Personality." *Journal of Personality,* 20:143–61, 1951.

Freedman, M. and Sweet, B. "A Theoretical Formulation of Some Features of Group Psychotherapy and Its Implications for Selection of Patients." *International Journal of Group Psychotherapy,* 4:355–68, 1954.

Frenkel-Brunswik, Else. "Psychoanalysis and Personality Research." *Journal of Abnormal and Social Psychology,* 35:176–97, 1940.

Frenkel-Brunswik, Else. "Motivation and Behavior." *Genetic Psychology Monographs,* 26:121–265, 1942.

Freud, A. *The Ego and the Mechanisms of Defense.* (Orig. publ. 1936.) New York: International Universities Press, 1946.

Freud, S. "On Narcissism." In *Collected Papers.* Vol. 4. London: Hogarth Press, 1934, pp. 30–59.

Freud, S. *New Introductory Lectures on Psychoanalysis.* 3rd ed. London: Hogarth Press, 1946.

Freud, S. *An Outline of Psychoanalysis.* (Orig. publ. 1940.) New York: Norton, 1949.

Freud, S. "Libidinal Types." In *Collected Papers.* Vol. 4. London: Hogarth Press, 1953.

Freud, S. *Inhibitions, Symptoms and Anxiety.* (Orig. publ. 1926.) Standard Edition, Vol. 20. London: Hogarth Press, 1959.

Freud, S. *The Ego and the Id.* (Orig. publ. 1923.) Standard Edition, Vol. 19. London: Hogarth Press, 1961.

Friedan, Betty. *The Feminine Mystique.* New York: Norton, 1963.

Fromm, E. *Man for Himself.* New York: Rinehart, 1947.

Funkenstein, D. H. (ed.). *The Student and Mental Health: An International View.* Cambridge, Mass.: The Riverside Press, 1959.

Gillespie, J. M., and Allport, G. W. *Youth's Outlook on the Future.* Garden City: Doubleday, 1955.

Glass, A. J. "Military Psychiatry." In Albert Deutsch (ed.), *The Encyclopedia of Mental Health.* New York: Franklin Watts, 1963.

Glazer, N., and Selznick, P. "Berkeley." *Commentary,* March 1965, pp. 80–85.

Goldstein, K. *The Organism.* New York: American Book, 1939.

Gough, H. G. *The California Psychological Inventory.* Palo Alto, Calif.: Consulting Psychologists Press, 1957.

Gough, H. G. "Techniques for Identifying the Creative Research Scientist." In D. W. MacKinnon (ed.), *The Creative Person.* Berkeley, Calif.: Institute of Personality Assessment and Research, 1961.

Gough, H. G., and Woodworth, D. G. "Stylistic Variations among Professional Research Scientists." *Journal of Psychology,* 49:87–98, 1960.

Greenblatt, M., Levinson, D. J., and Williams, R. H. (eds.). *The Patient and the Mental Hospital.* New York: The Free Press, 1957.

Group for the Advancement of Psychiatry. *The College Experience: A Focus for Psychiatric Research.* Report No. 52, 1962.

Hartmann, H. *Ego Psychology and the Problem of Adaptation.* New York: International Universities Press, 1958.

Hartmann, H. *Essays on Ego Psychology.* New York: International Universities Press, 1964.

Hartmann, H., Kris, E., and Loewenstein, R. M. "Comments on the Formation of Psychic Structure." In *The Psychoanalytic Study of the Child.* Vol. 2. New York: International Universities Press, 1946.

Hathaway, S. R., and McKinley, I. C. *The Minnesota Multiphasic Personality Inventory.* Rev. ed. New York: Psychological Corporation, 1943.

Havighurst, R. J. "Social Competence of Middle-aged People." *Genetic Psychology Monographs,* 56:297–375, 1957.

Helson, Ravenna. "Creativity, Sex and Mathematics." In D. W. MacKinnon (ed.), *The Creative Person.* Berkeley, Calif.: Institute of Personality Assessment and Research, 1961.

Hill, Evan. "How Successful Are College Marriages?" *Redbook,* May 1964.

Hollingshead, A. B., and Redlich, F. "Social Stratification and Psychiatric Disorders." *American Sociological Review,* 18:163–69, 1953.

Holmes, T. H. "Multidiscipline Studies of Tuberculosis." In Phineas J. Sparer (ed.), *Personality, Stress and Tuberculosis.* New York: International University Press, 1956.

Jaeger, Gertrude, and Selznick, P. "A Normative Theory of Culture." *American Sociological Review,* 29:653–68, 1964.

Jellinek, E. M. "The Problems of Alcohol." In *Alcohol, Science and Society. Quarterly Journal of Studies of Alcohol,* New Haven, Conn., 1945.

The Joint Commission on Mental Illness and Health, *Action for Mental Health.* New York: Basic Books, 1961.

Kahn, A. J. *Planning Community Services for Children in Trouble.* New York: Columbia University Press, 1963.

Katz, J., and Sanford, N. "The Causes of the Student Revolution." *Saturday Review,* December 18, 1965.

Kelly, E. L. "Consistency of the Adult Personality." *American Psychologist,* 10:659–81, 1955.

Kelly, G. *The Psychology of Personal Constructs,* Vol. 1. New York: Norton, 1953.

Keniston, K. "Social Change and Youth in America." *Daedalus,* 91:145–71, 1962.

Keniston, K. *The Uncommitted.* New York: Harcourt, 1965.

Kerr, C. *The Uses of the University.* Cambridge, Mass.: Harvard University Press, 1963.

King, S. H. "Emotional Problems of College Students: Facts and Priorities." *American Association of University Professors Bulletin,* Winter 1964, pp. 327–32.

Kinsey, A. C., and Gebhard, P. H. *Sexual Behavior in the Human Female.* Philadelphia: Saunders, 1953.

Klein, D., and Lindemann, E. "Preventive Intervention in Individual and Family Crisis Situations." In G. Caplan (ed.), *Prevention of Mental Disorders in Children.* New York: Basic Books, 1961.

Klein, D., and Ross, A. "Kindergarten Entry: A Study of Role Transition and Its Effects on Children and Their Families." In M. Krugman (ed.), *Orthopsychiatry and the School.* New York: American Orthopsychiatric Association, 1958.

Klein, G. S. "The Personal World Through Perception." In R. R. Blake and G. V. Ramsey (eds.), *Perception: An Approach to Personality.* New York: Ronald Press, 1951.

Klein, Melanie. "Contribution to the Psychogenesis of the Manic-Depressive States." In *Contributions to Psychoanalysis, 1921–1945.* London: Hogarth Press, 1948.

Kluckhohn, C., and Murray, H. A. "Personality Formation: The Determinants." In C. Kluckhohn and H. A. Murray (eds.), *Personality in Nature, Society and Culture.* New York: Knopf, 1948.

Kluckhohn, C., and Murray, H. A. *Personality in Nature, Society and Culture.* New York: Knopf, 1948.

Knight, R. P. "Introjection, Projection and Identification." *Psychoanalytic Quarterly,* 9:334–41, 1940.

Kroeber, A. L., and Parsons, T. "The Concepts of Culture and of Social System." *American Sociological Review,* 23:582–83, 1958.

Kruglak, T. *The Foreign Correspondents.* Geneva: Librairie E. Droz, 1955.

Kubie, L. S. "The Forgotten Man of Education." *Harvard Alumni Bulletin,* February 6, 1954.

Kubie, L. S. "The Fundamental Nature of the Distinction Between Normality and Neurosis." *Psychoanalytic Quarterly,* 23:167–204, 1954.

Levinson, D. J. "The Psychotherapist's Contribution to the Patient's Treatment Career." In H. H. Strupp and L. Luborsky (eds.), *Research in Psychotherapy.* Washington, D.C.: American Psychological Association, 1962.

Levinson, H., Price, C. R., Munden, K. J., Mandl, H. J., and Solley, C. M. *Men, Management and Mental Health.* Cambridge, Mass.: Harvard University Press, 1962.

Lewin, K. *Field Theory in Social Science.* New York: Harper, 1951.

Lindemann, E. "Symptomatology and Management of Acute Grief." *American Journal of Psychiatry,* 101:141, 1944.

Lindemann, E., and Caplan, G. *Explorations in Preventive Psychiatry,* unpublished manuscript, 1963.

Lindemann, E., and Dawes, L. "The Use of Psychoanalytic Constructs in Preventive Psychiatry." In *The Psychoanalytic Study of the Child,* Vol. 7. New York: International Universities Press, 1952.

Lipset, S. M., and Seabury, P. "The Lesson of Berkeley." *The Reporter,* January 28, 1965, pp. 36–40.

Lolli, G. "On Therapeutic Success in Alcoholism." *Quarterly Journal of Studies on Alcohol,* 14:238–46, 1953.

Lorr, M. "Relation of Treatment Frequency and Duration to Psychotherapeutic Outcome." In H. H. Strupp and L. Luborsky (eds.), *Research in Psychotherapy.* Washington, D.C.: American Psychological Association, 1962.

MacKinnon, D. W. "Creativity in Architects." In D. W. MacKinnon (ed.), *The Creative Person.* Berkeley, Calif.: Institute of Personality Assessment and Research, 1961.

Maslow, A. H. "A Test for Dominance-Feeling (Self-Esteem) in College Women." *Journal of Social Psychology,* 12:255–70, 1940.

Maslow, A. H. "Self-Esteem (Dominance-Feeling) and Sexuality in Women." *Journal of Social Psychology,* 16:259–94, 1942.

Maslow, A. H. *Motivation and Personality.* New York: Harper, 1954.

McCarthy, R. G., and Douglass, E. M. "Prohibition and Repeal." In R. G. McCarthy (ed.), *Drinking and Intoxication.* New York: The Free Press, 1959.

McConnell, T. R., and Heist, P. "The Diverse College Student Population." In N. Sanford (ed.), *The American College.* New York: Wiley, 1962.

McDougall, W. *Introduction to Social Psychology.* London: Methuen, 1908.

McGavran, E. G. "Facing Reality in Public Health." In *Key Issues in the Prevention of Alcoholism.* A Report of the Northeast Conference. Harrisburg, Pa.: Pennsylvania Department of Health, 1963.

McGee, H. Measurement of Authoritarianism and Its Relation to Teachers' Classroom Behavior. Doctoral thesis, University of California, Berkeley, 1954.

Meehl, P. Wanted: A Good Cook-Book. Presidential address, Midwestern Psychological Association, April 29, 1955. Dittoed.

Milbank Memorial Fund. *An Approach to the Prevention of Disability from Chronic Psychoses: the Open Mental Hospital Within the Community.* New York, 1958.

Morgan, C. D., and Murray, H. A. "A Method for Investigating Phantasies: The Thematic Apperception Test." *Archives of Neurology and Psychiatry,* 34:289–306, 1935.

Mowrer, O. H. *Learning Theory and Personality Dynamics.* New York: Ronald Press, 1950.

Mowrer, O. H. *Psychotherapy: Theory and Research.* New York: Ronald Press, 1953.

Moynihan, D. P. The Impact of Universal Opportunity for Higher Education on Manpower Development and Employment of Youth. Unpublished paper delivered by the Assistant Secretary of Labor at the Conference on Universal Higher Education, organized by the Institute for Higher Education, Columbia University, Dorado Beach, Puerto Rico, November 1964.

Murphy, G. *Personality.* New York: Harper, 1947.

Murphy, Lois. "Preventive Implications of Development in the Preschool Years." In G. Caplan (ed.), *Prevention of Mental Disorders in Children.* New York: Basic Books, 1961.

Murray, H. A., *et al. Explorations in Personality.* New York: Oxford, 1938.

Murray, H. A. "Preparations for the Scaffold of a Comprehensive System. In

S. Koch (ed.), *Psychology: A Study of a Science.* Vol. 3. New York: McGraw-Hill, 1959.

Murray, H. A., and Kluckhohn, C. "Outline of a Conception of Personality." In C. Kluckhohn, H. A. Murray, and D. M. Schneider (eds.), *Personality in Nature, Society and Culture.* Rev. Ed. New York: Knopf, 1955.

Myrdal, G. *An American Dilemma.* New York: Harper, 1944.

Neugarten, Bernice. "Personality Changes During the Adult Years." In R. G. Kuhlen (ed.), *Psychological Backgrounds of Adult Education.* Chicago: Center for the Study of Liberal Education for Adults, 1963.

Neugarten, Bernice. "A Developmental View of Adult Personality." In J. E. Birren (ed.), *Relations of Development and Aging.* Springfield, Ill.: Charles C Thomas, 1965.

Newcomb, T. M. *Personality and Social Change.* New York: Holt, 1943.

Newcomb, T. M. *Social Psychology.* New York: Holt, 1950.

Nurse, A. R. Personality and Behavioral Changes Relative to Therapy of Alcoholics. Unpublished paper presented before the 1964 convention of the American Psychological Association, Los Angeles, September 5, 1964.

Office of Strategic Services Assessment Staff. *Assessment of Men.* New York: Holt, 1948.

Ojemann, R. H. "Basic Approaches to Mental Health: The Human Relations Program at the State University of Iowa." *Personnel and Guidance Journal,* 37:198, 1958.

Ojemann, R. H. "Investigations on the Effects of Teaching an Understanding and Appreciation of Behavior Dynamics." In G. Caplan (ed.), *Prevention of Mental Disorders in Children.* New York: Basic Books, 1961.

Ojemann, R. H., Levitt, E. E., Lyle, W. H., Jr., and Whiteside, M. F. "The Effects of a 'Causal' Teacher-Training Program and Certain Curricular Changes on Grade School Children." *Journal of Experimental Education,* 24:95, 1955.

Pavenstedt, Eleanor. "A Study of Immature Mothers and Their Children." In G. Caplan (ed.), *Prevention of Mental Disorders in Children.* New York: Basic Books, 1961.

Pinner, F. "The Crisis of the State Universities: Analysis and Remedies." In N. Sanford (ed.), *The American College.* New York: Wiley, 1962.

Prescott, D. A. *The Child in the Educative Process.* New York: McGraw-Hill, 1957.

Prudential Insurance Company of America. *Facing Facts about the Two-Year College.* New York, 1963.

Redfield, R. *The Folk Culture of Yucatan.* Chicago: University of Chicago Press, 1941.

Reider, N. "Psychodynamics of Authority with Relation to Some Psychiatric Problems in Officers." *Bulletin of the Menninger Clinic,* 8:55-58, 1944.

Renaud, H. Clinical Correlates of the Masculinity-Femininity Scale of the Minnesota Multiphasic Personality Inventory. Ph.D. dissertation, University of California, Berkeley, 1950.

Richmond, J. B. "Some Observations on the Sociology of Pediatric Education and Practice." *Pediatrics,* 23:1175, 1959.

Riesman, D. *The Lonely Crowd.* New Haven, Conn.: Yale University Press, 1950.

Rogers, C. R. "A Theory of Therapy, Personality, and Interpersonal Relationships, as Developed in the Client-Centered Framework." In S. Koch (ed.), *Psychology: A Study of a Science,* Vol. 3. New York: McGraw-Hill, 1959.

Rogers, C. R., and Dymond, R. (eds.). *Psychotherapy and Personality Change.* Chicago: University of Chicago Press, 1954.

Rose, A., and Stub, H. "Summary of Studies on the Incidence of Mental Disorders." In A. Rose (ed.), *Mental Health and Mental Disorder: A Sociological Approach.* New York: Norton, 1955.

Rose, J. A. "The Prevention of Mothering Breakdown Associated with Physical Abnormalities of the Infant." In G. Caplan (ed.), *Prevention of Mental Disorders in Children.* New York: Basic Books, 1961.

Rose, J. A., and Ross, D. C. "Comprehensive Pediatrics: Post-graduate Training for Practicing Physicians." *Pediatrics,* 135:144, 1960.

Rosen, E. "Differences between Volunteers and Non-volunteers for Psychological Studies." *Journal of Applied Psychology,* 35:185–93, 1951.

Rosen, G. (ed.). "Public Health and Mental Health: Converging Trends and Emerging Issues." In *Mental Health Teaching in Schools of Public Health.* A Report of a Conference Sponsored by the Association of Schools of Public Health. New York: Columbia University School of Public Health and Administrative Medicine, 1961.

Rosenberg, Pearl, and Fuller, Myrtice. "Human Relations Seminar for Nursing Students." *Nursing Outlook,* 5:724, 1957.

Rosenstock, I. M. "The Motivation of Health Behavior." In *Key Issues in the Prevention of Alcoholism.* Report of the Northeast Conference. Harrisburg, Pa.: Pennsylvania Department of Health, 1963.

Sanford, N., *et al.* "Physique, Personality and Scholarship." *Monographs of the Society for Research in Child Development,* 8, No. 1, 1943.

Sanford, N. "Identification with the Enemy: A Case Study of an American Quisling." *Journal of Personality,* 15:53–58, 1946.

Sanford, N. (ed.). "Personality Development During the College Years." *Journal of Social Issues,* 12(4):1–70, 1956.

Sanford, N. "Is College Education Wasted on Women?" *Ladies Home Journal,* May 1957.

Sanford, N. "The Uncertain Senior." *Journal of the National Association of Women Deans and Counselors,* 21:9 15, 1957.

Sanford, N. "Ends and Means in Higher Education." In G. K. Smith (ed.), *Current Issues in Higher Education.* Washington, D.C.: Association for Higher Education, 1962.

Sanford, N., *et al.* "The Findings of the Commission in Psychology." *Annals of the New York Academy of Science,* 63:341–64, 1955.

Sanford, N., Webster, H., and Freedman, M. "Impulse Expression as a Variable of Personality." *Psychological Monographs,* 71:1–21, 1957.

Sanford, N. "Developmental Status of the Entering Freshman." In N. Sanford (ed.), *The American College.* New York: Wiley, 1962.

Sears, R. R. *Survey of Objective Studies of Psychoanalytic Concepts.* Social Science Research Council Bulletin, No. 51. New York: Social Science Research Council, 1943.

Seeley, J. R. "The Forest Hill Village Human Relations Classes." In *Basic Approaches to Mental Health in the Schools.* Washington, D.C.: American Personnel and Guidance Association, 1959.

Sheldon, W. *The Varieties of Human Physique: An Introduction to Constitutional Psychology.* New York: Harper, 1940.

Sheriffs, A. C., and McKee, J. P. "Qualitative Aspects of Beliefs About Men and Women." *Journal of Personality,* 24:451–64, 1957.

Silber, E., Hamburg, D. A., Coelho, G. V., Murphey, E. B., Rosenberg, M., and Pearlin, L. I. "Adaptive Behavior in Competent Adolescents: Coping with Anticipation of College." *Archives of General Psychiatry* 5:354–65, 1961.

Stern, G. G. "Environments for Learning." In N. Sanford (ed.), *College and Character*. New York: Wiley, 1964.

Stewart, G. *The Year of the Oath*. New York: Doubleday, 1950.

Strong, E. K., Jr. *Vocational Interests of Men and Women*. Stanford, Calif.: Stanford University Press, 1943.

Symonds, P. M. *Dynamic Psychology*. New York: Appleton, 1949.

Terman, L. M., and Miles, C. C. *Sex and Personality*. New York: McGraw-Hill, 1936.

Terman, L. M., and Oden, Melita. *The Gifted Group at Mid-Life*. Stanford, Calif.: Stanford University Press, 1959.

Thorndike, F. L., and Woodworth, R. S. "The Influence of Improvement in One Mental Function upon the Efficiency of Other Functions: I." *Psychological Review*, 8:247–61; "II. The Estimation of Magnitudes." *Ibid.*, 384–95; "III. Functions Involving Attention, Observation and Discrimination." *Ibid.*, 553–64, 1901.

Tolman, E. C. "Identification and the Post-war World." *Journal of Abnormal and Social Psychology*, 38:141–48, 1943.

Tomkins, S. S. *The Thematic Apperception Test*. New York: Grune & Stratton, 1947.

Tomkins, S. The Psychology of Knowledge. Unpublished address to Division 8, American Psychological Association, September 7, 1964.

United States Office of Education. *Summary Report on Bachelor's and Higher Degrees Conferred During the Year 1962–63*. Washington, D.C.: United States Government Printing Office, 1964.

Voth, H. M., and Mayman, M. "A Dimension of Personality Organization." *Archives of General Psychiatry*, 8:366–80, 1963.

Waldfogel, S., and Gardner, G. E. "Intervention in Crisis as a Method of Primary Prevention." In G. Caplan (ed.), *Prevention of Mental Disorders in Children*. New York: Basic Books, 1961.

Waldfogel, S., Hahn, Pauline, and Landy, E. "School Phobias: Causes and Management." *School Counselor*, 3:19, 1955.

Webster, H. "Some Quantitative Results." In N. Sanford (ed.), "Personality Development During the College Years." *Journal of Social Issues*, 12:29–43, 1956.

Webster, H., Freedman, M. B., and Heist, P. "Personality Changes in College Students." In N. Sanford (ed.), *The American College*. New York: Wiley, 1962.

Wedge, B. M. (ed.), *Psychosocial Problems of College Men*. New Haven, Conn.: Yale University Press, 1958.

Welsh, G. S. A Projective Figure-Preference Test for Diagnosis of Psychopathology: 1. A Preliminary Investigation. Unpublished Ph.D. dissertation, University of Minnesota, 1949.

White, R. W. *The Abnormal Personality*. New York: Ronald Press, 1944.

White, R. W. "The Dangers of Social Adjustment." *The Medical Press* (London), 228:9–15, 1952.

White, R. W. *Lives in Progress*. New York: Holt, 1952.

Witkin, H. A., Lewis, H. B., Hertzman, M., Machover, K., Meissner, Pearl B., and Wapner, S. *Personality through Perception: An Experimental and Clinical Study*. New York: Harper, 1954.

Wrightstone, J. W. "Discovering and Stimulating Culturally Deprived Talented Youth." *Teachers College Record*, 60:23–27, 1958.

Name Index

Subject Index